Historical Dictionaries of Ancient Civilizations and Historical Eras
Series editor: Jon Woronoff

Historical Dictionary of Ancient Israel

Niels Peter Lemche

Historical Dictionaries of Ancient Civilizations and Historical Eras, No. 13

The Scarecrow Press, Inc.
Lanham, Maryland, and Oxford
2004

SCARECROW PRESS, INC.

Published in the United States of America
by Scarecrow Press, Inc.
A wholly owned subsidary of
The Rowman & Littlefield Publishing Group, Inc.
4501 Forbes Boulevard, Suite 200, Lanham, Maryland 20706
www.scarecrowpress.com

PO Box 317
Oxford
OX2 9RU, UK

British Library Cataloguing in Publication Information Available

Library of Congress Cataloging-in-Publication Data

Lemche, Niels Peter.
  Historical dictionary of ancient Israel / Niels Peter Lemche.
    p. cm. — (Historical dictionaries of ancient civilizations and historical
eras ; no. 13)
  Includes bibliographical references (p.).
    ISBN: 978-0-8108-4848-1

  1. Jews—History—Dictionaries. 2. Judaism—History—Dictionaries. I. Title.
II. Series.
DS102.8 .L38 2004
933'.003—dc22
                                                        2003015311

♾ ™ The paper used in this publication meets the minimum requirements of
American National Standard for Information Sciences—Permanence of
Paper for Printed Library Materials, ANSI/NISO Z39.48-1992.
Manufactured in the United States of America.

Contents

Editor's Foreword

Of all the ancient civilizations that will be included in this series none is smaller than the ancient kingdoms of Israel and Judah, otherwise known as ancient Israel. Small both in geographical area and population, they were barely noticed by the major civilizations of the time in Egypt, Mesopotamia, and elsewhere, which either crushed or ignored them. Yet, several millennia later, ancient Israel is the civilization we remember most acutely, which we know (or think we know) the most about, and which has even been revived after a manner. Alas, what we know (or think we know) about Israel comes partly from the Old Testament and partly from fragmentary and sometimes distorted bits of historical evidence. So it has been doubly hard to figure out just what is true and what is false, what can be proven historically and what must be left to conjecture. This is a second way in which the subject matter of the *Historical Dictionary of Ancient Israel* differs notably from other books in the series.

This makes it considerably more problematic to determine the suitable coverage of a reference work, since it is necessary to include in the dictionary entries on persons, places, and events about which there is painfully little solid data and where even the Bible may be ambiguous or confusing. But they must be there, and they are, with as much information as can be mustered. The same applies to the broader environment: historical, political, and economic, as well as anthropological and sociological, since they give useful clues as to what life in ancient Israel was like. To put things in their proper place as much as possible, the introduction plays a significant role. And the chronology, actually this time two chronologies, can give us a feel for the sequence of events in Israel and surrounding areas. Naturally, since opinions still vary so much, from an older maximalist to a newer minimalist view, the bibliography is crucial not only to learn more and understand better but also to find different interpretations of the evidence.

Obviously, all this does not facilitate the compilation of the volume on ancient Israel. It is necessary for the author to acquire considerable information; part gleaned from the biblical and related literature, part won from archaeological and related research. And it is also essential to decide how much credit to give to the former and the latter. The author, Niels Peter Lemche, certainly has the background and experience. Receiving his doctorate at the University of Copenhagen in 1985, he had already served as an associate professor at the University of Aarhus, and after a brief stint at the University of Hamburg, he became and remains professor of theology at the University of Copenhagen. He has lectured and written widely on prehistoric and early Israel and on the Canaanites and other early peoples. He has a broad knowledge of the whole region, including the major civilizations. And he has also delved into the archaeology and anthropology of the period. It should doubtlessly be added that, although a minimalist, Dr. Lemche is aware of the maximalist positions, and therefore makes an attempt to encompass a broader view. For such reasons, he is an unusually reliable guide through an era that can be more confusing and misleading than most.

Jon Woronoff
Series Editor

Reader's Notes

The *Historical Dictionary of Ancient Israel* covers the history of Palestine to the conquest of Alexander in 331 B.C.E. with an emphasis on the periods reflected by the historiography of the Old Testament. It breaks off at the point when Judaism becomes the major intellectual and political factor of the country; the following history is not the history of ancient Israel but of early Judaism. Although any division made between historical periods is artificial and in a way unsatisfying, this division is a practical one, as the history of early Judaism also covers the history of early Christianity and the world of the New Testament.

The following sections show the complexity of the task of providing a historical dictionary of ancient Israel, as most of the historiography in the Old Testament is not history in the modern meaning of the word but will have to be characterized as narrative, tales from the past and legendary information.

At the same time, the history of Palestine followed its own course. It is as if two histories are present, the one in the Old Testament, and the one in the world outside the Old Testament, sometimes engaged in a dialogue, sometimes separating in two monologues. The dictionary has to cater to both subjects. This may leave the reader in confusion, but it is the hope that the preface will help the reader to understand the types of problems that are involved when dealing with biblical history. This preface discusses the merits of the historiography in the Old Testament and presents an overview of the history of Palestine in ancient times.

Terminology is a major problem. In this dictionary the "Old Testament" has been chosen as the name of the collection of biblical books otherwise known as the "Hebrew Bible." Although many biblical scholars seem to prefer the Hebrew Bible as the politically correct terminology, it also limits the Old Testament to its Hebrew (and Aramaic) version, thereby disregarding the far larger collection, otherwise known as the Greek Old Testament, or the Septuagint, the Old Testament of the Orthodox Church. Also, the Old Testament of the Roman Church includes more books than the Hebrew Bible.

The dictionary generally refers to Palestine. This will sometimes be seen as politically incorrect. However, most terminology relating to this country will in some way seem politically incorrect. Some may use the term "the Land of Israel," which is definitely wrong not only in the political sense of the word but also from a historical perspective as the historical State of Israel never ruled all of Palestine in ancient times. Probably a more correct terminology would be "the Holy Land." Since Palestine is holy to Jews as well as Christians and Muslims, "the Holy Land" would not be totally improper, although rather cumbersome. For this reason this option has been disregarded. Palestine is used in the traditional Christian sense and carries no intended political connotations.

Finally, instead of B.C. (before Christ), the dictionary uses B.C.E. (before the common era), as this is becoming the standard term used by most modern textbooks relating to ancient Israel and the Old Testament.

Preface

How to Read the Old Testament Historically— How to Read This Dictionary

Although small in scale, ancient Israel has received more attention than any other nation of the ancient world and for good reason as ancient Israel is believed to be the historical society described in the books of the Old Testament, a work of immense interest to most people of Western civilization. The study of ancient Israel is also highly interesting to the professional historian because of the conspicuous changes that have taken place within the last generation of scholarship changing this history from being a kind of rationalistic paraphrase of the tales and stories of the Old Testament into a secular history with a sophisticated methodology. Thus, if one compares the two classic textbooks among the many histories of Israel written over the last hundred years or more, John Bright's *A History of Israel* and Martin Noth's *Geschichte Israels*, both published in the 1950s, and a more recent contribution like J. Alberto Soggin's *An Introduction to the History of Israel and Judah* from 1993—now in its fourth Italian edition in 2002—the changes are enormous and the way in which the historical reconstruction has been liberated from the framework of the biblical narrative is astonishing.

A full-scale and up-to-date history of ancient Israel in English is still absent, although it is to be expected that such attempts will begin to appear in the near future. This situation creates some problems for the project of writing a historical dictionary of ancient Israel such as this and makes the enterprise seem a bit hazardous. Most readers will, without realizing the problems involved, turn to a dictionary to find information about the seemingly historical world of the Old Testament or about its great figures like Moses or David. How can this problem be handled in a dictionary if there was no historical Moses or David or if both persons were not actually the heroes of ancient Israel playing the roles they represent in the writing of ancient biblical historiographers? The solution chosen in this dictionary is to begin a major article like the one about Abraham with a résumé of the biblical narrative in the biblical Book of Genesis. After this introduction a discussion follows about historical problems connected with the hypothesis that there never was a historical Abraham or a historical Period of the Patriarchs which Abraham was a part of. This second part will generally present a historical scenario very different from the image of, for example, Abraham in the Old Testament, a fact that will probably disturb many laypersons but which nevertheless reflects the advances of biblical scholarship.

The narratives of the Old Testament were generally written much later than the historical events which they may reflect—sometimes many centuries if not millennia later. According to biblical chronology translated into a modern chronology, Abraham is supposed to have lived at the end of the Early Bronze Age. Although traditional scholarship has a long time ago moved him down into the Middle Bronze Age or even later, the tradition about this patriarch will have had to travel for many centuries before it was reduced into writing—according to the most conservative estimates in the 10th century B.C.E. (more recent dating will say the sixth century B.C.E. or even later). Of course, this interval between the assumed date of a biblical figure and the appearance of a written account of his or her life will narrow down as we proceed to later periods but the problem will basically be the same. As long as we have no contemporary source, i.e., information written at the same time as the events that are described in the written source took place, it is very difficult and in many cases impossible to extract reliable historical information from the historical narratives of the Old Testament.

This attitude to the historiography of the Old Testament is sometimes considered minimalist, if not directly nihilistic. But it reflects a growing awareness among biblical scholars of the character of the historiography of the Old Testament, of the motives behind this historiography, and of the techniques available to the historiographers of the ancient world, including the people responsible for the collection of stories included in the Old Testament. It is obvious that these writers cannot be evaluated according to the standards of modern historians and that they should not be condemned for not writing history in the modern scholarly meaning of the word. They had no tools to prepare themselves for such a task; it took Western civilization more than 2,000 years to acquire such tools. They did not invent the history of ancient Israel; they wrote this history in a way that was in their eyes best adapted to meet the requirements for a history of their own society. They included whatever traditions—written or oral—that were in their possession and handled the traditions in such a way that they became part of their important project of creating the world of ancient Israel. However, they had no critical ability to distinguish between a historically verifiable tradition or a legend from ancient times, and they did not possess any means telling them how to date the events described in these traditions in any accurate way—at least not before they were able to draw on synchronism such as the ones between kings of Assyria and Israelite and Judean kings. From the time when contacts were made between the rulers of the kingdoms of Israel, Judah and Assyria and, following the Assyrians, Babylonian kings, historical chronology seems fairly solid. The moment we cross into the Persian period, chronology may again be less accurate than hoped.

The Biblical History of Ancient Israel

A history of Palestine—a country that in the Iron Age also included the two kingdoms of Israel and Judah—will in many respects be different from the outline of the history of Israel presented by the Old Testament. This is not the place to present an extensive overview of this history. It is only necessary to present the major differences between the two kinds of history related to ancient Israel.

According to the biblical history of ancient Israel, the origins of Israel can be traced back to its first patriarch Abraham, whom God chose as the father of his chosen people after the dispersal of humankind all over the world. Basically, the history of the Period of the Patriarchs is presented as a family affair, concentrating on the whereabouts of the three patriarchs Abraham, Isaac, and Jacob, and Jacob's twelve sons. The Period of the Patriarchs came to an end when Jacob/Israel moved to Egypt with his family and stayed there for 400 years.

The sojourn of the Israelites in Egypt changed the structure of Israel from that of one family into that of a nation of twelve tribes counting hundred of thousands, if not millions, of men, women, and children. After 400 years, Israel left Egypt, persecuted by Pharaoh and his army that drowned in the Sea of Reeds while Israel continued its way out of Egypt to Sinai. After a migration in the desert that lasted for 40 years, Israel stood on the eastern banks of the Jordan River, ready to cross the river and conquer its land, the land of Canaan.

The conquest of Canaan followed, when the tribes of Israel invaded Palestine, massacred its Canaanite population, and distributed the country among the twelve tribes of Israel. After the death of the Israelite commander Joshua, a series of judges ruled Israel in the Period of the Judges, until the weak political organization of the Israelites was insufficient to protect the tribes against foreign enemies and internal strife. Facing new and more serious challenges, the Israelites were forced to look for a more permanent kind of leadership in the form of kings of Israel. The Israelite kingdom opened with a great success under David who expanded his kingdom to become a Levantine empire. However, the glorious days of ancient Israel soon came to an end when David's kingdom split into two independent states after the death of Solomon, its second king. The larger of the two states, the Kingdom of Israel, lasted for two centuries before it was crushed by the army of the Assyrians. The tiny Kingdom of Judah survived for another 140 years when it was also eliminated, this time by the Neo-Babylonian Empire under Nebuchadnezzar.

Ancient Israel was led into captivity in Mesopotamia that was to last for many years. The Jews, however, survived the Babylonian Exile and were allowed by Cyrus the king of Persia to return to their homeland and Jerusalem in 538 B.C.E. Here they reconstructed the temple of Jerusalem and continued their way of life first under Persian, later Macedonian and Roman, rule.

Traditional histories of Israel of the last 150 years have mainly followed the course of history as laid out by the Old Testament. The earliest period, the Period of the Patriarchs, was generally—not least in textbooks in English—considered a historical period although the historians were in doubt as to the exact time of the patriarchs. Already at the beginning of the 18th century a few scholars living in Germany had raised doubts about the historicity of Abraham, Isaac, and Jacob, but the general picture was that it was possible to defend at least the idea that the patriarchs represented an early stage in the development of the Israelite nation.

The exodus from Egypt had been questioned for a long time, because from a rationalistic point of view the number of Israelites that left Egypt was so enormous that the last Israelite would hardly have left Egypt before the first one entered Canaan. Whatever their personal preference and theological background, most scholars accepted that an exodus had taken place, probably involving far fewer Israelites than argued by the biblical historiographers.

In the eyes of traditional critical scholarship, the Period of the Judges definitely constituted a historical era and it was believed possible to translate the stories relating to the exploits of the judges into a historical textbook dealing with the history of Israel as a tribal society. When these textbooks arrived at the beginning of the Period of the Hebrew kings, they simply presented paraphrases of the biblical narratives. Thus the notion of a United Hebrew Kingdom remained in force, and the reasons for the break between Israel and Judah in the early days of King Rehoboam presented by biblical historiography were generally accepted as historically correct. Few objections were raised about the story of the divided kingdom, and the notion of the Babylonian Exile and the development of early Judaism as described by the Books of Ezra and Nehemiah were often accepted at face value.

A modern historical reconstruction of the history of ancient Palestine would in many respects present a rather different picture of ancient Israel. Few contemporary scholars would accept the idea of a patriarchal age, and they would be almost totally against the idea of an extensive Israelite exodus from Egypt. If anything happened, its scale was so insignificant that it never left any impression on Egyptian history as the exodus is not a part of Egyptian recollections about the past.

The history of the Israelite conquest of Canaan has been transformed into a history of social unrest and change among the inhabitants of Palestine already living in this place for centuries. Hardly any trace indicates an Israelite immigration, let alone conquest toward the end of the Late Bronze Age. Instead of a conquest followed by the rule of the judges, Palestinian society evolved over a period of several hundred years. It was a change that involved political rearrangements and allowed new political entities to appear but basically these changes happened among a population that had for centuries lived within the borders of ancient Palestine.

The thesis of the United Kingdom is in jeopardy today, as some leading scholars have begun to question its very existence. Thus we do not know if there ever was a historical David or Solomon, and if these figures ever existed, what kind of rulers they may have represented: kings, princes, or chieftains. Archaeological remains leave little evidence of Israelite greatness in the time normally allotted to David and Solomon—indeed, the very existence of the city of Jerusalem at this time has been questioned by recent scholarship.

When it comes to the history of the two kingdoms of Israel and Judah, a similar situation emerges. While it is normally accepted that the Kingdom of Israel existed for perhaps two centuries, say between 900 and 722 B.C.E., it is argued that no centralized state arose in the Jerusalem area, the core land of the Kingdom of Judah, before the late ninth or early eighth century B.C.E. This state only remained independent for a few generations. Already toward the end of the eighth century B.C.E., it became an Assyrian vassal-state. It was finally wiped out by the Babylonians in 587 B.C.E., if not already in 597 B.C.E. (there is no Babylonian confirmation of the conquest of Jerusalem in 587 B.C.E.).

The extent of deportations following the Babylonian conquest may have been considerable in relation to the limited number of inhabitants at that time in Judea. However, the level of destruction was likewise extensive, and for a very long period the effects of the Babylonian conquest were felt in Palestine, perhaps apart from the central territory of the ancient Kingdom of Israel which was seemingly left intact by the Babylonian conquerors. As a result of new investigations some scholars have begun to question not only the notion of the Babylonian Exile as expressed by the Old Testament, but also the usual reconstructions of the history of Palestine in the Persian Period.

As this dictionary is being published, it is still too early to say which way the study of the history of ancient Israel and Palestine will go. This is a time of transition between an old biblically oriented phase in scholarship and independent historiography with a different view of the value of the Old Testament as a historical source from the one entertained by earlier generations of historians of ancient Israel. Any reader and user of this dictionary should pay attention to this situation and accept the dictionary for what it is: an image of scholarship in transition.

The History of Ancient Palestine

The reader will, however, be entitled to put this question to the author: What did really happen in ancient Israel and Palestine? Maybe the historiography of the Old Testament does not provide an exact account of events of ancient times but this probably does not mean that nothing happened at all and that modern students of the ancient Near East are left in the void when it comes to the history of Palestine.

Functioning as a bridge between two great cultures, on the one hand Egypt, and on the other Mesopotamia, the inhabitants of ancient Palestine must inevitably have been the eyewitnesses not only of many great events but also of more mundane movements between these centers of people, goods, and knowledge. Somehow it must be reflected in the history of the country, and somehow it must be possible to describe the history of that part of the world.

In the broad perspective, the territory of Palestine is very restricted, amounting to only about 28,000 square kilometers. Yet, in spite of the smallness of scale, Palestine is subdivided into many different regions—mountains in the center and north, deserts in the south and east, plains in the north and along the sea, and highlands separating the coastal plain from the central mountains. These very different natural habitats have left their mark on the history of the country. The population has traditionally been split between several occupational zones, practicing husbandry in some areas including also nomadism, and agriculture in other parts of the country. The mountains and the highlands especially favored a mixed economy of husbandry and agriculture. Wine was produced on a large scale as well as olive oil, especially in the valleys of the mountains.

The economy was mixed and largely based on food production. Apart from wine and olive oil, Palestine produced nothing of value for international trade and did not possess any natural resources like gold, silver, copper, or precious stones. This fact, as well as the fragmented character of the country, did not allow for extensive political formations like major territorial states, and certainly not for the appearance of great cities as found in Mesopotamia and Egypt. Most Palestinian cities were extremely small, housing a few thousand inhabitants. Only occasionally did major cities appear, like Hazor in the Middle and Late Bronze Age, or Jerusalem in the later part of the Iron Age. In such cases special political developments may have facilitated a concentration of people in one place that was not natural for the country as a whole. Moreover, it has been suggested that Hazor was in the Bronze Age more of a Syrian city playing a power game in competition with other major Syrian cities of the second millennium B.C.E. Jerusalem only arose to greatness in the wake of the Assyrian destruction of the country at the end of the eighth century B.C.E., when it remained perhaps the only unharmed city within the territory of the king of Judah.

Should standards of life rise in Palestine above the level of basic food production and small-scale trade with agricultural products, this would depend on income that came from trade. In this way the well-being of at least the leading stratum of the Palestinian population, the part of the population that would benefit from income from trade, would depend on the international conditions, as Palestine functioned in most of antiquity as a transit area for international trade that crossed the country on established routes, and on its way left goods, mostly in the form of taxes and customs paid by the tradesmen to local chieftains and kings. Whenever international trade broke down, mostly because problems in one of the key areas of trade—either Mesopotamia or Egypt—disrupted the flow of goods between these centers, Palestinian society would decline making even the maintenance of the small cities of Palestine impractical.

Accordingly the history of Palestine in ancient times shows a remarkable uniformity that also has a kind of cyclical character. Sometimes city culture is blossoming—at least according to normal Palestinian standards—sometimes the cities are given up and replaced by a more rudimentary agriculture based on villages or nomadism.

Stone Age to Early Bronze Age

This cyclic pattern can be traced back to the Stone Age. It is not easy to tell the reasons for such changes when no written documents exist (writing only appeared in the ancient Near East toward the end of the fourth millennium B.C.E.). In Palestine the first examples of writing belong to the second millennium B.C.E. To present an example, the city of Jericho that had been in existence since the 10th millennium B.C.E. was deserted in the Neolithic period, although no natural conditions such as drought would have caused such a drastic move, as Jericho is located in an oasis in the rift valley of Jordan.

The rather dramatic change toward city culture in the Early Bronze Age—as far as Palestine goes it is still prehistory—may be explained as a consequence of the appearance of the Old Kingdom in Egypt, a period of immense wealth and the time of the great pyramid builders. There is clear evidence of an Egyptian interest in Palestine, although it is impossible to say anything about the precise character of the Egyptian presence. Thus it is not known if the Egyptians were masters of southern Palestine or only placed trade emporiums here. Toward the end of the Early Bronze Age, cities disappeared from the Palestinian countryside. Most were given up—some like Ai for good—and never resettled, others lay deserted for a period of some hundred years only to reemerge in the Middle Bronze Age as important Palestinian centers.

The biblical Period of the Patriarchs has been linked to these upheavals that toward the end of the third millennium B.C.E. transformed Palestinian society from being based on cities to a rural-like one. It has been guessed that the patriarchs represented a new population, the Amorites, who were supposed to have appeared in the Near East shortly before 2000 B.C.E. Modern scholarship has largely dismissed this idea of an Amorite immigration, seeing the Amorites as people already in the region for hundreds of years and probably the bearers also of the city culture of Palestine in the Early Bronze Age.

Middle and Late Bronze Age

When Egypt recovered from the weakness of the First Intermediary Period, a period of decline that followed the time of the great pyramid builders, when in Egyptian tradition everything was turned upside down, the rich becoming poor and the poor rich, Palestine also recovered and its urban culture started to reappear. Although little is known in the way of precise information—apart from special periods like the Amarna Period in the 14th century B.C.E., it seems that Palestine was subdivided into a great number of sometimes very small city-states, that is, political organizations based on the existence of a central town where the king of the state and his administration were located. The city was the center of the state and controlled all aspects of its economy and policies. It was the center of local trade and the place where products for export were handled.

Sometimes local kings acted as heads of independent states, but just as often they had to submit to foreign, that is, Egyptian, rule. This was the situation in the Late Bronze Age, when Egypt ruled most of the Levant. It is less certain that Egypt also controlled Palestine politically in the Middle Bronze Age. Much speaks in favor of local political independence, although an Egyptian presence was evident in the time of the Middle Kingdom. Toward the middle of the second millennium B.C.E., Egypt lapsed into a crisis when northern Egypt was ruled by the Hyksos kings, kings of foreign extraction, having Amorite names.

Politically, the rule of the Hyksos—by later Egyptian tradition considered the low ebb of Egyptian history—can be seen as a consequence of the extensive relations between Egypt and Palestine. Egypt presented an opportunity to people in Palestine looking for a better life and was therefore the place to go in order to find food and prosperity. The distance between Egypt and Palestine was of no concern, a little more than 100 kilometers, and the presence of the Hyksos rule in northern Egypt indicates a large-scale immigration of people from Asia that finally took over the political control in northern Egypt and ruled this territory for a couple of hundred years before they were thrown out of Egypt by energetic rulers from southern Egypt who boasted of having liberated Egypt from the rule of the foreign kings.

After having cleared Egypt of the Hyksos, the Pharaohs of the New Kingdom continued their advance, this time into western Asia where they reached as far as the eastern side of the Euphrates. In Palestine the activity of Egyptian armies can be seen in many places where destruction followed in their wake. Thus, in the middle of the 16th century B.C.E., many Palestinian cities were destroyed although most of them were soon rebuilt more or less as continuations of the cities of the previous period, reusing the fortifications of the past.

For the next many hundred years, Egypt controlled Palestine with as little effort as necessary. Now, documents begin to abound, at least in certain periods, allowing for an inside look into the political conditions in Palestine under the sway of Egypt. This documentation, mostly in the form of the Amarna Letters from the 14th century B.C.E., paints a picture of local disorder and lack of stability, but reality may have been very different from the impression one gets from these documents written by local Palestinian "kings"—the Egyptians used to call them "majors of cities." The Palestinian petty kings, all of them vassals of the Pharaoh, describe a situation of internal turmoil: everybody at the throat of his neighbor, and all planning for revolt against their Egyptian master. The Egyptians, safely in control, did not care much about the litany of complaints from their subjects. They demanded taxes and especially people since they saw impoverished Palestine mostly as a source of a labor force always in demand for maintaining the Egyptian economy and assisting the Egyptians in the great many building projects of the New Kingdom. As long as they received their revenues from Palestine, they left the Palestinian petty kings on their own, fighting their civil wars for eternity.

The situation changed in the 13th century, when Egypt had to fight for the survival of its empire in western Asia, now threatened by the appearance of a new major power, the Hittites of Asia Minor. In the end the competition for control over Syria between the Egyptians and the Hittites ended in a stalemate when the Pharaoh and the Hittite king concluded a covenant dividing western Asia between the two great powers of that time. However, the Egyptians seem to have tightened their grip on Palestine, exerting more control than previously, a fact that may have left less freedom of movement to the petty kings of Palestine and certainly created a safer life for its plagued inhabitants, formerly the victims of the eternal competition for local power between the petty kings.

The following centuries saw a new development that is marked by the decline of Palestinian cities and the rise of an extensive system of scattered and undefended villages, not least in the mountains. The exact reasons for this change of settlement in Palestine can only be guessed. It has often been considered the result of the breakdown of international trade at the end of the Late Bronze Age, that is, at the end of the 12th century B.C.E. It is certain that the blossoming culture of the Late Bronze Age in the Levant was dependent on trade and that secure international relations between the powers of that time promoted trade activities. This situation changed for the worse toward 1200 B.C.E., as trade relations were severely disturbed by developments in faraway places such as Greece, where the great sea empire of Mycenae broke down, or in Asia Minor, where Hittite rule succumbed to the pressure of local mountain tribes.

One of the consequences of the breakdown of the international political system and the trade nourished by it was the movement of the Sea Peoples, probably of European origins. This movement hit the Levant shortly before 1200 B.C.E. and brought havoc with it, although certain areas such as Phoenicia were left almost unharmed by the Sea Peoples. When it reached Egypt, it was stopped and the Sea Peoples were defeated in a sea battle commemorated on the walls of Ramesses III's mortuary temple at Medinet Habu. Among these Sea Peoples one finds the Philistines, later appearing in the Old Testament as the inhabitants of the coastal plain of Palestine. Although the Philistines were soon integrated into the population of Palestine and gave up their language in favor of a local variety of Amorite, they gave their name to the area inhabited by them, and later to all of Palestine, meaning "the land of the Philistines."

However, in spite of these upheavals, the Egyptian presence was still very much in evidence in Palestine to at least the latter part of the 11th century B.C.E., and perhaps even longer. Archaeologists have found evidence, for example, at Beth Shan, of an Egyptian military presence as late as the latter part of the 10th century, making the presence of a major Israelite empire in Palestine in this century highly improbable. As far as their interests went, at the end of the second millennium Egypt still controlled the part of Palestine, that was crucial to its own safety.

Evidence of this continuous interest of the Egyptians in Palestine is the so-called "Israel-stele" of Pharaoh Merenptah that includes the first mention of Israel as a people of Palestine that is no more— testifying that it must have been important enough to the Egyptians not only to include it among the nations of Palestine, but also to mention its passing.

While historical and archaeological analyses of the evidence from Palestine in the Late Bronze Age and in the Early Iron Age make it likely that there never was an Israelite conquest of Palestine as described by the Book of Joshua, the early vestiges of later Israel can be traced back to this period, c. 1200 B.C.E., although the exact historical developments that led to the appearance of this Israel and its relations to the later state of Israel cannot be traced in any detail. The way Israel is mentioned as well as internal information provided by the inscription makes it likely that it was a kind of tribal society located in central Palestine. If this is correct, then it is likely that the Israel said to have been destroyed by Merenptah in some way represented a core element in the later Kingdom of Israel, otherwise only attested in inscriptions from the mid-ninth century B.C.E.

The Iron Age

The year 1200 B.C.E. is the official date of the beginning of the Iron Age presented by most textbooks on the history of Israel. Such a date must be understood as symbolic more than real as the coming of the Iron Age involves an extremely complicated process that changed the world of the Bronze Age into that of the Iron Age. In Palestine this transition lasted for at least 300 years, and a fully developed Iron Age only existed from the latter part of the 10th century B.C.E. when technological improvements made it possible to transform the rather useless crude iron into steel, thus procuring the finest material for the fabrication of tools ever to exist.

As it happened, the coming of iron did not represent a cultural advance. Rather, iron replaced bronze as a result of the breakdown of international trade, making it impossible to import the materials needed for transforming copper into bronze, that is, tin and arsenic, none of these materials being available locally in the Near East.

Politically, the Iron Age led to a gradual development that not so much changed the general political structure of Palestine as it changed the names of the players in the political game. Many cities blossoming in the Bronze Age continued to exist, and although a certain setback for urban life was conspicuous already at the end of the Late Bronze Age, the cities did not totally disappear and many were after shorter or longer intervals reestablished and repopulated, some still to function as heads of city-states.

Most of these city-states were just as insignificant as the previous Palestinian states of, for example, the Amarna Age in the 14th century B.C.E. Only in one place at the end of the 10th century B.C.E. did a major political unity arise: in the northern part of the central mountains. This state was known as Israel, but more common ancient inscriptions refer to it as "the House of Omri," seeing King Omri as the founder of this state. Israel, alias the House of Omri, covered the northern part of the central mountains and at its height probably extended its sway to include also large parts of northern Palestine, including the Galilee and the western part of Transjordan. Its international importance is reflected by the Assyrian inscription mentioning the battle at the Syrian city of Qarqar in 853 B.C.E., where a coalition of Syrian states temporarily stopped the advance of the Assyrian army. King Ahab of Israel appears among the major contributors to this coalition.

Already in the second half of the ninth century, the kingdom of Israel began to crumble. The Aramaeans of Syria—especially Damascus—rose to power and united in a few major states forcing Israel into a conflict where Israel could not prevail. King Hazael of Damascus especially represented a serious threat to Israel, endangering its survival and despoiling Israel of its possessions east of the Jordan River. Only toward the end of the ninth century B.C.E. did the advance of Assyria against Damascus stop the Aramaeans from totally annihilating the Kingdom of Israel.

While Israel was certainly a major factor in international policies of the ninth century B.C.E., territorially it only controlled a part of Palestine, although a major one. Along the coast of the Mediterranean, a series of independent or quasi-independent small states survived, not least city-states ruled by the descendants of the Philistines. Israel never succeeded in subjecting the Philistines to its rule. In the northwestern part of the country, the Phoenicians controlled most of the cities along the coast, and they represented such an important factor in the economy of the world that they were generally left in peace. The story in the Old Testament of the marriage between King Ahab and the Tyrian princess Jezebel may well reflect the international rules of that age. Instead of making war against the Phoenicians, it was preferable to establish personal relations at the highest level and in this way to enjoy some of the benefits of the intensive Phoenician trade on the Mediterranean.

No state existed south of the Israelite border, at least not before the end of the ninth century B.C.E. Jerusalem was in this century hardly more than a provincial town with a few thousand inhabitants. The tradition of the greatness of Jerusalem in the time of King David and Solomon has little if anything to do with historical circumstances. At its largest, a small principality existed in this area, although it had perhaps already acquired its dynastic name of "the House of David," seeing David as the founder of this principality. In the ninth century B.C.E., this principality was probably allied to Israel or dominated by Israel.

Only in the eighth century B.C.E. did a state form in southern central Palestine. Nothing indicated that it was to become a major factor in later tradition. It was limited to the area around Jerusalem and included at its peak the northern Negeb and parts of the highland in the west where the most important city of the state, Lachish, dominated. It is known to posterity as Judah, although this name only appears in rather late documents. With the weakening of Israel, the Kingdom of Judah obtained a certain room of maneuver playing off the interests of Israel with those of, at first, the Aramaeans, and later, the Assyrians. It remained an unimportant political factor, although toward the end of the eighth century B.C.E., when Israel was no more, King Hezekiah of Judah instigated a major rebellion against the Assyrians that left him bereft of most of his kingdom with only Jerusalem remaining in his possession.

Shortly before the temporary rise of the kingdom of Judah to political importance, the Kingdom of Israel became a thing of the past. Its kings, seriously underestimating the destructive force of the Assyrians, the new major power of the ancient Near East in the Iron Age, began to look for ways of blocking the imperial aspirations of the Assyrians, often in alliance with their former foe, the Aramaeans of Damascus. This scheming met with absolutely no success. The opposing Assyrian armies were led by one of the ablest monarchs of the ancient world, King Tiglath-pileser III (744-727 B.C.E.), who in his usual energetic way handled the problems west of the Euphrates. In a series of campaigns he conquered all of Syria including Damascus, and reduced the Phoenician cities to vassalage. Then he turned upon Israel, which he stripped of all its possessions, leaving only the minor city-state of Samaria to the former king of Israel. A few years after his death, his successors dealt the final blow to the independent state of Israel, reducing the last part of the kingdom to the Assyrian province of Samarina.

When King Hezekiah of Judah ventured into a rebellion against the Assyrians, it took King Sennacherib of Assyria only one campaign to crush the revolt. In his own words, Sennacherib bottled up Hezekiah in his city "like a bird in its cage." For unknown reasons, the Assyrians never conquered Jerusalem but spared it, although for a price. Almost every other city within the confines of Hezekiah's kingdom, including Lachish, was destroyed and a heavy tribute was extracted from Hezekiah, including gold, silver, and his daughters.

The future of Palestine was for almost a century hidden in the shadow of the Assyrian Empire, and before the end of the Assyrian Empire there are no more signs of political upheavals.

Toward the end of the seventh century B.C.E., such disaster struck Assyria that within 20 years it was first reduced to a minor kingdom in northeastern Syria, then totally destroyed and the last traces of its former greatness wiped out. A coalition of its former enemies lurked behind these changes in the fortunes of Assyria. This coalition included Babylon, now ruled by a Chaldean dynasty, Media located in present-day Iran, and Lydia in Asia Minor. These new powers divided the world between them. Babylon and the Chaldeans received as their part the territories to the west of the Euphrates, including Palestine.

Ever since a show of force by Pharaoh Shishak toward the end of the ninth century B.C.E.—an event recorded by the Old Testament—Egypt played no important role in the policies of western Asia. Now it decided to interfere, but to no avail. In the first half of the seventh century B.C.E., Egypt had been totally humiliated by the Assyrians, who for a short while succeeded in conquering and occupying it. Although Egypt soon regained its independence, it never again rose to become a major power and was more likely to fall prey to future intruders, such as the Persians and the Greeks.

All attempts to cast off the yoke of Babylon were thwarted. For the Kingdom of Judah it meant the end of its political existence. In 597 and 587 B.C.E., the Babylonians crushed rebellions in Palestine. On the last occasion, they totally destroyed Jerusalem, and deported a great many of its inhabitants to Mesopotamia. The effects of this conquest are easy to trace in the archaeological remains not only in Jerusalem, but also in most of Palestine where an almost total destruction of urban life followed in the wake of the Babylonian advance. Present evidence suggests that only the territory of the former Assyrian province of Samarina—or Samaria—escaped the wave of devastation that in other places led to an almost complete collapse of Palestinian civilization.

The Old Testament explains that the exiled inhabitants of Jerusalem were allowed to return to Palestine when King Cyrus of Persia, the new great power that toward the end of the sixth century B.C.E. conquered all of the Near East, including Egypt and Asia Minor, and extended its empire as far as to the borders of India, in 538 B.C.E., after his conquest of the city of Babylon, allowed the exiled Jews to return to their homeland. Archaeology may present a very different view of the events of that time, showing resettlement to have started at a much later date.

Whatever happened, it seems certain that during the time of the Persian Empire that lasted until the arrival of Alexander the Great and his Macedonian army in the later part of the fourth century B.C.E. Judaism appeared in the area around Jerusalem leading to the refoundation of the city and its temple. The origin of Judaism is—in spite of the testimony of the Old Testament—veiled in mystery, but having established itself in Jerusalem, it changed character and in the Hellenistic period grew into the dominant political and religious factor in the country.

Chronology

The easiest way to illustrate the differences between the history of ancient Israel as told by the historiographers of the Old Testament and traditional studies of the history of ancient Israel and a modern reconstruction of the history of ancient Palestine including the two states of Israel and Judah is to present the chronology of ancient Israel as based on, for example, John Bright's *A History of Israel* (1st edition: 1959) and to compare it with a more modern one.

Chronology of Ancient Israel

Period of the Patriarchs	c. 1900-1700
Israel in Egypt	c. 1700-1280
Exodus	c. 1280
Conquest of Palestine	c. 1250-1200
Period of the Judges	c. 1200-1020
Saul	c. 1020-1000
United Monarchy	c. 1000-922
David	c. 1000-961
Solomon	c. 961-922
Divided Kingdom	922-597
Kingdom of Israel	922-721
Kingdom of Judah	922-587
Babylonian Exile	587-538
Persian Period	538-331

Chronology of Ancient Palestine

Chalcolithicum	c. 4300-3500
Early Bronze Age	c. 3500-2300
Intermediate Early-Middle Bronze Age	c. 2300-1900
Middle Bronze Age	c. 1900-1550
Late Bronze Age	c. 1550-1300
Intermediate Late Bronze-Early Iron Age	c. 1300-900
Iron Age	c. 900-600
Kingdom of Israel	c. 900-722
Kingdom of Judah	c. 800-587
Neo-Babylonian Period	c. 600-539
Persian Period	c. 500-331

ABBREVIATIONS

ET   English Translation

The Books of the Old Testament

Gen	Genesis
Exod	Exodus
Lev	Leviticus
Num	Numbers
Deut	Deuteronomy
Josh	The Book of Joshua
Judg	The Book of Judges
Ruth	Ruth
1 Sam	The First Book of Samuel
2 Sam	The Second Book of Samuel
1 Kgs	The First Book of Kings
2 Kgs	The Second Book of Kings
1 Chron	The First Book of Chronicles
2 Chron	The Second Book of Chronicles
Ezra	The Book of Ezra
Neh	The Book of Nehemiah
Job	The Book of Job
Ps	Psalms
Prov	Proverbs
Eccl	Ecclesiastes
Cant	Song of Songs
Isa	The Book of the Prophet Isaiah
Jer	The Book of the Prophet Jeremiah
Lam	Lamentations

Hez	The Book of the Prophet Hezekiel
Dan	The Book of the Prophet Daniel
Hos	The Book of the Prophet Hosea
Joel	The Book of the Prophet Joel
Amos	The Book of the Prophet Amos
Obad	The Book of the Prophet Obadiah
Jon	The Book of the Prophet Jonah
Mic	The Book of the Prophet Micah
Nah	The Book of the Prophet Nahum
Hab	The Book of the Prophet Habakkuk
Zeph	The Book of the Prophet Zephaniah
Hag	The Book of the Prophet Haggai
Zech	The Book of the Prophet Zechariah
Mal	The Book of the Prophet Malachi

THE DICTIONARY

- A -

AARON. The brother of **Moses** and his deputy during the migration of the Israelites in the wilderness (*see* **Desert, Migrations in the Desert**) and the eponymous ancestor of the Aaronite priesthood. The traditions about Aaron have been colored by the formation of the Aaronite priesthood that probably belongs to a relatively late phase of **Israel**'s history. In this way, the character of Aaron can be divided into, on one hand, a priest administering priestly duties, on the other, obligations connected with the leadership in combination with Moses. Sometimes he is called a "**prophet**" (Exod 7:1). One tradition stands apart: the story of the Golden Calf (Exod 32-34), where Aaron appears both as the leader of the people in Moses' absence, and as the priest in front of the idol. It has been customary within Old Testament scholarship to associate the image of Aaron the priest with the alleged late priestly strand of traditions in the **Pentateuch** (usually dubbed "P"), whereas other traditional layers (usually called the Yahwist ["J"] and the Elohist ["E"]) have a much more reserved view of this figure from the past.

According to the story of the call of Moses, Aaron was installed as Moses' assistant and spokesperson because of his claim that he was deficient in speaking properly (Exod 4:10-17). In this capacity, Aaron appears at the side of Moses in the confrontation with **Pharaoh** (Exod 5-11). He also appears in this role in other traditions, e.g., at **Sinai** (Exod 24:9-11), in the story about Moses' spies (Num 13:26; 14:26), and at Meribah where Moses struck water from the rock (Num 20:1-13). In the retelling of the desert stories in **Deuteronomy**, Aaron is almost totally missing, although Deuteronomy includes the information about his death at Mosera (Deut 10:6—in Deut 32:50 his place of death is given as Mount Hor—today identified with a mount overlooking the rock city of Petra in Jordan).

As is the case of almost every personality of the early traditions of Israel, it is practically impossible to verify any part of the tradition about Aaron as historical. He is a composite figure that has been reworked many times. If there ever was a historical Aaron, it is hardly the figure presented in the Old Testament.

ABDON. A **judge** in **Israel**, from Pirathon in **Ephraim**, who had 40 sons and 30 grandsons and judged Israel for eight years (Judg 12:13-15). He belongs to the list of five judges (Judg 10:1-5; 12:8-15) who together judged Israel for 70 years but left no records about their exploits.

ABEL. Meaning "stream," the name of a number of localities in **Palestine** mentioned in the Old Testament. Most important are Abel-Maachah or Abel-Beth-Maacah (Tell Abil), a town at the border between **Israel** and **Aram**, sometimes ruled by the Aramaeans, sometimes by the Israelites, and Abel-Mehola, the home of the prophet **Elisha**.

ABIATAR. One of **David's priests**, the son of **Ahimelech**, the priest at **Nob** (2 Sam 20:35). He escaped the fate of his father and fellow priests who were killed on **Saul's** request for supporting David fleeing from the wrath of the king. Abiatar joined David's men in the desert (1 Sam 22:20-23) and brought the ephod—an important cultic requisite—from Nob to David's camp (1 Sam 23:6). After David's conquest of **Jerusalem**, Abiatar became his priest together with **Zadok** (2 Sam 20:25). His career came to an end when he, after the death of David, supported **Adonijah** against **Solomon**. He was, however, spared by Solomon and allowed to retreat in peace to **Anatot** (1 Kgs 2:26-27). He has sometimes been considered a representative of old Israelite religious habits in contrast to Zadok, who has been seen as representing new and non-Israelite religious innovations. Speculation that Abiatar is the author of the "**Succession History**" (2 Sam 7-1 Kgs 2) is totally without foundation.

ABIEL. Two men of this name ("My father is El") are mentioned in the Old Testament: 1. King **Saul's** grandfather (1 Sam 9:1; 14:51), and 2. One of **David's heroes** (1 Chron 11:32).

ABIGAIL. One of **David's** wives, first married to **Nabal**, whose husband died from fear in a confrontation with David (1 Sam 25). In **Hebron**, she became the mother of Chileab, David's second son. Abigail's fate, being another man's wife before joining David, is paralleled by the story of **Bathsheba**, the wife of the **Hittite Uriah**, and perhaps also of **Michal**, the daughter of King **Saul**.

ABIJAH. A number of persons in the Old Testament carry the name of Abijah ("Yahweh is my father"). From a historical point of view, two persons are interesting:

1. The infant son of King **Jeroboam** of **Israel** who died after a curse was put upon his father by the prophet **Ahijah** from **Shiloh** (1 Kgs 14).

2. The successor of King **Rehoboam** of **Judah** (1 Kgs 14:31-15:8; a variant tradition presents the name as **Abijam**). His mother was **Maacah**, a daughter of **David's** son **Absalom** (1 Kgs 15:2). According to the Hebrew text, he reigned for three years (c. 915-913 B.C.E.); the Greek Septuagint, however, gives him a six-years reign. The biblical evaluation of Abijah is negative. He sinned against the Lord; however, at the same time he was able to fight off the Israelites under King Rehoboam.

ABIJAM. The name means "My father is [the god] Jam." Some are of the opinion that this was the real name of the king **Abijah**, suppressed by later biblical tradition, Jam being the **Canaanite** god of the sea.

ABIMELECH. Two persons of importance carry the name of Abimelek ("the king is my father").

1. The **Philistine** king of **Gerar** when **Abraham** and **Isaac** visited the city (Gen 20 and 26). The two occurrences are similar: The patriarch had left his own region in order to travel to a place where he could find food, and on both occasions almost lost his wife. However, something happens and the plot is solved without endangering the survival of the patriarchal family. The two stories are

variants of the narrative about Abraham in **Egypt** (Gen 12) and carry no independent historical information.

2. Abimelech, the son of the **judge Gideon** and a woman from **Shechem** (Judg 9). Upon his father's death, Abimelech used the support of his Schechemite relatives to obtain power, whereafter he disposed of his 70 brothers who were executed "on one stone" (Judg 9:5). Only one survived the ordeal, **Jotham**, the author of the Jotham fable about the trees looking for a king (Judg 9:7-21). A person of the name of **Gaal**, the son of Ebed (literally "the son of the slave"), instigated a rebellion against Abimelech in Shechem, but was outsmarted by Abimelech's agent, **Zebul**. Abimelech defeated Gaal, who was chased from Shechem by Zebul. After this, Abimelech took gruesome revenge on the people of the Tower of Shechem. When they looked for refuge in their stronghold, Abimelech had it burned down, and they perished. Abimelech met his death at the hand of a woman who threw a millstone on him when he entered besieged **Thebez**. No information about Abimelech can be found outside the Old Testament, although scholars have sometimes speculated about his relationship with the Shechemite champion of the Amarna Period (*see* **Amarna and the Amarna letters**), Labayu, who was a crafty and shifty local ruler of the central hill land around the middle of the 14th century.

ABINADAB. The Old Testament includes short notes about a number of persons of the name of Abinadab ("My father is noble"), among these:

1. A man from **Kiriath-jearim** housing the ark of the Lord for 20 years after it was conquered but not kept by the **Philistines** at the battle of **Aphek** (1 Sam 7:1-2).

2. An older brother to **David**, in the service of King **Saul** (1 Sam 16:8).

3. A son of King Saul who died together with his father and brother at **Gilboa** (1 Sam 31:2)

ABIRAM. Two persons of this name ("My father is exalted") are mentioned in the Old Testament.

1. Abiram, who in connection with Dathan instigated a rebellion against **Moses** and his leadership but was swallowed up by the earth (Num 16:1-40). The story is totally legendary, although

scholars have sometimes tried to extract tribal history from it, such as the demise of the tribe of **Reuben**.

2. The oldest son of **Hiel** of **Bethel**, who was probably sacrificed by his father when he rebuilt the city of **Jericho** (1 Kgs 16:34). The note in 1 Kgs 16:34 may reflect a custom attested in archaeological discoveries of child sacrifices in connection with foundation ceremonies.

ABISHAG. A handsome girl from **Shunem** who was brought to the royal court to revitalize the ailing King **David**—without much success (1 Kgs 1:1-4). The anecdote might reflect a custom when an old king is on trial in order to *see* that he is still fit for ruling his country. Instead of becoming the king's mistress, Abishag acted as the nurse of the old and sick David. After David's death and **Solomon's** assuming of power, Solomon's half brother **Adonijah** showed interest in the girl (1 Kgs 2:12-25), something Solomon recognized as a renewed bid for the kingship on the part of Adonijah. In this way Abishag became the indirect reason for Adonijah's death.

ABISHAI. A nephew of King **David**, the son of the king's sister Zeruah and brother of David's general **Joab**. The Old Testament narrative presents a portrayal of a split person: on one hand, a staunch supporter of the king and, on the other, a rather independent person who sometimes in combination with his brother carried on with a policy of his own, although always with the interest of the king in mind. He is said to be one of the chiefs of David's heroes, the elite force of David (2 Sam 23:18). He supported David in his early days: together with Joab he slew **Saul's** general **Abner** (2 Sam 3) and participated in quenching the rebellion of **Absalom** (2 Sam 18) and later of **Sheba** (2 Sam 20). Finally, he is said to have saved the life of the king by killing the **Philistine** hero Ishbi-benob (2 Sam 21:17).

ABNER. King **Saul's** cousin and general, son of Saul's uncle Ner (1 Sam 14:50, the name means "the father is Ner"). The books of Samuel (*see* **Samuel, Books of**) present an interesting portrayal of Abner as an ambitious politician whose plans are destined to end tragically, being crossed by the younger **David**, the very person

Abner had to look for on the king's request after he had killed **Goliath** (1 Sam 17:55-58). Abner remained loyal to Saul to the very end, and appeared regularly at the side of the king, thus during a festival (1 Sam 20:25), and again when he was reproached by David for not protecting his lord and master (1 Sam 26:15). After Saul's death at the battle at **Gilboa**, Abner was the person who ensured the kingship for Saul's family by bringing Saul's surviving son, **Ishboshet**, to **Mahanaim** where he was elected king of **Israel** (2 Sam 2:8-9). During the warfare that broke out soon after Ishboshet's enthronement between the armies of Ishboshet and David, Abner made a bid for the city of **Gibeon**. In the course of this campaign, Abner lost the battle but killed **Asahel**, the brother of David's general **Joab** (2 Sam 2). At a later date, Abner may have planned to become king himself by approaching Rizpah, Saul's concubine (2 Sam 3:7). A quarrel broke out between Abner and the king, and Abner opened negotiations with David in **Hebron**. When he returned from Hebron, Abner was killed by Joab, officially as revenge for the death of his brother but in light of the political situation probably to rid David of his fiercest competitor for the Israelite throne (2 Sam 3).

ABRAHAM. Or Abram (the name is changed in Gen 17:5). Abraham was the first among **Israel**'s three patriarchs. The name Abraham might either represent a learned "Aramaic" variant to the name of Abram, meaning "the father is exalted," or a peculiar dialectal form of the name Abram. The part of Genesis devoted to the story of Abraham covers chapters 11:26-25:10. Abraham is said to have left his parental home in **Ur of the Chaldaeans** (*see also* **Chaldaea, Chaldaeans**) in order to travel in the company of his father Terah and his nephew **Lot** to **Haran**. After Terah's death, Abraham together with his wife, **Sarah** (until Gen 17:15 Sarai), left Haran and traveled to **Canaan**, the country promised to him and his family by God. Shortly after his arrival in Canaan, Abraham was forced to leave the country because of a great **famine** and travel to **Egypt**. In Egypt he almost lost his wife to **Pharaoh**'s harem but Sarah was given back to Abraham by the direct order of God. Finally, Abraham returned to his own country a richer man than ever before. In Canaan, Abraham and Lot were forced to separate. Lot moved on to **Sodom**, no longer a part of Israel's future.

Abraham settled in **Mamre**, where he began to experience God's promises coming true. God concluded a covenant with Abraham including promises of a country and plenty of descendants. However, so far Sarah had not been able to give birth to a child. Abraham, and Sarah, endeavored to circumvent God's promise about a son, and Abraham begot a substitute heir, **Ishmael**, by the Egyptian slave girl **Hagar**, a futile project as Hagar and Ishmael were forced to leave Abraham because of Sarah's jealousy. A son had to be fathered by Abraham with Sarah as his mother. The promise of a son was repeated to Abraham by God who visited him at Mamre. The son, **Isaac**, is born, however, on the order of God only to be sacrificed to God, although spared in the last moment by God's personal interference. Now the last part of Abraham's life was approaching. Sarah died, and Abraham had to negotiate the acquisition of a grave cave for her from the local population at **Hebron**. After Sarah's death, Abraham provided a wife for his son, a girl, Rachel, coming from his own family back in Haran. Having provided for the future of his family, Abraham took his leave. He died and was buried next to his wife.

The story of Abraham is a comprehensive tale of the ancestor's life. Here it has only been possible to present a short summary. The summary might seem to reflect a homogenous narrative. It is far from being so. The narrative is a compositional story made by including a number of anecdotes and single stories, sometimes interrupted by additional stories about the fate of the minor characters of the narrative, such as Lot, Hagar, and Ishmael. At intersections the narrative also leaves space for the genealogies of a number of people in contact with Abraham. One of the anecdotic sections, Abraham's visit to Egypt (Gen 12), is repeated in Gen 20, although this time the scene has been removed to **Gerar**. Some stories have been classified as "legends of the sacred place," purportedly founded by Abraham, such as **Shechem** (Gen 12:6-7) and **Bethel** where Abraham installs an altar (Gen 12:8). Accordingly, scholars traditionally consider the Abraham story a redactional collection of narratives with a complicated history of compilation. On the other hand, the story is kept together by a thread that shows a compiler whose redaction was determined by the message to be included in the narrative, a message about devotion to the God of Israel, a devotion that is fully rewarded by God. The message is that Yahweh will never forsake his people, not even if they are not always absolutely obedient to the commandments of God, as sometimes happens in Abraham's relationship to his God. If Israel stays with Yahweh and scorns other gods, the promises will come true, Israel will become a great nation with its own country, and Yahweh will always remain faithful to his people.

The special qualities of the narrative about Abraham have to be evaluated on the basis of the message contained in this story. These qualities have little to do with external circumstances, such as historical events purportedly connected to the life of this patriarch. Historical-critical scholarship, however, normally aims at explaining the historical background of such narratives. Accordingly, scholars for more than a hundred years have tried to connect the person Abraham to specific periods in the history of the Holy Land and the ancient Near East at large. Sometimes attempts have been made to connect Abraham to real historical figures. It is a precondition that it can be demonstrated that there once existed in the prehistory of ancient Israel a special time, the period of the **patriarchs**. Such a period has turned out to be most elusive. Among the periods proposed as the time of Abraham may be mentioned the final part of the Early Bronze Age, that is, the end of the third millennium B.C.E. For a short while, following the discovery of ancient **Ebla**, and the decipherment of its inscriptions, Abraham was likened to a king of Ebla, who has, however, subsequently vanished as the reading of these texts became more solid. The period of the patriarchs has also been identified with the Middle Bronze Age—the first part of the second millennium B.C.E. From this period the cuneiform tablets from Mari are supposed to describe a nomadic society close to the one described in the Old Testament. Abraham and his two successors, Isaac and **Jacob**, have also been connected to the early part of the Late Bronze Age (c. 1500 B.C.E.) and the milieu of the text from Nuzi in **Mesopotamia**, purportedly—based on the text from ancient Nuzi—showing a juridical situation close to the one presumed by the patriarchal narratives. Finally, the early part of the Early Iron Age (c. 1200 B.C.E.) has been proposed, again based on information included in the patriarchal narratives.

This survey already shows that this direction within scholarship has met with little success. In present Old Testament scholarship it is becoming more and more evident that the ideological content of the patriarchal narratives is much more important than any possible historical content of the narratives. The narratives have been composed not in order to image the historical past but with regard to their ideological importance for early Judaism. Abraham is mentioned in only a few places outside Genesis, mostly in formulaic sentences like "I am the God of your fathers, the God of Abraham, of Isaac, and of Jacob" (e.g., in Exod 3:6 ff.). In Prophets and Psalms Abraham occurs sporadically, as in Ps 105:6-9. Generally, it is clear that such texts are totally dependent on the image of Abraham created by the narratives in Genesis. In this category must also be placed later Jewish speculation and tradition about Abraham.

ABSALOM. The third among **David's** sons, born in **Hebron**. His mother was **Maacah**, a royal princess from the **Aramaean** petty state of **Geshur** (2 Sam 3:3). Absalom's part in David's history (2 Sam 13-19) began when his half brother **Amnon** raped his sister **Tamar**. Absalom took his revenge on his brother and killed him. To escape his father's punishment he went to his mother's father, the king of Geshur, and hid there. After a while, David pardoned his son, who returned to the court of David in **Jerusalem**, only soon after to initiate a rebellion that almost overwhelmed his father. At the end of the day, David's general **Joab** subdued the rebellion and killed Absalom. David was hardly pleased by the news of his son's death. In spite of all the quarrels, Absalom remained to his death David's most beloved son.

Often, Absalom's rebellion against his father has been interpreted as reflecting a conflict between various power groups in the time of King David. One such explanation sees Absalom as the leader of a Judean rebellion against a king who, from his residence in neutral Jerusalem, not belonging to the land of any tribe of **Israel**, has allowed other tribes a leading role in his new kingdom. As proof it has been customary to point to the opening of the insurrection in Hebron, the ancient capital of Judah, but also David's withdrawal from exposed Jerusalem to his provinces to the east of the **Jordan River** might be understood in the light of the Judean origin of his son's betrayal.

A more recent interpretation of the story of David and Absalom generally disregards the possible historical content of the Absalom incident and sees it as a kind of narrative that explains the dangers of a father who, like the patriarch Jacob, loves one of his sons all too much—a preference that can only lead to disaster within the family, as was also the case in the **Joseph** story in Genesis. Within the compass of the David story, the narrative about Absalom illustrates how David's career took a bad turn after the violation of **Bathsheba**, the wife of the **Hittite Uriah**.

ACCO (or ACCHO). An important harbor and city c. 15 kilometers to the north of modern Haifa. It belonged to the tribal territory of **Asher** (Josh 19:30—according to the usual correction of the Hebrew text followed by modern scholars)—but according to Judg 1:31 was not conquered by the Asherites. Excavations at the place (Tell Fulkhar, less than a kilometer from the walls of the medieval city of Acre) demonstrate that it was a **Phoenician** city rather than an Israelite one. The tell was continuously settled from Chalcolithicum (fourth millennium B.C.E.) and until Hellenistic times when the population moved to the new city at the coast, the Acre of the Middle Age, or modern Acco. It is well documented in ancient sources from the Middle Bronze Age and onward and functioned for most of its history as an important trading center and production site.

ACHAEMENIDS. The name of the ruling house of the **Persian Empire** from 559 to 331 B.C.E. The Achaemenid dynasty produced a series of important kings of Persia known from Old Testament, Persian, and Greek sources and literary imagination, for example, **Xerxes**, the tragic hero of Greek tragedy (Aeschylus). Among the important kings are **Cyrus** II (559-530 B.C.E.), the founder of the Persian Empire, referred to with many hopes in the prophecies of Deutero-Isaiah (Isa 44:28; 45:1) and **Darius** I (522-486 B.C.E.), who consolidated the power of the huge Persian Empire. The dynasty was brought down when the last king, Darius III (335-330 B.C.E.), was defeated by Alexander the Great and subsequently killed by his own people.

List of Achaemenid kings:

Cyrus	(559-530)
Cambyses	(529-522)

Darius I	(522-486)
Xerxes I	(486-465)
Artaxerxes I	(465-423)
Xerxes II	(423)
Darius II	(423-405)
Artaxerxes II	(404-359)
Artaxerxes III	(358-338)
Arses	(337-335)
Darius III	(335-330)

ACHAN. A man of the tribe of **Judah** who stole from the war booty from **Jericho**. Therefore Achan became the direct reason for **Israel's** defeat in front of **Ai** (Josh 7). Achan was tried and punished with death, and the place where this happened is known to posterity as "the Valley of Achor." The story of Joshua 7 is most likely to be classified as an **etiological narrative**, presenting an explanation of the place name Achor.

ACHISH. King of **Gath** of the **Philistines, David's** contemporary and ally. Flying from **Saul**, David sought and obtained a safe asylum at the Achish court not totally in accordance with the inner hopes of the servants of Achish (1 Sam 27). When the Philistines mustered at **Aphek** before the battle at **Gilboa**, David was among Achish's retainers but was sent back at the demand of Achish colleagues, the assembly of Philistine rulers (1 Sam 27:1-2; 29). Otherwise nothing is known about this king of Gath. His name is certainly not Hebrew and may be Philistine in origin.

ACHOR. In the **etiological narrative** of Joshua 7, Achor got its name from **Achan**, who was executed and buried at this spot. The name means "to bring into trouble." It has been identified with the small valley in the Judean desert, El Buqeah, a few kilometers to the west of the Qumran settlement where remains of three small Iron Age II Settlements have been discovered.

ACHZIB. Harbor city some kilometers to the north of **Acco**. Reckoned as belonging to **Asher** (Josh 15:44), however—according to Judg 1:31—never conquered by **Israel**. The history of Achzib goes back to the Bronze Age, when the harbor was constructed, and it survived as a **Phoenician** city to **Persian** and Hellenistic-Roman times. Achzib was excavated in the 1960s.

ADMINISTRATION. Societies with an unsophisticated political structure likely to be found in **Palestine** in the Iron Age were in no need of an extended bureaucracy. The Old Testament includes very little in the way of precise information about the administration and officers of the two states of **Israel** and **Judah**. The lists of the **Officers of David and Solomon** (2 Sam 8:16-18; 20:23-26; 1 Kgs 4:1-6) are the only examples of a systematic description of the public administration. They indicate a tripartite system of administration that was divided between three departments: a civilian, a military, and a religious bureau. Next to the central administration, a system of **provinces** and provincial **governors** was established. Only in the Hellenistic and Roman periods did the need emerge for a more elaborate system of administration, serving not only the civilian and military interests, but which—alongside the enormous temple complexes of that time—demanded an elaborate system of **priests** of many categories.

ADONI-BEZEK. A **Canaanite** ruler who fought against the tribe of **Judah** at **Bezek** (Judg 1:5-7). Adoni-Bezek was caught and was mutilated—as he had formerly mutilated his own prisoners. He was brought in capture to **Jerusalem**, where he died. It has been proposed that Adoni-bezek, literally "the lord of Bezek," the place of the battle, is a corrupted form of **Adoni-zedek**, the king of Jerusalem slain by **Joshua** (Josh 10). Irrespective of the legendary character of the information about Adoni-bezek, it informs about the existence of a Jerusalem tradition that did not link the Israelite conquest of this city as firmly to the figure of King **David** as is generally the case in the Old Testament. There may have been traditions other than the ones in 2 Sam 5, telling stories about how Jerusalem became an Israelite city.

ADONIJAH. King **David**'s fourth son, born in **Hebron** (2 Sam 3:4). Adonijah—meaning "Yahweh is my lord"—may have been the oldest surviving son of David and accordingly the natural successor to the throne of **Israel**. In the quest for the kingdom, Adonijah sought support among David's old retainers, the general **Joab** and the priest **Abiatar**, but was subsequently outsmarted by his younger brother **Solomon** who through his mother, **Bathsheba**, had direct access to the old king (1 Kgs 1:5-53). After Solomon's accession to the throne, Adonijah retired and was at first left in peace. When he requested the hand of **Abishag** from **Shunem**, his action was seen by the king as a claim to the throne, and Adonijah was executed on the king's order. His supporters were either killed or banished from the country (1 Kgs 2:12-25).

ADONIRAM. Or Adoram or Hadoram, one of at first King **David's** (2 Sam 20:24) and later King **Solomon's** official (1 Kgs 20:24). Adoniram ("My Lord is exalted"—the variant names may mean "Ad[ad] or Had[ad] is exalted") was in charge of the forced labor necessary for the building activities of the king. In this capacity he directed the carving of cedar trees in **Lebanon** (1 Kgs 5:14). After Solomon's death, his successor, **Rehoboam,** during the negotiations with the representatives of the northern tribe, sent Adoniram to quench the impending rebellion of the infuriated Israelites. The Israelite representatives responded to this challenge by killing Adoniram (1 Kgs 12:18).

ADONI-ZEDEK. The **Canaanite** king of **Jerusalem** who assembled a coalition of five kings, of the cities of Jerusalem, **Hebron, Jarmuth, Lachish,** and **Eglon,** against **Joshua** and the Israelites. In the battle at the **Ajalon** Valley, Joshua was victorious. Together with his allies, Adoni-Zedek sought refuge in the cave of **Makkedah** but was caught by Joshua's men and together with the four other Canaanite kings he was executed (Josh 10). Adoni-zedek is sometimes believed to be identical with **Adoni-bezek** who fought against **Judah** (Judg 1:5-7). The narrative about Adoni-zedek in Josh 10 is sometimes considered an **etiological narrative** commemorating a landmark known in later times.

ADRIEL. The son of **Barzillai** from **Mehola** and the husband of **Saul's** oldest daughter **Merab** (1 Sam 18:18—but according to 2 Sam 21:8, he married younger daughter **Michal,** otherwise said to be **David's** first wife [1 Sam 18:20]). Five of his sons were executed by David at **Gibeon** (2 Sam 21:8).

ADULLAM. A place in southwestern **Judah,** sometimes identified with Tell esh Sheikh Madhkur, although the identification has never been confirmed by excavations at the site. The place is mentioned a number of times in the Old Testament, the first time indirectly by the reference to a friend of Judah, the son of **Jacob,** as being an Adullamite (Gen 38:12.20). An unnamed king of Adullam is mentioned in the **Book of Joshua** (Josh 12:15) as a **Canaanite** king defeated by **Israel.** A cave close to Adullam became the hiding place of **David** fleeing from Saul (1 Sam 22:1). According to **Chronicles, Rehoboam** fortified the city (2 Chron 11:7), and the prophet **Micaiah** mourned its fate.

AGAG. Two kings carry the name of Agag. 1. A legendary king mentioned by the sorcerer **Balaam** (Num 24:7). No more is known about this figure from the past, although there has been a lot of speculation but hardly any facts about his eventual connection to the traditional enemy from the north, Gog—a totally fabulous being. 2. An Amalekite king, an enemy of King **Saul.** He was spared by Saul but cut down by **Samuel** (1 Sam 15). It has been proposed that Agag was not a name but the title of the ruler of **Amalek.**

AGRICULTURE. *See* ECONOMY.

AHAB. King of Israel c. 874-853 B.C.E. and the most important ruler in his dynasty. The main source on the life of Ahab is supposed to be 1 Kgs 16-22. However, 1 Kgs 17-19 is part of the **Elijah** and **Elisha** legends, and 1 Kgs 20 and 22, that tell how intense warfare broke out between **Israel** and **Aram,** may have been wrongly placed by the editors of Kings as relevant to Ahab's time. Ahab is also mentioned in an Assyrian (*see* **Assyria and Babylonia**) inscription commemorating the battle at **Qarqar** in 853 B.C.E. as Ahabbu Sir'ilaja, that is, "Ahab of Israel," Sir'ilaja most likely being a corrupted form of Israel. He may also be mentioned by the **Mesha inscription** from ancient **Moab,** although without a name. Finally, his relations to the Tyrian King Ittoba'al (Old Testament: **Ethbaal** 1 Kgs 16:31) have been elaborated by **Josephus.**

   The description of Ahab's reign in the Old Testament is strongly biased and directly misrepresents the deeds of a great king. According to the Old Testament, Ahab was perhaps the most pathetic crook among all his fellow kings. This source can only be used as historical information with the utmost care when it comes to the reign of Ahab. According to the Old Testament, Ahab, provoked by his marital alliance with the Tyrian princess **Jezebel**, seduced his people into idolatry when he established a sanctuary for her god, Ba'al, at his capital, **Samaria**, in the heartland of Israel. It is also Jezebel who brought the conflict between Ahab and the Israelite nobleman **Naboth** to its gruesome conclusion. Ahab failed both when it came to his internal policies and in his foreign affairs. His policies brought upon him and his dynasty a conflict with the supporters of the traditional Israelite God, Yahweh—most notably the two prophets Elijah and **Micaiah**, the son of Imlah. His foreign policy is said to have ended in disaster when the Aramaeans laid siege to his capital. Finally, according to the Old Testament, Ahab succumbed to the Aramaeans in a battle close to **Rabba Ammon** (*see also* **Ammon, Ammonites**)—present-day Amman.

Although the Old Testament is highly critical of Ahab and his house, it cannot totally cover up that he was a king of eminent importance. Thus the biblical narrative includes some notes that describe his building activities (1 Kgs 16:32-33; 22:39—the last note said to come from "the **Chronicles of the Kings of Israel**"—by a number of scholars reckoned to have been the official annals of the kingdom of Israel). Furthermore, the note about Ahab's death in 1 Kgs 22:40 indicates that he did not die violently in a battle but peacefully in his own home at Samaria.

When all the information about Ahab is taken into consideration, a totally different picture emerges from the one in the Old Testament. Ahab inherited from his father, King **Omri**, a relatively wealthy kingdom and was able to hand over to his son and successor a well-established and consolidated kingdom. He established a series of connections to **Phoenicia** through his marriage policies, and entertained a perfect relationship with the important Aramaean state of **Damascus** to the east and its northern neighbor, the kingdom of **Hamath**. Between the state of Israel and its southern neighbor, the petty kingdom of **Judah**, another marital union was created, between Ahab's sister (2 Kgs 8:26) or daughter (2 Kgs 8:18) **Athaliah** and the king of Judah—either **Joram** or **Ahaziah**. According to the Moabite Mesha inscription, Mesha was able to liberate his kingdom from Israelite supremacy, although—

according to the OT—this only happened in the days of Ahab's successor, Joram. The clearest example of Ahab's greatness may be his contribution to the Syrian anti-Assyrian coalition that fought and won the battle of Qarqar. In this alliance between, among other states, Damascus and Hamath, Ahab contributed with an enormous contingent of chariots. It may be correct, as maintained by the Old Testament, that his religious policies created problems within his own kingdom, but excavations in Palestine show that his building activities were indeed considerable. Important remains from his time have been excavated—apart from Samaria—at **Megiddo, Hazor,** and **Jezreel.**

AHASUERUS. In the Book of **Esther** the king of **Persia** married the Jewish woman Esther and made her his queen. When a Persian courtier named **Haman** raised the king against the Jews, Esther saved her father and her people and Haman was executed. Ahasuerus is the Hebrew form of the Persian Chshajarsha ("the righteous king"), better known as **Xerxes.**

AHAZ. King of **Judah** c. 741-726 B.C.E. The complete name was Joahaz (meaning "Yahweh holds [him] firmly") mentioned in an Assyrian (*see* **Assyria and Babylonia**) inscription. Ahaz was the son and successor of King **Jotham.** According to the evaluation of the Old Testament historiographers, not much can be said in favor of Ahaz and his time (2 Kgs 16; 2 Chron 28; Isa 7). He had his son pass through fire—possibly a reference to a child sacrifice—and he plundered the temple and substituted the traditional altar with a new one constructed according to a foreign pattern. He sacrificed on the hills and, finally, he pledged his country in order to obtain the support of the Assyrian King **Tiglath-pileser III,** thereby showing contempt and lack of confidence in his God, Yahweh. Not even the name of his mother has been preserved, and according to 2 **Chronicles,** he was not found worthy to be buried in the royal cemetery outside the walls of **Jerusalem** among his predecessors, the former kings of Judah. According to the historical literature in the Old Testament, the reign of Ahaz was the turning point in the history of his country. The catastrophe was now imminent and unavoidable. The historical King Ahaz should perhaps be allowed greater respect than accorded him in the Old Testament. He was living in a difficult time when the Assyrian empire (*see* **Assyria and Israel**) was directing its interest against the territories to the west of the **Euphrates**. After his accession of power in 745 B.C.E., Tiglath-pileser III successively subdued Urartu in Asia Minor, and **Babylonia**. After 740 B.C.E. he conquered northern **Syria** and most of **Phoenicia**. Now his armies were directed to **Damascus** and southwestern Asia, including **Samaria**. In the tradition of former times (*see also* **Ahab**), Damascus and Samaria tried to revitalize an old anti-Assyrian coalition also including Judah. Ahaz refused to accept the offer. When the two powers in the coalition tried to replace Ahaz with a certain **Tabel**, he submitted to Tiglath-pileser's rule and became the vassal of Assyria, something he deemed preferable to serfdom under Samaria and Damascus. In this way, Jerusalem and Judah escaped the fate of the two states of the coalition. Damascus was sacked by the Assyrians in 732 B.C.E., while Samaria lost all its provinces except the city area of Samaria, and became an Assyrian puppet state. Ahaz's religious innovations have often been seen in the light of his pro-Assyrian policies, and he has been accused of introducing Assyrian religious beliefs and practices into his kingdom. This is hardly correct, although from his time Judah became part of the Assyrian sphere of interest.

AHAZIAH. ("Yahweh holds firmly") The name of two kings of the Old Testament.

1. Ahaziah king of **Israel**, the son of **Ahab** and **Jezebel**, who reigned for little more than a year (852/1 B.C.E.). Very little in the way of concrete information has been preserved about Ahaziah, except from the note on his ascension to the throne (1 Kgs 22:40). Ahaziah may be regarded as continuing his father's policies, especially entertaining good relations with **Damascus**, but virtually no information has survived, except that he invited **Jehoshaphat**, his colleague from **Judah**, to participate in overseas trade out of **Ezion-Geber**. The story about Ahaziah's death (2 Kgs 1:1-18) forms part of the circle of prophetic legends about **Elijah**. It says that Ahaziah suffered from a fall from a lattice in his upper chamber in the palace of **Samaria**. Ahaziah sent for an oracle from Baal-zebub (pejorative for "Baal-zebul, the "prince Baal") at **Ekron**, and was properly condemned by Elijah. As a consequence he died from his injuries and was followed on the throne by **Jehoram**.

2. Ahaziah king of Judah for only one year (842/1 B.C.E.), the son of King Jehoram and Queen **Athaliah**, the daughter of **Omri** or Ahab (2 Kgs 8:24-29). According to 2 Kings, Ahaziah joined King Jehoram of Israel in his fight against the **Aramaeans** from Damascus led by the warrior King **Hazael** and a battle was joined at **Ramoth-Gilead** to the east of the **Jordan River** (2 Kgs 8:28-29). This episode is said to lead to Ahaziah's death. At the same time the wounded King Jehoram was disposed of by the push of **Jehu**, the son of Nimshi, the future king of Israel, Ahaziah fled from Jezreel toward nearby **Megiddo** but, while making his escape, he was injured by Jehu's retainers. Although he succeeded in reaching Megiddo, he died there from his wounds (2 Kgs 9:27-28). Seventy of his male relatives (the Old Testament says "brothers") were executed in **Samaria** on Jehu's order (2 Kgs 10:12-14). 2 **Chronicles** has a different story of Ahaziah's life and death giving not only a different age at his ascension (42 years instead of 22 years, *see also* 2 Kgs 8:26/2 Chron 22:2), but also a variant story of his death saying that he was hiding in Samaria after the coup d'état of Jehu but Jehu's people found him and brought him to Jehu, who had him executed (2 Chron 22:7-9).

AHIJAH. A number of persons in the Old Testament carry the name of Ahijah ("Yahweh is my brother"). The most important is Ahijah, the prophet from **Shiloh**, related to the fate of King **Jeroboam** and his family (1 Kgs 11:29-30; 12:15; 14:2-18; 15:29). Ahijah prophesied to Jeroboam that the kingdom of **Solomon** would be split into two parts and the biggest part would follow Jeroboam. Later he turned against Jeroboam and prophesied about the death of the king and the destruction of his dynasty. Ahijah belonged to a series of prophets supposed to have acted as the strongest critics of monarchy. It should be noted that, according to **Chronicles**, one of the major sources for Solomon's reign is supposed to be "the prophecy of Ahijah" (2 Chron 9:29).

AHIKAM. The son of the high official **Shaphan** and the father of the governor **Gedaliah**, installed after the **Babylonian** conquest. Ahikam belonged to one of the leading families of administrators at the royal court in **Jerusalem**. He is said to have saved the life of the prophet **Jeremiah** (Jer 26:24), and he led a delegation in connection with the finding of the law book to the prophetess **Hulda**. During the conflicts that led to the destruction of **Judah** and Jerusalem, he may in his political orientation have been pro-Babylonian. As a testimony to his attitude against **Nebuchadnezzar**, his son was appointed governor by the Babylonians after they had brought down the traditional ruling house of Judah, the **house of David**. There is no information at the end of the Judean state of Ahikam's activities, nor is he included among the list of deportees from sacked Jerusalem. A safe guess is that he did not live to see the destruction of his nation.

AHIMAAZ. The son of **Zadok**, one of **David**'s two important priests (2 Sam 15:27.36). Together with **Jonathan**, the son of David's second priest **Abiatar**, Ahimaaz was used by David as an intelligence officer. In this capacity he stayed in **Jerusalem** when David fled from **Absalom** and provided the king with news about the whereabouts of Absalom (2 Sam 17:17-21). He was the first messenger who reached the king after the defeat of Absalom, bringing only good tidings while he at the same time "forgot" to tell the serious news about Absalom's death (2 Sam 18:17-33). In this way, the tale about Ahimaaz presents an interesting variant to the messenger stories of ancient tradition, telling of how a messenger may escape the risks of being the harbinger of bad news, bringing for his own part only the good news to the king.

AHIMELECH. (Meaning "my brother is king"). The name of three persons mentioned by the Old Testament.
1. Ahimelech, the priest at **Nob** who without knowing the true reason of **David**'s visit—running away from **Saul**—helped him by providing him with food and **Goliath**'s sword. **Doeg**, an **Edomite** retainer of Saul, refers the matter to Saul who ordered Ahimelech and the other priest at Nob killed. Only Doeg had the stamina to execute the king's order (1 Sam 21:2-10). Ahimelech is the father of **Abiatar**, one of David's associates since his days on the run from King Saul.
2. One of David's people who did not assist him when he forced his way to Saul, who was sleeping in his tent (1 Sam 26:6). This Ahimelech is called "a Hittite." This is not a reflection of his origin among the historical **Hittites** of the second millennium; it is rather

the result of a development of the tradition about the Hittites that was current in the first millennium when the inhabitants of Syria were sometimes named Hittites by Mesopotamian sources.

3. A priest, the son of Abiatar and the grandson of the priest Ahimelech who according to **Chronicles** helped **Zadok** in reorganizing the **priests** (1 Chron 24:3).

AHINOAM. The name (meaning "my brother is delightful") of two royal ladies of the Old Testament. 1. The wife of **Saul** and mother to most of his known children (1 Sam 14:50). 2. One of **David's** wives since his time in the desert (1 Sam 25:50). She belonged among the booty made by the **Amalekites** but was quickly saved by David (1 Sam 30). She was the mother of **Amnon**, David's firstborn son (2 Sam 3:2).

AHITOPHEL. A wise man (name partially incomprehensible) who first served as a counselor to **David** but changed sides during the **Absalom** rebellion and became Absalom's most important advisor (2 Sam 16:15-17.23). His advice was said to be as if it came from God (2 Sam 16:23). Ahitophel advised Absalom to violate David's harem in order to show that he was now the king. Absalom followed this advice, but he did not follow the advice immediately to continue his pursuit after David. This advice was countered by **Hushai**, David's agent among the retainers of Absalom. When Absalom followed the wrong advice, that allowed David to gain time and reassemble his forces; Ahitophel took his leave, went home, and hung himself.

AHITUB. The name (meaning "my father is good") of several persons in the Old Testament, among whom may be mentioned, 1. The father of **Ahimelech**, the priest at **Nob** (1 Sam 14:3), and 2. The father of **David's** priest **Zadok** (2 Sam 8:17).

AI. A city of the Old Testament, said to have been conquered by **Joshua** (Josh 8), almost universally identified with the modern ruined site of et-Tell (meaning "the Ruin," an exact rendering of the Hebrew name) close to present-day Beitin (**Bethel**). The city was extensively excavated during the British Mandate of Palestine, and again in the 1960s and 1970s. At the beginning of the Early Bronze

Age (c. 3100 B.C.E.), a fairly large urban settlement was founded here that was to experience a complex history of destruction and rebuilding that was to last until c. 2400 B.C.E., when the city was destroyed for the last time. After 2400 B.C.E and until the Early Iron Age (c. 1200 B.C.E), Ai was a desolate place without habitation. In the Early Iron Age (between c. 1200 and 1150 B.C.E.) a small unfortified village existed at Ai. After that time the place was never resettled.

From a historical point of view, Ai became a key location when the scholarly discussion about the Israelite settlement in **Canaan** (*see* **Settlement of Israel**) sharpened and it became clear that the image of a great conquest as described in the **Book of Joshua** had little or nothing to do with the process that changed the Late Bronze Age society of **Palestine** into the society of the Iron Age. Although scholars have tried to manipulate the dating of the conquest, Ai would still have been a desolate place when Joshua conquered it. The story about the conquest of Ai in Joshua 8 has therefore been interpreted as an **etiological narrative** of a traditional kind giving explanation to the place name of "Ai" and lacking any historical foundation.

AJALON. A city and a fertile valley about 18 kilometers to the northwest of **Jerusalem** where the sun stood still on **Joshua**'s request to provide time for the total defeat of the coalition of the **Canaanite** kings (Josh 8:12-14). The exact location of the city has not been finally settled, although the valley carrying its name is a well-known and fertile plain west of Jerusalem.

AKKAD. The name of a city and a state situated in central **Mesopotamia** and ruled by Semitic-speaking kings. It became the center of the first empire (2335-2154 B.C.E.). The empire was founded by **Sargon** (2335-2279) and consolidated and enlarged by his successors to also include southern Mesopotamia and western **Elam**. Sargon's grandson, Naram-sin, during his campaigns to the west reached the "Cedar mountains," that is, the Amanus mountain range in northwestern **Syria**, and the Mediterranean coast. After Naram-sin's death, the empire began to crumble and was soon to disappear from history, although in the historical tradition of later

Mesopotamia, the age of Akkad was a kind of golden past and King Sargon the epitome of a divinely inspired ruler.

AKRABBIM, THE ASCENT OF. According to the Old Testament, a pass leading from the southern end of the Dead Sea to the Judean plateau at the border between **Judah** and **Edom** (Num 34:4). The name means "the Pass of the Scorpions" and refers to the tortuous character of the ascent.

AMALEK, AMALEKITES. A desert people reckoned among the traditional enemies of early **Israel**. Amalek, their eponymous ancestor, belongs to the genealogy of **Esau** (Gen 36:15), making a close relationship with the **Edomites** more than likely. They also inhabited an area in southern **Palestine** and northern **Sinai** often associated with Edom. They were dependent on camels (1 Sam 30:17; see also Judg 6:5; 7:12), a fact that placed them alongside the Ishmaelites (*see* **Ishmael**) and **Midianites** as proto-Bedouins, representatives of the early phase of the development of the Arab Bedouin type of nomadism. Their way of living made them a highly mobile force that raided Palestinian territory from the north to the south, for example, in the **Jezreel** Valley (Judg 6:33), at **Jericho** (Judg 3:13), or at **Ziglag in Judah** (1 Sam 30). They appeared as mercenaries among **Philistine** troops (2 Sam 2:1-10) or in alliance with **Moabites** (Judg 3:12-14). The origin of the enmity between Amalek and Israel is supposed to go back to the time of the Israelite migrations in the desert (*see* **Desert, Migrations in the**) when they confronted but were defeated by Israel at Rephidim (Exod 17:8-16). They suffered a serious defeat at the hand of King **Saul** (1 Sam 15), and their King **Agag**, the only Amalekite mentioned by name in the Old Testament, was executed. They raided **David**'s home at Ziglag during his absence but were duly pursued and punished. After the period of David, they vanished from history, and may have joined one of the other Arab tribal coalitions of the first millennium B.C.E.

AMARNA AND THE AMARNA LETTERS. In the Late Bronze Age, **Egypt** ruled large parts of western Asia—for a short time as far north as the **Euphrates**. For the local rulers of **Syria** and **Palestine**, it was a period of adaptation to customs and rules very different from their own. In the history of the Late Bronze Age, the Amarna period played a special role, partly because of the religious sentiments of the time—it was the period of Pharaoh Akhnaten's break with tradition—partly because of a collection of letters in cuneiform writing found in 1887 at Akhnaten's residence in present-day Amarna, a ruined place c. 300 kilometers south of Cairo that got its name from the local Bedouin tribe. Apart from the Old Testament, the collection of Amarna letters is the most extensive source in existence of information about life and sentiments in Bronze Age Palestine, and indeed is valuable also for describing the conditions of life in the Iron Age. The collection of Amarna letters includes about 380 tablets in cuneiform writing, the majority being letters sent to the Pharaoh from abroad and a few going in the opposite direction. A minority of the letters includes the correspondence of the "great kings," that is, independent rulers with vassals of their own, such as the king of **Babylonia** or the king of the **Hittites**. The vast majority contains the remains of the correspondence between the Pharaoh and his vassals of Syria and Palestine and includes all kinds of trivia provoked by the everlasting rivalry between the governors of mostly small townships naming themselves "kings" but understood to be no more than low-standing public servants by their Egyptian masters. Being the patrons of their own society, they were in the eyes of the Egyptians little more than "dust"—a common metaphor in these letters.

Among the more interesting sections of the Amarna correspondence, several mentions can be found of a social group called **habiru**, homeless people who struggled for survival in a foreign habitat, but also local patrons denounced by their colleagues in front of the Pharaoh as "habiru," runaway slaves, paying no attention to their lords.

The social and political structure as described by the Amarna letters has been compared to the biblical portrayal of the **Period of the Judges**. To a large extent this is a correct observation, although there are no hints at the existence of a tribal system like the Israelite one of the Old Testament. Although tribal groups were present in the shape of Sutu nomads, small cattle nomads, they had no central role in the local power play between Palestinian potentates. On the other hand, a story like the one about **Abimelech's** rule over **Shechem** and its territory (Judg 9) may just as well have had Palestinian society in the Amarna age as its subject. The tribal society of early **Israel**, as told by the Old Testament historiographers, had much less influence than was usually assumed (*see also* **tribal society, patronage society**).

AMASA. A relative of **David** who was appointed commander of the army by **Absalom** when he rebelled against David (2 Sam 17:25). After having put down the rebellion, David kept him as his general, probably at the same time sacking **Joab** for having killed his son Absalom (2 Sam 20:4). When the rebellion of **Sheba** broke out, Amasa was ordered to assemble the troops in three days but failed miserably. When he joined David's forces at **Gibeon**, Joab treacherously murdered him and reinstated himself in the position as commanding general.

AMASIAH. (The name means "Yahweh supports"). An officer of King **Jehoshaphat** of **Judah** (2 Chron 17:16) praised for his piety. The text indicates that he had bound himself to serve the king by pledging himself to God.

AMAZIAH. (The name means "Yahweh has shown his strength") King of **Judah** 797-769, the son of King **Joash**. Most of the information about Amaziah's long reign comes from 2 Kings 14, but 2 Chronicles 25 includes additional material aiming at explaining Amaziah's disastrous war against Joash of **Israel**. Amaziah is supposed to have stabilized Judean rule by defeating **Edom**. He also occupied Sela, by many scholars identified as the city of Petra in Transjordan. According to 2 Chronicles 25, he employed Israelite mercenaries for his campaigns against Edom. When these soldiers were fired after the end of the war, they started plundering the cities of Judah, maybe a reason for the following hopeless war against Joash of Israel. The encounter between Amaziah's and Joash's armies was a disaster for the Judeans. The battle was fought at **Beth-Shemesh**, west of **Jerusalem**. The king was taken prisoner and Jerusalem sacked. Several years after the debacle at Beth-Shemesh, Amaziah fled to **Lachish** because of a coup d'état. Here he was killed, although brought back to Jerusalem and buried among the former kings of Judah. His son assumed power after his death.

AM-HA-ARES. Literarily "the people of the land," a Hebrew social term that appears a number of times in the Old Testament. It is rather difficult to define the exact meaning of the term, maybe because it has changed its content over time. It is possible roughly to divide the use of the term into three phases, an old pre-exilic usage when it referred to so-called "full citizens" in the southern kingdom, that is, wealthy landowners living outside the confines of the royal city of **Jerusalem**. This group was active on a number of occasions, including the coups that led to the institution of King **Joash** (2 Kgs 11) and King **Jehoahaz** (2 Kgs 23). In the post-exilic period the term lost importance and may have ended up as a term denoting people who did not take part in the exile. Finally, in later Jewish literature, the term Am-ha-ares was used about common people in contrast to law-abiding Jews.

AMMON. King of **Judah** 642-640 B.C.E. (1 Kgs 21:18-26). The only information about his reign is that he ruled for two years and was slain by his servants, who for their part were executed by the **Am-ha-ares**, and had his infant son **Josiah** installed on his throne. There have been many speculations about the reason for the murder: either older brothers who were passed over in the competition for the kingship, religious opposition (Ammon is supposed to have followed his father **Manasseh's** bad ways), or opposition to Ammon's pro-Assyrian (*see* **Assyria and Babylonia**) policy. Although such speculation is common in biblical studies, the Old Testament offers no reason for the murder. It just states it as a fact.

AMMON, AMMONITES. According to the Old Testament, the eponymous ancestor of the Ammonites, Ammon, was the result of the intercourse between **Lot** and his daughters (Gen 19:36-38). The Ammonites are mentioned in biblical, **Assyrian**, and local sources. When put together, the various sources allow for a reconstruction of a fragmentary list of eleven Ammonite kings and a likewise fragmentary reconstruction of Ammonite history. They inhabited an area in Transjordan with their capital **Rabbath-Ammon** (modern Amman) as the center. According to the Old Testament tradition they opposed the migrating Israelites who were forced to circumvent Ammonite territory (Num 25:24-35). Later they became the enemies of the **judge Jephthah** (Judg 11:4.12-33). They were the enemies of **Saul** (1 Sam 11:1-11) and were defeated by **David** and joined his empire as a vassal state (2 Sam 10-12). Renewed military confrontation arose during the time of King **Jehoshaphat of Judah** who was obliged to fight against a coalition from Transjordan (2 Chron 20), and again in the days of King **Jehoiakim**, this time in alliance with the **Chaldaeans** (2 Kgs 24:2). Little is known about the following history of Ammon, apart from the fact that the killers of **Gedaliah** escaped to Ammon (Jer 41:10.15), and that it became a **Persian** province ruled by a governor.

AMNON. **David's** firstborn son, born at **Hebron** (2 Sam 3:2). Amnon fell in love with his sister **Tamar** and raped her. His father pardoned him but not his brother **Absalom**. Later on he was invited to a party by his brother Absalom. Here Absalom killed Amnon, but also in this case David showed leniency toward his children and pardoned Absalom.

AMORITES. In the Old Testament the Amorites are counted among **Palestine's** pre-Israelite nations. The application of the term centers on four different usages: 1. The Amorites are the people living in the mountains whereas the **Canaanites** are identified as the inhabitants of the coast (Josh 5:1; 11:3); 2. The Amorites are simply one of the many nations who together with the Canaanites, the **Hivites**, the **Jebusites**, etc., appear in lists spread among the historical literature in the Old Testament (Gen 15:19-21); 3. The term Amorites embraces all the inhabitants of pre-Israelite Canaan (Josh 24:15.18); and 4. The Amorites are the people living in **Transjordan** who oppose the Israelites during their wanderings to the east of the **Jordan River**.

There is no correlation between the use of the term Amorite in the Old Testament and the historical references to Amorites found in ancient Near Eastern sources from the third and second millennia B.C.E. Indeed, the closest parallel to the biblical usage can be found in the **Mesopotamian** tradition of the first millennium, when "Amorite"—in Akkadian *Amurru*—was simply used as a designation of the people living to the west of the **Euphrates**, a development of a literary tradition from the past without actual relations anymore to the ethnic composition of **Syria** in the first millennium. The origin of the term Amorite should be sought back in the third millennium, in **Syria** and Mesopotamia in the Early and Middle Bronze Age (3200-2000 B.C.E. and 2000-1500 B.C.E. respectively). Amorite was simply the general Mesopotamian term for "Westerner."

The presence of Amorites in Western Asia was formerly attributed to the consequences of a great migration when Semitic-speaking people moved from the Arabian Desert into the cultural and developed zone of the Fertile Crescent. Influenced by a theory about major popular migrations, scholars reckoned a "Canaanite" migration to have taken place c. 3000 B.C.E., an Amorite migration c. 2000 B.C.E., and an **Aramaean** one c. 1000 B.C.E. This idea of the past as governed by a general exchange of population has by and large been given up by present-day scholarship. First of all, the Syro-Arabian Desert has never in historical times been able to support any large population. Secondly, Mesopotamian inscriptions indicate that Amorites were already living in Mesopotamia a long time before the assumed date of their migration. Finally, the excavations at **Ebla** in Syria have shown the presence of a social and political organization hardly expected to have existed in that part of the world as early as the middle of the third millennium B.C.E.

The Amorites could hardly have migrated to Syria, **Palestine**, or Mesopotamia c. 2000 B.C.E.; rather they constituted the majority element of the population of Syria and Palestine a long time before the turn of the third millennium. A number of common traits connected this population, the most important one being the fact that they all spoke the same language, worshipped the same deities, and basically shared a common material culture—of course, with many local variations. Among the peoples of Syria and Palestine in the latter part of the Early Bronze Age the rural districts were dominated by an Amorite speaking population. After the breakdown at the end of the Early Bronze Age and the reestablishment of Syrian urban culture in the Middle Bronze Age, the Amorites dominated Syrian city life. Furthermore, a number of Mesopotamian states, including Babylon, were in the first part of the second millennium B.C.E. ruled by Amorite dynasties, the best known being the dynasty of King Hammurabi of Babylon (1792-1750 B.C.E.).

In the 14th and 13th centuries B.C.E, in the Late Bronze Age, a short-lived Syrian state assumed the name of Amurru, playing on the traditions of the Amorites but not being the reason for the survival of the term.

AMOS. A Judean prophet from **Techoa** near **Bethlehem** said to have ministered in the days of King **Jeroboam** II of **Israel** (784-753 B.C.E.) and **Uzziah** of **Judah** (769-741) (Amos 1:1). He is reckoned to be a firsthand witness to the effects of the policies of the royal administration on the local population and is especially important because of the criticism of the social injustice that had created an intolerable gap between the rich and the poor. In this way, Amos's prophecies have been accepted as an important source that describes how the inner solidarity between the various parts of the population had broken down, preparing for the following political disasters that led to the downfall of the Kingdom of **Israel** a few decades after Amos's death. Most of his activity is placed in the Kingdom of Israel, and King Jeroboam belongs among the people especially addressed by him (Amos prophesies about the violent downfall of the royal house of Israel). He was confronted by **Amaziah**, the priest at **Bethel**, who forbade Amos to prophesy in the royal sanctuary of the north and urged him to return to his own country (Amos 7).

AMPHICTYONY. The name of a sacral league in ancient Greece. Members of the Amphictyony were either city-states or alliances of city-states. The temple at Delphi functioned as the center of the Amphictyony. A number of similar organizations are known from the history of the classical world. It was formerly common—following a proposal by the German scholars Albrecht Alt and Martin Noth—to see the Israelite tribal organization of twelve tribes in the **Period of the Judges** as a kind of Amphictyony organized according to the Greek model (*see also* **Tribal league**). The sacred center of this organization was supposed to be **Shechem** or **Shiloh**. The official title of **"judge,"** Hebrew *shofet*, should be interpreted in the light of this organization. In present scholarship, the Amphictyony has largely been given up as irrelevant to the understanding of early Israelite history and society. Most importantly, there is no information in the **Book of Judges** that indicates that any Amphictyony existed. Nor can it be shown that one particular sanctuary acted as the center of such a league.

AMRAPHEL. The king of **Shinar**, one of the great kings who was defeated by **Abraham** in the **Valley of Siddim** (Gen 14). Amraphel is sometimes identified with King Hammurabi of Babylonia (*see* **Assyria and Babylonia**) (1792-1750 B.C.E.). Recently scholars have proposed **Merodak-Baladan** as the historical figure behind this mythical king.

ANAK, ANAKITES. Anak is said to be the son of Arba (Josh 15:13), the founder of **Kiriath-arba** (**Hebron**) and the eponymous ancestor of the Anakites, said to be a giant race that inhabited **Canaan** before the arrival of the Israelites (Deut 2:10.21; 9:2). They appear in the story about **Joshua**'s spies sent in advance to Canaan (Num 13-14) as the inhabitants of the southern Judean hills. There are no extra-biblical references to the Anakites.

ANATOT. A city of **Benjamin**, a few kilometers north of **Jerusalem**, normally identified as Ras el-Kharrube not far from the Arab village of Anata that has preserved the name. Mentioned in the Old Testament as the home of two of **David**'s champions (2 Sam 23:27; 1 Chron 11:28; 12:3; 27:12), and as the place of banishment for David's priest **Abiatar** (1 Kgs 2:26). It is described as lying on the **Assyrian** line of advance toward Jerusalem (Isa 10:30). The prophet **Jeremiah** was born here (Jer 1:1).

ANER. An **Amorite** allied to **Abraham** together with his brothers, **Mamre** and **Eshkol**, and a participant in Abraham's campaign against the great kings of the east (Gen 14:13-14).

ANNALS. The great kingdoms of the ancient Near East normally compiled a system of yearbooks or annals that in shorthand listed the most important events of the year. Extensive annals have been found at Assyrian and Babylonian (*see* **Assyria and Babylonia**) sites, but also from the **Hittite** Empire of Asia Minor. Annals were also composed in the **Persian**, and later the Hellenistic and Roman, Empires.

Although no annals can be found in the Old Testament, there are, strictly speaking, a series of references to such annals. In 1 Kgs 14:19 and 2 Kgs 15:31, references are presented to "the Book of the Chronicles of the Kings of **Israel**," and in 1 Kgs 14:29 and

15:31 to "the Book of the Chronicles of the Kings of **Judah**." In 1 Kgs 11:41, the author refers to "The Book of the Acts of **Solomon**." None of these has survived and the content can never be reconstructed, although the note about **Sennacherib**'s campaign in 2 Kgs 18:13-14 might well be representative of such a source. The Old Testament books of the Chronicles have nothing to do with annals.

APHEK. Variant spelling Apheka. Place name, probably meaning "spring," or "riverbed." Up to five different cities of this name are mentioned in the Old Testament. The more important were: 1. Aphek of **Asher**, likely to be identified with modern Tel Kabri close to the modern city of Nahariya, a city not conquered by Asher (Judg 1:31); 2. Aphek in the Sharon, situated at the sources of the Yarkon River at Tel Ras el-'Ain, mentioned in the Old Testament as well as **Egyptian** and **Assyrian** sources. In the Old Testament, the **Philistines** mustered their troops at Aphek before joining the battle at **Ebenezer** (1 Sam 4:1), and probably again when moving on to do battle against Saul at Gilboa (1 Sam 28:1-2). In Hellenistic and Roman times, Aphek was known as Antipatris.

ARABAH. The biblical name of the **Palestinian** part of the rift valley that passes from **Syria** right down to Mozambique in Africa. Most often Arabah indicates the part of the valley between the Dead Sea and the Gulf of Aqabah, a dry and desolate spot (Arabah means "the dry country"), however rich in minerals, and exploited already in the Late Bronze Age by Egyptian mining activities, especially at **Timna'** some 16 kilometers to the north of present-day Elath. Apart from the legendary references to Arabah in the tales about the migration of the Israelites in the **desert**, Arabah seems in the Period of Kings to have been a contested area, sued for by Judaean as well as **Edomite** princes.

ARABIA, ARABS. From a linguistic point of view perhaps the most satisfying translation of Arab may well be the ancient Egyptian term for the inhabitants of the desert, the "sand-dwellers." Only later did the term "Arab" become an ethnic term, denoting people speaking a special language, "Arabic." Thus the words Arab and Arabia occur rather sporadically in the Old Testament, Arabia indicating, apart from the Arabian Peninsula, also the desert regions of **Syria** and **Transjordan** and their inhabitants. A reference to an Arab in the Old Testament is not necessarily a reference to an Arab in a strictly ethnic sense; it is a reference to an inhabitant of the desert. The origin of the Arabic-speaking people along the fringe of the Syro-Arabian desert should probably be dated back to the end of the Bronze Age and the beginning of the Iron Age (roughly 1200-1000 B.C.E.), and the development of this language group may be seen as parallel to the earlier appearance of the **Amorites** and the almost contemporary spread of the **Aramaeans,** in both cases better understood to be language groups than well-defined ethnic identities. A decisive reason for the development of the Arabs was that from the very beginning they had domesticated camels, something that only became common at the end of the second millennium B.C.E. Early Arabs can accordingly be defined as camel-breeding proto-Bedouins.

Among the early Arabs, two tribal organizations or coalitions come to mind: the **Midianites** and the **Amalekites** of the Old Testament. The Midianites had their homeland in the northwestern part of the Arabian Peninsula, the Amalekites in the **Negeb** and **Sinai.** With their base in these territories, both groups, encouraged by their way of living, raided, traded, and travelled all over the region, making the best of every opportunity, being a constant problem to the settled population of **Palestine** and Transjordan. Little if anything is known about these groups outside the Old Testament. **Assyrian** sources mention an Arab leader providing a contingent of a thousand camels to the anti-Assyrian coalition at **Qarqar** in 853 B.C.E., showing that Arabs were becoming a force to be reckoned with. Thus, already in the ninth century B.C.E., Arabs began to penetrate settled society and sometimes also assumed high positions like the professional soldier **Omri** (his name is most likely Arabic, like the name of his son Ahab, and the first part of the name of the royal princess **Athaliah**), who rose to become the founder of an important dynasty of Israelite kings.

In the eighth century a new phenomenon turned up in Assyrian sources that was to be characteristic of Arab tribal societies until modern times: the first major Arabian tribal coalition, the Shumuil, or **Ishmaelites,** who are supposed to have covered most of the regions of the Syrian and North Arabian Desert. The Shumuil coalition was a respected enemy and sometimes partner of great Assyrian kings. At a certain point, the Shumuil coalition was substituted by other coalitions, among them the Nabataeans of the Hellenistic-Roman period. It is characteristic of Old Testament tradition that it only hints at this development and position of the Shumuil in the genealogy of Ishmael (Gen 25:12-15) where most of the twelve sons of Ishmael also appear in extra-biblical evidence, the exception being Kedemah—probably a general name ("easterner") to bring the number of sons/tribes to twelve. Somehow these were related, if not identical, to the group of Hagarites (most likely a derivation of the name of **Hagar**, **Abraham**'s Egyptian second wife and Ishmael's mother), said to have opposed the forces of **Reuben**, **Gad**, and **Manasseh** (1 Chron 15:18-20).

Throughout history, Arabia and the Arabs played an important role in trade. Not only was Arabia itself considered the home of exotic items, spices, precious stones, etc., some of it probably being trade goods in transit from even more remote regions rather than local production, but Arab caravans were also now able to cross the desert because of the camels bringing and selling their merchandise and buying goods for export. Thus it is characteristic that the first note on Arabs in the Old Testament (1 Kgs 10:15) lists tributes from the kings of Arabia among the income of King **Solomon**. On top of this the Solomonic tradition speaks of the visit of the South Arabian queen from Sheba (*see* **Sheba, Queen of Sheba**) to Solomon's court (1 Kgs 10:1-13). Such contacts—although not on the personal level—were not unusual for the rest of the **Period of the Monarchy**.

ARAD. A royal **Canaanite** city of the Negeb (Num 21:1; 33:40), situated in the Negeb of Arad (Judg 1:16). The ruins of ancient Arad were discovered at Tell Arad some 23 kilometers east of **Beersheba**, and escavated from 1962-67, and again in 1976. The phases of inhabitance at Arad can mainly be divided into two: the first belonging to the Early Bronze Age, the second to the Iron Age. The heyday of Arad was the Middle Bronze Age, when a large and well-constructed city was placed here on the foundations of a village-like settlement with roots going back into the Chalcolithic Period. The Early Bronze Age city shows a connection to **Egypt** that includes the presence of Egyptian royal names, and pottery produced at Arad has been discovered in Egypt. Also the layout—or type of layout—of the city walls may be reflected in a pictorial presentation on the Egyptian Narmer palette from the Early Dynastic Period, c. 3000 B.C.E. About 2650 B.C.E., the city was destroyed and never rebuilt. Probably a climatic deterioration made such a rebuilding uneconomic.

In the Iron Age an unfortified village existed here, but was substituted by a proper fortress situated on the highest spot of the city from the Judaean Period of the Kings. According to the archaeologists who excavated Arad, the fortress was constructed in the 10th century B.C.E. and modified a number of times since then. Within the compound of the fortress a temple of Yahweh was constructed, but according to a recent reinterpretation of the archaeological evidence not before the late eighth or early seventh century B.C.E. The fortress was probably demolished by the troops of **Nebuchadnezzar** at the beginning of the sixth century B.C.E. Although rebuilding followed, Arad had only marginal importance and in the **Persian** period no settlement was found in this place.

The excavations of Arad had important consequences for archaeology in **Palestine**. By meticulously sorting and cleaning all the pottery found, an extensive number of inscribed ostraca emerged, adding considerably to the amount of written material from Palestine in ancient times. Since Arad, this has been common procedure at all archaeological excavations.

ARAM, ARAMAEANS. The eponymous ancestor of the Aramaeans, Aram, turns up in the "Table of Nations" (Gen 10:22) as one of the sons of Shem. The **patriarchs'** close relationship to the Aramaeans is a stereotype motive in the patriarchal narratives. Thus **Rebecca's** brother and **Jacob's** father-in-law is "the Aramaean **Laban**" (Gen 28:5). At a later date, the descendants of Aram, the Aramaeans, appear in the **Book of Kings** as the staunchest adversaries of the Israelite kingdoms. Especially crucial to the history of **Israel** is the rivalry between Israel and the Aramaean kingdom of **Damascus**. Israel sometimes got the upper hand, whereas Damascus at other times almost subdued Israel. This situation lasted until 734 B.C.E. when the **Assyrian** conquest of **Syria** put an end to the political independence of the Aramaeans and saved Israel from the Aramaean threat.

The inclusion of the Aramaeans in the patriarchal narratives has, in the light of biblical chronology, been seen as an anachronism. The historical Aramaeans do not show up on the historical scene before the Early Iron Age, shortly before 1000 B.C.E. whereas the patriarchs and "the Aramaean" Laban are supposed to have lived perhaps as early as the end of the third millennium B.C.E. It is also possible to roughly sketch the origin of the Aramaeans who—like the Amorites—may have originated at the fringe of settled Syrian society among a mixed population of partly nomadic, partly peasant background and merged into independent or quasi-independent rural societies outside the control of the centralized states of the Late Bronze Age. In connection with the breakdown of centralized state organization at the end of the Bronze Age, an opportunity arose for the people living at the fringe to extend their political control and to expand their territories toward Mesopotamia and toward the central parts of Syria.

Around 1000 B.C.E., a series of Aramaean states was founded, among the best known being Damascus. Other important Aramaean states included Bit Gusi in northern Syria and Bit Adini in the valley of the Euphrates. In the southeastern part of Mesopotamia the Chaldaeans, linguistically related to the Aramaeans, established a number of similar petty states. The political independence of the Syrian Aramaean states lasted from c. 1000 until 734 B.C.E. These were unruly times characterized not only by internecine warfare between the Aramaeans, but also by the ever existing external threat to their independence from Assyria. Sometimes the Aramaeans succeeded in fighting off the Assyrians as at Qarqar in 853 B.C.E. by forming a strong anti-Assyrian coalition including King Ahab of Israel. At other times they were forced to submit to Assyrian supremacy. The end came when Tiglath-pileser III in 734 B.C.E. subdued all of western Asia and pushed the Assyrian frontiers as far as the borders of Egypt. The Aramaeans never recovered their independence, but they lived on in tradition because until the Arab conquest in the seventh century C.E. their language functioned initially as the lingua franca of the Persian Empire and later as the ordinary language of common men.

ARAM-MAACAH. A small **Aramaean** kingdom in the northern part of the territories to the east of the **Jordan River**. Maacah was part of the Aramaean coalition that was defeated by **David** and became part of his kingdom (2 Sam 10). With the resurrection of Aramaean power in **Damascus**, the territory of Maacah became part of the new state.

ARAM-NAHARAIM. Meaning "Aram of the two rivers" (*see* **Aram, Aramaeans**), the last part of the name being linguistically an equivalent of the Greek **Mesopotamia**, meaning the same, although Aram-Naharaim did not include all of Mesopotamia but was limited to a region around the great bend of the **Euphrates** in northern **Syria**. According to Genesis, **Abraham's** servant travels to Nahor in Aram-Naharaim to find a wife for **Isaac** among Abraham's Mesopotamian relatives (Gen 24:10). Among the people coming from Aram-Naharaim belong the seer **Balaam** (Num 23:5) and **Cushan-Rishataim**, who oppressed **Israel** (Judg 3:10). The element Naharaim is well documented in extra-biblical sources from the second millennium B.C.E. In Egyptian sources, the name appears as *Naharina*, an area of interest to the Egyptian conquerors, and the **Amarna letters** sometimes also refer to this region, however never with any hint of an Aramaean presence.

ARAM-ZOBAH. An **Aramaean** kingdom situated in the northern part of the territories to the east of the **Jordan River**, and the adversary of **Saul** (1 Sam 14:47) and **David**. David defeated Aram-Zobah and its king **Hadadezer**, although he was an ally of **Damascus** (2 Sam 10). Aram-Zobah is not mentioned in ancient sources outside the Old Testament, although—according to the OT—a person from **Zobah**, **Rezon**, became the new founder of the Aramaean state of Damascus (1 Kgs 11:23-24).

ARAUNA'S THRESHING GROUND. When God punished **David** because of his census (2 Sam 24), God's revenging angel stopped at the border of the **Jebusite** Araunah's threshing ground. David bought the place and reserved it for the future temple. The name of Araunah is believed not to be Hebrew. It has been proposed that "Araunah" comes from **Hittite** or Hurrian, with the meaning "magnate." Araunah has accordingly been considered the last Jebusite king of **Jerusalem** before David's conquest. The question of whether or not the second **Book of Samuel** contains any historical information is without importance to the general meaning of the text: to provide legitimation for the **temple of Jerusalem**, understood to be a holy place.

ARCHAEOLOGY OF ISRAEL. The importance of archaeology for the study of the history of ancient **Israel** cannot be exaggerated. Before archaeologists began to roam the regions of **Palestine**, the Old Testament was the only source of information relating to the country's ancient history. The role of archaeology in Palestine started early. Its history can roughly be divided into five phases. In the 19th century archaeologists concentrated on soundings in the **Jerusalem** area. The technique was rather primitive with the organization lagging behind. Although local success was experienced and things of interest were found, the published results of the early excavations are mainly worthless by today's standards. The second phase began when archaeologists who had been working in **Egypt** started to drift to Palestine shortly before the turn of the 20th century. Especially British, German, and American archaeologists were very active here in the years preceding World War I. The period witnessed the first traces of stratigraphical archaeology, which although primitive in design nevertheless constituted a vast advance in comparison with the earlier period. The digs were generally extensive, and involved the removal of whole strata of occupation, sometimes almost down to bedrock. Very little of the published results have survived the scrutiny of time.

During the British Mandate of Palestine, in the 1920s and 1930s, extensive excavations took place in many important places. These excavations generally reached similar results as previous expeditions but got closer to developing a proper archaeological method that relied on a number of different techniques, including the establishment of a pottery chronology for dating occupation layers. The development of the British stratigraphical method at **Samaria** is especially worth mentioning. British archaeologists working here moved from horizontal excavations of whole city strata to limited selections that were carried down to bedrock whenever it was possible. The fruitful activity of the time of the British Mandate came to a partial end with the eruption of the first Palestinian revolt (1934–36) and it stopped totally at the outbreak of World War II.

When archaeological excavations were resumed after the formation of the State of Israel in 1948, it became to a large extent an Israeli enterprise, although especially American and British archaeologists were still active. The stratigraphical method became the only one accepted by the community of archaeologists and was perfected over the first 20 years to such a degree that a modern archaeological excavation is a highly sophisticated scientific enterprise including a meticulous recording of all kinds of small finds, objects, ceramics, bones, etc. It involves specialists from many branches of the sciences, including architects, medical experts, palaeobotanists, chemists, pottery experts, and many others. The postwar years can be divided into two phases: one devoted to biblical archaeology and one to independent Palestinian archaeology. Since the beginning of archaeological explorations in Palestine many archaeologists literarily dug with the spade in one hand and the Bible in the other, with the intention of illustrating the Bible with archaeological findings. The last 20 years have seen a change of attitude. It has become clear that archaeology cannot be used to prove that the Bible is true. It is an independent science with its own scholarly agenda, and this agenda is not always at ease with the agenda of biblical historiographers. In this way, archaeology has turned into a major player when it comes to modern reconstructions of the history of ancient Israel.

ARIOCH. King of Ellasar, and one of the four great kings who were defeated by **Abraham** in the **Valley of Siddim** (Gen 14). He is sometimes identified with Tukulti-Ninurta I of **Assyria** (1243-1207 B.C.E.).

ARK OF THE COVENANT. A cultic relic located in the time of the Israelite monarchy in the **temple of Jerusalem.** The traditions about its prehistory since the time of the Israelite migrations in the desert (*see* **Desert, Migrations in the Desert**) describe it as a movable shrine which the Israelites used to carry with them into war. The last time the Ark of the Covenant was taken into the field it was ignominiously lost to the **Philistines,** although in the event the Philistines were not able to keep it but had to send it away (1 Sam 4-6).

ARNON. A mighty river in **Transjordan** forming the natural border of **Moab** to the north. It runs through the present Wadi el-Mudjib, a huge canyon to the east of the Dead Sea.

AROER. Name of a number of cities in **Transjordan.** The more important are:

1. Aroer at the **Arnon**, in a number of places reckoned to be at the **Moabite** border. It was conquered by the Israelites migrating through Transjordan (Deut 2:36) and was supposed to be part of the territory of the tribe of **Reuben** (Josh 13:16), although other information lists it as part of the tribe of **Gad** (Num 32:34). In the inscription of the Moabite King **Mesha** (c. 8730 B.C.E.), Mesha boasts of having fortified Aroer. About 800, according to the Old Testament, it marked the southern border of **Hazael's** kingdom (2 Kgs 10:33). Later it returned to Moabite rule (Jer 48:18). It has been located at Arair, an Arab village at the fringe of the Wadi-Mujib canyon in Jordan, and was excavated in the 1960s. Here remains of a fortress or small city were found.

2. The **Ammonite** Aroer was situated east of Rabah (present-day Amman) forming the border between the tribe of **Gad** and **Ammon** (Josh 13:15). Its present location has not yet been established.

ARTAXERXES. The name of three kings of **Persia.** 1. Artaxerxes I Longimanus (465-425 B.C.E.) who made peace with the Greeks c. 450 B.C.E. and consolidated his realm after troubles following the death of **Xerxes** and rebellion in **Egypt.** 2. Artaxerxes II Mnemon (404-358 B.C.E.), who stabilized the situation of the empire in Asia Minor but had to quell rebellions in Egypt. 3. Artaxerxes III Ochus (359-338 B.C.E.), the last important king of Persia, who reconquered Egypt, but was murdered by his eunuchs.

Artaxerxes I is normally associated with the mission of **Nehemiah** to Jerusalem, whereas Artaxerxes II is seen as the master of **Ezra** the scribe. The Old Testament makes no distinction but simply uses Artaxerxes of any king of this name.

ASA. The third king of **Judah,** who reigned for 41 years (traditionally 913-873 B.C.E.), and the son of **Abijah** and **Maacah,** the daughter of **Absalom.** Asa's reign thus paralleled the reign of Israelite kings from **Jeroboam** to **Ahab.** The information about Asa can be found in 1 Kgs 15:9-24 and 2 Chron 14-16. The expanded version of Asa's reign in **Chronicles**, however, is constructed on the basis of the shorter version in **Kings** but has been supplemented by information not from an independent source but from the need of the Chroniclers to provide more information about this pious king. 1 Kings describes Asa as the initiator of the reform of the cult in **Jerusalem**. He fought successfully against **Baasha**, the king of **Israel**, and concluded a defensive alliance with the **Aramaeans** against the kingdom of Israel. Mention is also made of his sickness, death, and burial in Jerusalem, and that he was followed on the throne by his son **Jehoshaphat**. From a literary point of view, the Asa story shows remarkable similarity to the narratives about **Ahaz** and **Hezekiah**. It is possible that the author of 1 Kings 15 composed the story about Asa on the basis of the tradition of other pious kings of Judah rather than using old source material. No source outside the Old Testament mentions him, nor can any remains be found that can safely be attributed to the reign of Asa.

ASAHEL. "And Asahel was as light of foot as a wild roe" (2 Sam 2:18). Asahel (the name means "God has made") was **Joab's** younger brother who was killed at the battle at **Gibeon** by **Abner** (2 Sam 2:18-23). Later this became Joab's pretext for killing Abner in revenge for his brother's death (2 Sam 3:27).

ASHDOD. A **Philistine** city about 4 kilometers from the Mediterranean coast. It never became part of either the kingdom of **Judah** or **Israel** but remained independent until Hellenistic times. In the Old Testament it is reckoned—without regard for reality—as part of Judah's inheritance (Josh 11:21-22). In the narrative about the loss of the **Ark of the Covenant** in 1 Samuel 4-6, Dagon's temple in Ashdod was imagined as the new home of the ark. However, history turned out otherwise, and the Philistines had to give up the idea of controlling the ark. Ashdod was extensively excavated between 1962 and 1970. The city was founded in the later part of the Middle Bronze Age, c. 1650 B.C.E. and existed as Azotus well into Hellenistic-Roman times, when it was gradually superceded by nearby Azotus Paralios (Ashdod Yam). Apart from casual notes in the Old Testament, Ashdod appears in texts from ancient Ugarit, and in **Sargon's** inscriptions pertaining to the year

713 B.C.E. That year the **Assyrians** had to put down a rebellion caused by a certain Yamani. The city was destroyed but was rebuilt and regained a part of its former status under **Esarhaddon**, who mentions it in his inscriptions. Later it became a province under the Neo-Babylonian Empire (*see* **Assyria and Babylonia**).

ASHER. The northwestern Israelite tribe, said to be the descendants of Asher, the son of **Jacob** and his second wife Zilpah. However, the name of Asher turns up in Egyptian sources from the 13th century B.C.E. Accordingly the ranking of Asher among the tribes of **Israel** may be secondary and reminiscent of the Israelite control over the coastal plain bordering on the **Phoenician** cities in the **Period of the Monarchy**. The tribal borders of Asher are described in Josh 19:24-31). A special branch of this tribal group appears in central **Ephraim** (see also 1 Chron 7:30-40). Not much information about the Asherites has survived. They are said to be rich and fat (Gen 49:20, see also Deut 32:24-25), and are reproached for not participating in the battle against **Sisera** (Judg 5:17), although they sided with **Gideon** against the **Midianites** (Judg 6:35).

ASHKELON. A major city and important harbor on the southern coast of **Palestine** about 50 kilometers south of modern Tel Aviv. It was excavated in 1920, and again in ongoing excavations since 1985. Traces of a settlement reaching back to the third millennium B.C.E. have been found but a major city with strong fortifications may only have appeared in the Middle Bronze Age, at which time it is mentioned in a number of Egyptian "**execration texts**"—formulaic curses directed against **Egypt**'s enemies. In the Late Bronze Age it was part of the Egyptian Empire and is mentioned in several documents including the **Amarna letters**. After the migration of the **Sea People** it became one of the major **Philistine** cities—together with **Ashdod, Ekron, Gath,** and **Gaza**. The Old Testament mentions that Joshua did not conquer Ashkelon (Josh 13:3). As a matter of fact, it remained a Philistine town to the end of the Iron Age, although it had to cede to the power of the **Assyrians** and became an Assyrian vassal state. Although destroyed by the Babylonians in 604 B.C.E., it was soon rebuilt and remained an important center of trade not only in **Persian** times but actually until the

Middle Ages when it was finally destroyed by **Arab** rulers after their victories over the crusaders.

ASHTEROT-KARNAJIM (also ASHTAROTH). A city in the northern part of **Transjordan**, said to have been formerly inhabited by the **Rephaites** (Gen 14:5). Later, it was the capital of the **Amorite** King **Og** (Deut 1:4). Today it is identified with Tell 'Ashtara in southern **Syria**. In extra-biblical documents, it is mentioned in Egyptian sources and in the **Amarna letters**, as well as **Assyrian** war reports. The double name may indicate that there were as a matter of fact two interrelated towns, Karnajim sometimes being identified with Tell Sa'd a couple of kilometers to the north of Tell 'Ashtara.

ASHURBANIPAL. King of **Assyria** 668-c. 627 B.C.E. Although the youngest son of **Esarhaddon,** Ashurbanipal was designated by his father as the heir to the throne of Assyria, while at the same time the prestigious but less politically influential office as governor of Babylonia was given to his older brother Shamash-shum-ukin. Ashurbanipal was the first king of Assyria who did not lead his armies in the field. The king's interest lay in the maintenance of the ancient culture of **Mesopotamia** and he invested most of his energy in creating a cultural milieu in his capital second to none. In **Nineveh** he collected the literary treasures of all of Mesopotamia in his famous library. He consolidated the power of Assyria over western Asia by, for example, giving up overambitious conquests such as **Egypt,** his father's conquest. On the eastern border he defeated **Elam** and conquered its capital **Susa,** ironically providing an opportunity for the rise of the Medes (*see* **Media**) to statehood. He also had to stand up against his brother who was heading a coalition against Ashurbanipal. Shamash-shum-ukin ended his days in the burning ruins of his palace, and peace was restored. About 627 B.C.E., when Ashurbanipal died, the Assyrian Empire looked healthier than ever. The fact was that it was already doomed. Less than 20 years after Ashurbanipal died, his empire had ceased to exist.

ASHURNASIRPAL II. King of **Assyria** 883-859 B.C.E. Ashurnasirpal inherited from his father, Tukulti-Ninurta II (890-884 B.C.E.), an expanding kingdom that had provided Assyria with a safe border to the north. Now, Ashurnasirpal turned the armies of Assyria toward the west against the **Aramaean** states in northern **Syria**. After having subdued these states, Ashurnasirpal pushed on to the coast of the Mediterranean where he received tribute from the cities of **Phoenicia**. He founded a new capital, Kalhu (Nimrud) and initiated the creation of a proper provincial administration. The relationship to Babylonia could best be described as a kind of armed neutrality.

ASSYRIA AND BABYLONIA. Together Assyria and Babylonia formed the two dominating states of **Mesopotamia** in ancient times. Assyria and Babylonia is often used synonymous with Mesopotamia. Although both of the names of Assyria and Babylonia go back to ancient cities, Ashur and Babylon respectively, they were not the oldest center of power in the region. In the Bronze Age, the center of political gravity was to be sought in the northern part of Mesopotamia. Until c. 2900 B.C.E., a rich urban culture dominated the area. In the so-called "proto-dynastic" period, that is, between 2900 and 2350 B.C.E., this culture spread to other parts of Mesopotamia, including the region closest to the Persian Gulf where a number of Sumerian city-states appeared, among the best known Ur (*see* **Ur of the Chaldeans**), Uruk, and Lagash. In this period Mesopotamia was not a politically unified country but split between innumerable small political units.

Toward the end of the period, a new development started that was to become characteristic of the next 2,000 years of Mesopotamian history, when one of the petty states began to dominate the rest of the territory. About 2350 B.C.E., the first Mesopotamian empire emerged ruled by **Sargon**, the king of **Akkad**, a city situated in the center of the country close to Babylon and modern Baghdad. He initiated his imperial aspirations by assuming control over central and southern Mesopotamia. The second phase was devoted to the expansion of his rule toward the north and west to the border of **Syria** at the upper course of the **Euphrates**. The third and final phase saw the successor of Sargon pushing the borders of the empire to the east into the Iranian plateau, and toward the west until the Mediterranean. However, as fast as the empire was established, it also crumbled and was replaced by other kingdoms, including the Sumerian kingdom of Ur that toward the end of the third millennium controlled all of southern Mesopotamia. The development leading to one imperial political construction substituting a previous one was repeated several times as the centuries went by.

Another political development characteristic of Mesopotamian history was the replacement of local dynasties with new ruling houses originating on the fringe of the political centers. In the beginning of the second millennium, a number of **Amorite** dynasties assumed power over most of the important Mesopotamian centers including Babylon itself. The early second millennium was also the period when Mesopotamian history began to split into two polar political societies, in the north Assyria and in the south Babylonia. This polarization persisted until the **Persian** conquest in the sixth century. About 2000 B.C.E., Mesopotamia was divided into a number of small states. However, in northern Mesopotamia the city-state of Ashur developed into the first Assyrian state under Shamshi-Adad I (1812-1780) who ruled large parts of upper Mesopotamia and the eastern part of Syria, including Mari at the Euphrates, where Shamshi-Adad placed his son as a puppet king. After Shamshi-Adad's death, his state dissolved, and Assyria was again reduced to an insignificant small kingdom in northern Mesopotamia.

Now Babylon took over and for the first time became the center of an important Mesopotamian state under King Hammurabi, the most important king of the Amorite first dynasty of Babylon. This period that lasted from 1894-1595 B.C.E. is generally considered the golden age of Mesopotamian civilization. In spite of this, Hammurabi's empire was soon to disappear, and Babylon returned to its former status of a local power in central Mesopotamia. Until Hellenistic times, Babylon was considered the cultural center of the region but was not able to be the dominant political power for almost a millennium after the fall of the Amorite dynasty.

From c. 1550 B.C.E., Babylonia was ruled by another dynasty of foreign origin, this time consisting of Kassite kings whose home should be sought in the mountains to the east of Babylonia. In the same period, Assyria was involved in a protracted struggle for survival against, among others, the Hurrite kingdom of Mitanni in upper Mesopotamia. Toward the middle of the fourth century B.C.E., this struggle led to the appearance of the Middle Assyrian Kingdom, the usual name for a rather unstable major Assyrian political construction that survived to the middle of the 11th century B.C.E. and at least at one point, during the reign of Tukulti-Ninurta I (1243-1207 B.C.E.) was able to occupy Babylonian territory. At the beginning of the first millennium B.C.E., a political situation emerged when history almost repeated itself, and the political structure of Mesopotamia resembled the one in c. 2000 B.C.E. In southern Mesopotamia, Babylon was still the most important power that was sometimes able also to interfere with policies in neighboring regions like **Elam** in present-day western Iran. Assyria was once again reduced to an insignificant political existence. At the same time, at the fringe of Mesopotamian society, a number of new states appeared, ruled by dynasties of **Aramaean** or **Chaldaean** origin.

In the period that followed to the middle of the first millennium B.C.E., the political history of Assyria and Babylonia was to become very different. Assyria was forced to fight for survival against a series of Aramaean states to the west, against states of Asia Minor—the more important being Urartu—to the north, and against tribal coalitions in the Zagros Mountains to the northeast and east. Until c. 900 B.C.E., the basic problem that confronted the rulers of Assyria was simply survival. However, after c. 900 B.C.E., the Assyrians had learned their lesson and out of this continuous struggle for survival a state of conquerors emerged, the Neo-Assyrian Empire (c. 900-612 B.C.E.), whose destiny was to conquer all of western Asia, and at the end of the line even **Egypt**. Babylonia continued to exist in the shadow of Assyria until another foreign dynasty, the Chaldaean, assumed power. For most of a century, Babylon was allowed to play the role as capital in a major empire of western Asia, the Neo-Babylonian Empire (625 B.C.E.-639 B.C.E.).

The heyday of this Neo-Babylonian Empire came in 612 B.C.E., when the king of Babylonia, Napolassar, joined forces with the Medians (*see* **Media**), the rulers of Iran, and succeeded in conquering and destroying **Nineveh**, the capital of Assyria. The last traces of Assyrian resistance were extinguished at **Charchemish** in northern Syria in 605 B.C.E., and Assyria vanished forever from history. The Neo-Babylonian Empire witnessed a period of cultural nostalgia when its rulers tried to revitalize the great moments of the past.

However, it was to become the last independent Mesopotamia realm for a period of almost 2,500 years.

Between 539 and 331 B.C.E., Mesopotamia was ruled by the Persians as one of their provinces, to be substituted after the conquest of Alexander the Great by the empire of the Seleucids who moved their capital from old Babylon to their new city of Seleucia—later to become Baghdad—no more an oriental but a Hellenistic city.

The reasons for this vexed history of Assyria and Babylonia must be sought in a general factor that was decisive. From a geographical point of view, Mesopotamia is not a unit, nor has it stable and well-defined borders against the outside world. Although at a later date, when Assyria and Babylonia no longer existed, they were almost understood to be synonymous, especially when it came to culture and ethnicity, this first impression is far removed from the political, economic, and demographic realities of ancient times. The Assyrians who inhabited a mixed geographical environment, partly a mountainous region, were formed into a tough and well-organized nation of warriors, culturally not on the level of the sophisticated Babylonians who thrived along the lines laid out by Sumerian culture. Naturally, the Assyrians were generally superior to the Babylonians when it came to military exploits but they were never able to obtain full recognition from their Babylonian neighbors as their peers. The Babylonians continued to the very end to see the Assyrians as brutes, barbarians without culture, and they never accepted the Assyrian domination. The Assyrians did not even reside in the city of Babylon; they sacked it. The political power structure of Assyria and Babylonia was also very dissimilar. Assyria was for all of its history ruled by Assyrians—in theory by members of the same dynasty. Babylonia for its part saw a succession of ruling houses of foreign extraction: Amorites, Kassites, and Chaldaeans. The Amorites ruled for 300 years, the Kassites even longer, c. 350 years, and although the rule of the Chaldaeans was limited to c. 90 years, their time represented the acme of Babylonian greatness.

The openness to foreign rule was because of the open borders. During the period of political instability that followed the demise of the empire of Sargon of Akkad, the Amorites, who at the end of the third millennium formed the majority of the population at the fringe of Babylonian society and in Syria, were able to penetrate the political scene in Mesopotamia. The story was repeated after the fall of the Amorite ruling house, when the Kassites and later the Chaldaeans rose to power over Babylonia. These substitutions had little to do with big migrations of thousands if not hundreds of thousands of people that changed the composition of the Babylonian population. Rather, they were the result of a changing orientation of the Babylonian population as a whole. In the third millennium the Sumerians gradually assimilated Akkadian-speaking people, and Akkadian replaced Sumerian as the common language. The process was repeated in the second millennium, although Akkadian remained the official language. However, when it was repeated in the first millennium, Aramaic began to replace Akkadian as the language of ordinary persons.

The complicated and changing history of Mesopotamia also accounted for the peculiar development of Assyrian and Babylonian culture and civilization that displayed an extraordinary diversity at the same time as an astounding unity. The diversity was the result of the many and variable inputs from the countries and peoples around Mesopotamia proper. It would be safe to say that everybody with business in mind, whether economic or political, would sooner or later arrive in Babylon. The pressure from tribal peoples—Amorites or Aramaeans in the west, and mountaineers in the north and east—oriented against the center of the world, central Mesopotamia with its rich urban culture, also influenced the ethnic and cultural composition of the local civilization.

On the other hand, the culture also showed this special homogeneity that was peculiar to it. The people of Mesopotamia, whether Assyrians or Babylonians or immigrants, where held together by a common tradition that reached back to the third Sumerian dominated millennium, and probably to cultures only known from material artifacts from an even earlier time. It was a very conservative tradition that kept its treasures for millennia, until the second century B.C.E., when the special Mesopotamian culture began seriously to break down under the impact of Hellenistic culture. The survival of the tradition was dependent on the existence of a network of scholarly institutions, so-called "scribal schools" where the students were educated in using the difficult cuneiform system of writing. Most of the education was based on copying ancient, classical texts from the Mesopotamian past. In this way any person who could read and write would be familiar with this tradition that also included the knowledge of Sumerian, the original language of cuneiform writing.

However, the education was not limited to writing lessons; it also included a series of scholarly subjects such as ancient mythology, astronomy—or rather astrology, for which enterprise exact astronomic knowledge was essential—medicine, and natural sciences, mostly preserved in long lists. Also classical texts from the legal tradition were preserved, read, and discussed. This antiquary domination of the Mesopotamian mind culminated when **Ashurbanipal**, the last great king of Assyria, established his famous library in order to preserve the Mesopotamian literary tradition in one place.

The reason for entertaining the costly and prolonged educational system had to do with the need for well-educated people with the ability to read and write. The often huge urban centers of Mesopotamia, housing sometimes several hundred thousand people, made a complicated administrative organization a necessity. The activities of the scribes and scholars were present in every sector of Mesopotamian society. Moreover, they followed the merchants and armies of Mesopotamia to the rest of the ancient Near East to such a degree that Akkadian in the second millennium B.C.E. became the lingua franca of the whole territory. The influence of Assyria and Babylonia on the society of **Palestine** and Syria in antiquity, an influence that is also evident on the pages of the Old Testament, was not only one of military conquest and suppression of local civilization, but it was also the influence of a superior culture that made its impression on every society that came into contact with it.

Lists of kings of the Neo-Assyrian Empire and of the Neo-Babylonian Empire:

Assyria:

Adad-Nirari I	(911-891)
Tukulti-Ninurta II	(890-884)
Assurnasirpal II	(883-859)
Shalmaneser III	(858-823)
Shamshi-Adad V	(823-811)
Adad-Nirari II	(810-783)

Shalmaneser IV	(782-773)
Ashur-Dan III	(772-755)
Ashur-Nirari V	(755-745)
Tiglath-pileser III	(744-727)
Shalmaneser V	(726-722)
Sargon	(721-705)
Sennacherib	(704-681)
Esarhaddon	(680-669)
Ashurbanipal	(668-627)

Ashurbanipal is followed by a succession of four insignificant kings who carried Assyria to its end.

List of synchronism between Assyrian kings and kings of **Israel** and **Judah**:

853	Shalmaneser III/Ahab of Israel
c. 830	Shalmaneser III/Jehu of Israel
c. 740	Tiglath-pileser III/Azariah of Israel
c. 735	Tiglath-pileser III/Menahem of Israel
c. 730	Tiglath-pileser III/Ahaz of Judah
c. 701	Sennacherib/Hezekiah of Judah
c. 680	Esarhaddon/Manasseh of Judah
c. 660	Ashurbanipal/Manasseh

Babylonian kings:

Napolassar	(625-605)
Nebuchadnezzar II	(604-562)
Evil-Merodach	(561-560)
Neriglissar	(559-556)
Labashi-Marduk	(556)
Nabonidus	(555-539)

ASSYRIA AND ISRAEL. At the beginning of the ninth century B.C.E., after a period of weakness, as **Assyria** was reduced to an insignificant north Mesopotamian city-state, **Ashurnasirpal** of Assyria initiated a new period of Assyrian greatness that led to an expansion of Assyrian territory to the west, to the borders of the Mediterranean. The first phase of the Assyrian expansion did not affect **Israel**. However, in 853 B.C.E. at **Qarqar** in **Syria**, direct contact was made when King **Ahab** joined an **Aramaean** coalition to fight off the threat from Assyria. For a moment the Assyrian onslaught was impeded. After the fall of the dynasty of **Omri**, the coalition was dissolved and replaced by prolonged fighting between the former allies, not least **Damascus** and Israel, an opportunity not to be missed by the Assyrians who continued their advance toward the west. Already in 843 B.C.E., **Jehu** of Israel was forced to submit to the might of Assyria.

None of these events have been recorded by the Old Testament historiographers. They show more interest in the events that followed the ascension of **Tiglath-pileser III** to the throne of Assyria in 745 B.C.E., when the final phase in the history of the Assyrian Empire began. Over a period of just a few years, Tiglath-pileser received tribute from King **Menahem** of Israel and pushed his armies to the border of **Palestine**. Here he and his successor, **Shalmanaser V,** succeeded in connection with the so-called "Syro-Ephraimite" war to reduce the states of Palestine into either Assyrian provinces or Assyrian puppets. Israel was limited to only its capital and the territory of the city itself. In 722 B.C.E. **Samaria** also fell to the soldiers of **Sargon,** and parts of the Israelite population were sent into exile in **Mesopotamia. Judah** had little to do with this event. Already before the fall of Samaria it had accepted the Assyrians as its overlords. Only when **Hezekiah** rebelled against Assyria, disaster struck, and Judah was almost totally destroyed by **Sennacherib**, while the king was forced behind the walls of **Jerusalem**. For unknown reasons Sennacherib did not conquer Jerusalem but left after having received an impressive tribute from the Judean king, including—according to his own royal annals—the daughters of Hezekiah. Only a small city-state with Jerusalem as its center remained as an Assyrian puppet state. From the middle of the seventh century B.C.E., the grasp of the Assyrians diminished in force and made some kind of independence possible for the local powers of Palestine. In the time of King **Josiah,** Judah seems to have regained its independence from Assyria.

It is difficult to find evidence of a direct Assyrian influence on the civilization of Palestine during its hegemony over the territory. Instead, one should think of an immense indirect influence, not least on religion. Scholars have generally understood the references pertaining to this period to astral religion in the Old Testament as a reflection of this influence.

ATHALIAH. (Meaning of name contested). Queen of **Judah** 842-837. Athaliah was the daughter of **Ahab** of **Israel** (2 Kgs 8:18), or of **Omri** of Israel (2 Kgs 8:26: The text probably means that she was a princess of the royal house of Omri), and the mother of King **Ahaziah** of Judah. After the murder of her son, she liquidated the house of **David** and assumed royal power for herself. Only an infant son of the king was saved by the **priests** of the temple in **Jerusalem**. After a seven-year period, Athaliah was removed and killed by a putsch that reinstated **Joash**, the infant, as the true successor of the Davidic line of kings of Judah (2 Kgs 11).

AZARIAH. The name of several persons in the Old Testament. The only Azariah of historical importance is Azariah, king of **Judah** 769-741 B.C.E. Better known as **Uzziah**.

AZEKAH. A city and fortress in the Judean **Shephelah**, overlooking the **Elah Valley**. In the Old Testament Azekah is mentioned a couple of times in connection with early warfare, in Josh 10:10-11 as the end place of the Israelite pursuit of the five **Amorite** kings, and in 1 Sam 17:1 as part of the description of the site for the duel between **David** and **Goliath**. **Rehoboam** is said to have fortified the place (2 Chron 11:9). Azekah turns up in some extra-biblical inscriptions, thus in **Assyrian** texts relating to campaigns in **Palestine**. It and **Lachish** were the last surviving localities of **Judah** during **Nebuchadnezzar**'s campaign against **Jerusalem** (Jer 34:7); information often compared to the famous text of Lachish letter No. 4: "Let him also know that we are watching for the beacons of Lachish, in accordance with all the code-signals that my lord has given; but we do not see Azekah" (transl. Gibson). Excavations were carried out at the usual place of identification, Tell Zakariya, in 1898-99. Remains were found which according to a modern archaeological estimate can be dated to at least the eighth century B.C.E.

- B -

BAAL-MEON (also BETH BAAL MEON and BETH MEON). A city in the tribal territory of **Reuben** (Num 32:38; Josh 13:17), somewhere to the east of the Dead Sea. It was fortified by **Mesha** of **Moab** in the middle of the ninth century but probably returned to Israelite control if the Baal-Meon of the **Samaria Ostraca** refers to the same site. The prophet **Jeremiah** considered it a Moabite city (Jer 48:23).

BAASHA. King of **Israel** (c. 910-887), the son of Ahijah of the tribe of **Issachar.** He murdered King **Nadab** who was besieging the Philistine (*see* **Philistines**) town of **Gibbethon,** and extinguished the royal house of **Jeroboam** I (1 Kgs 15:27-32). The Old Testament has few details about his long reign, except that he competed with King **Asa** of **Judah** for many years over the control of the passes to the north of **Jerusalem.** Thus he fortified **Ramah** only a few kilometers north of Jerusalem. Asa approached the crisis by allying himself with Bar-Hadad (*see* **Ben-Hadad**) of **Damascus**—Baasha's former ally—and encouraged Bar-Hadad to attack **Israel,** advice the **Aramaean** king was all too ready to follow. As a consequence Baasha was forced to retreat from Judah to his royal city **Tirzah** (1 Kgs 15:16-22). The evaluation of Baasha's reign in the Old Testament is highly negative. He was no better a king than Jeroboam, and according to a prophecy formulated by **Jehu the son of Hanani** the fate of his family was going to be the same as the one he measured out for Jeroboam's dynasty (1 Kgs 16:1-4). Baasha died peacefully and was buried at Tirzah.

BABEL, TOWER. In Genesis 11 it is told how humankind aspired to enter God's world by constructing a tower that reached to heaven. God thwarted human scheming and dispersed humankind all over the earth. Although the tale of the tower of Babel has no historical foundation, the idea of Babel as housing a mighty tower may reflect the temple towers of old **Mesopotamia,** including the famous tower of the temple of Marduk at **Babylon** itself. These towers were called ziggurats, and their remains can still be seen, for example, at Babylon and **Ur.**

BABYLON, BABEL. The center of Mesopotamian culture, a famous city of central **Mesopotamia** that rose to power and glory under the **Amorite** dynasty in the beginning of the second millennium B.C.E., especially under King Hammurabi (1792-1750 B.C.E.) who founded the first Babylonian Empire. For most of its history, Babylon was ruled by dynasties of foreign extraction, either directly by Amorite or Kassite dynasties residing in the city itself, or by **Assyrian** overlords, ruling the city by help of Assyrian vice kings. The city was destroyed by **Sennacherib** at the beginning of the seventh century B.C.E but reestablished and partly rebuilt by **Esarhaddon** after Sennacherib's death. It remained in existence for another 400 years and became the center of the Neo-Babylonian Empire (605-639 B.C.E.). It continued its existence as a famous cultural and administrative center under the **Persians** and was visited by Alexander the Great who died there in 323 B.C.E. After Alexander's death, his successor Seleuchus I founded a new city (Seleucia alias Baghdad of modern times) near old Babylon. The old city was given up by its inhabitants who moved to the more comfortable quarters in the Hellenistic city. That was the end of Babylon and its glory. The city was left, never sacked, and became a memory of the past—a fate probably reflected in the story of the **tower of Babel** (Gen 11).

BABYLONIA. *See* ASSYRIA AND BABYLONIA.

BABYLONIA AND THE KINGDOM OF JUDAH. In spite of Babylonia's (*see* **Assyria and Babylonia**) position as the center of the ancient world, and in spite of the biblical tradition about the patriarchs as coming out of **Mesopotamia,** historical relations between Babylonia and **Israel** were late. The first historically feasible connection was established in the days of **Hezekiah,** when negotiations were held between Hezekiah, himself an instigator of a rebellion against the **Assyrians,** and the fierce Babylonian opponent of the Assyrians, **Merodak-Baladan,** in the very last years of the eighth century B.C.E. (2 Kgs 20:12-13). Nothing came of the negotiations; Hezekiah had to surrender to Assyrian power, and in the end Merodak-Baladan lost his prolonged fight against Sennacherib. A century later, the Neo-Babylonian Empire was to spell the end of the independent **Kingdom of Judah**. It began in 597 B.C.E. when **Nebuchadnezzar** for the first time conquered **Jerusalem** and removed King **Jehoiachin**, installing **Zedekiah**, in the wording of the **Babylonian Chronicle** "a king of his own liking." Ten years later, when Zedekiah joined an anti-Babylonian rebellion, Nebuchadnezzar wiped out the Kingdom of Judah, destroyed the capital with its **temple**, and removed a part of its population to **Mesopotamia** (*see* **Babylonian Exile**). Less than 50 years later, Babylonia itself lost its independence to the **Persians**.

BABYLONIAN CHRONICLE. A Babylonian historical chronicle that covers the period from 626-594 B.C.E. It includes important information about **Nebuchadnezzar's** first conquest of **Jerusalem** in 597 B.C.E. but, alas, is broken before it comes to his second and final conquest and destruction of the city.

BABYLONIAN EXILE. The rulers of the Neo-Babylonian Empire continued the practices of the **Assyrians** to deport parts of the conquered populations (*see* **Deportation**). When the Babylonians conquered **Jerusalem** in 597 B.C.E., they removed 7,000 persons of substance to **Mesopotamia** (2 Kgs 24:16), among them the prophet **Ezekiel**. More deportations followed the destruction of Jerusalem in 597 B.C.E (2 Kgs 25:11). The exiled Judeans were settled in agricultural colonies. The best known was **Tel-Abib** close to the ancient Mesopotamian city of Nippur where the exiled Judeans enjoyed a life hardly less prosperous than the one they were used to in their homeland. Although the traditions of the Old Testament prefer to talk about **Jews** being persecuted in Mesopotamia and remember the exile as a time of distress (e.g., Ps 137), living conditions were generally preferable in the fertile river valley of ancient Mesopotamia to the ones to be found in the barren Judean hill land. The Old Testament presents very little in the way of historical information concerning the Babylonian exile. The final note of the 2 **Book of Kings** mentions the release of King **Jehoiachin** from his prison after the death of Nebuchadnezzar (2 Kings 25:27-30). The second part of the Book of **Isaiah** is attributed to an anonymous prophet who prophesied about **Cyrus's** conquest of Babylon and the impending return of the Jews to Jerusalem, but it has little to say about the living conditions of the Jews in Mesopotamia.

The official date of the end of the Babylonian Exile is 538 B.C.E., when Cyrus after his conquest of **Babylonia** allowed the Jews to return to their homeland. The **Book of Ezra** states that following Cyrus's decree of freedom, 42,360 persons returned from the exile (Ezra 2:64). However, it is well documented from Mesopotamian and Jewish sources that a large part of the Jews in Mesopotamia chose to remain in Mesopotamia, where a large Jewish community—belonging to the *golah*, the "Dispersal" of later Judaism—was continuously present until modern times. However, in Jewish tradition, the Babylonian Exile became the great divide between ancient Israel and the Jewish society that emerged from the ruins of the former **Kingdom of Judah**.

BALAAM. Son of Beor. A seer or **prophet** from Peor in **Aram-Naharaim** who was invited by the **Moabite** King **Balak** to curse the Israelite tribes during their migration in **Transjordan** (Num 22-24). As it turned out, Balaam did not curse but blessed **Israel**. Other traditions associate Balaam with the apostasy of the Israelites with the **Midianite** women at Peor (Num 31:16; see also Num 25), and it is recorded that the Israelites killed him in a battle against the Midianites (Num 31:8). An Aramaic inscription from Deir 'Allah in Transjordan dating from the eighth or seventh century B.C.E. provides a different and imaginative image of Balaam who may have been a traditional religious figure from Transjordan.

BALAK. King of **Moab** and son of Zippor, who according to the Old Testament invited the seer **Balaam** to curse **Israel** during its camping at the plains of Moab. As it turned out, Balaam blessed Israel to Balak's frustration (Num 22-24). Apart from this story and a few references to it in other parts of the Old Testament (e.g., Josh 24:9-10; Judg 11:25; Mic 6:5), nothing is known about Balak.

BARAK. The son of Abinoam, from Kedesh-**Naphtali**, called upon by the prophetess **Deborah** to oppose the **Canaanite** forces of **Sisera** of Haroshet-of-the-Gentiles (Judg 4). When he hesitated, Deborah promised to assist him but at the cost of the glory of victory: The enemy leader will be killed by a woman. Barak's forces met the Canaanites at the spring of **Kishon**—in the version of the battle given in the "**Song of Deborah**" (Judg 5), the battle took place at **Taanach** at the waters of **Megiddo**—and routed them in spite of their huge force of chariots. Sisera fled from the battle and looked for refuge in the tent of the **Kenite** woman **Jael**, who killed him in his sleep.

BARUCH. The son of Neriah, **Jeremiah's** scribe, who according to biblical tradition is the author of a large part of the Book of Jeremiah. His name appears among the **seals** found in **Jerusalem**.

BARZILLAI. The name of three men in the Old Testament. Two are of historical interest.
   1. Barzillai, a wealthy man from **Gilead**, who supported **David** with food and materials during his flight from **Absalom** (2 Sam 17:27-29). As a reward he was invited by David to accompany the king to his residence in **Jerusalem**. Barzillai declined with a reference to his old age and sent his son. In his instructions to **Solomon** toward the end of his life, David expressly ordered Solomon not to harm Barzillai or his family.
   2. Barzillai from **Abel-Mehola** and the father of **Adriel** the husband of **Saul's** daughter **Merab** (1 Sam 18:19) whose children were executed by the **Gibeonites** with David's assistance (2 Sam 21:1-14).

BASHAN. A geographical name of the plateau east of Lake Kinnereth. It appears for the first time in a Sumerian text from the third millennium. In the Late Bronze Age it appears in Egyptian sources as part of the Egyptian Empire. It was inhabited at least since the fourth millennium. It is said to be the territory of King **Og** of Edrei (modern Der'a), who was defeated together with all his men by **Moses** (Num 21:33-35; Deut 3:1-9). Bashan was later a contested area, the scene of many battles between the Israelites and the **Aramaeans** until matters were settled by **Tiglath-pileser III**, who removed Bashan from **Israel**. One of the cities of Bashan was Golan (Deut 4:43) from which the modern name of the region, the Golan Heights, derives.

BATHSHEBA. The daughter of Eliam and wife first of the **Hittite Uriah,** and secondly of **David** king of **Israel,** and the mother of King **Solomon.** She was destined to become the scandalous source of the troubles that plagued the latter part of David's reign. The story about David and Bathsheba in 2 Sam 11-12 reports how the king seduced the wife of one of his officers and made her pregnant. When her husband on leave from the army declined to have intercourse with her, the scandal was complete, and the only way to escape an open scandal left to the king was to have Uriah killed. **Joab,** David's faithful general, made it sure that it happened, but David was properly condemned by the prophet **Nathan.** The first-born son of David and Bathsheba died, but Bathsheba played a decisive role at David's death when she secured the kingship for her second son, Solomon (1 Kgs 1:11-31). She was also the mastermind behind the death of Solomon's brother **Adonijah** when she revealed his wish to marry the handsome **Abishag** from **Shunem,** one of David's concubines, to the king, who had Adonijah executed as a pretender to the throne (1 Kgs 2:13-25). The portrayal of Bathsheba in the Old Testament is a highly literary one and should not be confused with a historical report. Whoever she was, she has been a great inspiration of art and literature to this very day.

BEERSHEBA. A city in the northern **Negeb,** the place of a royal city in the Iron Age II—roughly the period of the Israelite monarchy. Settlements in the vicinity of the modern city of Beersheba go back to the fourth millennium B.C.E., but after that followed a gap that lasted until the Iron Age. In the Iron Age it is necessary at Beersheba to distinguish between two types of settlement: 1. a settlement of uncertain extension partly uncovered beneath the city limits of the modern city and only excavated by rescue operations in combination with construction work relating to the modern city. This settlement seems to have existed in the Iron Age. 2. The fortified city on Tell es-Saba' at the eastern outskirts of modern Beersheba, extensively excavated between 1969 and 1976. The excavations uncovered a city of many strata that developed on the place of an unfortified village settlement in the early part of Iron Age I. In the 10th century it became the place of a major, well-planned fortresslike city with strong walls, a well dug out within the city confines (*see also* **fortifications**), and a centralistic layout of the city. It existed for most of Iron Age II but was sacked and burned, probably by **Sennacherib**, in 701 B.C.E. No city was ever reestablished in this place.

In the Old Testament, Beersheba is located at the southern end of Israelite territory sometimes summarized as going from **Dan** in the north to Beersheba in the south. Its name is differently explained in the patriarchal narratives as "the seven wells" or "the well of the oath" (see Gen 21:31; 26:33). It was reckoned as originally belonging to **Judah** but later was transferred to the tribe of **Simeon** (Josh 19:9).

BELSHAZZAR. The son of **Nabonidus** and the last king of Babylonia (*see* **Assyria and Babylonia**) (556-539 B.C.E.), who acted at least for a period of three years as his father's coregent and vice king during Nabonidus's self-imposed exile at the oasis of **Tema**. After 543 B.C.E., the sources pertaining to Belshazzar and his administration come to an end. Thus it is not known what happened to him after the **Persian** conquest of **Babylon** (539 B.C.E.). He is the antihero of the story about the writing on the wall (Dan 5). According to the Book of Daniel he was killed when **Darius the Median** conquered Babylon (Dan 5:30-6:1), information that makes little sense, as there never was a Darius of the Medes, nor did any historical Darius of the Persian Empire conquer Babylon.

BENAIAH. One of **David's** heroes, the commander of the **Cherethite** and **Pelethite** guards (2 Sam 8:18). He joined the party of **Solomon** during the struggle for the succession after David (1 Kgs 1:38), and acted as the king's executioner in the killing of **Adonijah** and **Joab** (1 Kgs 2:25; 34). After Joab's death, Benaiah was entrusted with the command of the army (1 Kgs 2:35).

BEN-HADAD. The Hebrew form of the Aramaic name Bar-Hadad ("Son of Hadad"). In the Old Testament, Ben-Hadad is used as the name of several **Aramaean** kings. Only two among these are historically verifiable. Other cases where the name of Ben-Hadad shows up may be in the form of pseudonyms—Ben-Hadad became a kind of common name attributed to Aramaean kings—or they are simply invented.

Such invented episodes involving a Ben-Hadad can be found in 1 Kings 20 and 22, the tale of unsuccessful wars against **Aram Damascus**, the leading Aramaean state of **Syria**. The king of **Israel** is said to be **Ahab**, but nothing indicates that the period of Ahab witnessed any serious confrontation between Israel and Damascus. On the contrary, **Assyrian** inscriptions make it clear that an alliance had been firmly established between Ahab and his Damascene colleague whose real name, however, was **Hadadezer**. The episodes of 1 Kings 20 and 22 are either misplaced and belong to the time of **Jehoash** of Israel, or they are simply invented.

Among the historical kings of Damascus of the name of Bar-Hadad, Bar-Hadad I ruled c. 900 B.C.E. He is said to have waged war against Baasha of Israel (1 Kgs 15:16-22). Bar-Hadad II, the son of **Hazael,** is better known from history. He ruled c. 800 B.C.E. but saw the realm of Hazael, his father, fall apart, torn by rebellions in Syria proper. Thus **Hamath** broke with Damascus as told by the Aramaic Zakur Inscription from Hamath. In the west, Jehoash of Israel reconquered the **provinces** lost to Hazael. Finally, Bar-Hadad II had to yield to Assyrian power after their conquest of Damascus in 796 B.C.E. which led to heavy taxation and vassalage. An inscription formerly attributed to a Bar-Hadad from Damascus may have nothing to do with either of these kings.

BENJAMIN. Meaning "son of the right side" or "son of the happy side." An Israelite **tribe** whose eponymous ancestor was Benjamin, the youngest son of **Jacob** and **Rachel** (Gen 35:16-18). After having lost **Joseph**, Benjamin's older full brother, Jacob kept Benjamin at home when his brothers were sent to **Egypt** to buy provisions, but they were asked by Joseph, whom they did not recognize, to return and bring their youngest brother. When they returned to Egypt, Benjamin was accused of stealing Joseph's silver goblet. Benjamin was arrested and together with his brothers placed in front of Joseph who this time revealed his true identity to his brothers (Gen 42-45).

The territory of the tribe of Benjamin should be sought in the hill land to the north of **Jerusalem**. In the south it was bordering on **Judah's** territory while in the north it shared borders with **Ephraim**. The traditions of the Old Testament provide a mixed picture of this tribe. In the **Period of the Judges**, **Ehud**, the son of Gera, one of the saviors of Israel, belonged to the tribe of Benjamin (Judg 3). However, the gruesome story about the rape of the Levite's wife at **Gibeah** in Benjamin's territory led to the almost total extinction of the tribe of Benjamin when the other Israelite tribes waged war against Benjamin who sided with the inhabitants of Gibeah. Only a remnant was spared in order to keep the number of tribes of Israel at twelve (*see also* **Twelve tribe system**) (Judg 19-21). Saul, the first king of Israel, was from Benjamin. In spite of a promising opening, Saul's reign ended in disaster with a king forsaken by God and people. After the futile rebellion of **Absalom** against **David**, **Sheba**, a Benjaminite, united the Israelite tribes in a new rebellion against the house of David. It took **Joab** only a short time to crush the rebellion of Sheba, who was killed by the inhabitants of Abel-Beth-Maacah (*see* **Abel**). When the kingdom of David and Solomon was divided into two independent states after the death of Solomon, half of Benjamin sided with **Rehoboam** and Judah, the other half with **Jeroboam**. Little more is known about this tribe, except that it helped Judah in rebuilding the **temple of Jerusalem** (Ezra 1:5).

It is uncertain, although not totally impossible, that there existed some sort of relationship between the biblical Benjaminites and a nomadic tribe at the time of the Kingdom of Mari in the 18th century B.C.E. called the Binujaminu, although the character of such a relationship is totally unknown.

BETH-AVEN. A city in the tribal territory of **Benjamin** (Josh 18:12), mentioned in connection with **Jonathan's** victory over the **Philistines** as close to **Michmash**. In the Book of **Hosea** a warning is issued to Beth-Aven together with **Gibeah** and **Ramah** of impending invasion, most likely from **Assyria** (Hos 5:8). Scholars have proposed many candidates for the location of Beth-Aven but so far no safe identification has been made. It is, however, highly possible in spite of the inclusion of Beth-Aven among the cities of Benjamin in the **Book of Joshua** that it—meaning "the house of wickedness"—is no more than a derogatory surname for **Bethel**, meaning "the House of God," a surname reflecting the status of Bethel in the **Deuteronomistic History** as the home of Jeroboam's golden calf and therefore a challenge to true Yahwism understood to be the legitimate religion of ancient Israel.

BETHEL. An important city c. 15 kilometers north of **Jerusalem**, situated on the crossroad of one of the most important roads of **Palestine** leading from the coastal plain to the **Jordan** Valley and the principal mountain route from north to south, close to the watershed. Apart from Jerusalem, no other city appears as frequently as Bethel in the Old Testament. **Abraham** is reported to have placed an altar at Bethel (Gen 12:8), **Jacob** had his famous dream at Bethel and set up a holy stone in commemoration of his dream, in which connection the ancient name of the place, **Luz**, is mentioned (Gen 28:10-22), and he established an altar there after his return from **Aram** (Gen 35:14-15). Later it became the subject of contest between the tribes of **Benjamin** and **Ephraim** (cf. Josh 18:22 and Judg 1:22). It was a religious center in the **Period of the Judges**, and the tribes assembled there after the war against Benjamin (Judg 21:2). Before the introduction of the monarchy, **Samuel** judged at Bethel. Later, King **Jeroboam** turned Bethel into a royal shrine and placed one of his golden calves at Bethel (see 1 Kgs 12:26-31 and Amos 7:13). Although the holy place at Bethel was condemned by the "Man of God," a **prophet** from **Judah** (1 Kgs 13), it remained in function until King **Josiah** destroyed the sanctuary (2 Kgs 23:15-18). The city survived into **Ezra's** time as a Judean city (Ezra 2:28).

Bethel is identified with the Arab town of Beitin, founded in the 19th century C.E. It was partially excavated in 1934 and again in 1954, 1957, and 1960. Remains of settlements at Bethel go back to the Chalcolithic Period and the Early Bronze Age. However, a fortified city was first built on this place in the Middle Bronze Age. There may have been a gap in the settlement sometime during the Late Bronze Age but the city was rebuilt and then—according to the excavators—again destroyed shortly before 1200 B.C.E., and again rebuilt. The historical implications of the excavations have recently been severely contested by other archaeologists.

BETH-HORON. The name of two cities overlooking the descent from **Gibeon** toward the coastal plain. The Old Testament sometimes distinguishes between the Upper Beth-Horon and the Lower Beth-Horon but just as often refers to both cities as simply Beth-Horon. Upper Beth-Horon was located on the border between **Ephraim** and **Benjamin** (Josh 16:5) and Lower Beth-Horon in the territory of Ephraim. The cities are said to have been conquered by the Israelites in Joshua's time, when Joshua slew the five Amorite kings at Gibeon and pursued them down past Beth-Horon to Azekah and Makkedah (Josh 10:5-11). The Philistines let their attack on Saul follow the route via Beth-Horon (1 Sam 13:18). Beth-Horon was rebuilt by Solomon (1 Kgs 9:17). Beth-Horon is also mentioned in Chronicles when the disbanded Israelite mercenaries in Amaziah's army plundered the towns of Judah "from Samaria to Beth-Horon" (2 Chron 25:13). Upper and Lower Beth-Horon is without doubt identical with the two Arab villages of Beit 'Ur el-Foqa' and Beit 'Ur et-Tahta that preserve the names. They have never been excavated but surface surveys have discovered mostly Iron Age pottery here. Their situation is strategically important, commanding one of the major routes from the coastal plain into the central highland of Palestine.

BETHLEHEM. A city in the territory of **Judah** about 10 kilometers south of **Jerusalem**, reported to be the burial place of **Rachel** (Gen 35:19) and the traditional home of the family of **David**, whose father **Jesse** lived there, and here David was anointed king by **Samuel** (1 Sam 16:1-13). Before that, in the **Period of the Judges**, the incident that led to the almost total annihilation of the tribe of **Benjamin** began when the wife of a person from **Ephraim** escaped to her family in Bethlehem (Judg 19). A note among the stories of **David's heroes** reports that a **Philistine** garrison was present there in David's days—a note hard to reconcile with other parts of the Davidic tradition (2 Sam 23:14). The city was fortified by **Rehoboam** (2 Chron 11:6). Not much is known about Bethlehem's fate after that date. Its future greatness was foreseen by the Prophet **Micaiah** (Mic 5:1-5). It is sometimes also called **Ephrata** and in this way is genealogically related to **Caleb**. No proper excavation has ever been carried out in Bethlehem. But a surface survey has discovered pottery from the Bronze Age and Iron Age close to the Church of Nativity on a site where ancient Bethlehem may have been situated. Speculations about the name of Bethlehem, in Hebrew "the house of Bread," relating the second part of the name to the Mesopotamian god Lahamu, have led to theories that it is mentioned in the **Amarna letters** from Jerusalem as Bît NIN.URTA. This reading has been rejected in recent studies.

BETH-PEOR. A place in **Transjordan** where the Israelites camped before the conquest of **Canaan** (Deut 3:29; 4:46; 34:6). The place was given to the tribe of **Reuben** (Josh 13:20). The name is related to a local deity, Baal-Peor, worshipped by Israelites as well as **Moabites** at **Shittim** (Num 25), and might well mean "the temple of Peor," and to Peor described as a mountain in Moab from where **Balaam** is supposed to have cursed **Israel** (Num 23:27-30). There have been many proposals for the location of Beth-Peor but no agreement has been reached as to the exact place.

BETH-SHAN. A major city c. 23 kilometers south of the Sea of Galilee that has been continuously inhabited from the Chalcolithic period until modern times. The ancient site was located on the impressive Tell el-Husn overlooking the vast ruined Hellenistic-Roman city. It was part of **Issachar's** tribal territory but was passed on to **Manasseh** (Josh 17:11), although it was never under Israelite control before the days of the monarchy (see also Judg 1:27). In the stories about the death of **Saul**, Beth-Shan was evidently under **Philistine** control, since the bodies of Saul and his sons were exposed by the Philistines on the walls of Beth-Shan (1 Sam 31:8-13). Beth-Shan was excavated in the 1920s and 1930s, and again in the 1990s. Extensively populated in the Early Bronze Age, it suffered the usual fate of **Palestinian** urban culture at the end of this period but reemerged as a major town with strong fortifications in the Middle Bronze Period. In the Late Bronze Period it was a center of Egyptian control, and is mentioned in an **Amarna letter** from **Jerusalem**.

Excavations at Beth-Shan have unearthed several remains from the time of the Egyptian Empire (*see* **Egypt**), including important inscriptions from the time of Seti I (c. 1290-1279 B.C.E.), **Ramesses II** (c. 1279-1213 B.C.E.), and Ramesses III (c. 1187-1156 B.C.E.). One of these inscriptions—from the time of Seti I—commemorates a victory over tribal people and the **Habiru** living in the vicinity of Beth-Shan. The Egyptians seem to have been in control of Beth-Shan at least until the end of the 11th century B.C.E. It has been guessed that the Philistines were also present, perhaps as mercenaries in Egyptian service. This proposition is based on the stories in the Old Testament about Saul's death and on the discovery of a special type of anthropoid coffins found in burials at Beth-Shan and assumed to be Philistine. So far no other evidence supports this assumption, and—apart from a single shard—no Philistine pottery has so far been found at this site.

BETH-SHEMESH. City in the northern sector of the tribal territory of **Judah** bordering on **Dan's** southern territory (Josh 15:10), c. 25 kilometers southeast of Jerusalem. When the **Philistines** had to give up the Ark of Yahweh that had destroyed the idol of Dagon in their temple at Ashdod, they let it go, dragged by oxen and unguided by men. It was carried to Beth-Shemesh where it was at first well received by the local population. Then it became a problem to the inhabitants of Beth-Shemesh who invited the people of **Kiriath-jearim** to take it away (1 Sam 6:7-16). At a later date, in the time of the **Hebrew** Monarchy, a battle was fought here between **Amasiah** of Judah and **Joash** of **Israel**, with the king of Israel leaving the field as victorious (2 Kgs 14:8-14). In the time of **Ahaz**, the Philistines conquered Beth-Shemesh. The city (the name means "the house of the son [god]"), has been located at Tell er-Rumeileh close to the Arab village of Ein Shems that preserved the name. It was excavated between 1928 and 1934, and remains turned up at this site of a fortified city dating back to the Middle Bronze Age.

BETH-ZUR. A city in the Judean Hills c. 35 kilometers south of **Jerusalem**. It is reckoned to be part of **Judah** (Josh 15:58) although other information relates it to **Caleb** (1 Chron 2:42-50). Excavations conducted at Khirbet et-Tubeiqeh—supposed to be ancient Beth-Zur—in 1931 and 1957 discovered remains from the Early Bronze Age and a fortified city from the Middle Bronze Age. The place was abandoned in most of the Late Bronze Age but a new settlement was established in the 12th century and destroyed again less than a hundred years later. It is remarkable that the city in spite of its commanding position on a hilltop was not fortified by **Rehoboam**. Thus it remained an unfortified settlement until it eventually became a victim of **Sennacherib's** invasion in 701 B.C.E. Over the following centuries only small insignificant and short-lived settlements were occasionally founded at this site. Only in the Hellenistic period, when the border between **Judea** and Idomea ran close to Beth-Zur, did a city develop at this site.

BEZEK. 1. The place where the Israelites defeated the **Canaanite** King **Adoni-bezek** (Judg 1:4-5). Some scholars propose a place for this Bezek in the vicinity of **Gezer**; other scholars think of the episode of Adoni-Bezek as a corrupted duplicate of **Joshua**'s victory over **Adoni-zedek** from **Jerusalem** and his coalition of five **Amorite** kings (Josh 10). 2. The place where **Saul** mustered his troops before he went to the rescue of **Jabesh** (1 Sam 11:8). The usual location of this Bezek, at Khirbet Ibzik c. 25 kilometers southwest of **Beth-Shan**, has recently been challenged, and Khirbet Sallab, a couple of kilometers west of Khirbet Ibzik is proposed in its place.

BLESSING OF JACOB. A collection of sayings that describes the character of the tribes of **Israel** (Gen 49). The collection is generally supposed to be very old, and a useful source if not of a detailed history of the tribes of Israel, then at least of their general status within the Israelite tribal system. See also TWELVE TRIBE SYSTEM.

BLESSING OF MOSES. Like the **Blessing of Jacob**, a collection of sayings about the tribes of Israel (Deut 33). The collection is generally held to be somewhat younger than the Blessing of Jacob but is still a useful source of knowledge about the status of the various tribes of Israel.

BUREAUCRACY. See ADMINISTRATION.

BYBLOS. Ancient Gubla, Hebrew Gebal, and the modern Jubail (the name means "the Mountain"), an ancient **Phoenician** city on the coast of **Lebanon** c. 35 kilometers north of Beirut. Inhabited since the fifth millennium B.C.E, it developed into an important seaport in the third millennium when it became the principal trade partner of **Egypt**, exporting cedar, wine, oil, and leather. Although destroyed sometime during the latter part of the third millennium, it remained an important city of trade, and the Egyptians continued to consider Byblos an important asset of theirs. The city has gained notoriety in the **Amarna letters** as an Egyptian puppet state when one of its rulers, Rib-Adda, seemingly wrote more letters of complaint to **Pharaoh** than all Pharaoh's other vassals put together, certainly too many for the comfort of the Egyptian court. The

Egyptian story from c. 1100 B.C.E. about the servant of Amun in Thebes, Wen-Amon, who traveled to Byblos to buy trees for building activities at home but received a very cold and disdainful reception here, illustrates the consequences of the diminishing of Egypt's power. In the Old Testament, the people of Byblos are known as skilled stonecutters (1 Kgs 5:18) and boatbuilders (Hez 27:9). **Assyrian** sources refer to Byblos as a member of the alliance of Syrian states who fought against the Assyrians at **Qarqar** in 853 B.C.E. A small series of inscriptions in Phoenician has been discovered at Byblos and dating from c. 1000 B.C.E. to the early Hellenistic period (c. 300 B.C.E.) makes it possible tentatively to set up a (fragmentary) list of kings of Byblos ranging from Ahiram c. 1000 B.C.E to Ayineel c. 333 B.C.E.

- C -

CALEB, CALEBITES. Caleb, the ancestors of the Calebites, the representative of the Tribe of **Judah** among the Israelite spies, was out from **Kadesh** by **Moses** to collect information about **Canaan** (Num 13-14). After the immigration, Caleb, now described as a **Kenizzite**, received from the hand of **Joshua** the area around **Hebron** and **Debir** that was from the beginning intended to be part of the territory of Judah (Josh 14:6-14). Through his relations with the Kenizzites, Caleb was related to the **Edomites**, although other traditions reckon him a Judean. Next to nothing is known about the history of his descendants, the Calebites. They may have represented a mixed population that included Judean as well as Edomite elements. They lived in southern Judah and in the northern part of the **Negeb**. A more elaborate genealogy of Caleb can be found in 1 Chron 1. The tradition about Caleb and Hebron may accordingly reflect demographic circumstances pertinent to the post-exilic period, when the border between Judah and Edom was pushed as far north as **Beth-Zur**, 10 kilometers north of Hebron. The name Caleb means "dog."

CANAAN, CANAANITES. Canaan is used in the Old Testament as the name of **Palestine** and its original population in pre-Israelite time. According to the Old Testament, Canaan is a descendant of Ham (Gen 9:18; 10:6). When the Israelites migrated to Canaan in order to subdue it, they had to kill a great number of Canaanites. A total destruction of the Canaanites had been planned. No trace of them should be left to posterity. However, the plan was never fully executed. The story of the Gibeonites (*see* **Gibeon**) in Joshua 9 reports that at least some Canaanites (the Gibeonites) saved their lives—in a most improper way—by cheating **Joshua**. The narrative in Judges 1 elaborates on the inability of the Israelites to live up to the command of the Lord that they should kill every Canaanite in sight. Judges 1 reports that many Canaanite cities survived the Israelite conquest (*see* **Settlement of Israel**), and because of this failure on the part of the Israelites, many Canaanites remained among the Israelites. The Israelites were not in complete control of all of Canaan before **David**'s conquest of **Jerusalem** (2 Sam 5).

The impression of Canaan obtained from the Old Testament is one of a well-defined geographical and ethnic term. The host of references to Canaan and its inhabitants in ancient Near Eastern sources hardly provides a picture of Canaan as well defined. The first reference to Canaan appears in inscriptions probably already from the end of the third millennium (in an inscription from **Ebla**). The number of references increases during the second millennium B.C.E. but diminishes again in the first millennium B.C.E. Many of these references to Canaan are not very precise. Some are of a very general nature or they refer to a territory that seems much larger than the one described by the Old Testament. This is also true of references found in inscriptions coming from sources situated within the very same territory that is called Canaan in the Old Testament, for example, the **Amarna letters**. Only in inscriptions dating from the last phase of the Egyptian Empire in Asia, that is, the final part of the Late Bronze Age, does Canaan assume a more precise meaning as a name of one of the Egyptian provinces in western Asia. However, one cannot be certain that the Egyptian province of Canaan was identical in extension with the geographical and ethnic designation of Canaan in the Old Testament. In first millennium references, Canaan tends to be used about **Phoenicia**.

The discrepancy between the idea of Canaan in the Old Testament and the references to a Canaan in ancient Near Eastern documents may well be that the Old Testament historiographers used

Canaan as an ideological concept rather than as a piece of historical and political information. In the Old Testament, Canaan and the Canaanites are presented as the antithesis of Israel and the Israelites. The Canaanites play the role of the "bad guys" of a literary plot, the Israelites of the "good guys." To their role belongs the dubious honor of being slaughtered by the Israelites during the Israelite migration into Palestine. In light of the conquest stories of the Old Testament, it is interesting that modern scholarship has shown that from a cultural perspective the ancient Israelites belonged among the Canaanites sharing their material culture and religious practices. The historical Israelites originated in Palestine and were not foreign invaders. The difference between the Israelites and the Canaanites is exclusively ideological and part of the ideological framework for the historical traditions as narrated by the historiographers of the Old Testament. It has nothing to do with the historical realities of the ancient Near East. Israelite culture developed from the pattern set by the ancient peoples of Palestine in the Bronze Age and the Israelite religion represented a restructuring of religious ideas current among the peoples of Palestine and **Syria**.

Scholarship has used the term Canaan in a rather dubious way to define the culture and civilization of the Levant as if this culture were totally different from the Israelite one. The Canaanite civilization with its imagined fertility religion—based on the evidence of the **Ugaritic** epics and the testimony of the Old Testament—has been vilified as inferior to the monotheistic Israelite belief in Yahweh as Israel's only God. In this way, the view of the Old Testament emerged that Israel's history was no more and no less than a continuous struggle between Yahweh and Baal, the foremost Canaanite deity. Scholars will in the future have to replace this polarization of Israel and Canaan presented by the Bible with a more precise terminology in order to classify the civilizations of Syria and Palestine in ancient times.

CAPHTOR. According to the Old Testament the original homeland of the **Philistines** (Amos 9:7; Jer 47:4) who are reported to have destroyed the Avvim before they settled at **Gaza** (Deut 2:23). In the table of nations (Gen 10:14), the Philistines are reckoned as the descendants of the Caphtorites. Jer 47:4 makes it likely that Caphtor was an island ("the isle of Caphtor"—the Hebrew word for "island" might also be translated "seashore"), and Caphtor has usually been identified with Crete and equated with Egyptian Keftiu or Akkadian Kaptara. This identification has been challenged in recent times, and other candidates proposed, especially Cyprus.

CARMEL. Meaning "orchard."
1. A mountain range of limited height (c. 550 meters at the highest) in northwestern **Palestine**, running from Haifa in the west and almost 50 kilometers in southeastern direction. It is the main dividing line between the coastal plain and the **Valley of Jezreel** and is known from history as a difficult area to pass. The pass at **Megiddo**, the scene of many battles, is especially famous. Here **Pharaoh** Thutmose III (c. 1479-1425 B.C.E.) fought against a coalition of local chieftains, and in this place King **Josiah** of **Judah** lost his life in 609 B.C.E., when he tried to block the road before the advancing Egyptian army. Carmel's role as a sacred mountain is mirrored by the story of the prophet **Elijah** killing the **priests** of Baal (1 Kgs 18:20-40).
2. A city in southern Judah (Josh 15:55), generally identified with modern Kurmul, 15 kilometers south of **Hebron**. King **Saul** raised a victory monument here in remembrance of his victory over the **Amalekites** (1 Sam 15:12).

CHALDAEA, CHALDAEANS. In the Old Testament Chaldaea is considered the original home of **Abraham** whose family traced their origin back to the **Ur of the Chaldaeans** (Gen 11:28.31). The Chaldaeans, who appear in **Assyrian inscriptions** since the first half of the ninth century B.C.E., inhabited southern **Babylonia**, including the marsh areas close to the Persian Gulf. They spoke a language related to Aramaic, if not Aramaic proper, but are never in Assyrian sources identified with the **Aramaeans**. Their place of origin is unknown—northeastern **Arabia** has been proposed—but they appear originally as a tribally organized group of people who as time went by partly settled in the Babylonian cities, and finally became rulers of all of **Mesopotamia**. Chaldaean leaders had Babylonian names, like **Merodak-Baladan** (Marduk-apal-iddina), who for many years fought against **Sennacherib** and negotiated with **Hezekiah** of **Judah** (2 Kgs 20:12-13), probably in order to find allies against Assyria. In the late seventh century, the Chaldaeans combined with the **Medes** and overran Assyria, conquering **Nineveh** in 712 B.C.E. and extinguishing the last vestiges of the Assyrian empire a few years later at **Haran**. Under mighty kings— especially Napolassar (625-605 B.C.E.) and **Nebuchadnezzar** II (604-562 B.C.E.)—they almost reestablished the Assyrian Empire as a Neo-Babylonian Empire. After the **Persian** conquest of **Babylon** in 539 B.C.E., "Chaldaean" was used in later oriental and Greek tradition about the sages of Babylon. In this latter capacity Chaldaeans turn up at the royal court in the stories of the **Book of Daniel** (Dan 2:2.4.5.10)

CHARCHEMISH. An important city and trade center at the upper course of the **Euphrates**, mentioned in documents from c. 2500 to 600 B.C.E. It already appears in the **Ebla** texts and remained an important and contested city during the second millennium, when it became the residence of the **Hittite** vice king of **Syria**. In the first millennium a dynasty supposed to have a Hittite background reigned at Charchemish. Charchemish fought successfully against **Assyria** in the ninth century but finally had to yield to Assyrian power in the days of **Tiglath-pileser III** (745-727 B.C.E.) and, after a rebellion, was reduced to an Assyrian province by **Sargon** (721-705 B.C.E.). Again Charchemish moved into the center of history when **Nebuchadnezzar** in 605 B.C.E., in alliance with Egyptian troops garrisoned at Charchemish, crushed the last vestiges of the former Assyrian Empire (see also 2 Chron 35:20). There are no records indicating that Nebuchadnezzar sacked the city which seems, however, since his time to have been left largely unpopulated until the Hellenistic period.

CHEDORLAOMER. King of **Elam**, and one of the four great kings who were defeated by **Abraham** in the **Valley of Siddim** (Gen 14). The name represents a distortion of the Elamite name Kutur-lagamar, but no king of that name is known from historical sources. Among the kings of Elam proposed as the prototype of the mysterious King Chedorlaomer of Genesis 14 is Kutur-Nahhunte of the 12th century B.C.E.

CHERETHITES AND PELETHITES. The name of **David**'s guard under command of **Benaiah**. It has been proposed that David raised his guard already while he was residing at **Ziklag**, and that the term referred to soldiers whose origin should be sought among the **Sea Peoples**. Some have understood the Cherethites to be mercenaries from Crete, but their home was more likely somewhere in the **Negeb** region (see also the Negeb of the Cerethites, 1 Sam 30:14).

CHRONICLES. An official, mostly state-sponsored literary genre listing the great events on a yearly basis. *See also* ANNALS.

CHRONICLES, THE BOOKS OF. The two books of Chronicles constitute the major part of the **Chronistic History**. They tell the story of humankind from Adam to the destruction of **Jerusalem**, with an appendix reporting how **Cyrus** ordered the temple rebuilt. However, until the death of **Saul** at **Gilboa**, the history is only in the form of a long genealogical listing of biblical figures from Adam to Saul. From the ascension of **Rehoboam** to the throne of **Judah** and the division of his kingdom into two parts, Chronicles concentrate on episodes relevant to the history of Judah, almost forgetting the existence of the **Kingdom of Israel**. It is generally assumed that the **Books of Kings** constituted the most important source for the writers of Chronicles. However, sometimes Chronicles deviate from Kings, for example, in their evaluation of the respective reigns of **Hezekiah** and **Josiah** of Judah by downplaying the importance of Josiah. A famous incident in Chronicles not narrated by Kings is the conversion of King **Manasseh** after his exile to **Babylon** (2 Chron 33).

CHRONICLES OF THE KINGS OF ISRAEL. In a number of places, the authors of the **Books of Kings** and **Chronicles** refer to the existence of a chronicle of the Kings of **Israel** as a source of further information. Thus, after having allowed for only a short note with scant information about the important King **Omri** of Israel, the authors of the Books of Kings refer the reader to the Chronicles of the Kings of Israel in this way: "Now the rest of the acts of Omri which he did, and his might that he showed, are they not written in the book of the chronicles of the kings of Israel?" (1 Kgs 16:27). Nothing from this source has been preserved.

In spite of the fact that the Chronicles of the Kings of Israel have often been regarded by scholars as a valuable source, absolutely nothing is known about them. It is not known if they belonged among the official genre of chronicles known from other ancient Near Eastern societies or included merely a mixed collection of tales from the past. It has also been suggested that the references to these chronicles as well as to the **Chronicles of the Kings of Judah** represent literary style and convention without any basis in any existing collection of documents.

CHRONICLES OF THE KINGS OF JUDAH. The southern equivalent to the **Chronicles of the Kings of Israel.** What has been said about the former chronicles can just as well be repeated here. Thus nothing is known about them, except that the authors of Kings and Chronicles occasionally refer to them as additional sources: "And the rest of the acts of Joash, and all that he did, are they not written in the book of chronicles of the kings of Judah?" (2 Kgs 12:19).

CHRONISTIC HISTORY. The second among the historical collections of the Old Testament, generally assumed to include the two **books of Chronicles** and the books of **Ezra** and **Nehemiah.** Their composition is normally considered quite late, dating to perhaps the **Persian** period (fifth century B.C.E. or even the fourth century B.C.E.), and of secondary importance in comparison to the **Deuteronomistic History.** Moreover, it is generally accepted that the Deuteronomistic History has been the source of information for the authors of the Chronistic History.

CHRONOLOGY IN THE OLD TESTAMENT. The chronology of the Old Testament basically takes one from creation to the time of **Ezra**'s return to **Jerusalem.** Although a British bishop a couple of centuries ago was able to reconstruct the history of the world according to biblical chronology, it is not the task here to discuss the legendary chronological information included in the Primeval History. Such a chronology is beyond history and serves different interests. Basically, the discussion has to do with real chronology and real time placing the events and personalities of the Old Testament within a chronological framework that from a historian's point of view makes sense and is operable.

In a discussion of the chronology of the Old Testament, it has—as the starting point—to be admitted that it is with a few exceptions impossible to create total harmony between the chronological information found in the Old Testament and the information coming from other parts of the ancient Near East, not to speak of modern chronological reconstructions. The aim and scope of chronology in the historical books of the Old Testament is vastly different from what is found in modern history books. The historical literature of the Old Testament was never written in order to explain exactly what may have happened and when it did happen. The chronology was not even intended to be exact in a way that resembles modern chronological concepts. The ideological aspects of chronology were generally more important than exact chronology. Thus the Old Testament allows for a span of time between the **Exodus** and the building of **Solomon**'s temple of 480 years, which cover twelve generations, each of 40 years. This is not an exact indication of time, but rather ideological numbers bearing a meaning not limited to the measure of real time. Both 12 and 40 function as round numbers. Such round numbers could also be used about a more limited span of time.

In this way King **David** is allowed to rule for 40 years, Solomon, his son for another 40 years, but Solomon's two successors, **Rehoboam** and **Abijah** together ruled for only 20 years (17 + 3 years), that is, half the time of David and Solomon. The mania for using ideological numbers is also apparent in lists such as the one of the so-called "minor judges" (*see* **Judge**) in Judg 10:3-5; 12:8-13. Here five judges functioned together for 70 years (23 + 22 + 7 + 10 + 8 years), or also for structuring the chronology of kings of less importance than David or Solomon. Thus the four rulers in Jerusalem, who follow **Asa** of **Judah**, together rule for 40 years (25 + 8 + 1 + 6). It is obvious that Old Testament historiographers were not fundamentally interested in real chronology and nowhere any critical note is found referring to chronological problems. This is obvious in the case of Israel's history before the introduction of the monarchy. The chronological framework, dividing this period into the time of the **patriarchs**, the sojourn in **Egypt** and the **exodus**, the conquest and the **Period of the Judges**, has nothing to do with history.

When it comes to the chronology of the **period of the Monarchy**, that is, the first half of the first millennium B.C.E., things gradually begin to change, not because the historical information in the Old Testament relevant to this period is by necessity more "historical" than the information about the previous periods, but because it is possible to establish a series of synchronisms between kings mentioned in the Old Testament and information from other parts of the ancient Near East, especially from **Assyria and Babylonia**. Assyrian and Babylonian records show much more interest in chronological precision, a fact that may have to do with the preoccupation in **Mesopotamia** with astrology that demanded exact observation and registration. Accordingly Assyrian and Babylonian documents sometimes included chronological information of a quality quite different from what is found in records from **Syria** and **Palestine** where exact dating was very unusual until the time of the **Persian Empire**. Thus no **Amarna letter** is ever dated. In his administrative documents, no king of **Ugarit** mentioned the exact date of the document in relation to, for example, his regnal years.

In Mesopotamia, the interest invested in astrological matters allowed the Assyrians and Babylonians to create chronological tools in order to distinguish precisely between different years. These precise observations occasionally permit the modern scholar to reconstruct the ancient chronology in a very precise way. Thus a reference to a solar eclipse included in an ancient source may allow the modern scholar to look for an absolute date of a certain event that happened in the same year. It has in this way been possible to establish the exact date of **Ahab's** participation in the battle of **Qarqar** in 853 B.C.E., because of a solar eclipse in the same year recorded by Assyrian scribes. It has also been possible on the basis of Assyrian documents to almost exactly place the tribute from **Jehu** to the Assyrians to the year of 841 B.C.E., from **Jehoash** to 796 B.C.E., from **Menahem** to 740 B.C.E. and 738 B.C.E., and from **Ahaz** to 734 B.C.E. Assyrian documents present the date of the fall of **Samaria** as 722 B.C.E., and Babylonian ones indicate that **Nebuchadnezzar** conquered **Jerusalem** for the first time in 597 B.C.E. Thus the chronology of the period of the kingdoms of Israel and Judah is at least correct in outline. But after the fall of Jerusalem, the ideological numbers return. Modern scholarship has established that the **exile in Babylon** lasted from 587 to 538 B.C.E., roughly 50 years. However, this date cannot be found in the Old Testament that only gives 70 years as the time of the exile, clearly on ideological grounds.

CITY, CITY-STATE. Although agriculture was the main occupation of the peoples of ancient **Palestine** and more than 90 percent of the population was engaged in basic food production, the city was the landmark of civilization, the center of districts, regions, and states. In the ancient Near East, including Palestine, urban civilization went back to the end of the Chalcolithic period (end of fourth millennium B.C.E.) and dominated the economic and political structure in the Early Bronze Age. At the end of the Early Bronze Age it broke down, but was reestablished in the Middle Bronze Age. The evidence from the Late Bronze Age indicates that the cities were struggling for survival, thus preparing for the breakdown of urban life at the end of the Bronze Age. In the first millennium B.C.E., the cities reappeared, although they never reached the level of the Bronze Age which was not to be surpassed before the Hellenistic period.

In Palestine, cities were normally small in extension but heavily fortified (*see* **Fortifications**)—an indication of the dangers of political life at that time, but also of a fragmented political structure, the country being divided into a series of petty **kingdoms** or city-states. The city was the center of administration and government and often identified with the state which it dominated. Thus with few exceptions, the **Amarna letters** continuously refer to the cities of **Syria** and Palestine as the name of states. In ancient Near Eastern documents of the Iron Age, the **Kingdom of Israel** was identified as **Samaria**, its capital. The name of **Jerusalem** does not turn up as the name of the **Kingdom of Judah**, although **Mesopotamian** references to "the city of Judah," meaning Jerusalem, show how important the city was.

CITY OF DAVID. Used in the Old Testament as an alternative name for **Jerusalem**, since **David**'s conquest of the **city** (2 Sam 5:7.9). Sometimes a distinction is made between the City of David situated on the southeastern hill (the "Ophel") and the Temple Mount (**Zion** in the proper sense).

CLAN. In traditional societies such as ancient **Israel**, the local community is divided into different levels of social organization. In most such societies where a centralized state does not exist or is only of minor importance to local people, the usual social organization will be the **tribe**, the **lineage**, and the **family**, probably allowing for a number of subdivisions as well. A tribal society may contain clans but the clan level is not always present. In general anthropological theory, it is difficult to distinguish between a clan and a lineage, both being extended family groups, although the connection between members of a clan often seems to be less important than is the rule in the lineage. It is not absolutely certain that ancient Israel included clans, although most commentators accept their presence. The Hebrew word normally associated with the clan is *mishpacha*, but it may also mean "lineage."

CONQUEST OF CANAAN, THE ISRAELITE. *See* SETTLEMENT OF ISRAEL.

CLIENTELISM. The technical term of a sociopolitical system that basically reckons with only two categories of people, the clients and their patrons. It is sometimes maintained that the presence of a sociopolitical system building on clientelism indicates the lack of a developed bureaucracy enabling the centralized state to exert control over its citizens. It is also called the "traditional Mediterranean family system" and has been operative not only in Rome, where it was the official political system in the time of the Roman Republic, but all over the Mediterranean world, including the ancient Near East, where the control (administration) of the centralized state was weak or absent. *See also* PATRONAGE SOCIETY.

COVENANT. Or constitution of **Israel**. According to the deuteronomistic (*see* **Deuteronomism**) theology of the Old Testament, the relationship between Israel and its God Yahweh is controlled by a covenant dictated by God to Israel at **Sinai** and later confirmed when **Joshua** summoned the people to **Shechem** for his farewell speech. Although the idea of the divine covenant is definitely a theological point made by the deuteronomists, it reflects the basic importance of the covenant system in a society where matters were normally decided through a person-to-person relationship, a kind of written or unwritten deal concluded among persons of an equal standing, that is, tribal leaders, great men, or kings. Basically, the system of **patronage**—the way to organize social differences into the haves and the have-nots—relied on an extensive system of covenants when great men attached ordinary people to their power group by setting up personal contracts or covenants. It is hardly surprising that language has survived in the Old Testament that reflects the function of the system of covenants as a protecting device, for example, in God's speech to the Israelites where he promised to send his angel in front of Israel to cut down its enemies (Exod 23:20-33).

CUSH. In translations since the King James Version normally translated "Ethiopia" (but cf. *The Revised English Bible*). Cush was in the Old Testament the name of the Valley of the Nile between the first and fifth cataract, in classical sources called Nubia, in modern times Sudan. Cush was famous for its treasures and its Negroid population that often served as mercenaries. In **Jeremiah's** time, a Cushite named Ebed-Melech served in the palace of **Jerusalem** (Jer 38:7-13).

CUSHAN-RISHATAIM. An oppressor of **Israel** (Judg 3:7-11), reported to be the king of **Aram-Naharaim. Othniel,** the brother of **Caleb,** put an end to his regime of terror. Cushan-Rishataim (meaning "double wickedness") is often seen as a legendary figure, not from **Aram** but from **Edom** (the writing of Edom and Aram is very similar in Hebrew), probably a personification of Cushan (Hab 3:7), an area related to the **Midianites** possibly located in northeastern Arabia.

CYRUS. King of **Persia** 539-530 B.C.E., and the founder of the Persian Empire. At the beginning of his career, Cyrus was the vassal of the Medes (*see* **Media**) but he threw away the Median yoke and started a process of expanding Persian territory into an empire of a size never previously witnessed. After having subdued the territories of present-day Iran, he turned to the northeast and conquered Asia Minor. Having settled affairs to the east and in the north and northeast, he turned his attention of **Babylonia.** His Babylonian campaign was crowned with success, when Cyrus entered the city of **Babylon** in 539 B.C.E. Now he was the master of all of the Near East from the borders of **Egypt** to India. He died battling in Bactria (present-day Afghanistan).

In the Old Testament, Cyrus has obtained a position unknown to any other foreign ruler. In the Book of **Isaiah**, he is reckoned the hope of freedom of the exiled Judeans and the anointed of the Lord (Isa 44:28; 45:1). The Old Testament records that a year after his ascension to the throne of Babylonia (538 B.C.E.), he issued a decree announcing freedom for the exiles, and the rebuilding of the **temple of Jerusalem**, an event that was regarded as the official end to the **Babylonian Exile** (1 Chron 36:22-23; Ezra 1:1-4). In **Hebrew** as well as Greek tradition, Cyrus was seen as the paragon of the just king, and was also accepted as such by Alexander the Great.

- D -

DAMASCUS. An important city of southern **Syria**, today the capital of Syria. Damascus is located in an oasis created by the river Barada, and at an important crossroad for international trade. The earliest reference to Damascus is found in Thutmose III's war accounts from the first part of the 15th century B.C.E. It remained a part of the **Egyptian** Empire during the Late Bronze Age. Thus it is mentioned in a number of **Amarna letters** as one of the petty vassal kingdoms of the Egyptians. Its subsequent fate during the Early Iron Age is unknown, but at the beginning of the first millennium B.C.E. it was the head of a minor **Aramaean** state conquered by **David** and lost again in the days of **Solomon**. After the separation from Israel, the fate of Damascus and Israel seemed linked together until the very end of both states. Only fragments of this history exist. From **Assyrian** sources, there is information about a coalition between **Israel** and Damascus and other Syrian states that fought at **Qarqar** in 853 B.C.E. At a later date, in the time of King **Hazael** of Damascus and **Jehu** of Israel, the good relations between Israel and Damascus broke down and Damascus became a deadly enemy to Israel that was saved by the Assyrian conquest of Damascus in 796 B.C.E. Around the middle of the eight century B.C.E., Damascus reemerged as an independent state now cooperating with Israel. It was part of the ill-fated coalition against the Assyrians led by **Tiglath-pileser III**. In 732 B.C.E., Tiglath-pileser reduced Damascus to an Assyrian province, and although the Assyrians were forced to deal with a short-lived anti-Assyrian rebellion in **Syria** including Damascus in 720 B.C.E., Damascus's role as an important political center was a thing of the past. From the end of the eighth century and onwards, practically nothing is known about the fate of the city before Hellenistic times.

DAN, CITY. A city of the Old Testament named after the tribe that lived there (*see* **Dan, tribe**). The city used to be called **Laish**, a name that occurs in Egyptian **Execration Texts** and in the text from Mari, and again in Thutmose III's inscriptions. It was located at the sources of the **Jordan River** in Upper **Galilee** (Judg 18:29), no doubt to be identified with Tell Qadi. The Arab name (meaning "the tell of the judge," playing on the meaning of Arabic *din* versus Hebrew *dan*) represents a kind of popular translation of the ancient Hebrew name. It housed a royal sanctuary since **Jeroboam** I (1 Kgs 12:29). It has been the center of extensive archaeological excavations since 1966. The first settlement at Dan goes back to c. 5000 B.C.E., although Dan was not going to house a city before the Early Bronze Age. From the Early Bronze Age and until Iron Age II, the time of the Israelite monarchy, Dan was continuously settled. The place may have been deserted in the **Persian** period but was soon rebuilt as a Hellenistic city with an important shrine.

DAN, TRIBE. The son of **Jacob** and Bilhah, and the eponymous ancestor of the tribe of Dan, one of **Israel**'s twelve tribes (*see* **Twelve tribe system**). Information about the tribe of Dan relates only to the oldest history of Israel. After the introduction of the monarchy, Dan disappears from the narratives of the Old Testament. Furthermore, the sources concerning the fate of the tribe of Dan are confusing and seemingly contradictory. According to the Old Testament, Dan settled in the hill lands, along the coastal range on the border between the tribal territory of **Judah** and the land of the **Philistines**. However, because of pressure from the **Amorites** they were forced out of their territory and migrated to the north ending up at **Laish** in Upper **Galilee** at the foot of Mount Hermon. Here was the future tribal territory of Dan (Judg 17-18). This migratory phase of the history of Dan seems connected with the legendary exploits of **Samson** (Judg 13-16).

Some sources in the Old Testament place Dan alongside **Naphtali** and the other tribes of the north, thus also the assumed oldest reference in the **Song of Deborah** (Judg 5:17), a note that makes many scholars doubt the historicity of the Samson figure and the references to an original home of Dan to the south. Because of the relations between Dan and the Philistines, some scholars have speculated about a relationship between this tribe and the Danuna of the **Sea People**, among whom the Philistines were also counted. Apart from this, Dan's reputation in the Old Testament is a mixed one. Their great hero Samson courted Philistine women—something that led to his downfall, and they stole their idol from an **Ephraimite** (Judg 17-18), although this narrative may be an ironic diatribe ridiculing the establishment of the royal sanctuary at Dan in the days of King **Jeroboam I** (1 Kgs 12:29).

DAN INSCRIPTION. In 1993, a fragment of an inscription in Aramaic was found at Dan (*see* **Dan, city**). Additional fragments appeared in 1995. The inscription includes the word *bytdwd*. In the preceding line, **Israel** is mentioned. The first publishers of the text were certain that *bytdwd* should be read as "the house of **David**" as a reference to the **kingdom of Judah**. Other scholars understand the text as a proof of the historicity of King David. The text was believed by the excavators to belong to the mid-ninth century B.C.E. It is probably more likely that it dates to c. 800 B.C.E. or even later. The interpretation of *bytdwd* has also been called into question, because of the peculiar way of writing and because of certain other difficulties connected with the context in which it appears. Some scholars have maintained that *bytdwd* does not refer to the Kingdom of Judah as its dynastic name but to a local place or shrine in the vicinity of Dan. The inscription has sometimes been considered a fake. The Dan inscription is currently part of the archaeological exhibition of the Israel Museum in **Jerusalem**.

DANIEL AND THE BOOK OF DANIEL. In the Christian Old Testament, the Book of Daniel is reckoned among the **prophets**, but in the Hebrew Bible it belongs to the third part, the Scriptures. It tells the story of the pious Daniel in the service of **Nebuchadnezzar**, the conqueror of **Jerusalem**, and goes on to narrate about the fate of King **Belshazzar** and the ascension of **Darius the Median** to the throne of **Babylon**. The final part of the book includes visions of the empires that are to come after Daniel's time. Although supposed to include events of the sixth century B.C.E., it is certainly much younger presenting a spurious and corrupted history of the past. It most likely presupposed events of 165 B.C.E. and can be dated to the middle of the second century B.C.E. Daniel appears in Ezek 14:14.20 together with Job and Noah as one of the three wise men from ancient times. It is sometimes believed that this figure from tradition appears in an early form in the **Ugaritic** epic of Dan'el.

DARIUS. The name of three **Persian** (*see* **Persia, Persian Empire**) kings. 1. Darius I (the Great), king of Persia 521-486 B.C.E. He consolidated the empire after the death of **Cyrus's** son Cambysses who had conquered **Egypt**. When he initiated a Persian expansion into the Mediterranean, his army was defeated by the Greeks at Marathon in 490 B.C.E. He is the king of the Medes (*see* **Media**) in the **Book of Daniel** (Dan 6:1), which otherwise mixes up information about this great king, making him the predecessor of Cyrus (Dan 6:29). The rebuilding of **Jerusalem's temple** is attributed to his time (Ezra 5-6). 2. Darius II, king of Persia 425-405 B.C.E. The letters from the Jewish colony at Elephantine (*see* **Elephantine papyri**) in Egypt belong to his time. 3. Darius III, king of Persia 335-331, who perished fighting Alexander the Great.

DARIUS THE MEDIAN. In the **Book of Daniel**, Darius the Mede (*see* **Media**) assumed kingship over **Babylon** after the death of **Belshazzar** (Dan 6:1). The note about Darius the Mede represents a corrupted historical tradition. There never was a Darius of the Medes. Darius was a **Persian** royal name, and the last **Chaldaean** king of Babylon was followed by **Cyrus**.

DAVID. The second king of **Israel**, the son of **Jesse** of **Bethlehem**, normally considered to have reigned from c. 1000-960 B.C.E.
    The David narratives are divided into two major collections: 1. the story of his ascension to the throne of Israel (1 Sam 16-2 Sam

6), and 2. the narrative about the succession to the throne of David (2 Sam 7-2 Kgs 2) (*see also* **Succession History**). The first collection describes the career of David from the moment when he was anointed by **Samuel** to the conquest of **Jerusalem** and the transportation of the Ark of God to its lasting place where **Solomon's** temple was later to be built (2 Sam 6). After his anointment and after having killed **Goliath**, the champion of the **Philistines**, David was accepted at the court of **Saul**. He became Saul's personal retainer and married his daughter, **Michal**. Then all was lost, when the king grew suspicious about his successful vassal, and David had to flee to save his life. David now lived as an outlaw. In the end he was forced to become the servant of **Achish**, the king of the Philistine city of **Gath**, to get protection from the persecutions of Saul. After Saul died battling the Philistines at **Gilboa**, David was elected king of **Judah**, while Saul's surviving son **Ishboshet** became the new king of Israel. A period of war followed when David moved against Ishboshet. Ishboshet's most important servant, his uncle **Abner**, treacherously approached David but was killed by David's general **Joab**. Following the killing of Abner, Ishboshet lost ground, and was subsequently murdered by two officers, who were executed by David, probably in order to escape accusations of having instigated the murder of Ishboshet. After the death of Ishboshet, the house of Saul was almost extinguished, leaving only a crippled child of **Jonathan** alive. The Israelites now turned to David as their savior and David ascended to the throne of Israel. In this position, he went on to conquer **Jebusite** Jerusalem that was to become the future capital of his kingdom and the center of royal worship.

The second collection of stories about David tells the sad story of the struggles among David's children for the succession to his throne. The reason for the tragedy that bereft David of his most able son, **Absalom,** is attributed to the crime he committed when fornicating with **Uriah's** wife **Bathsheba**. The tragedy opens when David's son **Amnon** raped his half sister **Tamar**, and was killed in revenge by Tamar's brother Absalom. Then, after an initial reconciliation, Absalom tried to dispose of his father and take over kingship, but was thwarted in his plans by Joab. Now, relations deteriorated between Israel and Judah, the two main parts of David's kingdom and Joab had to put down the dangerous rebellion of

Sheba, a Benjaminite probably acting against what he might have seen as the man behind the downfall of the family of Saul, the royal Benjaminite house, a suspicion supported also by the execution of seven of Saul's sons. Toward the end of his time, David was left in his palace as an old and lonely man, while at the same time his surviving children Solomon and **Adonijah** entered the last act of their notorious struggle for power.

The stories about David have often been considered an important historical source for the history of Israel in the 10th century B.C.E. Thus it was supposed that the second part, the Succession Story, was written by an eyewitness to the events, maybe **Abiatar**. However, modern research has to a large degree settled on the opinion that most of the traditions about David cannot be historical reports from David's own time, or from the time of Solomon. They are elaborate fictitious literature more resembling a Greek tragedy. The first part about David's career shows remarkable likeness to ancient Near Eastern literature, and may be patterned on a popular fairytale about the young prince who, although the youngest among his brethren, obtains for himself the throne and the princess.

From a historical point of view, the claim of the Old Testament that David conquered and ruled an empire reaching from the Euphrates in the north to **Egypt** in the south has little to recommend itself and creates many problems. The 10th century is in Near Eastern history a kind of dark age—little in the way of written sources has survived from **Mesopotamia** dating to this period, and Egypt has little to contribute to the history of **Palestine** until **Pharaoh Shishak**'s campaign there in the years following Solomon's death (1 Kgs 14:25-26). In spite of the dearth of written sources from Palestine itself and from the ancient empires of the ancient Near East, the sources are remarkably silent about the existence of an Israelite empire in the 10th century. Furthermore, archaeology has created a situation where the monumental buildings that were formerly attributed to Solomon are now generally down dated to the time of the dynasty of **Omri**. Archaeology has even cast doubts on the very existence of Jerusalem in the 10th century B.C.E. Some archaeologists flatly deny that anything has been found in Jerusalem dating to this period, while other archaeologists are of the opinion that there was a Jerusalem, although hardly an imperial capital but a small town of less than 2,000 inhabitants. If David is a historical person, which is still the majority view among biblical scholars, he at most ruled over an insignificant kingdom in central Palestine.

DAVID, HOUSE OF. The name of the royal family of **Judah** and the dynastic name of the **Kingdom of Judah**. In the first millennium, it was common in **Syria** and **Palestine** to name states after their ruling houses. Thus a series of **Aramaean** states from Syria is rather common that carry names of the type "House of NN." In Palestine, the **Kingdom of Israel** is also known from ancient Near Eastern documents as "the **House of Omri**." The House of David did not appear in extra-biblical documents until the discovery in 1993 of the **Dan Inscription**.

DAVID'S HEROES. A group of elite soldiers in **David's** service (2 Sam 23:8-39); (see also 1 Chron 11:10-47). They were divided into two groups, a minor one of three warriors who had distinguished themselves with extraordinary exploits, and a major one of 30 warriors who were led by **Abishai**, the brother of **Joab**. The list of David's heroes has often been considered very old, perhaps reaching back to David's rule at **Hebron** since all the heroes come from the tribes of **Judah, Benjamin, Dan,** and **Ephraim**. It is impossible to say how old the list really is, and it cannot be left out of consideration that it might have been concocted by the author of 2 Samuel.

DEBIR. A city in the mountains of **Judah**, formerly **Kiriath-Sepher** (Judg 1:11), conquered by **Joshua** (Jos 10:38-39) or **Othniel** (Judg 1:11-15). A levitical city (Josh 21:15). Formerly believed to be situated at Tell Beit Mirsim southwest of **Hebron**, it was excavated in the 1930s. Modern archaeologists prefer to identify it with Khirbet Rabud closer to Hebron.

DEBORAH. A prophetess and **judge** in **Israel** (Judg 4:4), who according to tradition rallied the Israelite forces against the **Canaanites** led by **Sisera**, and composed the victory hymn, "**the Song of Deborah**" (Judg 5). Her home is said to have been located between **Ramah** and **Bethel**, perhaps because she in tradition has been identified with Deborah, the nurse of **Jacob**, who was buried near Bethel (Gen 35:8).

DEBORAH, SONG OF. The victory hymn in Judges 5, celebrating the Israelite victory over the **Canaanite** coalition headed by **Sisera**. The Song of Deborah thus represents the poetic parallel to the prose account of the events in Judges 4. It includes some minor differences like the place of the battle. In Judges 4 the battle took place at the brook of **Kishon**, in Judges 5 at **Taanach** by the waters of **Megiddo**. The Song of Deborah has often been taken to be very old, for many people the oldest part of the Old Testament, probably reaching back to the time of the battle itself. Though this claim is not verifiable, the language of the song is different, archaic or archaizing, from most other Old Testament literature, a fact that indicates a special origin.

DELILAH. The wife of the **Judge Samson** who caused the downfall of her heroic husband and delivered him into the hands of his **Philistine** enemies (Judg 16).

DEPORTATION. Among the empires of the ancient Near East it was customary to remove large population groups from conquered territories to other parts of the empire in order to break up the local power structure (*see also* **patronage**) by blending the different populations of the empire. The two states of **Israel** and **Judah** suffered several such deportations, after the fall of **Samaria** in 722 B.C.E. (2 Kgs 17:3-6.24), during **Sennacherib's** campaign in Judah in 701 B.C.E. (2 Kgs 18:13-16), and again at the beginning of the sixth century B.C.E., when the **Babylonians** subdued the **Kingdom of Judah**, in 597 B.C.E. and 587 B.C.E. (2 Kgs 24:16; 25:11).

DESERT, MIGRATIONS IN THE DESERT. In the literature of the ancient Near East, the desert plays a role similar to that of the woods in European fairy-tales. It is a kind of middle world that intersects human-inhabited territories. It is a world of demons, monsters, and ghosts. In this world the hero must prove his abilities before he can move on to his glorious future as the leader of kingdoms and armies in the inhabited world. This function of the desert is obvious the moment one turns to the story of **Israel's** migrations in the desert (Exodus–Deuteronomy). The Israelite migration from **Egypt** to **Canaan**—two inhabited "cultural" countries—involved Israel in a long march from the **Sea of Reeds** to the border of Canaan, passing by the mountain of **Sinai** and onward to the Gulf of Aqaba and to **Kadesh Barnea.** After the stay at Kadesh, where the Israelites were condemned to continue their traveling in the desert for 40 years because of their faintheartedness, and after the aborted invasion of Canaan from the south (Num 13-14), their migration took the Israelites to **Transjordan, Edom,** and **Moab.** It involved Israel in fights against desert people like the **Amalekites** (Exod 17:8-13), or against monster kings like **Sihon** and **Og** (Num 21). The tale of Israel's migrations in the desert includes stories of apostasy such as the incident of the golden calf (Exod 32) and of the Israelites fornicating with **Midianite** women at **Beth Peor** (Num 25). It also includes the story of the encounter with God at Sinai (Exod 19-24). Fundamental institutions of Israelite society were established in the desert such as the institution of the ark (*see* **ark of the covenant**) and the tent of meeting (Exod 25-30). Also the Law of God was given to Israel on Mount Sinai (Exod 20; 35-Num 10).

Historically, the migration in the desert as described in the books of the Old Testament has little to do with life in the desert as it really was. It is described more like the procession of an immense number of people nourished from the desert but by God himself. Scholars usually dismiss the description of the desert migrations as historically unfeasible but sometimes entertain the idea that the tradition about the desert may go back to a minor migratory group that had its original home in the desert regions south and east of **Palestine.**

DEUTERO-ISAIAH. *See* ISAIAH.

DEUTERONOMISM. Among biblical scholars deuteronomism is used as the name of the ideology that not only forms the background of the **Deuteronomistic History,** but also constitutes the governing idea of other parts of the Old Testament. The fundamental idea of deuteronomism is related to the centralization of Israelite religion and worship in **Jerusalem,** making Jerusalem the center of the world. The origin of this ideology is often traced back to the **Kingdom of Israel**. Thus, after the fall of **Samaria** in 722 B.C.E. refugees from Israel brought this ideology to Jerusalem where it established itself as the ideological background of **Josiah's reform** in 623 B.C.E.

DEUTERONOMISTIC HISTORY. The name used among Old Testament scholars for the collection of historical books from the **Book of Joshua** to 2 Kings (*see* **Kings, books of**). Sometimes scholars also include the Book of **Deuteronomy** in the Deuteronomistic History. According to current scholarship these books represent one single work, a major history of **Israel** from the conquest of **Canaan** (*see* **Settlement of Israel**) to the end of the **Kingdom of Judah**. As a literary composition it displays a lack of homogeneity owing to the different nature of the sources included in this history. Thus it has been possible to isolate a series of compositions that were only secondarily incorporated into the Deuteronomistic History, such as the stories of the **judges** who saved Israel (Judg 3-11), the **Samson** narrative (Judg 12-16), the story of young **David**'s career (1 Sam 16-2 Sam 7), the **Succession History** (2 Sam 8-1 Kgs 2), and the complex of **Elijah** and **Elisha** stories (1 Kgs 17-2 Kgs 9). On several occasions the compilers of the Deuteronomistic History break into the narrative in sections that were written to explain the reasons for the cause of history leading to the tragic fate of the Israelites because of their haunted relationship with their God (e.g., Judg 2; 2 Kgs 17)

The attitude to history displayed by the Deuteronomistic History is mainly negative as it foresees and describes the disappearance of the Jewish presence in Canaan as the end of history. The Deuteronomistic History has been dated to either the late seventh century B.C.E., or to the time of the **Babylonian Exile** (sixth century B.C.E.). Recent scholarship has proposed to date it to either the **Persian** period (539-331 B.C.E.) or to the early Hellenistic period (late fourth century-early third century B.C.E.).

DEUTERONOMISTIC REFORM. *See* JOSIAH'S REFORM.

DEUTERONOMY. The usual name in the English-speaking world of the fifth Book of Moses (*see also* **Pentateuch**). The name means "the second law" and refers to the content of the book understood to be a new formulation of the legislation presented by God to **Moses** at **Sinai.** The book opens with a review of the migrations in the **desert** that is not absolutely in accordance with the version presented in the books of **Exodus** and **Numbers.** When the law is presented to **Israel,** it does not happen at Sinai but on the plains of **Moab.** The formulation of the new law occupies most of the book (in total chapters 5-26—in a more narrow sense chapters 12-26). This law includes a new version of the Ten Commandments (Deut 5:6-21; see also Exod 20). The law section concludes with curses on the person who breaks the law and instructions for a ritual of blessing and cursing (Deut 27-28). The remaining chapters include the farewell speech of Moses, his blessings, and the story of his death at Mount **Nebo** (chapters 29-34).

The Book of Deuteronomy is literarily and ideologically linked to the **Deuteronomistic History.** If it is not a part of this history, it has been composed by people belonging to the same intellectual circle that wrote the Deuteronomistic History. The central part of the book has sometimes been linked to the law book found in the **temple of Jerusalem** and brought to King **Josiah** of **Judah** and in this way became the official reason for his reform (2 Kgs 22:8-20; *see also* **Josiah's Reform**).

DIBON. A royal city of ancient **Moab** located at Dhiban c. 65 kilometers south of modern Amman. Conquered by the **Amorite** King **Sihon** from the Moabites (Num 21:26), but taken by the Israelites and allotted to **Reuben** or **Gad** (Num 21:30; 32:34; Josh 13:17). King **Mesha,** himself a "Dibonite," retook the city and fortified it. It seems to have remained part of Moab to the end of the Iron Age (see also Isa 15:2; Jer 48:22). Excavations in the 1950s discovered a settlement from the Early Bronze Age, and again in the Iron Age. At the beginning of the sixth century B.C.E. the place was destroyed by the Babylonians (*see* **Assyria and Babylonia**) and not rebuilt before Roman times.

DINAH. The daughter of Jacob who was raped by **Shechem,** the son of **Hamor,** the leader of the city of Shechem. Her rape led to the death of the male population of Shechem when her brothers **Simeon** and **Levi** revenged their sister (Gen 34). Dinah has sometimes been taken by Old Testament scholars to be the name of an Israelite tribe that disappeared at a very early moment in Israel's history. *See also* TWELVE TRIBE SYSTEM.

DOEG. An **Edomite** in the service of King **Saul,** who witnessed the **priest** of **Nob** providing **David** with food and weapons. On the king's order, Doeg executed 85 priests from Nob (1 Sam 21).

DOR. A city on the coast of Palestine, c. 15 kilometers south of Haifa. Dor was a member of the coalition of **Canaanite** kings who fought against **Joshua** (Josh 11:2; 12:23). Dor was allotted to the tribal territory of **Manasseh** (Josh 17:11). It is mentioned in Egyptian documents of the New Kingdom, and again in the Wenamon report from c. 1100 B.C.E. as inhabited by the Tjeker, a **Sea people.** After the **Assyrian** conquest, it became the center of the Assyrian province of Duru, and later belonged to **Sidon.**

DOTHAN. The place where **Jacob's** sons attacked their brother, Joseph, and sold him as a slave (Gen 37:15-36). It is mentioned in the **Elisha** story (2 Kgs 6:13), but is otherwise unknown in spite of being a well-defined and imposing site 20 kilometers north of Nablus. It was excavated in the 1950s and 1960s but the results were never published and little is known except that Dothan was settled in the Bronze and Iron Ages.

- E -

EBAL. A mountain to the north of ancient **Shechem** close to the modern city of Nablus, and the place of the ceremony of curses in **Deuteronomy** 27. **Joshua** built an altar at Ebal (Josh 8:30-35). According to the excavator of the summit of Ebal, this altar has been recovered. His claim has, however, been severely disputed by other archaeologists.

EBENEZER. The place where the Israelites lost the ark of God (*see* **Ark of the Covenant**) to the **Philistines** (1 Sam 4:1-11). It has tentatively been identified with 'Izbet Sartah close to ancient **Aphek.**

Ebenezer (meaning "stone of help") shares its name with the stone put up by **Samuel** between **Mizpah** and Jeshanah (1 Sam 7:12) commemorating his victory over the Philistines.

EBLA. A city of ancient Syria, located at Tell Mardikh c. 70 kilometers south of Aleppo. Although it is not mentioned in the Old Testament, Ebla gained notoriety in the 1970s, when a large archive was found in this place dating back to the second half of the third millennium B.C.E. In the third millennium B.C.E., it was probably the political center of northern **Syria** but was destroyed c. 2250 B.C.E. It was rebuilt in the Middle Bronze Age but destroyed again by the **Hittites** c. 1600 B.C.E. Its archive, counting as much as 17,000 clay tablets, partly in a hitherto unknown West-Semitic language, was formerly believed to include important information about biblical figures. Thus the name of Abraham was identified among the kings of Ebla. However, recent analysis of the written sources from Ebla has made any equation with biblical personalities impossible.

ECONOMY. Ancient Israel was technologically a traditional Mediterranean society. Its survival was based on a mainly agrarian economy, involving more than 90 percent of the total population in the production of basic means of livelihood. That society could also afford to produce food for people in other sectors, such as administration, the army, and the palace including the royal family. The majority of the population was engaged in agriculture including animal production on a limited scale. More specialized animal production was left in the hands of herders and nomads always present but never representing more than a fraction of the total number of people in food production. Most Palestinian **cities** were small but heavily defended and provided shelter for the peasants in time of distress. The city would have been the center of more specialized crafts and the place where the agricultural sector sold its products. **Palestine** has little in the way of special products of interest to foreign traders. Its most important crop was probably olives, and the oil produced from olives. Evidently, international trade was a more important source of income, although this trade may not to any great extent have involved products of Palestine itself. However, Palestine's location as a kind of bridge leading from western Asia to **Egypt** allowed for an extensive transit of goods from **Mesopo-**

tamia to Egypt and vice versa, always offering an opportunity for taxation as the trade caravans moved across the Palestinian countryside.

EDOM, EDOMITES. In the Old Testament, Edom and the Edomites are the descendants of **Jacob's** brother **Esau.** Because of this relationship, the reputation of the Edomites in the Old Testament is mixed. Sometimes they were the allies of **Israel,** at other times they were the subjects of Israelite kings as in the days of **David** and **Solomon.** However, more often they acted as enemies to Israel. Thus, in the time of the Israelite migrations in the desert (*see* **Desert, Migrations in the Desert**), they denied the Israelites free passage through their country (Num 20:14-21). Historically, the first references to Edom can be found in Egyptian documents of the New Kingdom. However, outside of the Old Testament no evidence is in existence that identifies Edom as a state. Basically, the material culture of the Edomites seems to have been nomadic, and settled communities were rare until late in the Iron Age. However, when Edom emerged as a state, it soon began to compete with the **Kingdom of Judah** for control of southern **Palestine** and access to the Gulf of Aqaba. When the Judean state gradually lost importance until it was finally wiped out by the Babylonians (*see* **Assyria and Babylonia**), Edom's influence grew and it gradually won control not only over the **Negeb,** but also over the southern part of the Judean hill land. In the Hellenistic period, the border between Judea and Edom ran at **Beth-Zur** between **Jerusalem** and **Hebron.**

EGLON, PERSON. The king of the **Moabites,** who was killed by **Ehud** (Judg 3:12-30). Eglon, who is described as a "very fat man," was killed in his bathroom, according to a story that plays mercilessly with his fatness and his servants' inability to comprehend what was taking place.

EGLON, CITY. A city in the Judean **Shephelah,** conquered by **Joshua** (Josh 10:34-35). Its king took part in the **Canaanite** coalition against Joshua and the Israelites headed by the king of **Jerusalem** (Josh 10). Its location is disputed, many scholars believing it to be Tell el Hesi in the southern Shephelah c. 10 kilometers south of modern Qiriath Gath. A dissonant voice claims that it should be sought at Tell 'Aitun c. 40 kilometers southwest of Jerusalem.

EGYPT. Israel's great southern neighbor and always an important player in the history of ancient **Israel** and **Palestine**. Egypt was united at the end of the fourth millennium B.C.E. into one state stretching from the first cataracts of the Nile in the south to the Mediterranean in the north. Egypt's history can roughly be separated into three periods of greatness—respectively the Old, Middle, and New Kingdom—and three intermediary periods. Its history is subdivided into 30 dynasties or royal families that, according to the list of Egyptian kings presented by the Hellenistic Egyptian historiographer Manetho, ruled Egypt for all of its history until Hellenistic times.

The Old Kingdom was introduced by the Early Dynastic period (c. 3100-2686 B.C.E.), covering dynasty 1-2. This early phase of the history of Egypt was followed by the blossoming era of the Old Kingdom (c. 2686-2183 B.C.E.), the period of the pyramid builders. At the end of the Old Kingdom, the First Intermediary period (c. 2181-2040 B.C.E.) followed—a period of decline and, in the eyes of later Egyptian writers, also of social unrest. In this Intermediary period the natural order was, according to later Egyptian sources, turned upside down: the rich became poor and the poor rich.

The Middle Kingdom (c. 2040-1795 B.C.E.) was the classical period of Egyptian culture and civilization. This period was also followed by one of decline, the Second Intermediary period (c. 1795-1550 B.C.E.). In the eyes of the Egyptians, the most infamous part of this period was dominated by the presence in northern Egypt of foreign rule in the time of the 15th dynasty, the **Hyksos** dynasty, believed to have consisted of princes of Asiatic origin. The New Kingdom (c. 1550-1069 B.C.E.) followed, a period of greatness when Egypt invaded western Asia and turned into an imperial power that ruled large parts of western Asia, bringing in its early period Egyptian armies to the banks of the **Euphrates**. Later, during the time of the 18th dynasty, the **Hittites** forced the Egyptians to reduce their presence in **Syria** and they had to move back to a line north of **Damascus**.

The New Kingdom included the Amarna period (*see* **Amarna and the Amarna letters**) as well as the time of the Ramessides. **Ramesses II** (1279-1213 B.C.E.)—often believed to be the **Pharaoh of the Exodus**—stands out among its many great rulers, not only because of the duration of his reign that covered most of the 13th century B.C.E. but also because of his political achievements and especially the number of monuments from his time that literally litters Egypt. The New Kingdom deteriorated into the Third Intermediate period (c. 1069-656 B.C.E.), when Egypt was not only seriously weakened but also at times ruled by dynasties of foreign origin, including Libyan or Ethiopian dynasties. Egypt never recovered from this weakness to regain its former greatness.

The lowest point of its political history before the conquest of Alexander the Great was reached when **Esarhaddon of Assyria** in 671 B.C.E. invaded Egypt. However, in the time of the 26th dynasty (664-525 B.C.E.) Egypt experienced its last political successes as an independent state before it was swallowed up at first by the **Persian Empire**, and, following Alexander the Great's victory over the Persians, by the Macedonian Empire. After Alexander's death in 323 B.C.E., Egypt was ruled by the Ptolemies (305-30 B.C.E.), a dynasty named after Ptolemy, one of Alexander's generals. It finally became part of the Roman Empire, when Augustus removed the last traces of Egyptian independence.

EGYPT AND ISRAEL. Archaeology has excavated many indications of Egyptian presence in southern **Palestine** already in the days of the Old Kingdom. Indeed, the remains pointing to an Egyptian presence indicate that the southern part of the country was already in the third millennium controlled by Egypt. This presence of Egypt in southern Palestine continued during the Middle Kingdom. From this period, the collections of **Execration Texts** show an intimate knowledge of rulers and places in Palestine. This period ended by a reversal of fortune when Asians who had migrated to Egypt established a rule in northern Egypt that followed an Asian rather than an Egyptian pattern. It was the time of the **Hyksos** kings bedeviled by later Egyptian tradition. When the last **Pharaohs** of the 17th dynasty expelled the Hyksos rulers, Egypt in the time of the 18th dynasty (c.1550-1295 B.C.E.) pressed on and sent its armies into the rear area of the Hyksos and in this way conquered western Asia up to the **Euphrates.** Until the fourth century, when the **Hittites** appeared on the **Syrian** scene, Egypt ruled western Asia, including all of Palestine. From the middle of the fourth century B.C.E., Egypt was challenged by the Hittites and pressed into the defensive until **Ramesses II** negotiated a lasting peace with the Hittite king that divided Syria between the two great powers of that time, the Hittites and the Egyptians. To the end of the New Kingdom Egypt stayed in control of Palestine.

New studies of the evidence from **Beth-Shan,** a traditional Egyptian stronghold, have shown that the Egyptians were present here in force as late as the 10th century. Toward the end of the 10th century **Pharaoh Shishak** directed a campaign against several Palestinian cities, an event also remembered by the Old Testament tradition (1 Kgs 14:25-26), although Shishak in his inscription commemorating the campaign does not mention any Judean city including **Jerusalem.** After his time, any Egyptian presence in Palestine was sporadic and generally thwarted by other more powerful states. Thus **Tirharkah's** abortive campaign in 701 B.C.E. against **Sennacherib** ended in defeat at Elteqeh. During the revival of Egyptian political aspirations in the time of the Saite dynasty, Pharaoh **Necho** in 609 B.C.E. moved his army against **Charchemish** and the **Babylonians.** On his way he engaged and defeated **Josiah** of **Judah** at **Megiddo,** but his campaign also ended in disaster when his army was routed by the Babylonians (*see* **Assyria and Babylon**) at Charchemish.

The biblical traditions about Egypt that concern relations between **Israel** and Egypt before the time of the monarchy, including the visits of **Abraham** and **Jacob** in Egypt, and **Joseph,** and the **Exodus,** are all legendary and the reflection of later ideas about Egypt, colored by many years of experience of being the neighbor of Egypt.

EGYPT, RIVER OF. The traditional border between **Canaan** and **Egypt,** and the southern border of **Judah** (Num 34:5). It is located some 10 kilometers south of **Gaza.** Its modern name is Nahal Besor, in Arabic Wadi Ghazzeh.

EHUD. A **Benjaminite** who became **judge** over **Israel** after having killed the fat King **Eglon** in his bathroom and in this way liberated

Israel from **Moab**. Although the length of his office is not mentioned, he created a peace for Israel that was to last for 80 years (Judg 3:15-29).

EKRON. In the Old Testament together with Gath, Gaza, Ashkelon, and Ashdod, mentioned as one of the five leading **Philistine** cities (Josh 13:3). Although it was considered a part of the tribal territory of **Judah** (Josh 15:11), it never was in Israelite possession. It participated in an anti-**Assyrian** rebellion but was conquered by **Sargon** in 712 B.C.E. and became Assyrian territory. Recent excavations at Tel Miqne, the place of ancient Ekron, discovered a major Palestinian city that was founded in the Bronze Age but flourished during the Iron Age. During the excavations, a royal inscription surfaced dating from the early seventh century B.C.E. This inscription mentions a series of kings of Ekron, some of them already known from Assyrian sources.

ELAH. The Old Testament knows of several persons of the name of Elah. The most important is King Elah of **Israel** (c. 887-886 B.C.E.). He was the son and successor of Baasha but only ruled for two years before he was murdered together with his family in his palace by **Zimri**, an officer of the chariots (1 Kgs 16:8-14). Apart from the circumstances of his killing, nothing is known of his reign.

ELAH, VALLEY OF. Meaning "the Valley of the Terabinth," the scene of the duel between **David** and **Goliath**, normally identified with Wadi es-Sant c. 23 kilometers southwest of **Bethlehem**.

ELAM. Since the end of the third millennium B.C.E., Elam was an important state located on the Iranian plateau with **Susa** as its capital. Most information about Elam comes from **Assyrian** and Babylonian documents, mainly records of wars and conquests. Toward the middle of the seventh century B.C.E., the Assyrians finally settled with Elam, when they conquered and destroyed Susa, although unable to permanently occupy its territory. In this way they paved the way for **Media**, a competing power of the region to the east of **Mesopotamia** that was to become one of its main foes toward the end of the Neo-Assyrian Empire. The tradition of Elam including its language—not related to Persian or any Semitic language—survived into the time of the **Persian Empire**, and this may form the backdrop of the Old Testament tradition about **Chedorlaomer**, the king of Elam who together with three other great kings invaded **Canaan** but was defeated by **Abraham** (Gen 14).

ELEPHANTINE PAPYRI. A collection of Aramaic papyri belonging to a Jewish military colony of the fifth century B.C.E. stationed at the island of Elephantine in Upper **Egypt** close to Assuan. Although not mentioned in the Old Testament, the documents from this colony provide interesting information that illuminates the history of post-exilic Judaism.

ELHANAN. The name of two of **David**'s heroes. 1. Elhanan the son of Jair (or Jaare). According to the **books of Samuel**, Elhanan killed **Goliath** (2 Sam 21:19); in **Chronicles**, he killed Goliath's brother Lahmi (1 Chron 20:5). It has since ancient times been proposed that Elhanan was David's first name. In this case the name of David may have been a throne name which he acquired upon his ascension to the throne. 2. Elhanan, the son of Dodo from **Bethlehem** (2 Sam 23:24), sometimes identified with Elhanan, the son of Jair.

ELI. The **priest** of **Shiloh** in **Samuel**'s time (1 Sam 1-4). He is also called a **judge** in **Israel** (1 Sam 4:18). His sons took advantage of their position as priests. As a punishment for their misbehavior they were killed in the battle against the **Philistines** at Ebenezer, although they had carried the **ark of the Covenant** with them into the battle. The ark was lost to the Philistines. When the message of the catastrophe reached Eli, he fell down from his seat and died. Among his descendants, **Ahijah** served as a priest at **Nob** in the days of King **Saul** (1 Sam 14:3).

ELIAKIM. 1. The original name of King **Jehoiakim of Judah** (2 Kgs 23:34). 2. The son of **Hilkiah** and the vizier in **Hezekiah**'s days who on the kings's order negotiated with the **Assyrian** envoys who were sent from **Lachish** to Jerusalem during the siege in 701 B.C.E. (2 Kgs 18:18-36). When he returned from the negotiations to the king with a harsh answer, Hezekiah sent him to the prophet

Isaiah asking for advice and consolation to the king (2 Kgs 19:1-7).

ELIASHIB. **High priest of Jerusalem** in the days of **Nehemiah.** During Nehemiah's first visit to Jerusalem, Eliashib supported his building project, the restoration of the city defenses (Neh 3:1). When Nehemiah returned from **Persia**, Eliashib (if it is the same priest of this name) appeared in an alliance with Nehemiah's enemies, especially **Tobiah the Ammonite** (Neh 13).

ELIJAH. (Meaning "My God is Yahweh"). A **prophet** from Tishbe in **Gilead** who was in opposition to King **Ahab** and his religious policies. The Old Testament includes a comprehensive tradition about Elijah, mostly legendary but conforming to the Old Testament tradition of the **prophets** as being the opponents of kings (1 Kgs 17-2 Kgs 2). Elijah is especially famous for his harsh treatment of the priest of Baal after the ordeal at **Carmel** where he killed 450 prophets of Baal at the brook of **Kishon** (1 Kgs 18), and for his cursing **Jezebel**, Ahab's queen (1 Kgs 21:23-24). This curse was fulfilled when Jehu had her killed at **Jezreel** (2 Kgs 9:30-37).

ELISHA. The son of Shaphat. Elisha was chosen to be a **prophet** by **Elijah** (1 Kgs 19:19-21). The comprehensive corpus of Elisha narratives (2 Kgs 2-13) is mostly legendary and without historical merit but his role as a forceful opponent of the **House of Omri** may reflect religious competition in the **Kingdom of Israel**. Elisha was the prophet that anointed **Jehu** to be the new king (2 Kgs 9:1-13). According to legend, he was also involved in choosing **Hazael** as the new king of **Aram Damascus** (2 Kgs 8:7-15).

ELKANAH. The Zuphite, who fulfilled his wife's vow to God at **Shiloh** to present her firstborn, the later **prophet Samuel**, to the **temple** (1 Sam 1-2).

ELON. A **judge in Israel**, from the tribe of **Zebulon**, who was in office for 10 years (Judg 12:11). He belongs to the list of five judges (Judg 10:1-5; 12:8-15) who together judged Israel for 70 years but left no records about their exploits.

ELOTH, ELATH. A city at the northern end of the Gulf of Aqaba close to **Ezion-geber.** Eloth was **Solomon's** seaport and the center of his overseas trade enterprises (1 Kgs 9:26). Eloth probably belonged to the **Kingdom of Judah** from **David** to **Joram,** when it became an **Edomite** possession (2 Kgs 8:21-22). It was retaken by **Uzziah** (2 Kgs 14:22), and lost again under **Ahaz** (2 Kgs 16:5-6). Its present location is still the subject of discussion.

EMPIRE OF DAVID AND SOLOMON. According to the Old Testament, **David** succeeded in creating an extensive empire that—apart from **Israel** and **Judah**—also included the territories to the east of the **Jordan River.** Here, David either conquered the states of **Ammon, Moab,** and **Edom,** or made them tributaries to Israel. In **Syria,** most of the **Aramaean** states of western Syria, including **Damascus,** submitted to Israelite rule, and the **Euphrates** became the ideal—if not practical—northern border of the Davidic-Solomonic Empire (1 Kgs 5:1: ET 4:24). The **Philistines,** although never defeated, probably became tributary to Israel, and good relations were entertained with **Phoenicia.** The Old Testament speaks of insurrections against David's rule, by his son **Absalom** and by the tribes of northern Israel (the Rebellion of **Sheba**), however not about problems with the vassal states at the periphery of the empire.

Things changed during the rule of David's successor, **Solomon.** Toward the end of Solomon's rule, the empire began to fall apart. Edom and Damascus regained their independence, while Solomon handed over a part of northeastern Palestine to the Tyrians (*see* **Tyre**) as payment for their contribution to his building activities in Jerusalem. Discontent also grew among the northern Israelite tribes, and a pretender to the throne, **Jeroboam,** the son of Nebat, had to flee for his life to **Egypt,** where he was received well.

In recent years, historians have increasingly expressed doubts as to the historicity of the description of the great Israelite empire which has normally been dated to the 10th century B.C.E. One way to minimize the importance of this empire is to reduce its size considerably, claiming that it hardly covered more than **Palestine,** or perhaps even less, only the basic Israelite territory reaching from **Dan** in the north to **Beersheba** in the south. Some scholars simply deny its existence for a number of reasons. Some of these reasons are based on a reevaluation of the archaeological material traditionally dated to the 10th century B.C.E., including many monumental buildings formerly attributed to Solomon but increasingly felt to belong to the time of the dynasty of **Omri**, but also involving the very existence of Jerusalem in the 10th century B.C.E., which is now contested by a series of archaeologists. Some scholars have pointed to the impossibility of a great Israelite empire in the 10th century because of the international political situation at that time, but this evidence is less conclusive as the 10th century is in general considered a "dark" period which has left little in the way of written documents or monuments. *See also* UNITED MONARCHY.

EN-GEDI. A spring and oasis in the Desert of Judah close to the Dead Sea c. 55 kilometers southeast of **Jerusalem**. Mentioned as a **city** belonging to **Judah** (Josh 15:62), although the settlement in this place was only founded c. 600 B.C.E. En-Gedi (meaning "the Spring of Goats") served as a place of refuge for **David** and his men when he was fleeing from **Saul** (1 Sam 24).

EPHRAIM (TRIBE). Ephraim was the eponymous father of the **tribe** of Ephraim. He was the youngest son of **Joseph** and the brother of **Manasseh** (Gen 41:52; 48:5). In spite of being the minor, Ephraim was blessed by his father. The tribe of Ephraim was the most important tribe living in the northern part of the central highlands of **Palestine**. It has been proposed that, historically, the name of Ephraim may be based on a geographical name, the Mountains of Ephraim. If this is a correct observation, the tribe of Ephraim is likely to be of Palestinian origin. The historical origin of the tribe cannot be traced in detail, but it must be related to the appearance of an extensive village culture in the highlands between 1200 and 1000 B.C.E. In the **Period of the Monarchy**, Ephraim seems to have lost ground to its northern neighbor, the tribe of Manasseh. The capital of the Northern **Kingdom of Israel** was placed, not within the territory of Ephraim, but on Manassite soil and this in spite of the fact that **Jeroboam**, the first king of Israel, was a man from the tribe of Ephraim. In the prophetic literature of the Old Testament, Ephraim is often used as a second name of the Kingdom of Israel.

EPHRAIM (PLACE NAME). The name of the place where **Absalom** murdered his brother **Amnon** (2 Sam 13:23), normally identified with Baal-Hazor 22 kilometers north of **Jerusalem.**

EPHRATA. In the Old Testament Ephrata appears as the name of a lineage or **clan** within **Caleb** or **Judah.** This family group was related genealogically to the family of **David.** Thus David's father **Jesse** is reckoned among its members (1 Sam 17:12). At the same time Ephrata may also mean the area inhabited by this group, including **Bethlehem,** and finally Bethlehem itself.

EPHRON. A **Hittite** who sold his field with its cave to **Abraham** as Abraham's grave cave (Gen 23).

ESARHADDON. King of **Assyria** (681-669 B.C.E.), the son and successor of **Sennacherib.** Esarhaddon was appointed heir to the Assyrian throne by his father, who at the same time ignored his older brothers. After the murder of Sennacherib (see 2 Kgs 19:37), Esarhaddon had to defend his claim to the throne against his brothers. Esarhaddon changed the Assyrian Babylonian policy that during the reign of Sennacherib had led to the destruction of the city of **Babylon.** Esarhaddon procured the means for the rebuilding of the famous cultural center of **Mesopotamian** civilization. His military activities were mostly restricted to restoring order in rebellious provinces and securing the borders of the empire. One campaign went to the capital of Urartu to arrest the murderers of Sennacherib who had fled to Urartu. From 679 B.C.E., his foreign policy changed and he sent his armies against **Egypt,** an enterprise that was crowned with success eight years later, in 671 B.C.E. Two years later he died on the way to Egypt, on a campaign intended to consolidate the Assyrian control over that country. Esarhaddon is only mentioned in the Old Testament in connection with the note about the murder of Sennacherib (2 Kgs 19:37). However, in his inscriptions, Esarhaddon mentions among his vassals King **Manasseh** of **Judah.**

ESAU. The oldest son of **Isaac** and **Rebecca,** and the brother of **Jacob** who cheated him for his right as firstborn (Gen 27). Esau married two **Hittite** women (Gen 26:34). With his Hittite wives he moved to **Seir** (Gen 36). When Jacob returned from his service in the house of his uncle **Laban**, he encountered Esau at **Penuel** and the two brothers were reconciled (Gen 33). In the Old Testament Esau is reckoned the heroic ancestor of **Edom** and the Edomites.

ESHKOL AND THE VALLEY OF ESHKOL. Eshkol (meaning "cluster") was an **Amorite** united with **Abraham** (Gen 14:13-14). He is generally reckoned a personification of the valley of Eshkol close to **Hebron**, and visited by **Moses'** spies (Num 13:23) who brought back a cluster of grapes from the Valley of Eshkol that could only be transported by two grown-up men.

ESHTAOL. A **city** in the territory of **Dan** (Josh 19:41), in the homeland of the hero **Samson** (Judg 13:25). Eshtaol is usually identified with an archaeological site near the Arab village of Ishwa, a few kilometers northeast of **Beth-Shemesh.**

ESTHER, THE BOOK OF ESTHER. The Book of Esther tells the story about Esther the Jewish queen of King **Ahasuerus** (that is, **Xerxes**) of **Persia** who saved her father **Mordecai** and her people from death and persecution. It is a romantic novel from the Hellenistic period with little or no historical foundation. It is often assumed that the name of Esther is based on the name of the Mesopotamian goddess Ishtar, and the name of her father on the name of the Babylonian god Marduk.

ETHBAAL. King of **Tyre** and the father of **Jezebel** (1 Kgs 16:31). According to **Josephus,** who calls him Itobalos (Phoenician Ittoba'al), he ruled Tyre for 32 years (c. 887-856 B.C.E.). The Old Testament reckons Ethbaal to be king of **Sidon,** a confusion created by the Tyrian conquest of Sidon.

ETHIOPIA. *See* CUSH.

ETHNICITY. *See* NATION.

ETIOLOGY, ETIOLOGICAL NARRATIVES. The Old Testament includes a series of stories and short notes supposed to explain the name of a number of localities in ancient **Palestine**. Normally, such a place is connected with a person or event relating to **Israel's** early history. Thus **Achan** died in the Valley of **Achor** (Josh 7), and the **Midianite** princes **Oreb and Zeeb** were executed on the Rock of Oreb and the winepress of Zeeb (Judg 7:25). Sometimes the Old Testament adds a note, "to this day," as in the story of the conquest of **Ai** that was reduced to the ruin "it remains to this day" (Josh 8:28). It is generally assumed that such names are older than the stories attached to them as etiological narratives.

EUPHRATES, THE. One of the two great rivers, the Euphrates and **Tigris,** that run through **Mesopotamia.** The Euphrates flows to the west of the Tigris. Its offspring is in Armenia in Asia Minor, and its outlet is in the Persian Gulf. In the Old Testament it is considered one of the four rivers that come out of Paradise (Gen 2:10-14), and it serves as the ideal northern border of the Davidic-Solomonic Empire (1 Kgs 5:1: ET 4:24) (*see* **Empire of David and Solomon**). In the Old Testament, it is also called "the Great River" or just "the River"—a testimony to its importance. Also other texts of the Old Testament entertain the idea that the land of **Israel** ideally runs from the Euphrates to the Mediterranean. Thus, the farewell speech of **Joshua** at **Shechem** has a reference to the original homes of the forefathers of the Israelites east of the Euphrates (Josh 24:3), and Abraham transgressed all of **Canaan** to the west of the Euphrates. This distinction between the territories located east and west of the Euphrates is typical of the Mesopotamian tradition according to which the country to the west of the Euphrates was inhabited by **Amorites** and Hittites.

EVIL-MERODACH. (Babylonian Amel-Marduk) King of Babylonia (*see* **Assyria and Babylonia**) 561-560 B.C.E. Almost no details have survived from his short reign, apart from the important notice in 2 Kings that he freed **Jehoiachin** from prison and entertained him at the palace, something that is also illustrated by a fragmentary Babylonian inscription recording provisions for the king of **Judah.**

EVOLUTION MODEL. *See* SETTLEMENT OF ISRAEL.

EXECRATION TEXTS. The Execration Texts include two collections of Egyptian inscriptions dating from the time of the Middle Kingdom. These texts formed part of a ritual including the cursing of **Egypt's** foreign enemies. The Execration Texts mention a series of **Palestinian cities**—including **Jerusalem**—and the names of their rulers. These names mainly belong to the **Amorite** language family. In this way they contribute considerably to the knowledge of the political and social structure of the country in the Middle Bronze Age.

EXILE. *See* BABYLONIAN EXILE.

EXODUS, BOOK. The second Book of **Moses.** The Book of Exodus can basically be divided into three sections. The first section includes the story of Moses' birth and miraculous saving, his wrestling with the **Pharaoh** about the liberty of the Israelites. It also includes the narrative about the plagues of **Egypt** and the installation of the Passover (Exod 7-13), and the escape of the Israelites into the **desert** (Exod 14-15). The second part follows the route of the Israelites to **Sinai** where God gave his **covenant** and the Ten Commandments to his people. This section also includes the story of the Golden Calf (Exod 32). The final part includes the first part of the comprehensive legislation at Sinai that only ends in **Numbers** 10.

EXODUS, HISTORY. The story of the escape of the Israelites from **Egypt.** The only source of the exodus available is the **Book of Exodus** 1-15, recording the tribulations of the **Hebrews** when a **Pharaoh** assumed power who did not know **Joseph** (Exod 1:8). This story has been paraphrased by **Josephus** who enters additional material into his account of the exodus, and by a Jewish Hellenistic writer, Hezekiel, the tragedian (third century B.C.E.) who wrote a tragedy based on the exodus tradition. The Pharaoh of the exodus, who did not know Joseph, put the Israelites to work on the storage cities of **Pithom** and **Rameses** (Exos 1:11), but he also wanted to extinguish the Hebrew nation by killing the male children of **Israel.** The narrative in the Book of Exodus goes on to tell the story of **Moses'** miraculous salvation, his life at the Egyptian court, and his escape to **Midian.** Moses returned from exile to free his people, and after the ten plagues, the Pharaoh felt compelled to let them go.

When the Pharaoh followed the fleeing Israelites with his army, the miracle at the **Sea of Reeds** allowed the Israelites to pass unharmed but the Pharaoh and his army perished when the waters returned. The debate about the historicity of the exodus has been intense since the 18th century C.E. when doubts were cast on the great number of Israelites leaving Egypt counting 600,000 men plus women and children (Exod 12:37), perhaps as many as 3,500,000 people. As it was said at that time, given the short distance from Egypt to **Canaan**, the last Israelite would not have left Egypt before the first had entered Canaan. In the 19th and 20th centuries, when scholars became able to read the Egyptian documents and inscriptions after the deciphering of the hieroglyphs, it was soon recognized that no Egyptian source mentions an exodus of any large population group as described in the Old Testament. Since the discovery of the mummies of the Pharaohs in the royal cache it has also been difficult to maintain that an Egyptian Pharaoh of the 18th or 19th dynasty drowned in the Sea of Reeds—especially not Ramesses II (1279-1212 B.C.E.), usually considered the Pharaoh of the exodus narrative. The tendency among scholars is either to reject any historicity of the exodus event, or to reduce the scale of this event considerably, turning it into an insignificant occasion totally ignored by the Egyptian authorities of the past. A third possibility is to consider the exodus story an Israelite variant of the Egyptian tradition about the expulsion of the **Hyksos**, something that happened not in the fourth century but in the sixth century B.C.E. This possibility was already chosen by the Jewish historiographer Josephus.

EZEKIEL. The third of the great **prophets** of the Old Testament. He was one of the people deported by King **Nebuchadnezzar** after his first conquest of **Jerusalem** in 597 B.C.E. He lived in the colony of deported people at Tel-Abib close to the ancient city of Nippur at the Kebar canal in central **Mesopotamia**. His book includes information relating to the final fall of Jerusalem in 587 B.C.E., something that indicates that he worked and prophesied between 593 and 573 B.C.E. His prophecies concentrate on the reasons for the catastrophe that struck **Judah** and Jerusalem. The last chapters in his book include a vision of the new temple that was going to be built sometime in the future (Ezek 40-48). Thus the Book of Ezekiel is generally believed to be a testimony to the feelings and sentiments among the exiled Judeans during the first part of the **Babylonian exile.**

EZION-GEBER. A seaport at the Gulf of Aqabah mentioned as a campaign station of the Israelites during their migrations in the desert (*see* **Desert, Migrations in the Desert)** (Num 33:35). It was the basis of **Solomon's** trade on Ophir (1 Kgs 9:26), an enterprise which **Jehoshaphat** failed to reestablish (1 Kgs 22:49). Its location has not yet been firmly established, although several places have been proposed, such as Tell el-Khuleifeh close to modern Elath, and Djezirat Far'un south of Elath.

EZRA, THE BOOK OF EZRA. In the Book of Ezra, Ezra "the Scribe" is characterized as the father of Judaism. He was sent to **Jerusalem** in the seventh year of **Artaxerxes,** the king of **Persia.** The aim of his mission was to teach the Jews the Law. When Ezra, himself a descendant of **Aaron** and of the family of the **high priest,** arrived, he was shocked by the general religious situation and began to reform the Jewish community in Jerusalem, among other things by banishing mixed marriages between **Jews** and non-Jews (Ezra 9-10). The **Book of Nehemiah** adds more traditions about Ezra's mission to Jerusalem. He recited the Law of **Moses** in front of the assembled Jews (Neh 8), arranged for the festival of the Succoth (Neh 8), and after having confessed its sins, the people was obliged to keep the **covenant** (Neh 9-10).

Historically, the mission of Ezra is difficult to access. According to the Old Testament, he was the son of **Sereiah** and the great grandson of the high priest **Hilkiah,** although Sereiah was executed by the Babylonians (*see* **Assyria and Babylonia)** in 587 B.C.E. Also the date of his arrival is uncertain. He arrived in Jerusalem in Artaxerxes' seventh year. However, there were three kings of Persia of this name, all three of them possible candidates. Ezra thus arrived in Jerusalem either in 459 B.C.E., 398 B.C.E., or 352 B.C.E. Most scholars have agreed on the year of 398 B.C.E., but the two other possibilities cannot be totally excluded. Although the Book of Nehemiah reckons Ezra to be a contemporary of Nehemiah, most scholars are of the conviction that Ezra's mission followed later than Nehemiah's appearance in Jerusalem and rebuilding of the city. A few scholars have entertained the idea that Ezra was a legendary rather than a historical figure.

Apart from the history of Ezra, the book carrying his name constitutes a continuation of the **Books of the Chronicles**. It opens with a description of the return from the **Babylonian Exile** and the rebuilding of the **temple of Jerusalem**.

- F -

FAMILY. In traditional societies like ancient **Israel**, the family constitutes the center of each person's life. The Old Testament reckons the family—in Hebrew the *beth 'ab*, a "father's house"—the basic organization on top of which other layers are placed like the **lineage** or **clan**, and at the top the **tribe**. Apart from the royal family, only a few of the families were politically important. Most families were small. Calculations based on information from other parts of **Syria** and **Palestine** in ancient times indicate that the average family may not have exceeded five to six persons. Only well-to-do families might have developed into so-called "extended families" including perhaps a score of people or more. Politically the ordinary family would be subordinated to the noble families in a system of **patronage** while the noble families would normally have to proclaim their loyalty to a royal family, the patron family of the whole society.

FAMINE. Famine was a matter of great concern to the peoples of ancient **Palestine**. The opening story about **Abraham** includes reflections on the dreadful consequences of famine. Abraham had hardly arrived in **Canaan** before famine forced him to leave his new country and travel to **Egypt** (Gen 12). Also **Jacob** and his sons had to go into exile in Egypt to escape the famine that had become a burden to their country—a major theme of the **Joseph** history (Gen 37-50). After these stories, the Old Testament occasionally refers to droughts and famines, and in the Old Testament the effects of famine are common metaphors for the desolation that is going to strike the country, for example, because of foreign conquest and destruction. Historically, the climate of Palestine only provides a marginal living for its inhabitants who have to expect famines on a regular basis, on the average about three times within a period of ten years.

FORTIFICATIONS. Since the Early Bronze Age, fortifications were major structural features of the **cities** of **Palestine.** Palestine was never a safe place to live and a source of booty for many armies— from other Palestinian states or from the great powers outside of Palestine. Fortifications sometimes assumed a size that was so clearly disproportioned in comparison to the size of the cities they protected that Palestinian cities looked more like citadels or fortresses than proper cities. The fortifications adopted many forms, and generally developed in response to technical developments within siege techniques. Thus the glacis embankments supporting the walls of the Middle Bronze Age cities were probably constructed as an answer to the needs created by the development of siege machines. Massive stone walls were also the order of the day in the Middle Bronze Age creating serious opposition to any attacker. In the Iron Age a new style of walls appeared. They were built in two layers creating a hollow space between them, also called casemates. These walls may have served as storage rooms in peacetime but could be filled with dirt in expectation of an impending siege and make the walls serve as an elastic bulwark against rams.

The gate was the focal point in the defense circle and at the same time its weakest point. Accordingly, gates became more and more sophisticated denying the enemy direct access to the entrance of the city. In Palestine the gate achieved its most elaborate forms in the Iron Age I, including a fourfold obstacle to intruders. According to some scholars these gates were built in the days of **Solomon;** according to others in the time of **Omri** and **Ahab.** The elaborate water systems that were constructed in the Iron Age were of special importance for the defense of the cities. The generally hot weather of Palestine made it mandatory to the defense of a city that its inhabitants have ample and continuous access to water. Such water systems that allowed for access from within the city confines even in the event of a siege have been found among other places at **Hazor, Gibeon, Megiddo, Beersheba,** and **Jerusalem.** *See also* SILOAM.

- G -

GAAL. The son of Ebed (literarily "the son of the serf") who stirred up discontent among the inhabitants of **Shechem** against **Abimelech**. As a consequence, Abimelech returned to Shechem and brought vengeance and destruction upon the city. Abimelech's henchman **Zebul** contemptuously threw Gaal out of Shechem (Judg 9).

GAD. One of **Jacob's** sons and the name of an Israelite **tribe**. Gad was the seventh son of Jacob. His mother was Zilpah, one of Jacob's midwives (Gen 30:11). He got his name because of a play on words with Hebrew *Gad*, "happiness." His descendants constituted the tribe of Gad. On the basis of the Old Testament it is only possible to create a very fragmentary history of this tribe. Their historical origin is unknown, although it is likely that the tribe emerged in connection with the social and political turmoil that spelled an end to the society of **Palestine** in the Late Bronze Age and inaugurated the beginning of the Iron Age. The tribal area of Gad was to the east of the **Jordan River** (see also Num 32:33-38), more exactly the central part of **Transjordan**, northeast of the Dead Sea.

The information in the Old Testament about the tribal area of Gad finds support in the **Moabite Mesha inscription** from the middle of the ninth century that mentions Gad in connection with Mesha's conquest of their territory. It might have been the end of historical Gad. At least there is no safe information that Gad existed after this date, and the lack of security when it comes to exactly defining Gad's territory in the Old Testament might have to do with the virtual disappearance of the tribe at an early date. In the Old Testament, Gad's territory is sometimes mixed up with the one of **Reuben**, probably because neither of the two tribes existed when the texts about their homeland were compiled.

GALILEE. In contrast to the importance of Galilee in the New Testament, but also in the writings of the Jewish historiographer **Josephus**, Galilee plays only a minor role in the Old Testament, and the term is never used with precise indication of its boundaries. The name—perhaps meaning "circle"—may refer to the part of

Galilee known from Josephus as "Lower Galilee," that is, the valleys in the southern part of Galilee opposing "Upper Galilee," the mountain ridges to the north bordering on the Lebanese mountains. In the expanded meaning, Galilee may refer to the northern part of **Palestine**, including the Valley of Esdraelon to the west and the **Valley of Jezreel** to the south; it includes the territory around the Sea of Galilee, otherwise known as Kinnereth or Genezareth. Some authorities will reckon the Valley of Huleh to the northeast as part of Upper Galilee, whereas to the north it may be difficult to decide where Galilee ends and **Lebanon** begins. Galilee is the most fertile part of Palestine, with a yearly rainfall of about 1,000 millimeters, and especially the valleys function as the breadbasket of the country.

Relatively few sources have survived relating to Galilee's history in pre-Hellenistic times, but the region has been settled since the Stone Age. A flourishing culture of many **cities** existed in the Middle Bronze Age that ended with the Egyptian occupation (*see* **Egypt and Israel**) of the land in the 16th century B.C.E. Several localities in Galilee appear in Egyptian war reports, including **Megiddo** that functioned as a gate at the entrance to the valley of Jezreel. The **Amarna Letters** provide more information showing Galilee to be split into a number of small city-states, a political system that most likely dominated the political structure of Galilee for all of the Bronze Age.

In the Iron Age, Galilee—according to the Old Testament settled by the **tribes** of **Naphtali, Zebulon, Asher,** and **Issachar**—belonged to the **kingdom of Israel**, although Israel's rule of Galilee was at times challenged by the **Aramaean** state of **Damascus**. In the second half of the eighth century B.C.E., the **Assyrians** gained control over Galilee and divided the territory into a number of provinces ruled by Assyrian governors. Galilee never returned to Israelite rule but after the Assyrians, the Neo-Babylonian kingdom took over, followed by the **Persians**.

GARIZIM. A mountain in central **Palestine**, close to the modern city of Nablus. In the Old Testament, Garizim is the place of blessing in contrast to **Ebal**, the mountain of curse. From Garizim **Jotham** proclaimed his fable about the trees looking for a king (Judg 9). In

Samaritan tradition Garizim was identified as the holy mountain of God and they built their temple on the top of the mountain.

GATH. An important **Philistine city** that together with **Ashkelon, Ashdod, Ekron,** and **Gaza** formed the center of Philistine power. It is normally located at Tell es-Safi c. 40 kilometers southeast of **Jerusalem,** at the foot of the Judean Hills. Gath turned into a place of refuge for **David** when he was fleeing from **Saul,** when David became a vassal of **Achish,** the king of Gath (1 Sam 27; see also 1 Sam 21:10-15, where he is not accepted by the **Philistines** as part of the army moving against Saul). At a certain time it was integrated into the Israelite kingdom, and **Rehoboam** is said to have fortified the city (2 Chron 11:8), but in the days of **Jehoash,** it was lost again to **Hazael.** Again a Philistine city, it appears among the conquered cities in **Sargon's** annals.

GAZA. A major **city** in southwestern **Palestine** and, together with **Gath, Ekron, Ashkelon** and **Ashdod,** one of the five important **Philistine** cities of the Old Testament. Ancient Gaza is located at Tell Harube within the city limits of modern Gaza. It has never been properly excavated. It appears to have been an important city already in the annals of **Pharaoh** Thutmose III (early 15th century B.C.E.) as a base of his campaigning in Asia. For the rest of the Bronze Age it remained an Egyptian stronghold in Palestine and the center of the provincial administration and appears in this capacity in the **Amarna Letters.** In connection with the migrations of the **Sea People,** it became the new center of Philistine power, and it is as a Philistine city that Gaza appears in the Old Testament. In spite of the claim that **Judah** conquered it (Judg 1:18), it never belonged to Israel. The **Assyrian** annals from the eighth to seventh centuries B.C.E. include a number of references to Gaza that became a vassal to Assyria in the days of **Tiglath-pileser III.** It later changed hands between Assyria, **Egypt,** Babylonia, and **Persia,** and was the last stronghold in western Asia to be conquered by Alexander the Great (333 B.C.E.).

GEBA. A **city** within the tribal territory of **Benjamin** (Josh 18:24). It was fortified by **Asa** of **Judah,** who was suspicious of the intentions of the **Kingdom of Israel** (1 Kgs 15:22). Geba is usually located at Djaba, an Arab village c. 10 kilometers north of **Jerusalem**. It has never been excavated but surveys have discovered traces of occupations in the Iron Age, and in the **Persian** period. Geba may be the same as **Gibeah**, otherwise known as **Saul's** hometown (see also 1 Sam 10:5; 13:3 where the text creates doubts as to the identity of Geba or Gibeah).

GEBAL. *See* BYBLOS.

GEDALIAH. The son of Ahikam and grandson of **Shaphan**, appointed governor over **Judah** by the Babylonians (*see* **Assyria and Babylonia**) after the fall of **Jerusalem** in 587. He resided at **Mizpah** a few kilometers north of ruined Jerusalem. Although tradition has him providing for the welfare of the Judeans left behind by the Babylonians, he was soon killed by **Ishmael**, a member of the royal house of Judah. The murder resulted in panic among the Judeans and a large part of the population sought safety in **Egypt**, bringing the **prophet Jeremiah** with them (2 Kgs 25:22-26; Jer 40-41).

GENEALOGY. In English translation often rendered as "generations" (e.g., in Gen 36:1: "These are the generations of Esau"). In traditional societies such as ancient **Israel**, it was of paramount importance to belong to an organization beyond the level of the **family**, such as the **lineage**, the **clan**, or the **tribe**. In practice, genealogies could be manipulated and some of the confusion in the Old Testament concerning such groups as the **Calebites** or the **Jerahmeelites** may be due to exactly this manipulation that allows for new members to be grafted onto the genealogy of an already existing group. Thus both the Calebites and the Jerahmeelites may at a certain point have been accepted into the larger tribe of **Judah** and their genealogy changed in order to make them acceptable among their new fellow tribesmen. How important the genealogy was is illustrated by the ethnic cleansing carried out by **Ezra** (Ezra 10).

GENESIS, BOOK OF. The first book of the Old Testament and of the **Pentateuch**, and the source of the earliest history of the human race. Genesis may be divided into three sections. The first section tells the story of humankind from its very beginning to the dispersal after it tried to build the **tower of Babel** (Gen 1-11). The second section includes the biographies of the **patriarchs, Abraham, Isaac,** and **Jacob** (Gen 12-36).The third section consists of the **Joseph novella** (Gen 37-50). Formerly, the oldest sources of Genesis were believed to go back to the period of **Solomon,** although the composition of Genesis that brought the different strands of tradition together was much later. Today, scholars are generally divided as to its period of composition between a late pre-exilic date and an early post-exilic one. From a historian's point of view, the Book of Genesis is viewed not as history but as a story, the Israelites' way of recounting their earliest history and the origin of the world very much along the lines also followed by other nations, for example, the Greeks and Romans, when they constructed their stories of origin. As to its contents, the Book of Genesis lacks homogeneity, a fact reflected by its complex history of composition.

GERAR. A **city** at the western end of the **Negeb** located at Tel Haror c. 20 kilometers west of **Beersheba.** It is known from the patriarchal narratives (*see* **Patriarchs, Period of the Patriarchs**) as the scene of the two stories about **Abraham** and **Sarah** and **Isaac** and **Rebecca** visiting Gerar of the **Philistines** (Gen 20; 26). **Asa** is said to have defeated an Egyptian army and pursued it as far as Gerar (2 Chron 14:12-15). Excavations at Tel Haror in the 1980s have discovered a settlement that goes back to the Middle Bronze Age but continued with interruptions to the **Persian** period.

GESHEM. Together with **Sanballat the Horonite,** and **Tobiah the Ammonite,** a fierce opponent of **Nehemiah's** building projects in **Jerusalem.** He was probably of **Arab** origin (Neh 2:19).

GESHUR. A small state located on the Golan heights northwest of the Sea of **Galilee.** It was allied with **David,** who married **Maacah,** the daughter of the king of Geshur and the mother of **Absalom** (2 Sam 3:3). It did not join the **Aramaean** cause against David but remained loyal to the **kingdom of Israel.** It was at a later date incorporated into the Aramaean kingdom of **Damascus.**

GEZER. A **city** located at an important crossroad at the foot of the Judean hill land. Gezer is identified with Tell Gezer c. 8 kilometers southeast of modern Ramleh. The king of Gezer participated in the coalition of **Canaanite** cities against **Joshua** (Josh 10:33) but it was not conquered by the Israelites (Josh 16:10). In the days of King **Solomon**, Gezer was captured and burnt down by the **Egyptians** and presented to Solomon as a gift from the **Pharaoh** (1 Kgs 9:16). It was rebuilt and fortified by Solomon (1 Kgs 9:17).

Excavations at Gezer in the 1960s and 1970s discovered a major fortified city with roots reaching back into the Chalcolithic period. It flourished in the Middle Bronze Age but was sacked by Thutmose III in the 15th century B.C.E. and included in his list of conquered Palestinian cities. From the Amarna period (*see* **Amarna and the Amarna letters**) a number of letters from the king of Gezer has survived. It is mentioned on Merenptah's **Israel stele** as a city conquered by the Pharaoh. Later occupation shows **Philistine** presence. Heavy **fortifications** have been dated to the time of Solomon, although this date is now contested.

GIBBETHON. A **city** in the territory of the tribe of **Dan** (Josh 19:44) and a so-called "city of the Levites" (Josh 21:23). It is mentioned two times in the Old Testament in connection with dynastic problems in the **Kingdom of Israel**, when **Baasha** killed **Nadab** who was besieging Gibbethon (1 Kgs 15:27), and again when **Omri** was chosen by his soldiers also besieging Gibbethon as the new king of Israel after **Zimri** had eliminated the house of Baasha (1 Kgs 16:15-17). Gibbethon is mentioned among Thutmose III's conquests in **Palestine** at the beginning of the 15th century B.C.E., and again by **Sargon II** who conquered Gibbethon c. 712 B.C.E. It is generally accepted that Gibbethon should be located at Tell Malat c. 8 kilometers south of Ramleh.

GIBEAH. Meaning "hill," the name of a number of localities in the Old Testament. Among these, the Gibeah of **Saul** is the best known, a **city** in **Benjamin** (Josh 18:28), and the place of the crime that almost led to the extinction of the **tribe** of **Benjamin** (Judg 19-21). Gibeah is sometimes identified with Tell el-Ful c. 5 kilometers north of Jerusalem. An alternative theory holds that Gibeah is only a variant name for **Geba**.

GIBEON. A **city** of **Benjamin** c. 8 kilometers north of **Jerusalem**. Gibeon was not conquered by **Joshua** but was by treason accepted into an alliance by the Israelites (Josh 9). After the death of **Saul**, **David**'s and **Ishboshet**'s forces fought a battle at the pool of Gibeon (2 Sam 2). Gibeon was the place where David had the sons of **Saul** executed (2 Sam 21). It was also famous because of its sanctuary visited by **Solomon** (1 Kgs 3:4-14). Excavations between 1957 and 1959 discovered a fortified city founded c. 1200 B.C.E. and a huge water system that has sometimes been identified as the scene of the battle in David's time.

GIDEON. A **judge** in **Israel** who liberated his people from the **Midianites** (Judg 6-8). When Gideon of the family of Abiezer of the tribe of **Manasseh** was called upon by an angel of God to liberate Israel from its enemies, he summoned the men of the tribes of Manasseh, **Asher**, **Zebulon** and **Naphtali**, but returned most of them and only kept a token force of 300 people. By using a sophisticated stratagem, he succeeded in defeating the Midianites, and he pursued them to **Transjordan** where he caught the two Midianite kings **Zebah and Zalmunna** and put them to death. He refused the offer of kingship presented to him by the Israelites (Judg 8:22-23) but like a king he had many wives and 70 sons (Judg 8:30). He was the father of **Abimelech**.

GIHON. A spring at the western slope of the Kedron Valley where **Solomon** was anointed king of **Israel** (1 Kgs 1:33.38-40), of vital importance for the water supply of ancient **Jerusalem**. Identified with modern 'En Sitti Maryam, it was located just outside the walls of the **city**, but made accessible from the inner side of the city by the construction of a water shaft, probably in the 10th or ninth century B.C.E. **Hezekiah** constructed his water tunnel leading water from Gihon to the **Siloam** pond at the southern end of the **Ophel** (*see also* **Siloam inscription**) thus securing water for the city during periods of siege (2 Kgs 20:20). As a reflection of its importance for Jerusalem, Gihon appears among the four rivers of Paradise (Gen 2:10-14). *See also* SILOAM, POOL OF.

GILBOA. A mountain overlooking the southern end of the **Jezreel Valley**, and the scene of the final battle between **Saul** and the **Philistines** (1 Sam 28; 31).

GILEAD. Roughly spoken, Gilead is the ancient name of the territory to the east of the **Jordan River** between **Arnon** in the south and **Bashan** in the north. According to the Old Testament, Gilead got its name from the Israelite **tribe** or tribal segment that settled in its territory (cf. Num 26:29). Although archaeology has begun to cast light over the early history of Gilead, very little is known. Archaeology has shown the area to have been settled at least in the Late Bronze Age. It was part of the **kingdom of Israel**, but was lost to the **Aramaeans** of **Damascus** at the end of the ninth century B.C.E. Although Israel regained possession of Gilead toward the middle of the following century, it was soon after lost forever to the **Assyrians,** who established a province of the name of Gilead here. The name of Gilead has been preserved in the Arab name of the region, *Ajlun.*

GILGAL. Meaning "circle (of stones)," Gilgal is in the Old Testament the name of a number of places. The most important place among these is Gilgal close to **Jericho, Joshua**'s base after having crossed the **Jordan River** (Josh 3-5). Here Joshua circumcised the Israelites after their migrations in the desert (*see* **Desert, Migrations in**), and celebrated the first Passover after the **exodus.** He also established the circle of twelve stones taken from the bed of the Jordan River. When **Ehud** killed the fat **Moabite** King **Eglon,** he twice passed by the stone circle of Gilgal (Judg 3:19.26). Gilgal is connected with **Samuel** who judged Israel here (1 Sam 7:16) and here the army chose **Saul** to be king of Israel (1 Sam 11:15). The final break between Samuel and Saul occurred at Gilgal, when Saul offered here without waiting for Samuel to come (1 Sam 15:12-33). In the prophecies of **Amos** and **Hoshea,** Gilgal is mentioned as a place of apostasy, and its cult condemned. In spite of many efforts, it has been impossible to propose an exact location for this Gilgal. Another Gilgal was located close to **Shechem.** Although it has sometimes been proposed that this was the actual place of ancient Gilgal—a proposal that is based on the traditions of the **Samaritans**—scholars generally agree on the principal location of Gilgal at Jericho.

GIRGASHITES. One of the nations of pre-Israelite **Canaan.** (Gen 15:21). They only appear in lists of the inhabitants of Canaan.

GOG, THE LAND OF MAGOG. In Ezekiel 38, Gog is the mysterious enemy of **Israel** who in the future will lead an army including **Persians** and the people of **Cush** against the land of Israel but who will also be defeated by God. The text is totally fabulous, having no bearing on historical events, although some have speculated about a faint relationship to the Lydian king Gyges.

GOLIATH. The champion of the **Philistines** from **Gath** who was killed by **David** in the **Elah Valley** (1 Sam 17). Another source has **Elhanan**, one of **David's heroes**, killing Goliath (2 Sam 21:19). In **Chronicles**, Elhanan killed the brother of Goliath (1 Chron 20:5). It has been proposed that Elhanan was David's original name, the name of David being his throne name. It is supposed that the name of Goliath derives from Lydian Alyattes.

GOMORRAH. One of the cities destroyed by God because of the wickedness of their inhabitants (Gen 19:24-25). As is the case of the other city, the **Sodom** of ancient traditions, the information of Gomorrah's destruction like that about Sodom's is totally fabulous. It is not known if any city of this name ever existed and its name is never attested in any ancient source, except in the Old Testament.

GOSHEN. A region in **Egypt** where the Israelites were allowed to settle (Gen 45:10). Its precise location is unknown but it was probably located in the eastern part of the delta of the Nile. **Pithom** and **Rameses**, the storage cities of **Pharaoh** were located at Goshen.

GOVERNORS. According to the Old Testament (1 Kgs 4:7-19), **Solomon** organized his realm as a system of twelve **provinces** with twelve governors, each of them entrusted with the provisions for the royal household for a month. The system was directed by a high official of the court. This system is normally understood to have been a permanent organization that divided the country into twelve parts. There was no necessary overlap between these provinces and the traditional **tribal** territories of Israel. In recent times, scholars have proposed a different interpretation of Solomon's provincial system. The governors were not permanently in office. Rather, they were royal emissaries whose job it was to extract taxes from different parts of the kingdom.

GREEKS. Greeks are almost totally absent from the pages of the Old Testament, although **Javan**, their ancestor, is considered a son of Japheth and the grandson of Noah. Historically, they were less invisible in the Iron Age, at least since the eighth to seventh centuries B.C.E. when Greek mercenaries were employed by the rulers of the Near East. Scholars have sometimes proposed to link the **Cherethites** to the Greeks as evidence of a Greek presence in **Palestine** already in the **Period of the Monarchy**. This proposal is hardly likely; however, at a certain time, the **Kittim** of the Old Testament became another name of the Greeks.

- H -

HABIRU. The name of a special category of people in western Asia in the second millennium B.C.E., although the exact meaning of Habiru is unknown. When the name of the Habiru first turned up, it was in connection with the discovery of the **Amarna letters** in **Egypt** dating back to the Late Bronze Age. In the letters from **Jerusalem**, they were mentioned by name; however, it soon became clear that most of the Amarna letters following the tradition of Mesopotamian scribes used a Sumerian name for the Habiru, SA.GAZ (probably a transcription into Sumerian of the Akkadian word *Shaggashu*, "murderer"). These SA.GAZ people had been known for long and now it became possible because of the equation between Habiru and SA.GAZ to trace their history in the Middle and Late Bronze Ages. The oldest source that definitely refers to the Habiru belongs to the 19th century B.C.E. and has its origin among the **Assyrian** trade colonies in Asia Minor in the period of the First Assyrian Empire. The last mention of the Habiru comes from Egypt in the 12th century B.C.E. Evidence is found of the Habiru all over the ancient Near East from Asia Minor in the north and Egypt in the south and from the coast of the Mediterranean in the west to Iran in the east.

Habiru is not an ethnic term. It is a social designation meaning
"refugee." The sources normally characterize a Habiru as a person
uprooted from his home and living in a foreign country. They were
generally employed as an unskilled labor force, either in public
service as private soldiers, stonecutters or the like, or hired by private people. The documents from Nuzi in northeastern **Mesopotamia** in the 15th century B.C.E. especially provide extensive information about the conditions of their private employment. Sometimes the sources mention Habiru making a life as highwaymen and
outlaws outside the control of the centralized states of the Bronze
Age. In this capacity they made up for a feared and notorious prole-
tariat and a source of discontent that might at the end have endangered the existence of many a petty state of **Syria** or **Palestine**. A
special application of the term is found in the Amarna letters where
Habiru is sometimes used, not as a social designation but as a nick-
name for the enemies of the **Pharaoh**, including princes and governors who are slandered as rebels against the rule of Egypt. The
presence of the Habiru in seemingly great numbers must be understood as one of the more important indications of the kind of social
problems in western Asia in the Bronze Age that contributed to the
fall of this civilization and the rise of a less differentiated society in
the Early Iron Age.

The Habiru have often been identified with the **Hebrews** of the
Old Testament. This identification is no more considered correct
because of spatial as well as chronological problems. However, the
Habiru share some of the social characteristics of the Hebrews of
the Old Testament, when the Israelites living in exile in Egypt before the **exodus** are repeatedly called Hebrews.

HADAD. A prince of **Edom** who in the time of **David** escaped to
Egypt. With the help of the **Pharaoh**, he succeeded in regaining
his kingdom in **Solomon's** days (1 Kgs 11:14-22). Hadad—
probably a hypocoristicon of a more elaborate name like **Ben-
Hadad**, Hadad being the name of a leading deity of the West Se-
mitic pantheon—may have been a traditional royal name in Edom.
The list of kings "who ruled over Edom before there were kings in
Israel" conventionally includes a Hadad (Gen 36:35; 1 Chron 1:46).

HADADEZER. 1. Hadadezer of the Old Testament, the king of **Aram-Zobah**, who is supposed to have fought against **David** on at least two occasions. In the first battle, Hadadezer was defeated by David and lost a great part of his army that was taken into captivity. When he was assisted by **Damascus**, David also destroyed their forces and made the **Aramaeans** tributary to his royal rule (2 Sam 8:3-8). The second time, Hadadezer assisted the **Ammonites** in their resistance against David but again David's army led by **Joab** came out victorious after having killed Hadadezer's general Shobach in the battle (2 Sam 10:6-19). The stories about these victories are a bit confusing, making all kinds of speculations about the sequence of the Aramaean kings possible. Thus it is not known whether the two battles were as a matter of fact one and the same, or two separate occasions, and also in the last case it is impossible to say which one was first. Hadadezer also appears in a note concerning **Rezon**, the new king of Damascus in **Solomon**'s days, and the son of one of Hadadezer's retainers who had deserted his master (1 Kgs 11:23-25).

2. Hadadezer of Damascus not mentioned by the Old Testament (where his name might have been conventionally changed to **Ben-Hadad**) but allied with **Ahab** in 853 B.C.E. at the battle at **Qarqar** against **Assyria**. Hadadezer is mentioned in the Assyrian report of the battle, as well as in Assyrian texts relating to battles against **Aram** in the years following Qarqar.

HAGAR. Abraham's Egyptian secondary wife who on the request of **Sarah** gives birth to Abraham's oldest son **Ishmael**. Because of Sarah's treatment, Hagar chose to leave Abraham, but in the first instance she returned (Gen 16), only at a later date to be sent away from Abraham when her son threatened the position of Abraham's second son **Isaac** (Gen 21). The nature of the legends and tales about Abraham makes it unlikely that Hagar was a historical person.

HAMAN. An important officer in the service of King **Ahasuerus** (*see* also **Xerxes**) of **Persia** who was scheming against the **Jews** but whose plans were thwarted by Queen **Esther**. As a consequence of his failure, Haman was hanged.

HAMATH. A major Syrian city, modern Hama on the upper course of the Orontes River. Its southern border is sometimes considered the ideal northern border of **Israel** (1 Kgs 8:65; 1 Chron 13:5). It was excavated between 1931 and 1938. The earliest settlements at Hamath go back to the Stone Age. In the Bronze Age, a fortified city developed but only obtained political importance in the Iron Age, when it became the center of an **Aramaean** state of the name of Hamath. According to the Old Testament, cordial relations were established between the king of Hamath and **David** (2 Sam 8:9-12). It participated together with Israel and **Damascus** in the anti-**Assyrian** coalition at **Qarqar** in 853 B.C.E. but was reduced to vassalage by **Tiglath-pileser III** in 738 B.C.E., and totally lost its independence to Assur in 720 B.C.E. Part of its population was **deported** and settled in **Samaria**. An important Aramaic inscription relating to Hamath was found at Afis in **Syria**. It was commissioned by King Zakur of Hamath and records wars with Bar-Hadad (*see also* **Ben-Hadad**), the successor of **Hazael**.

HAMATH-ZOBAH. A place in **Syria** fortified by **Solomon** (2 Chron 8:3). The note about Hamath-Zobah may be late and reflecting a time when **Zobah** was part of the **Persian** province of **Hamath**.

HAMOR. Meaning "he-ass," the head of the city of **Shechem** in the days of the **patriarch Jacob**. Jacob bought a piece of land from the sons of Hamor, that is, the family of Hamor (Gen 33:19), but Hamor's son Shechem raped Jacob's daughter **Dinah**. As a result Jacob's two sons **Simeon** and **Levi** killed the male population of Shechem (Gen 34). The sons of Hamor were in the **Period of the Judges** the ruling class of Shechem (Judg 9:28).

HARAN, HARRAN. A city in northern **Mesopotamia** about 45 kilometers south of modern Urfa. Haran was the home of the **patriarchs'** Mesopotamian relatives, and a station on **Abraham's** migrations between **Ur of the Chaldaeans** (*see* also **Chaldaea, Chaldaeans**) and **Canaan** (Gen 12). The name means "road" or "caravan-station" and relates to its importance as a trading center with a history that became important in the early part of the second millennium B.C.E. Later it was dominated by the Hurrians (*see* **Horites, Hurrians**) in the time of the Kingdom of Mitanni (Late

Bronze Age). In the ninth century B.C.E., it was conquered by the **Assyrians** and remained in Assyrian possession. After the fall of **Nineveh** in 612 B.C.E., Haran became the last capital of Assyria (612-609 B.C.E.).

HAROSHET-HAGOIM. The home of the **Canaanite** general **Sisera,** who led a coalition of Canaanite cities against the Israelites under **Deborah** and **Barak** (Judg 4-5). Its present location is unknown. It has been proposed that the name of Haroshet-Hagoim does not indicate a city but perhaps a region, especially if the element of the name *Hagoim* is a corrupted form of **Galilee** as sometimes assumed.

HAZAEL. King of **Damascus** c. 842-800 B.C.E. According to the Old Testament, Hazael, although "the son of nobody," as told by a contemporary Assyrian (*see* **Assyria and Babylonia**) inscription, that is, a usurper to the throne, murdered his predecessor, **Hadadezer**—not **Ben-Hadad** as the Old Testament maintains (2 Kgs 8:7-15)—inspired by the prophet **Elisha.** In the first part of his reign, Hazael had to defend his kingdom against the onslaught from the Assyrians that reached as far as the gates of Damascus. After 836 B.C.E. Hazael diverted his interest to conditions in **Syria** and especially **Palestine** and **Transjordan** and he succeeded de facto in subduing most of these countries. In a series of campaigns he destroyed the considerable military power of the **Kingdom of Israel** and annexed its provinces in Transjordan; the **Philistine** states on the Palestinian coast, and in the end also the **Kingdom of Judah** had to submit to Damascus and accept its leadership. After the reduction of Palestine into a number of vassal states, Hazael may have turned his armies to central and northern Syria, although nothing is known about such campaigns. He kept Assyria in check for the rest of his reign, but shortly after his death, when he was followed by his son Ben-Hadad, Damascus was hard pressed by Assyrian armies to the east, and in the west by the growing power of the renewed Israelite kingdom under **Jehoash.**

HAZOR. A major **city** in northern **Galilee** c. 12 kilometers north of the Sea of Galilee, by far the biggest pre-Hellenistic city in **Palestine.** Under its king **Jabin** Hazor led a coalition of **Canaanite** cities that fought against **Joshua** at the waters of **Merom**. Joshua crushed the Canaanite opposition and went on to burn Hazor down to the ground (Josh 11:1-11). In the Period of the Judges (*see* **Judges, Period of**), Jabin of Hazor is also said to have been the agent who brought about the coalition of Canaanite cities that fought against **Deborah** and **Barak**, although in the event the Canaanite general was **Sisera** from **Haroshet-hagoim** (Judg 4-5). It was together with **Gezer** and **Megiddo** fortified by **Solomon** (1 Kgs 9:15), but destroyed again by **Tiglath-pileser III** in 732 B.C.E.

Major excavations between 1955 and 1969 and again in the 1990s have uncovered for the standards of that time an enormous city probably housing more than 25,000 people. The layout of the city distinguishes between an upper city or acropolis, the home of the official buildings, and a lower city that was not rebuilt after the end of the Late Bronze Age. Traces of settlements go back to the Early Bronze Age, but the city reached its maximum extension during the Middle Bronze Age. After its destruction, probably c. 1200 B.C.E., only the acropolis was resettled. Here remains of the Iron Age fortified city have been found, dated by archaeologists to the 10th century B.C.E., the time of Solomon, or to the ninth century, the time of **Omri** and **Ahab**.

HEBREW BIBLE. The Hebrew text of the Old Testament that provides the foundation of all modern translations of the Old Testament. Although it includes the most important sources for the history of ancient **Israel**, it is based on rather late manuscripts, dating from the 10th and 11th centuries C.E. Now, the discovery of the Dead Sea manuscripts have changed our knowledge of the history of biblical books because all the books of the Old Testament apart from the **Books of Ezra** and **Nehemiah** and **Esther** have shown up among the scrolls found after 1947 at Qumran close to the Dead Sea. These manuscripts and fragments of manuscripts allow scholars to reconstruct at least in part the prehistory of the present Hebrew Bible going back to the beginning of the Common Era.

HEBREW KINGDOM. The traditional name in Anglo-Saxon literature of the Israelite monarchy. There is no equivalent to the term

"Hebrew Kingdom" in the Hebrew Old Testament. *See also* IS-
RAEL, KINGDOM.

HEBREWS. (In Hebrew *'ibrîm*), the descendants of Eber (Gen
10:21-26). Hebrew is sporadically used in the Old Testament as a
name of the people of **Israel** or of Israelite individuals. Hebrew is
mainly used in three limited parts of the Old Testament, in the Joseph novella (*see* **Joseph [Person], and the Joseph Novella**) (Gen
37-50), in the stories about Israel in **Egypt** (Exod 1-15), and in
connection with the **Philistine** wars before the introduction of the
monarchy (1 Sam 4; 13; 14, and 29). In **Genesis, Abraham** is one
time called a Hebrew (Gen 14:13). The **prophet Jonah** described
himself in confrontation with Philistine sailors as a Hebrew (Jon
1:9). Finally, the so-called "Book of the Covenant" (Exod 21-23)
opens with a couple of laws about Hebrew slaves, repeated in the
legislation about the Sabbatical Year (Deut 15) and in the narrative
about the planned manumission of slaves in the days of **Zedekiah**
of Judah (Jer 34:8-22).

The etymology of the word Hebrew has not been solved. The
Hebrews are often related to the social designation **Habiru**, known
from ancient Near Eastern documents—not least the Palestinian
Amarna letters—meaning "refugee" or "outlaw." If this linguistic
identification is correct, the origin of the term Hebrew in the Old
Testament may be traced back to Habiru-elements in the Late
Bronze Age and this group's involvement in the social turmoil that
contributed to the downfall of the civilization of the Late Bronze
Age and the emergence of Iron Age society in **Palestine.** Because
Habiru is a social and not an ethnic term, it is premature to see the
Hebrews of the Old Testament as direct descendants of Habiru, but
the use of the term indicates that the ancient Israelites originated in
the melting pot of ethnic and social elements that existed at the end
of the Bronze Age.

In the Old Testament, Hebrew is primarily an ethnic designation
meaning an Israelite. This means that the content of the word
Habiru must have changed from a social designation into a national
one. However, it is important that Hebrew is only used in a few
places in the Old Testament and not as the usual term for Israelites
and always in such a way that traces of the social background of
the term have been preserved. In the Joseph novella and in the story

of Israel in Egypt, the Israelites are in exile in Egypt, either as refugees from Palestine or as their descendants. In 1 Samuel, Hebrew is used only by the Philistines as a kind of derogatory term about the Israelites who have revolted against their master. Finally, when Jonah presents himself as a Hebrew, he has fled his land and is running away from Yahweh. When Abraham is called a Hebrew, the meaning is less clear. Maybe the term is used to describe Abraham as a newcomer to **Canaan** (the Greek Bible translated the term as "wandering"). In the slave law in the **Book of Exodus,** a Hebrew must serve his master for seven years before he can call himself a free person. In this way, whenever Hebrew is used in the Old Testament, it carries a national as well as a social meaning that can be compared to the status of the Habiru in the Late Bronze Age. Furthermore, when the Philistines call the Israelites Hebrews, they use the word in a derogatory manner not far from the one also found in the Amarna letters when it is used about the enemies of the **Pharaoh** in a general sense.

In recent scholarship, this identification of the Hebrews with the Habiru has been severely questioned, mostly because all texts that mention the presence of Hebrews are very late, or so it is maintained.

HEBRON. An important city in the Judean hill land, located almost halfway between **Jerusalem** and **Beersheba. Abraham** bought his family grave cave here from the **Hittites** (Gen 23), and settled at **Mamre** close to Hebron. Later Hebron belonged to the inheritance of **Caleb** (Josh 14:13-14). While king of **Judah, David** chose Hebron as his capital and resided there for seven-and-a-half years (2 Sam 2; 5:5). Hebron was also the base of **Absalom**'s rebellion against David (2 Sam 15:7-12). Hebron was also called **Kiriath-Arba** (Josh 14:15). Historical Hebron traces its roots back to the Early Bronze Age and it became a fortified city in the Middle Bronze Age. No Late Bronze Age city seems to have been located at Hebron but it was rebuilt again in the Iron Age. The ancient city is located on a tell within the city limits of the modern city of Hebron.

HESHBON. The capital of King **Sihon** of the **Amorites,** conquered by the Israelites (Num 21:21-31). Later it was successively reckoned a part of the territory of **Gad**, as belonging to **Moab**, or to **Ammon**. It is located at Tell Hesban c. 20 kilometers southwest of Amman, where excavations between 1968 and 1976 uncovered remains of a city reaching back to the beginning of the Iron Age (c. 1200 B.C.E.).

HEZEKIAH. (Meaning "Yahweh is my strength"), King of **Judah** c. 726-697 B.C.E. In the Old Testament Hezekiah stands out as a king who did "what was right in the eyes of the Lord" (2 Kgs 18:3). Hezekiah is described as a pious king who trusted God and fought successfully against the **Assyrians**, who unsuccessfully besieged **Jerusalem** but had to leave with empty hands, beaten by the Lord. The Assyrian **annals** of **Sennacherib** have a different story to tell. Hezekiah was the mastermind behind a major rebellion against the Assyrians in the southern Levant. Sennacherib reacted swiftly. The Assyrian army destroyed most of Judah, including **Lachish**, and bottled up Hezekiah in his royal **city** of Jerusalem "like a bird in its cage." After having extracted a heavy tribute from Hezekiah, including his daughters, the Assyrian army spared Jerusalem and Hezekiah, now reduced to an insignificant vassal in southern Palestine ruling a territory of a few hundred square kilometers. In the Old Testament Hezekiah is praised as the king who did construction work in Jerusalem, including the water shaft (*see* also **Siloam inscription**) and entertained diplomatic relations with **Merodak-Baladan**, the Babylonian adversary of Sennacherib. In **Chronicles** Hezekiah is also said to be the great reformer of the **temple of Jerusalem**.

HIEL. A man from **Bethel** who rebuilt **Jericho** but because of **Joshua**'s curse on Jericho (Josh 6:26) it cost him the lives of his two sons (1 Kgs 16:34).

HIGH PRIEST. In the post-exilic period, the high priest of **Jerusalem** may have been the most important person in Judea, the leader of religious as well as political affairs. This position was new in comparison to the role played by the high priest during the time of the monarchy, when the king not only headed the political affairs of the state of **Judah** but most likely also the religious establishment in Jerusalem. The **temple of Jerusalem** built by **Solomon**

was a minor affair in comparison to the **palace** complex and was located within the palace compound. Occasionally, a high priest could rise to political importance, like **Jehoiada**, who played a decisive role in the overturning of **Athaliah**'s rule and the election of **Joash** as king of Judah (2 Kgs 11). **Hilkiah**, another high priest, played a decisive role during **Josiah's reform**.

HILKIAH. The **high priest** of the **temple of Jerusalem** in **Josiah**'s time (1 Kgs 22:4). Hilkiah played an important role in **Josiah's reform** of the religious establishment in his kingdom and the centralization of the cult in **Jerusalem**. It is Hilkiah who found the ancient law book in the temple that triggers the reformation.

HIRAM. King of **Tyre** (c. 969-936 B.C.E.), a contemporary of **David** and **Solomon**. According to the Old Testament, he entertained good relations with David (2 Sam 5:11), and assisted Solomon in building his **palace** and the **temple of Jerusalem** (1 Kgs 5:15-26), however, for a heavy price that left him in control of northwestern Palestine (1 Kgs 9:10-14). He also assisted Solomon in establishing a commercial fleet running from **Ezion-Geber** to **Ophir** (1 Kgs 9:26-28). **Josephus** provides more information about the reign of Hiram, probably based on the **annals** of **Tyre**.

HISTORICAL-CRITICAL SCHOLARSHIP. For almost two centuries the dominant school of biblical studies. It developed since the time of the Enlightenment and reached its largest number of followers in the 20th century when it was the universal methodology of almost every student of the Bible. It is one of the school's basic assumptions that although most narratives in the Old Testament were only written down after a certain period—sometimes centuries later than the events which they covered—it is still possible by applying a critical analysis to distinguish between original information and later notes of redaction. In the study of the **Pentateuch**, it developed a theory according to which the Pentateuch is a complex composition based on four originally independent strands or sources, dating the oldest one, the Yahwist to the time of **David** and especially **Solomon**, and the most recent, the Priestly Source, to the **Persian** period. Recent studies of early Israelite history may have made this kind of historical analysis obsolete by demonstrating that many narratives of the Old Testament are without any historical foundation at all. Thus the description of the Israelite settlement in **Canaan** (*see* **Settlement of Israel**) in the Old Testament is totally without historical merits; it is a construction belonging to a period perhaps more than 800 years later than the events of the **Book of Joshua**. Historical-critical scholarship in its late form still lives on in the present controversy between **maximalism** and **minimalism**.

HITTITES.   One of **Canaan**'s pre-Israelite nations (Gen 15:20). Apart from being included in the lists of Canaan's early inhabitants, they appear in the story of **Abraham**'s acquisition of a grave cave at **Hebron** (Gen 23).

Historically, the Hittites founded one of the great nations of the past. Being an Indo-European-speaking people, the Hittites between c. 1700 and 1180 B.C.E. established a major empire with its capital at Hattushash (modern Bogazkale), some 200 kilometers east of Ankara in Turkey. From Hattushash, the Hittite armies penetrated as far as **Babylon**, which they sacked (end of 17th century B.C.E.). In the fourth century B.C.E. they challenged the Egyptian Empire in western Asia pushing the Egyptians back toward southern **Syria** and **Palestine**. In the beginning of the 13th century B.C.E., after the advance of the Hittites had been checked by **Ramesses II** at Kadesh in Syria, the Hittites entered into a peaceful relationship with the Egyptians and the two great powers of that time simply divided Syria between them. Palestine remained an Egyptian possession. However, a century later the Hittite Empire ceased to exist when Hattushash fell, most likely to roaming mountain tribes of Asia Minor.

The tradition of the Hittites lived on in northern Syria where several small states boasted of dynasties of Hittite origin. Although Hittite emissaries may have occasionally passed through Palestine on their way to **Egypt**, they never settled here. When the Old Testament includes the Hittites among the nations of Canaan, it is not in accordance with historical realities. The use of the term "Hittite" in the Old Testament may reflect traditional **Assyrian** and Babylonian terminology of the first millennium B.C.E. according to which the territories to the west of the **Euphrates** were inhabited by **Amorites** and Hittites. Thus, when **Nebuchadnezzar** prepared for the campaign that led to the conquest of Jerusalem in 597 B.C.E., he, according to the **Babylonian Chronicle**, went to "the land of the Hittites."

HIVITES. One of **Palestine's** pre-Israelite nations (e.g., Josh 9:1). They are related to the people of southern **Lebanon** (Judg 3:3), to the inhabitants of **Shechem** (Gen 34), or **Gibeon** (Josh 9). According to the table of nations in Genesis 10, they were the descendants of Ham. No references to the Hivites are found outside the Old Testament. Their name has sometimes been considered a corrupted form of the name of the **Horites**, or simply a pseudoethnicon, that is, the name of a people that has never existed in history.

HORITES, HURRIANS. The tradition of the Old Testament places the Horites southeast of **Palestine**. From this place they were expelled by the **Edomites** (Deut 5:2.12-22). Their equation with the Hurrians—a non-Semitic-speaking population element of **Syria** in the second millennium B.C.E.—is likely although not indisputable. Thus one of the names used by the Egyptians about Palestine and **Syria** was "Haru land," the land of the Horites. In the middle of the second millennium B.C.E., they established a major state of the name of Mitanni in Upper **Mesopotamia**.

HORMA. A city of the **Negeb** mentioned in connection with the abortive Israelite invasion of **Canaan** from the south (Num 14:45). Its present location is unknown.

HOSHEA (PROPHET). The first among the twelve minor prophets of the Old Testament, who prophesied in the days of **Uzziah, Jotham, Ahaz**, and **Hezekiah**, although nothing in his book seems to indicate a date later than c. 730 B.C.E. His prophecies concentrate on the pending doom of his people because of their apostasy. He is considered a firsthand witness of the religious conditions in the **Kingdom of Israel** in the decades preceding the fall of **Samaria**. He probably did not live to see the end of the **Northern Kingdom**.

HOSHEA (KING). The last king of the **Kingdom of Israel** (732-722 B.C.E.). He murdered his predecessor **Pekah** and with the help of the **Assyrians** he rose to the throne of Israel. The Assyrians saw him as their vassal, and Assyrian inscriptions refer to him in this quality. After the death of **Tiglath-pileser III**, he probably joined a coalition with **Egypt** and rebelled against the Assyrians, his masters, who reacted instantly and started a three-year-long siege of his capital, **Samaria**. Shortly before the fall of Samaria, the Assyrians captured Hoshea and put him in jail.

"HOUSE-OF-DAVID INSCRIPTION." *See* DAN INSCRIPTION.

HULDA. A **prophet**, who may have been attached to the royal court of **Jerusalem** and active during **Josiah's reformation** (2 Kgs 22:14-20). She is said to have prophesied about the happy fate of the king and about the evil outcome of the inhabitants of Jerusalem. Although the last part is clearly **deuteronomistic**, many scholars consider the first part to be genuine and going back to the prophet. Josiah's ultimate fate was not to be a happy one as he was killed by the **Egyptians** at **Megiddo**.

HUSHAI. Of the Archite clan from **Benjamin** who, being "the king's friend," acts as **David**'s spy among **Absalom**'s retainers. When David fled to **Mahanaim**, Hushai was instructed to stay behind and oppose the advice of **Ahitophel**, Absalom's vice counselor. This he did so well that Absalom's rebellion was doomed and ended in disaster, while Ahitophel committed suicide (2 Sam 15:32-37; 16:15-19; 17:1-17).

HYKSOS. The Greek rendering of an Egyptian name for the Semitic immigrants in **Egypt** linked to the 15th Dynasty (c. 1650-1550 B.C.E.). They were officially expelled from Egypt by **Pharaoh** Ahmose I (c. 1552-1527 B.C.E.). Since antiquity, their expulsion has often been linked to the **exodus** of the Israelites, ignoring the point of the narrative that the exodus constituted liberation and not a forced **deportation** from Egypt.

- I -

IBZAN. From **Bethlehem**, a **judge** in **Israel**, who functioned for a period of seven years. He was renowned for having 30 sons and 30 daughters (Judg 12:8-10). He belongs to the list of five judges (Judg 10:1-5; 12:8-15) who together judged Israel for 70 years but have left no records about their exploits.

INSCRIPTIONS. Texts written on stone, clay tablets, papyri, tree, or metal. Over the period of the last 200 years, literally hundreds of thousands of inscriptions have emerged from the soil of the ancient Near East. These inscriptions have illuminated many aspects of life not only of the ancient Near East in general, but also of **Palestine** in biblical times. Thus several inscriptions have been found relevant to persons or events mentioned in the Old Testament. Most references to Old Testament personalities are short. However, some inscriptions provide additional information not included in the Old Testament and may elucidate episodes of history as preserved by the Old Testament. Generally speaking, the inscriptions from the ancient Near East should be considered a kind of "reservoir." Their importance is indirect rather than direct. They contain a wealth of information about living conditions, the enactment of justice, religious beliefs, and literary conventions, common to the world also shared by the authors of Old Testament literature.

Nevertheless, their value is limited. First of all, scholars are depending on luck. Only inscriptions found by excavators are known. There can be no idea of what may still be hidden in the ground. Neither is it known how many inscriptions have been lost over time. The present may possess a fairly extensive collection of information but there is no reason to believe it to be complete. Rather, what is left is a highly fragmentary image of the past. Second, inscriptions found in the ground are often in bad shape. Sections have been lost, tablets have partly crumbled, inscriptions on stones have been obliterated either intentionally or in the course of time, or they are incomprehensible. Interpretation is often problematic.

The more important discoveries of inscriptions and assemblages of inscriptions have been made not in Palestine but in the great cultures of **Egypt, Mesopotamia,** and Asia Minor—especially at Hattushash, the **Hittite** capital—and **Syria.** Inscriptions from Palestine are far apart and mostly very short.

Apart from the casual historical information in official war reports or victory hymns, the Egyptian inscriptions have only minor interest for the study of Palestinian society—with some notable exceptions. Among the important collections of references to Palestine may be mentioned the **Execration Texts** from the Middle Kingdom, at the beginning of the second millennium B.C.E. These are small inscriptions on figurines intended for magical purposes, mentioning leaders of Palestinian cities. The **Amarna Letters** from the Late Bronze Age are most important. Several of these include messages sent from Palestinian potentates to the **Pharaoh.** Merenptah's victory inscription (c. 1208 B.C.E.) (*see* **Israel Stele**) is of special importance for the early history of **Israel** as it—apart from mentioning a number of localities such as **Ashkelon** and **Gezer**—also includes Israel among the vanquished foes of the Pharaoh: "Israel is destroyed. Its seed is no more"—the first known reference to Israel in any ancient text. Among the inscriptions of the first millennium, a list of conquered Palestinian cities included in a victory inscription of Pharaoh **Shishak** has direct relevance as it is likely to refer to events also mentioned by the Old Testament (1 Kgs 14:25-27).

In Mesopotamia, literally hundreds of thousands of inscriptions have been unearthed, including all possible genres of literature and other documentation. Only a few among them mention people known from the Bible. On the other hand, several compilations of law have been discovered, the most famous being the Code of King Hammurabi of Babylon (1792-1750 B.C.E.), and thousands of documents from the courts of Mesopotamia provide an unparalleled insight into the life of ordinary people. Huge mythological texts have also been extracted of the utmost importance for the study of Old Testament literature and religious imagination. Sometimes the parallels are so close that the world of the Mesopotamian inscriptions has been identified also as the world of the biblical authors. Thus the texts from Mari and Nuzi have been understood as reflecting the milieu of the **patriarchs.** The **Assyrian** and later Babylonian war records of the first millennium sometimes provide direct information of relevance for the study of Israel's history. Dating from the ninth century, Assyrian inscriptions mention both **Ahab** and **Jehu**, and from the eighth century also **Hoshea** of Israel. Doubtless the most famous Assyrian inscription pertaining to the Old Testament is **Sennecherib**'s description of the campaign that led to the siege of **Jerusalem** in 701 B.C.E. The **Babylonian Chronicle** that records **Nebucadnezzar**'s conquest of Jerusalem in 597 B.C.E. is almost in the same category. Belonging to a later period, the private archive of the Murashu family includes references to the Jewish exilic society in Mesopotamia in the sixth and fifth centuries B.C.E.

The Hittite archive from the Late Bronze Age includes only very few references that have to do directly with matters in southern Syria or Palestine. From an Old Testament point of view, the religious and mythological texts are more important. In contrast, texts from Syria are often very important, although their significance has sometimes been exaggerated, for example, as happened when the archives from **Ebla** in northern Syria were discovered in the 1970s. The famous texts from the Late Bronze Age discovered at **Ugarit** since 1929 include several items of extraordinary importance, however not so much for history. The great Ugaritic texts are epics about gods and heroes from the past. Historical information can be found in letters and documents of law, but this has very little to do with Palestine. The **Phoenician** inscriptions of the first millennium, although important, have only little to say of interest to the student of Israelite history. However, some inscriptions from **Transjordan**—especially the **Mesha inscription**—are very important in this respect.

Inscriptions from Palestine in pre-Hellenistic times are relatively few and insignificant as they mainly consist of short notes and messages. Cuneiform documents—both Akkadian and Ugaritic—have been found, for example, at **Taanach** and **Lachish**, dating from the Late Bronze Age. From the 11th century an "ABC" turned up in excavations at Izbet Sartah in the form of a Hebrew alphabet. From the 10th century, the Gezer calendar is noted for its layout of the agricultural year. From the ninth century come the **Samaria** ostraca, administrative documents from the royal court at Samaria. From the ninth or eighth century comes the Tel **Dan inscription**, the so-called "House of **David**" text, perhaps referring to an **Aramaean** victory over a coalition between Israel and **Judah**. From the eighth century the **Siloam inscription** is of special interest, recording the carving out of the water tunnel under Jerusalem (see also 2 Kgs 20:20). From the early part of the sixth century are the letters from Lachish recording the situation in Judah on the eve of the Babylonian conquest. On the other hand, the **Persian** period has yielded very few inscriptions, although the Wadi Daliyah papyri may help throw light on living conditions in Palestine in the fifth or fourth centuries B.C.E. On the other hand, the **Elephantine Papyri** sometimes have a direct bearing on conditions in Palestine.

ISAAC. The second among the three **patriarchs** of Israel, the son of **Abraham** and **Sarah** and the brother of **Ishmael**. The name—sometimes spelled differently (e.g., in Jer 33:26; Amos 7:9.16)—means "he who laughs" or "he is kind." The name may be a shortened form of Isaac-El, that is, "God laughs/God is kind." The name is not attested in any ancient Near Eastern documents outside the Old Testament. The story about Isaac includes several examples of playing with the meaning of his name, including his "play" with Ishmael that leads to the expulsion of Ishmael and his mother from Abraham's household (Gen 21). Although Isaac is the hope of old Abraham, he, on the order of God, travels to Mount Moriah to sacrifice his son, but Isaac is saved at the last moment (Gen 22). The story continues to tell how Abraham sent his servant to his relatives in **Haran** to claim **Rebecca** as the wife of Isaac (Gen 24). The marriage between Isaac and Rebecca results in the birth of the twins **Esau** and **Jacob** (Gen 25) and the ensuing competition between the two brothers that led to the dissolution of Isaac's family when Jacob fled to **Laban**, his mother's brother in Haran, and Esau moved to **Seir**. When he died, Isaac was buried next to Rebecca in the cave of Machpela at **Hebron** (Gen 35:27-29).

Scholars have paid attention to the fact that the story about Isaac is limited in extent and almost engulfed by the respective stories about Abraham and Jacob. It has been argued that Isaac as an independent patriarch has been "squeezed" by the two more important patriarchs who have usurped most of the traditions about Isaac. His real home is supposed to have been in the **Negeb**. Such speculations presuppose that Isaac is a historical person, which is a rather doubtful assumption. Rather, the stories about Abraham and Jacob manipulate the Isaac tradition and partly decide its content. Thus the story about Isaac and Rebecca in **Gerar** (Gen 26) is no more than a vague retelling of Abraham's visit to the **Pharaoh** (Gen 12) and to Gerar (Gen 20).

ISAIAH. A major **prophet** of the Old Testament, supposed to have prophesied in the days of **Uzziah, Jotham, Ahaz,** and **Hezekiah** (Isa 1:1). Thus he lived to see not only the **Assyrian** mutilation of the **Kingdom of Israel** in 732 B.C.E., when a greater part of this kingdom was made into an Assyrian province, but he also experienced its destruction in 722 B.C.E. At a later date, he was present in **Jerusalem** during **Sennacherib's siege of Jerusalem** in 701 B.C.E. His prophecies are generally accepted as an important testimony not only to the history of Israel and **Judah** toward the end of the eighth century B.C.E., but also concerning moods and policies—he, so to speak, represents the look behind the curtain. The sayings of Isaiah are covered by the first part of the prophetic book in the Old Testament carrying his name (chapters 1-39). The second part of the Book of Isaiah (Isa 40-55) is attributed by biblical scholars to an anonymous prophet who lived at the end of the **Babylonian exile** and prophesies about **Cyrus's** conquest of **Babylon** and the return of the **Jews** to their homeland, while the third part (chapters 56-66) is believed to come from the hand of a postexilic source of the **Persian** period.

ISHBOSHET. The youngest son of King **Saul,** who after the battle at **Gilboa** and his father's death succeeded Saul. **Abner,** his uncle, was the instrument in the rise of Ishboshet to the throne (2 Sam 2:8-10). In the time following his ascension to the throne, Ishboshet continuously lost territory to **David.** When he also lost the support of Abner, who initiated negotiations with David but was killed at **Hebron,** Ishboshet's fate was sealed. Soon after Abner's abortive mission to David, Ishboshet was killed, whereupon his kingdom transferred its loyalty to David (2 Sam 4). Ishboshet means "man of evil." It is most likely a pejorative form of Ishba'al, "the man of Baal" (see also 1 Chron 8:33).

ISHMAEL, ISHMAELITES. Ishmael, the eponymous ancestor of the Ishmaelites, was the oldest son of **Abraham** with his Egyptian secondary wife **Hagar** (Gen 16; 21). In this way the Ishmaelites are related to the **patriarchs**. Between c. the eighth and the fifth centuries B.C.E., the Ishmaelites formed the members of the first major **Arab** tribal coalition known from history—in **Assyrian** sources they are called the Shumuil. The home of this coalition was the Syrian and North Arabian Desert. The membership of the Ishmaelite coalition also counted "the sons of Ishmael" (Gen 25:12-18). Several among these names are known from Assyrian sources that record numerous encounters with these roaming camel nomads. The later Nabateans may be descendants from the Ishmaelite coalition.

ISHMAEL. A member of the royal house of **Judah**, who murdered **Gedaliah** a few months after he had been installed as governor over Judah by the **Babylonians** (2 Kgs 25:25; Jer 41:2).

ISRAEL. The name of Israel has never been explained. The last element of the name may refer to the West Semitic god El, but no convincing explanation of the first element has ever been proposed. Outside the Old Testament, the references to Israel are few and far between. The name appears for the first time in **Pharaoh Merenptah's Israel stele** (c. 1208 B.C.E.) among the vanquished foes of the Pharaoh. The next time it appears is as Serilaya, evidently a corrupted form, in the **Assyrian** record of the battle at **Qarqar** (853 B.C.E.). Otherwise the Assyrians referred to Israel as Bit Humriya, "the House of **Omri.**" Around the middle of the ninth century B.C.E., King Mesha of **Moab** mentions Israel in his famous inscription (*see* **Mesha and the Mesha inscription**). Finally, the **Dan inscription** refers to the king of Israel, maybe as a parallel to the king of "the house of David" mentioned alongside the king of Israel. In the Old Testament, Israel is the name of a **patriarch**, a nation, and a state. It is the second name of the patriarch **Jacob**, who was officially accorded the name of Israel following his fight with God at night (Gen 32:22-32). From its apical ancestor, the chosen people of God carried the name of Israel and Israel is identified as the Jewish people. However, in the **Period of the Mon-**

archy, Israel became the name of the Northern Kingdom in contrast to **Judah**, its southern neighbor.

ISRAEL, KINGDOM OF. The usual name of the northern part of Solomon's kingdom that gained political independence from **Judah** and the Davidic dynasty in the time of King **Jeroboam** I. In Old Testament scholarship it is also called the Northern Kingdom.

ISRAEL STELE. An Egyptian inscription put up by Pharaoh **Merenptah** (1213-1203 B.C.E.) in commemoration of his victory over the Libyans in his fifth year. The final part of the inscription consists of a hymn praising the Pharaoh for his victory over Asia. This hymn includes the earliest known mention of **Israel** and has since its discovery been considered the decisive argument for dating the Israelite settlement in **Palestine** to the end of the 13th century B.C.E. *See also* SETTLEMENT OF ISRAEL.

ISSACHAR. The fifth son of **Jacob** and **Leah**, and the eponymous ancestor of the **tribe** of Issachar. Little is known about the tribe of Issachar's early history, although the **Blessing of Jacob** describes Issachar as a strong ass who submitted to forced labor (Gen 49:14-15). Issachar's tribal territory was eastern **Galilee** close to Mount **Tabor**, a holy place that may have been the common sanctuary of the tribes of **Zebulon**, **Naphtali**, Issachar and probably also **Asher**. The Song of **Deborah** reckons Issachar among the tribes that fought the **Canaanite** coalition led by **Sisera** (Judg 5). In Hebrew Issachar means "a hired worker," and it has been proposed that the tribe originated as a social term denoting workers living in the Valley of **Jezreel** who revolted against their Canaanite lords and joined the Israelite tribes.

- J -

JABBOK. A major river in **Transjordan**, identified with Nahr ez-Zerqa, a tributary that enters the **Jordan River** c. halfway between the Sea of **Galilee** and the Dead Sea. Here **Jacob** brings his family into safety before his meeting with **Esau** (Gen 32). Later it was considered the northern border of the territories that were awarded the tribes of **Reuben** and **Gad** after the victory over **Sihon** (Deut 3:16).

JABESH. A **city** in **Gilead** of importance to **Israel**'s early history. In the Period of **Judges**, the men from Jabesh did not participate in the campaign against **Benjamin**. As punishment, every person in the city apart from the virgins were killed and the maidens given to the surviving Benjaminites (Judg 21:7-14). Later **Saul** came to their assistance when the **Ammonites** besieged Jabesh (1 Sam 11:1-11). The people of Jabesh paid the debt because of the help from Saul as they took his body from the walls of **Beth-Shan** and buried his bones at Jabesh (1 Sam 31:11-13).

Jabesh is normally located somewhere alongside the Wadi el-Yabis in **Transjordan** that has preserved the name.

JABIN. A King of **Hazor** who rallied the **Canaanites** against **Joshua** and the Israelites. His coalition included the kings of **Galilee**, and the kings of the Jordan Valley south of Lake Kinneret, but also the northern part of the coastal plain. The battle took place at the Waters of **Merom** but was a lost cause for the Canaanites. Following his victory, Joshua conquered Hazor and burned it to the ground (Josh 11). This tradition from **Israel**'s past may be in conflict with the narrative in Judges 4 about **Deborah**'s and **Barak**'s victory over a Canaanite coalition headed by **Sisera**, "the captain" of Jabin's army (Judg 4:2). Since Sisera is the principal enemy of the story of Judges 4-5, it is sometimes asserted that Jabin is an intruder in this text.

JACOB. The third **patriarch** and the son of **Isaac** and **Rebecca**, and the brother of **Esau**. Jacob was the father of twelve sons, the apical ancestors of the twelve tribes of **Israel**. He also fathered a daughter, **Dinah**. Jacob's importance for the biblical tradition is evident. After having wrestled with God/the angel of God (Gen 32:23-30), he was accorded the name of "Israel," because he fought against God and was victorious—a word play on the popular interpretation of the name of Israel.

The traditions about Jacob are mainly found in the complex of narratives that goes from Genesis 25 to Genesis 36, although Jacob also has a role to play in the **Joseph novella** (Gen 37-50). The Jacob tradition opens when Jacob was born as a twin, the younger brother of Esau who treacherously lost his right as the firstborn to Jacob (Gen 25:19-34), and it comes to its first conclusion when he returned from his exile in **Mesopotamia** and reunited with his family. The first part of the tradition narrates how Jacob was forced to leave his country after having cheated Esau. In Mesopotamia he found a new family in the house of **Laban,** his mother's brother, and here he married the two daughters of Laban, **Rachel** and **Leah.** The second part of the Jacob tradition has him moving back to **Canaan** as a very rich man reconciled with his brother. In the center of the Jacob tradition stands the narrative about the birth of his sons (Gen 29:31-30:24, with an appendix on **Benjamin's** birth and Rachel's death in Gen 35:16-20). In the Joseph Novella, Jacob appears mostly in the role of the old father. The initiative is left to his sons. Jacob ended up in **Egypt,** where he died, but his body was brought back to **Hebron** and buried in the cave acquired by **Abraham** (Gen 50).

The story about Jacob is an artful and highly literary narrative built up as a kind of "ring composition," ending very much in the same way as it started. In the beginning of the narrative, Jacob breaks with his father and brother; at the end they are all reconciled. In the beginning, God appears in front of the sleeping Jacob and promises him a safe journey and return (Gen 28:10-22), and toward the end of the story God approaches Jacob, seemingly with less friendly intentions (Gen 32:23-30).

Generally, modern readings of the Jacob narratives pay little attention to its value as a historical source but are more interested in its literary meanings. Formerly, scholars used to link events in the narratives to episodes in Israel's historical past. Thus the reconciliation between Jacob and Esau (Gen 33) was seen as a reflection on peaceful coexistence in **Transjordan** between Israelite and **Edomite tribes** in the days of the kings of Israel and **Judah.**

Mostly the Old Testament let Jacob have a very high standing among its heroes. However, a different image of Jacob appears in the Book of **Hoshea** (Hoshea 12) where he is blamed for his moral conduct. In spite of this, it is the general opinion that Jacob was truly the *heros eponymos* of the **Kingdom of Israel** in ancient times. Thus, the name of Jacob is sometimes used—for example, in prophetic literature—in biblical books as a second name of this kingdom.

JAEL. A **Kenite** woman, who after the battle between the Israelites and the **Canaanites** at the Brook of **Kishon**, killed the fleeing Canaanite general **Sisera** when he rested in her tent (Judg 4:17-22). For this deed she is praised in the Song of **Deborah** (Judg 5:24-27).

JAFO. Joppa in the New Testament, modern Jaffa. A city on the Mediterranean coast, located at the southern end of modern Tel Aviv. Mentioned in Egyptian documents of the New Kingdom, when Thutmose conquered the city c. 1500 B.C.E., and again in the **Amarna Letters**. Although said to be in the territory of **Dan** (Josh 19:46), Jafo was not an Israelite or Judean city but evidently populated by the **Philistines**. It was conquered by **Sennacherib** in 701 B.C.E. during his campaign against **Hezekiah** of **Judah**. According to an inscription from **Sidon**, in the sixth century B.C.E. the city was donated by the king of **Persia** to Eshmunezer, the king of Sidon. In the Old Testament prophetic Book of **Jonah**, it is narrated how the prophet Jonah fled by ship from Jafo.

JAIR. A **judge** in **Israel**, from **Gilead**, who functioned for 22 years (Judg 10:3-5). He belongs to the list of five judges (Judg 10:1-5; 12:8-15) who together judged Israel for 70 years but left no records about their exploits.

JARMUTH. A **Canaanite city** that participated in the coalition headed by the king of **Jerusalem** against **Joshua** (Josh 10). It is normally located at Tel Jarmuth, 25 kilometers southwest of Jerusalem. It was part of the tribal territory of the **tribe** of **Judah** (Josh 15:35). A second Jarmuth was located within the confines of **Issachar** but considered a city of the **Levites** (Josh 21:29). Although it is mentioned in an Egyptian inscription of Sety I (c. 1294-1279 B.C.E.) as located in the vicinity of **Beth-Shan**, its present location is unknown.

JAVAN. The Hebrew rendering of Greek Ionian, in the Old Testament one of the sons of Japheth (Gen 10:2). *See* also GREEKS.

JEBUS, JEBUSITES. According to the Old Testament, Jebus is the old name of **Jerusalem,** and the Jebusites its inhabitants. The Jebusites belonged among the pre-Israelite nations of **Canaan** (Gen 15:21) and according to the traditions of the Old Testament they lived traditionally in the central highlands of **Palestine.** The identification of Jebus with Jerusalem is, however, a problematic one. Every document from the ancient Near East that refers to Jerusalem lists the city as Jerusalem. Thus in the **Amarna Letters,** Jerusalem is called Urusalimmu. There is no evidence of Jebus and the Jebusites outside of the Old Testament. Some scholars reckon Jebus to be a different place from Jerusalem; other scholars prefer to see the name of Jebus as a kind of pseudo-ethnic name without any historical background.

JEHOAHAZ, JOAHAZ. The name of a king of **Israel** and a king of **Judah.**
1. The son of **Jehu** and king of Israel (815-799 B.C.E.). The Old Testament describes his period as a low point in the history of Israel, when **Hazael** of **Damascus** had almost crushed Israel and only a vestige of its former greatness was left. The story about the **Aramaean** siege of **Samaria** (1 Kgs 20), which the Old Testament places in the reign of **Ahab,** may describe events in the time of Jehoahaz.
2. The son of **Josiah,** king of **Judah** 609 B.C.E. He reigned for only three months before being dethroned by **Necho** and imprisoned in **Egypt,** where he died (2 Kgs 23:30-34). He was also called Shallum (Jer 22:11).

JEHOASH, JOASH. The name of a number of persons in the Old Testament, including a king of **Judah** and one of **Israel.**
1. Jehoash the Abiezrite, an influential man from **Manasseh** and the father of the **judge Gideon** (Judg 6:11).
2. Jehoash, king of Judah (c. 836-797 B.C.E.) and only surviving son of **Ahaziah** of Judah. The infant Jehoash was spared the fate of his family, which Queen **Athaliah** wiped out after the death of her son, Ahaziah. He was hidden from Athaliah within the temple complex in Jerusalem (*see* **Temple, temple of Jerusalem**). The high priest **Jehoiada,** who had directed the revolt against Athaliah, brought him from the temple and presented him to the people and

had him elected as king of Judah (2 Kgs 11). The only events of importance from his reign narrated by the Old Testament include the repair of the temple of Jerusalem and his tribute to **Hazael** of **Damascus** who had attacked Judah but spared the city of Jerusalem (2 Kgs 12). Joash was assassinated by his own people.

3. Jehoash, king of Israel (799-784 B.C.E.), the son of **Jehoahaz** and grandson of **Jehu**. In his time, the fortunes of war between Israel and **Damascus** changed when the **Assyrians** conquered Damascus c. 800 B.C.E., and Jehoash succeeded in recovering parts of the territories lost to Damascus (2 Kgs 13:22-25). When **Amaziah** of Judah challenged Jehoash, Jehoash defeated the Judean forces at **Beth-Shemesh** and went on to plunder the temple of Jerusalem (2 Kgs 14:8-14).

JEHOIACHIN. The son and successor of **Jehoiakim**. He had only reigned for three months when the Babylonians (*see* **Assyria and Babylonia**) conquered **Jerusalem** in 597 B.C.E. and carried the young king away to a lifelong exile in **Mesopotamia** (2 Kgs 24:8-17). After the death of **Nebuchadnezzar** in 562 B.C.E., Jehoiachin was released from the prison and lived at the Babylonian court (2 Kgs 25:27-30). Babylonian documents show that his prison may have been a kind of "golden cage," where the royal family of **Judah** was kept under relatively comfortable conditions.

JEHOIADA. The **high priest** of Yahweh at the **temple of Jerusalem**. Jehoiada organized the revolt against Queen **Athaliah** who had eliminated the royal house of the **Kingdom of Judah**—except the infant **Jehoash** and promoted the election of the seven-year-old Jehoash—the last surviving prince of **David's** line—to be king of Judah (2 Kgs 11).

JEHOIAKIM. The son of **Josiah** who was placed on the throne of **Judah** by **Pharaoh Necho**, who had arrested his brother and brought him to **Egypt**. Necho also ordered the name of the king changed from Eliakim to Jehoiakim, who was obligated to pay a heavy tribute to Egypt (2 Kgs 24:33-35). Jehoiakim reigned for eleven years (609-598 B.C.E). Following **Nebuchadnezzar's** victory over the Egyptians in 605 B.C.E., Jehoiakim was forced to submit to the **Babylonians** but he soon revolted. As a consequence,

Nebuchadnezzar moved against **Judah** and **Jerusalem** and conquered the city in 597 B.C.E. By that time Jehoiakim had died. The Old Testament has little good to say about Jehoiakim, who is also described as the adversary and tormentor of the **prophet Jeremiah**.

JEHORAM, JORAM. The name of a king of **Israel** and a king of **Judah**.
1. Joram, king of Israel 853-842 B.C.E. He succeeded his brother **Ahaziah** on the throne (2 Kgs 3:1). In alliance with **Jehoshaphat** of Judah, he conducted a campaign against **Mesha** of **Moab** (2 Kgs 3). He died at **Megiddo** from the wound he received from **Jehu** (2 Kgs 9:24).
2. King of **Judah** c. 849-842 B.C.E., the son of **Jehoshaphat**. Married to **Athaliah**, the daughter of **Ahab** (2 Kgs 8:16-24.26). In his time **Edom** rejected the yoke of Judah and liberated Tibna.

It has been proposed that these two Jehorams are as a matter of fact one and the same person, a theory not without foundation, the confusing information in the Old Testament about the kings of this period taken into consideration.

JEHOSHAPHAT. King of **Judah**, 974-850 B.C.E. Jehoshaphat, and his father **Asa**, are praised by the historiographers of the Old Testament but little in the way of real information has been preserved from his time, except that his trade enterprise out of **Ezion-geber** met with little success (1 Kgs 22:41-50).

JEHU. King of Israel 842-815 B.C.E. Jehu, the son of Nimshi, was an Israelite general who was anointed king by a **prophet** sent out to **Ramoth-Gilead** by **Elisha**. He returned to **Jezreel** where he killed King **Jehoram** of **Israel** and King **Ahaziah** of **Judah, Jezebel**, the queen of **Ahab**, as well as the royal family of Israel and a number of Judean princes (2 Kgs 9-10). His period was one of decline for Israelite power. The alliance between a series of **Syrian** and **Palestinian** states that fought successfully against the **Assyrians** at **Qarqar** in 853 B.C.E. soon broke down and fierce competition broke out between its members, especially Israel and **Damascus**, now ruled by **Hazael**. When the Assyrians attacked Damascus (841 B.C.E.), Jehu submitted to Assyrian power and paid tribute, an event not recorded by the Old Testament but presented on a famous inscription of **Shalmaneser III** (858-823 B.C.E.) that also carries a portrait of Jehu, the son of **Omri** (meaning Israel). In spite of his political problems, Jehu founded a dynasty that was to last for almost a hundred years.

JEHU, THE SON OF HANANI. A **prophet** from the time of **Baasha** who prophesied about the downfall of the house of Baasha (1 Kgs 16:1-4). In the Books of **Chronicles**, the chronicles of Jehu is supposed to be one of the sources of knowledge about King **Jehoshaphat** of **Judah** (2 Chron 20:34).

JEHU, DYNASTY. The royal house of the **Kingdom of Israel** that ruled the country from c. 842-752 B.C.E. The kings belonging to this dynasty were **Jehu, Jehoahaz, Joash, Jeroboam II,** and **Zechariah.** Jehu, the founder of the dynasty, inherited a politically mighty and economically affluent country but in his time most of the former glory of **Israel** vanished in fights for survival against the **Aramaeans** from **Damascus** who stripped Israel of most of its possessions east of the **Jordan River.** The latter part of the rule of the House of Jehu witnessed a certain restoration of Israelite power, especially in the days of Jeroboam II when Israel returned to a state of relative, if short-lived, prosperity.

JEPHTHAH. A **judge** in **Israel** whose office lasted for six years (Judg 11). Jephthah, a man from **Gilead** and an outlaw and head of a gang of highwaymen, was called upon by his fellow countrymen to help them against the **Ammonites.** Jephthah was victorious but lost his daughter because of a vow to God to sacrifice the first living being of his household to greet him when he returned from the war—a motive for the sacrifice of the child well-known from Greek tradition (Judg 11). Later he led the Gileadites in a war against the **Ephraimites** that led to the "Shibboleth" incident when fleeing Ephraimites were executed when they failed to pronounce the Hebrew word *shibboleth* correctly **(Judg 12).**

JERAHMEEL. Either once an independent **tribe** or a branch of the tribe of **Judah,** in the Old Testament considered the brother of **Caleb** (1 Chron 2:25-29). Their tribal area should be sought in southern Palestine or in the **Negeb.**

JEREMIAH. The son of **Hilkiah**, of the priestly family of **Anatot**. The second among the great **prophets** of the Old Testament, who, according to the book carrying his name, prophesied in the days of **Josiah, Jehoiakim**, and **Zedekiah** of the **Kingdom of Judah** (Jer 1:2-3). Jeremiah survived the fall of **Jerusalem** in 587 B.C.E.; indeed, he was rescued by the **Babylonians** from his prison at **Nebuchadnezzar's** instruction to **Nebuzaradan**. He opposed the policies of the last kings of Judah and, while he foresaw the destruction of the city and its temple (Jer 7; 26), he also, on the brink of disaster, redeemed his family possessions at Anatot as a sign that there would be a future for his people in spite of the impending national disaster (Jer 32). After the fall of Jerusalem, he was entertained by the Babylonian governor **Gedaliah**, but after Gedaliah's death he was forced by other Judeans to seek refuge in **Egypt**. His book is generally considered a firsthand source of information about the last years of the Kingdom of Judah. It is, however, a problem that he, although he should have begun his office in 626 B.C.E. (Jer 1:2), does not mention **Josiah's reform**, which according to 2 Kings took place in 623 B.C.E. (2 Kgs 22:3).

JERICHO. An important **city** and oasis located in the Jordan valley c. 10 kilometers northwest of the Dead Sea. It is located c. 250 meters below sea level in an almost tropical and highly fertile environment. In the Old Testament it is also occasionally called the "City of Palms" (e.g., Deut 34:3). It was conquered by **Joshua** (Josh 5-6) and totally destroyed. A curse was put on the man who was going to rebuild Jericho that he shall lose his two sons (Josh 6:26), and it falls on **Hiel**, who in the days of **Ahab** rebuilt the city (1 Kgs 16:34).

Jericho is located at Tell es-Sultan on the eastern outskirts of the modern city and oasis of Ariha. It was excavated in the 19th century, and again at the beginning of the 20th century. Excavations were resumed during the British mandate and again between 1952 and 1958. On Tell es-Sultan a settlement existed with roots reaching far back into the Mesolithic period (10th millennium B.C.E.). It was continuously inhabited for most of the Stone Age, abandoned sometime in the fourth millennium, but rebuilt in the Early Bronze Age, and after a new hiatus in its settlement again in the Middle Bronze Age. The city was destroyed c. 1550 B.C.E. and not rebuilt before the seventh century B.C.E. The Iron Age settlement was destroyed probably in connection with the Babylonian conquest of the **Kingdom of Judah** in 587 B.C.E. The tell was never resettled.

JEROBOAM. The name of two kings of Israel.
1. Jeroboam, the son of Nebat, the first king of post-Solomonic **Israel** (932-911 B.C.E.) (1 Kgs 11:26-14:20). Jeroboam was in **Solomon**'s service but was forced to flee to **Egypt** where he was received at the court. After Solomon's death he returned and participated in the meeting at **Shechem** between **Rehoboam** and the representatives of the northern tribes. When the negotiations broke down, Jeroboam was elected as king of Israel. Among his acts, the Old Testament sees his installation of the royal worship of golden calves at **Bethel** and **Dan** as proof of his wickedness and condemns him as the archetypical bad king. The downfall of his dynasty was foreseen by the prophet **Ahijah** of **Shiloh**.
2. Jeroboam II, the son of King **Jehoash** of the **Kingdom of Israel** (784-753 B.C.E.). In spite of the negative evaluation of Jeroboam in the Old Testament, he not only reconquered lost parts of the kingdom, but also **Damascus** and **Hamath**. In conclusion, his period may represent the last flourishing of the Kingdom of Israel (2 Kgs 14:23-29).

JERUBBAAL. The second name of **Gideon**. The name includes a play on words. Jerubaal means, according to the Old Testament, "he who fought against Baal," but according to normal rules for Hebrew names, the true meaning of the name should be "Baal fights" (in favor of the carrier of the name).

JERUSALEM. The capital of **David** and **Solomon**, and following the dissolution of their empire, the capital of the **Kingdom of Judah**. Jerusalem belonged to the tribal area of **Judah**, although the Judeans were not able to conquer it (Josh 15:63; see, however, also Judg 1:8). The **city**, formerly known as **Jebus**, was conquered by David and turned into his capital and the center of official religion (2 Sam 5-6). It kept its status, and was even enlarged in the days of **Hezekiah**, as the center of **Judah** until it was destroyed by **Nebuchadnezzar** in 587 B.C.E. Rebuilt during the **Persian** period, it survived the vagaries of war and peace until 70 C.E., when the

Roman army led by the later emperor Titus copied Nebuchadnezzar's deed from more than 600 years before.

Historically and archaeologically Jerusalem poses a number of problems. It is mentioned in the Egyptian **Execration Texts** but at the beginning of the Middle Bronze Age was hardly a well-fortified city of notice. It is also mentioned in the **Amarna letters**. Some letters carry the name of the king of Jerusalem, but so far Jerusalem of the Late Bronze Age has not appeared in the archaeological remains, although Jerusalem has been extensively but at the same time—because it is now a modern densely populated city—sporadically excavated over a period of more than 130 years. Jerusalem of the **Empire of David and Solomon** also presents a problem as until now very little if anything has emerged from the ground dating to the 10th century B.C.E., conventionally the century of David and Solomon.

Although the dating of discoveries from the 10th and ninth century is the subject of a heavy debate among archaeologists and historians, little speaks in favor of a major city located at Jerusalem at this time. The city began to flourish as a provincial town in the ninth century B.C.E. Its first period of greatness came after **Sennacherib**'s siege of the city that left it unharmed while at the same time most other Judean cities, including the former important city of **Lachish**, were destroyed. **Hezekiah** enlarged the city limits of Jerusalem considerably. It has been estimated that toward the end of the Kingdom of Judah, Jerusalem housed more than 20,000 people (in contrast to the maximal 2,000 of the 10th century B.C.E.). The effects of the Babylonian conquest are easy to recognize not only because of the massive destruction layers dating from this time, but also because of the poor resettlement of the city in the fifth-fourth century B.C.E. Only in the Hellenistic period did Jerusalem regain its former greatness.

JESSE. An **Ephratite** from **Bethlehem**, the grandson of the **Moabite** woman **Ruth**, and the father of **David** (1 Sam 16:1; see also Ruth 4:17.22). In his house, the **prophet Samuel** anointed David to be the future king of **Israel** (1 Sam 16:1-13).

JETHRO. The **priest of Midian**, and the father-in-law of **Moses** (Exod 3:1). Jethro is also called **Reuel** (Exod 2:18), or Hobab (Jud

4:11). He acted as the advisor of Moses in juridical matters (Exod 18:13-27). The connection between Jethro the Midianite and Moses the **Levite** has often been seen as an indication of an early relationship between the Israelites and the Midianites.

JEWS. The terms "Jew" and "Jewish" are rather confusing as far as the Old Testament is concerned. Christian scholarship has regularly distinguished between Israelites and Jews, the former denoting the population of ancient **Palestine** organized as the twelve tribes of **Israel** (*see* **Twelve tribe system**), and Jews becoming the name of the post-exilic population that centered on **Jerusalem** and the worship of YHWH in its temple. Sometimes the distinction is made in a rather confusing way between people of Palestinian origin—that is, the Israelites—before and after the exile—that is, the Jews. Thus the inhabitants of Elephantine (*see* **Elephantine Papyri**) are often seen as members of a Jewish colony. Jew is a late development of Judean, a person coming from **Judah**—or *Jehud*. In Western tradition, it was related to the practitioners of a special religion, Judaism, sometimes also but erroneously referred to as a special race, and this distinction was probably already made in antiquity, distinguishing the Jews from other segments of the Palestinian population such as the **Samaritans** and the **Philistines**.

For reasons of clarity, Israelites are the descendants of **Jacob**, alias Israel, in the Old Testament considered one nation until they were divided after **Solomon's** death. Then the distinction applies between the inhabitants of the **Kingdom of Israel** and the **Kingdom of Judah**. It has sometimes been assumed that the Judeans adopted the term Israelite after the fall of the Kingdom of Israel in 722 B.C.E. Nevertheless, all sources point to the term "Judean" being used about the subjects of the king of Judah until exilic times in the early sixth century B.C.E. Only after the establishment of the modern State of Israel in 1948 did Israel become the common name of the new Jewish nation, although its inhabitants are generally called Israelis, not Israelites.

JEZEBEL. A Tyrian (*see* **Tyre**), the daughter of King **Ethbaal** (Ittobaal) who was married to **Ahab** of Israel (1 Kgs 16:29-31). The portrait of Jezebel in the Old Testament is extremely negative, making her the source of much of the calamity that befell the **house**

of Omri. The Old Testament also shows her to have been a very active queen handling state business on her own and interfering in juridical matters as well, as when she arranged for the execution of **Naboth** (1 Kgs 21). She is said to have been highly active in religious affairs supporting the cult of (presumably) the Tyrian god of Baal Shamen. When victorious **Jehu** entered **Jezreel**, she ridiculed him as a wretched usurper and was instantly killed on his order (2 Kgs 9:30-37).

JEZREEL. A city at the foot of **Gilboa** overlooking the eastern section of the **Jezreel Valley**, identified as Tel Jezreel c. 4 kilometers east of modern Afulah. In the Old Testament, it is a royal city, the place of the **Naboth** incident (1 Kgs 21) and here **Jezebel** the queen of **Ahab** met her cruel end at the hands of **Jehu** (2 Kgs 9:30-37). Excavations at Jezreel in the 1990s have discovered extensive **fortifications** from the ninth to eighth century but hardly a royal palace.

JEZREEL, VALLEY OF. An important and fertile valley in northern **Israel** that goes from modern Haifa along the northern slope of **Carmel** and **Gilboa** to **Beth-Shan**. This valley was the site of a series of important **cities** including **Taanach, Megiddo, Jezreel,** and Beth-Shan. It was a contested area and the scene of the decisive battle between **Israel** and the **Philistines** that led to the death of **Saul** (1 Sam 31).

JOAB. **David's** nephew and general (2 Sam 8:16) and one of **Zeruiah's sons.** Joab was David's most loyal henchman, never failing in his obligations to the king but often acting as a very independent person, although always with David's interests in mind. During the negotiations between **Abner** and David, Joab killed Abner at **Hebron** (2 Sam 3:26-27). He was the first Israelite to enter Jebusite **Jerusalem** (1 Chron 11:6). He conquered in David's name **Rabba Ammon** (*see* **Ammon, Ammonites**), but at the same time had **Uriah** killed (2 Sam 12:26-31). He negotiated the reconciliation between David and **Absalom** (2 Sam 14:28-33), but later he killed Absalom against the king's clear order to spare his son (2 Sam 18:9-17). When David dismissed him as his commander in chief and put **Amasa** in his place, he murdered Amasa and regained his position as the commanding officer of David's forces against **Sheba** (2 Sam 20). On his deathbed, David instructed **Solomon** to get rid of Joab, and when Joab supported **Adonijah** against Solomon, he was killed at the altar of the sanctuary by **Benaiah** (1 Kgs 2:28-31).

JOAHAZ. *See* JEHOAHAZ.

JOASH. *See* JEHOASH.

JONADAB. The name of two persons in the Old Testament.

1. A relative of **David** who acted as counselor to **Amnon** who planned to rape his half sister **Tamar** (2 Sam 13:3-5).

2. The head of the **Rechabites** who participated in **Jehu's** rebellion against the **house of Omri** (2 Kgs 10). At a later date, the Rechabites reckoned Jonadab as their eponymous ancestor (Jer 35).

JONAH. The son of Amittai who in the prophetic book carrying his name was sent to **Nineveh** to preach to the Ninevites. Instead of traveling to Nineveh, Jonah fled by ship from **Jafo** but ended up being swallowed by a "big fish." When he escaped from the fish, he decided it was wise to obey the Lord and travel to Nineveh to deliver his preaching to its inhabitants who—contrary to his expectations—responded positively to his demand for conversion. The Book of Jonah is a comic narrative without relation to any historical event, although Jonah is supposed to have been active as a **prophet** in the days of **Jeroboam** II of **Israel** (2 Kgs 14:25).

JONATHAN. Several persons share the name of Jonathan. The more important are:

1. Jonathan, the oldest son of King **Saul** and his designated heir to the throne. As told by the Old Testament, the opening of Jonathan's career was auspicious. In an audacious military feat, Jonathan surprised a **Philistine** contingent at the pass of **Michmash** and slaughtered it (1 Sam 13-14). However, he broke the king's order to fast during the battle. Divine intervention exposed his crime but he was saved from punishment by the intervention of the army. The incident shows that Jonathan could not be the person chosen for kingship by Yahweh. He could not be the successor of Saul. Thus

the way was paved for David's advance toward kingship. Jonathan became the friend of young David and they concluded an alliance (1 Sam 19). At a later meeting, he accepted David as the future king (1 Sam 23:16-18) but was killed together with his father and most of his brothers at the battle at **Gilboa** (1 Sam 31). It is impossible to know the historical accuracy of the information about Jonathan. The Jonathan story follows the theme of the tragic hero so beloved by people of ancient times. In spite of all his qualities, he lost his life in order to give place to a more successful contender.

2. The son of the **priest Abiatar** who acted as David's spy together with **Ahimaaz**, the son of the priest **Zadok** (2 Sam 17.17-21). After David's death Jonathan joined his father in supporting **Adonijah** and it was his destiny to be the one to break the news about **Solomon**'s ascension to Adonijah and his party (1 Kgs 1:42-48).

JORAM. *See* JEHORAM.

JORDAN RIVER. The name of, by far, the greatest river in the land of the Bible, normally considered the eastern border of the land of **Canaan** and often functioning as the border of the Israelite kingdoms, although part of the area to the east of the river was also inhabited by the Israelite tribes of **Reuben, Gad,** and **Manasseh.** The sources of the Jordan River are in **Lebanon** and especially on the slopes of Mt. Hermon. It follows a north-south course bringing it down to Kinnereth (the Sea of **Galilee**). To the south of Kinnereth it continues its course to the Dead Sea. In spite of the importance attached to this river, it is not very broad, more a brook than a proper river, and fordable in several places.

JOSEPH (PERSON), AND THE JOSEPH NOVELLA. Joseph was the firstborn son of **Jacob** and **Rachel** whose arrogance awoke the envy of his brothers who sold him to **Midianite** or **Kenite** traders, who again sold him to **Potiphar**, the captain of the **Pharaoh's** bodyguard. After having been to the jail because of the false accusation of rape, he was enlisted by the Pharaoh as supervisor of the grain supply and in this position he saved **Egypt** during a seven-year-long famine. He married Asenath, the daughter of the Egyptian priest at On. Finally, he was joined by his family in Egypt. The

Joseph novella (Gen 37-50) is a highly sophisticated novel, by some Egyptologists held to be very late (from the Saitic Period, that is, seventh-sixth century B.C.E.). Although little in the story of Joseph is historical, it has a historical backdrop in Egyptian history where people from Asia occasionally rose to very high positions, although Joseph has never been identified among these officials.

JOSEPH (TRIBE). Sometimes also called "the House of Joseph," that is, the descendants of **Jacob**'s son **Joseph**. Joseph appears in tribal lists in the Book of Genesis. From the **Book of Exodus** and onward, the **tribe** is replaced by **Ephraim** and **Manasseh**, reckoned to be the two sons of Joseph (*see also* **Twelve tribe system**). Probably there never was a tribe of Joseph. The distribution in the tribal lists may be the result of literary considerations rather than historical remembrance.

JOSEPHUS. A Jewish historian who participated in the Jewish rebellion against the Romans (66-70 C.E.). When he was captured, he went into Roman service supported by the imperial Flavian family, including the emperors Vespasian, Titus, and Domitian. In Rome he wrote "The Jewish Antiquities," a history of ancient **Israel**, and "The Jewish War," a report of the abortive rebellion against the Romans. He died c. 100 C.E. In his Jewish Antiquities, his main source is the Old Testament and he has little additional information, although he sometimes includes traditions of his own.

JOSHUA. 1. Joshua (the name means "Yahweh is salvation") was the Israelite conqueror of **Canaan**, nominated as "the servant of **Moses**" already in the desert (Exod 24:13) and installed by Moses as his successor (Num 27:12-23). After Moses' death he took command over the Israelite tribes and commanded the campaign in **Canaan**. Here he conquered **Jericho** and **Ai**, and reduced the Canaanites to servants of the Israelites (Josh 6-9). When he had finished the conquest, he distributed the territories of Canaan between the Israelite **tribes**. At the end of his life, he summoned the leaders of Israel to **Shechem** in order to renew Israel's **covenant** with Yahweh (Josh 24). When he died, he was buried at **Timnath-serah** in the hill land of **Ephraim** (Josh 24:30).

While Joshua and the conquest tradition were formerly believed to be historical information, at least in part, historical and archaeological investigations have now created a scenario for the history of **Palestine** in the late second millennium B.C.E. that makes an Israelite conquest of Canaan as described in the **Book of Joshua**, our main source of knowledge about Joshua, totally unlikely. See also SETTLEMENT OF ISRAEL.

2. The son of Jozadak, the high priest who after the exile and together with **Zerubbabel** rebuilt the **temple of Jerusalem** that was finished in 516 B.C.E. (Hag 1:12-15; Ezra 3).

JOSHUA, BOOK OF. The sixth book of the Old Testament and normally considered the opening of the **Deuteronomistic History**. The main subjects of the Book of Joshua are the Israelite conquest of **Canaan** (see also **Settlement of Israel**) and the partition of the country among the **tribes of Israel** (see also **Twelve tribe system**). The first part of the book is devoted to the description of the conquest of the two Canaanite **cities** of **Jericho** and **Ai** (Josh 2; 6, and 8, respectively), and the covenant with the inhabitants of **Gibeon** (Josh 9). After these war stories, a more general description follows of the Israelite conquest of the central and southern part of the country (Josh 10), and following this the northern part (Josh 11). The distribution of the land of Canaan among the nine tribes destined to live to the west of the **Jordan River** occupies the central part of the book (chapters 13-19). Because it was a tribe of **priests**, the tribe of **Levi** was not allowed a territory of its own. Nevertheless, a series of cities distributed all over the land of **Israel** was placed under Levite control (Josh 21). The final part of the Book of Joshua includes two occasions where Joshua summoned the leaders of the tribes to farewell meetings at **Shiloh** and **Shechem** (Josh 23-24). At the last occasion, Joshua pledges the people of Israel to take up the **covenant** with the Lord as a guarantee that they will stay in the country.

Scholarship gave up the Book of Joshua a long time ago as a valid source of knowledge of the Israelite settlement in Canaan. The **Book of Judges** presents a different and less complete picture of the conquest (Judg 1). Modern scholarship has demonstrated how far from reality the war history of the Book of Joshua really is. Nothing in the archaeological material indicates a violent shift of power in **Palestine** in the time of Joshua. It is clear that the Book of Joshua includes a kind of political program for the possession of the land of Israel that has little to do with history. The list of tribal territories in the central part of the book is often seen as a rather late compilation, dating at the earliest to **Solomon**'s time, but it could be much later. Some scholars have suggested a date as late as the time of **Josiah**.

JOSIAH. King of **Judah** 639-609 B.C.E. Josiah is best known from his extensive religious innovations in combination with his concentration of all official religion to the **temple at Jerusalem** (2 Kgs 22-23). This reform is said to have been inspired by an old law book found in the temple, sometimes identified with at least a part of the Book of **Deuteronomy**. **Josiah's reform** therefore generally carries the name of the **Deuteronomistic Reform**. His acts at **Bethel,** where he destroyed the local sanctuary that was established by **Jeroboam,** the first independent king of **Israel,** and his move to **Megiddo** in order to confront **Pharaoh Necho,** where he was killed by the Egyptians, indicate that he had included in his kingdom much of the territory of central **Palestine** formerly belonging to the **Assyrians.** 2 Kings reckons Josiah the greatest king of Judah after **David. Chronicles** is less positive, saying that he died because he disobeyed the Lord (2 Chron 35:20-25).

JOSIAH'S REFORM. A religious reform with political overtones that took place in **Jerusalem** in 623 B.C.E. (2 Kgs 22-23). King **Josiah** centralized the official worship of Yahweh, the state god of **Judah,** at Jerusalem and banned local sanctuaries and moved their **priests** to Jerusalem. The reform is said to be based on the discovery of an old law book—some scholars say **Deuteronomy** or parts of Deuteronomy—within the temple compound (*see* **Temple, Temple of Jerusalem**). The reform is accordingly sometimes called "the **Deuteronomistic Reform**." The reform was short-lived. Josiah's son and successor abandoned its program. Archaeologically, there is little evidence of a change of religious habits within the territory of the **Kingdom of Judah** at the end of the seventh century B.C.E.

JOTHAM. 1. The youngest son of the **Judge Gideon**, who escaped the fate of his many brothers. These were executed by **Abimelech** (Judg 9:5). Jotham was the author of the famous fable about the trees seeking a king for themselves. They opted for a noble tree but in the end they got the thorn (Judg 9:7-15). 2. King of **Judah**, co-regent with his father **Uzziah** c. 750-742 B.C.E, and king c. 741-734 B.C.E. (2 Kgs 15:32-38). The Old Testament has little to say about Jotham but evaluates him positively.

JUDAH, KINGDOM OF. The name of the part of **David's** and **Solomon's** kingdom that remained in the possession of the Davidic dynasty after the division of the kingdom. After his death, the kingdom of Solomon was split into two sections: the **Kingdom of Israel**, also called "the Northern Kingdom," embracing most of Solomon's extensive realm, and the Kingdom of Judah, or the Southern Kingdom. Judah was soon to become a minor player in comparison to the Kingdom of Israel, although it reentered the scene of international politics after the **Assyrian** destruction of the Kingdom of Israel between 732 and 722 B.C.E. The Kingdom of Judah was destroyed by the **Babylonians** in 587 B.C.E.

Historically, the story of the Kingdom of Judah preserved in the Old Testament will have to be revised as modern historical and archaeological investigations have made it likely that Judah only arose as a centralized state c. 800 B.C.E. Most of the previous history must be considered legendary.

JUDAH, TRIBE. Judah was the youngest son of **Jacob** and **Leah**, and the eponymous ancestor of the tribe of Judah. After the division of **David's** and **Solomon's** kingdom, Judah was also the name of the Southern Kingdom, in contrast to **Israel**, the Northern Kingdom.

The **patriarch** Judah saved the life of his brother **Joseph** (Gen 37:26-27). Another story describes his relation to his daughter-in-law **Tamar**, a relationship that led to the birth of Zera, an ancestor of the future king of Israel, David.

Historically, the name of Judah may at first have been linked to a region in ancient **Palestine**. The tribal territory of Judah was located south of **Jerusalem**, bordering in the south on the **Negeb** desert. In the east, the Desert of Judah marked the end of inhabitable land. Altogether the territory of Judah may not have exceeded c. 2,000 square kilometers. It has been suggested that the **tribe of Judah** may have been a relative newcomer among the tribes of Israel, tracing its historical origins back to Palestinian soil. Probably it was a coalition of tribes including **Simeon, Caleb, Jerahmeel,** and **Othniel.** The important part played by Judah in the Old Testament may have been colored by the fact that the **Kingdom of Judah** based its existence on the support of this tribe.

JUDGE. The conventional translation of Hebrew *shophet,* the title of the governors of **Israel** in the **Period of the Judges.** In the linguistic context of the West Semitic languages, *Shophet* is used about a magistrate who rules and makes decisions, in court as well as elsewhere in public service. Thus the term appears in later Punic and Roman sources as the name of the magistrates of Carthage, originally a **Phoenician** colony. In the **Book of Judges** the judges are described as saviors of Israel, a kind of dictator (in the Roman sense of the word) who appeared when Israel was in distress. The list of these savior judges includes **Othniel,** who saved Israel from **Cushan-rishataim, Ehud** (Judg 3:7-11), who killed the **Moabite** King **Eglon** (Judg 3:12-30), **Deborah** and **Barak,** who rallied the tribes to fight against **Sisera** and the **Canaanites** (Judg 4-5), **Gideon,** who disposed of the **Midianite** intruders (Judg 6-8), and **Jephthah,** who liberated Israel from the threat of the **Ammonites** (Judg 11).

In the narratives about these saviors of Israel, a list of judges appears that includes the names of a number of judges and a few particulars about them but no important information about their exploits. This list is broken up into two parts. The first part includes **Tola** and **Jair** (Judg 10:1-5), the second mentions **Ibzan, Elon,** and **Abdon** (Judg 12:8-15). Altogether these five judges ruled Israel for 70 years. They have sometimes been seen as representatives of a different type of judge, officers of the Israelite **tribal league.** In the Book of Judges, **Samson** is the last savior of Israel in the Period of the Judges (Judg 13-16), but the Samson story is normally considered to belong to a different strand of tradition than the other stories about the heroic acts of the judges.

JUDGES, BOOK OF. The seventh book of the Hebrew Bible that covers the **Period of the Judges**. It is divided into the following sections: a review of the conquest that includes a more limited view of the Israelite conquest of **Canaan** sometimes believed to present a more historically correct picture of the early days of **Israel** in Canaan (Judg 1), the narratives about the saviors of Israel (Judg 2-12) (*see* **Judge**), the story about **Samson**, the great champion of Israel (Judg 13-16), and finally stories illustrating the dangers of being without a king (Judges 17-21).

JUDGES, PERIOD OF. In the Old Testament the period that connects the days of the conquest with the installation of the **Hebrew kingdom**. In the biblical literature, it was the time when the Israelite **tribes** acted more or less as autonomous political entities, although sometimes "governed" by a savior, who whenever **Israel** was in distress liberated it from its enemies. The pattern of political developments described by the **Book of Judges** includes an Israel that after the death of **Joshua** disobeyed the Lord and worshipped other gods. As a consequence, God sent enemies against Israel, and when Israel cried to the Lord for help, a savior appeared who liberated Israel. When the savior, for example, **Ehud** or **Gideon**, died, the process was repeated. As time went by, the institution of the savior was corrupted by more dubious savior figures like **Jephthah** and **Samson**. At the end of the Period of the Judges, the system broke down. In the words of the Old Testament, "in those days there was no king in Israel; every man did that which was right in his own eyes" (Judges 21:25). The end of the Period of the Judges came with gruesome crimes and destructive wars among the Israelite tribes (Judges 19-21).

Although historical-critical scholarship has generally considered the Period of the Judges to constitute a historical phase in Israel's early history, it has in recent scholarship become obvious that the Period of the Judges is a literary construct with little historical background. In historical terms the Period of the Judges belongs to the transition period between the Late Bronze Age and the Early Iron Age, that is, c. 1250 and 950 B.C.E. Its chronology as described by the Old Testament is highly artificial, in many cases made up by so-called "round" numbers. Thus a period of 40 years follows **Othniel**'s disposal of **Cushan-rishataim** (Judg 3:11), a period of 80 years (2 x 40 years) comes after Ehud's killing of **Eglon** (Judg 3:30). After **Deborah's** and **Barak's** victory over the **Canaanites**, there was peace for 40 years (Judg 5:31), and Gideon caused peace to prevail for another 40 years. Altogether the five judges **Tola, Jair, Ibzan, Elon,** and **Abdon** judged Israel for 70 years (Judg 10:1-5; 12:8-15). Instead of seeing the Period of the Judges as a historical period, scholars tend to consider it a "heroic time," including stories of very much the same kind as Greek, Roman, or Germanic prehistory.

- K -

KADESH, KADESH-BARNEA. An oasis in northern **Sinai** that functioned as the base of the Israelites under **Moses** before the abortive invasion of **Canaan** from the south (Num 13-14). In Kadesh, **Miriam,** the sister of Moses, died and was buried (Num 20:1). The name of the place (meaning "holy" in Hebrew) and the importance of the traditions connected with Kadesh have led scholars to assume that it was an early center of the Yahwistic religion of **Israel,** eventually visited by Israelite as well as **Midianite** and **Kenite** tribesmen. Kadesh is located at 'En el-Qudeirat close to a road junction leading from Suez to **Beersheba** and from el-'Arish to 'Aqaba. Excavations at Kadesh between 1972 and 1982 uncovered remains of an Iron Age **fortress.**

KADMONITES. One of **Canaan's** pre-Israelite nations (Gen 15:19). The word Kadmonites means "Easterners" or even "people of the past." Nothing is known about them.

KEDESH-NAPHTALI. A city within the tribal territory of **Naphtali** and the home of the **judge Barak** (Judg 4:6), and known also as a Levitical (*see* **Levites**) city (Josh 21:32), conquered by **Tiglath-pileser III** in 732 B.C.E. Kedesh-naphtali is normally identified with Tell Qadesh to the north of **Hazor.** However, Tell Abu-Qudeis in the **Valley of Jezreel** has also been proposed as the place of Kedesh-naphtali.

KEDORLAOMER. *See* CHEDORLAOMER.

KENITES. The biblical Kenites are considered the descendants of Kain (Gen 4:24:21-25; cf. Num 24:21-22). Several specialized crafts are attributed to Kain's relatives, including music, nomadic cattle breeding, and smiths. The Kenites may therefore have constituted at gypsy tribe of some sort. Its home was southern **Palestine**, the **Sinai** Peninsula and northwestern **Arabia**, and they are sometimes related to the **Midianites**. They occasionally appear in connection with narratives about **Israel's** early history. Thus, in the Old Testament, the father-in-law of **Moses** is sometimes reckoned to be a Kenite (Judg 4:11)—in other places he is a Midianite (Exod 2-3). They were the allies of the **Amalekites** in the days of King **Saul** (1 Sam 15).

KENIZZITES. One of **Canaan's** pre-Israelite nations (Gen 15:19). Nothing is known about the history of the Kenizzites, except that tradition connects them to, on one side **Edom**, and on the other **Hebron**. **Caleb** is supposed to have been a Kenizzite. The tradition about the Kenizzites may reflect post-exilic political conditions when the border between Edom and **Judah** lay to the north of Hebron.

KINGDOM. A. *The kingdom as institution.* Most specialists in the development of political organization consider traditional states, which base their economy on agriculture but are, on the other hand, already complex systems, to be organized as kingdoms. As the center of political power, a kingdom often substitutes a previous chiefdom. In the ancient Near East, states were almost without exception kingdoms. Without much protest, all citizens accepted a king as the head of their society. In **Mesopotamian** tradition, the institution of the kingdom originated in heaven. In Egypt the king was considered a god.

B. *The kingdom in the ancient Near East.* Two categories of kingdoms were in evidence: the major imperial states ruled by great kings, and vassal states also ruled by kings, however, subordinated to the great kings and tied to the policies of their master kings. Thus, in the terminology of ancient times, the great kings were "followed" by minor kings in great number. However, on the ideological level, the minor kings adopted the ideology of their masters in dealing with their own subjects. Thus the phraseology of royal greatness may also appear in inscriptions belonging to minor vassal kings as well as in the description of the Israelite kingdom in the Old Testament.

C. *The kingdom in ancient Israel.* The importance of the kingdom as an institution is reflected by the interest shown by large parts of the Old Testament in the fate of the Israelite kingdoms. On the other hand, the Old Testament also gives space to a different voice raising criticism against the kingdom as an institution. In the **Deuteronomistic History** and in other deuteronomistic literature such as the Book of **Deuteronomy**, both open and implied criticism can be found. Thus, the so-called "King's Law" (Deut 17:14-20) includes a program for the future Israelite kingship that stresses among other things the importance of the king being elected by the Lord, but also that the kings should be modest and, especially, that he should not have too many wives and concubines because these may lead his heart astray. The king should not seek personal fortune but act as the wise counselor for his subjects. The warnings of the **prophet Samuel** against the introduction of the Israelite kingdom (1 Sam 8) present a different image of kingship. Here the king is characterized as a tyrant who will turn his subjects into slaves and confiscate their possessions for his own ends. In the development of the history of the Israelite kingdom(s) in 1-2 Samuel and 1-2 Kings, each king is valued according to his deeds. The general attitude toward the Israelite kings is a highly negative one and the kingdom is seen as representing a rejection of the just rule of the Lord. According to 1-2 Kings, there were few exceptional kings who proved themselves, like **David, Solomon,** and **Josiah,** but most kings failed miserably and their misbehavior led directly to the destruction of the Israelite states and the exiles in **Assyria and Babylonia.**

KINGS, BOOKS OF. The two Books of Kings cover the tragic history of the **Hebrew** kingdoms, the **Kingdom of Israel** and the **Kingdom of Judah,** from the days of King **Solomon** to the end of the Judean state, **Nebuchadnezzar**'s destruction of **Jerusalem** and its **temple,** and the exile of the Judeans in **Babylonia** (*see* **Babylonian Exile**). The first part deals with the final act in the prolonged strife among **David**'s children for the succession to the throne of Israel (1 Kgs 1-2). Thereupon follows the description of **Solomon**'s glorious days, including his construction of the **temple of Jerusalem**. This story about Solomon, however, also tells about a monarch and an empire in decay, something that inaugurates the end of the united Israelite monarchy after Solomon's death (1 Kgs 3-11). The remaining parts of Kings describe the fate of the two independent Israelite **kingdoms**. A large section is made up by stories about two important prophets, **Elijah** and **Elisha**, who were in opposition to the **house of Omri** until its very end (1 Kgs 17-2 Kgs 9). The Books of Kings remain the most important source to the history of the two kingdoms of Israel and Judah which can—at least from the days of Omri—be reconstructed in outline. Parts of the Books of Kings may only be judged as containing legendary stories rather than history, but they also include very exact information, for example, about the campaigning of **Sennacherib** of **Assyria** in **Palestine** in 701 B.C.E. The Books of Kings are generally reckoned a part of the **Deuteronomistic History**.

KIRIATH-ARBA. ("City of Four") According to the Old Testament, the original name of **Hebron**.

KIRIATH-JEARIM. ("The Forest city") Also known as Kiriath-Baal (Josh 15:60) or Baala (Josh 15:9), a **city** belonging to the tribal territory of **Judah** (Josh 15:9), alternatively of **Benjamin** (Josh 18:28). It was the home of the **Ark of the Covenant** after the **Philistines** gave up the hope of keeping it (1 Sam 6:21-7:1) and until **David** brought it to **Jerusalem** (2 Sam 6).

KIRIATH-SEPHER. ("City of the Book") Another name for **Debir**.

KISHON. A brook in northern **Israel** where **Deborah** and **Barak** vanquished their **Canaanite** foes (Judg 4-5). It is normally identified with Wadi al-Muqatta—in modern Hebrew renamed the Nahal Kishon north of the **Carmel** range. However, this location has been contested. Another candidate is Wadi el-Bira—now Nahal Tabor—to the east of the **Tabor** Mountain.

KITTIM. According to the Table of Nations, Kittim was the son of **Javan** (Gen 10:4). Otherwise it is a place name and the name of a population group. The name is believed to be a derivative of Kition, a city of ancient Cyprus, close to the modern city of Larnaka. Although Kittim may sometimes refer to Cyprus and its inhabitants, it lost this specific meaning and was used about **Greeks**, **Macedonians**, and **Romans**. The oldest occurrence of Kittim appears on an ostracon from **Arad** (late seventh century B.C.E.). It may be evidence of the presence at Arad of Greek mercenaries in the time of **Josiah**.

- L -

LABAN. **Jacob's** maternal uncle and the brother of **Rebecca**, from **Haran** in upper **Mesopotamia**. When Jacob escaped to Haran fearing the revenge of his brother **Esau**, he joined Laban's household and served Laban for seven years in order to receive **Rachel** in marriage. Laban cheated Jacob and gave him **Leah**, obliging Jacob to serve for another seven years for the sake of Rachel. Laban is called "the **Aramaean**," reflecting the ethnic composition of Haran in the first millennium B.C.E. The name means "white" and has sometimes been related to the worship of the moon god Sin who had one of his centers at Haran.

LACHISH. A major city in the hill lands of **Judah**. Lachish is mentioned among the **Canaanite** cities that opposed **Joshua** (Josh 10). King **Amaziah** of Judah was murdered at Lachish (2 Kgs 14:19). It is mentioned as the base of **Sennacherib** during his siege of **Jerusalem** (*see* **Sennacherib's siege of Jerusalem**) (2 Kgs 18:13).

Extensive excavations at Tell ed-Duweir, reckoned to be the site of ancient Lachish, from 1932-1938 and 1973-1987, have unearthed a major town with settlements reaching back to the Early Bronze Age. It was heavily fortified during the Middle Bronze Age. A number of **Amarna letters** were written by the ruler of Lachish. However, the city was destroyed sometime in the 12th century and only rebuilt c. 200 years later. It became the largest city of Judah until it was destroyed by Sennacherib, a feat commemorated by the **Assyrians** on a famous relief from **Nineveh**—now in the British Museum in London. **Jeremiah** mentions Lachish as one of two remaining Judean cities on the eve of the Babylonian conquest of Jerusalem (Jer 34:7). The city was deserted in the early Hellenistic period.

LACHISH LETTERS. During the excavations at **Lachish** in the 1930s, 21 inscribed ostraca turned up in a closure near to the city gate, among them 13 letters, dating from the last stratum of the city, probably shortly before the Babylonian (*see* **Assyria and Babylonia**) conquest of Lachish in 587 B.C.E. Altogether they constitute a significant collage of administrative information relevant to the province of the **Kingdom of Judah**, among them military information. One phrase in letter 4, "we are watching for the signals of Lachish for we do not see **Azekah**," is often taken to reflect a situation where Azekah, a **fortress** a few kilometers northeast of Lachish, had already fallen victim to the Babylonian army, although Lachish was still defending itself. The Book of **Jeremiah** mentions the same two cities (34:7). According to Jeremiah, Azekah and Lachish had not yet been conquered by the Babylonians. In this connection the Lachish inscription no. 4 may show what happened next.

LAISH. The original name of the biblical city of **Dan**. Together with **Hazor**, Laish is mentioned in an Egyptian **Execration text**, and in a document from ancient Mari (18th century B.C.E.).

LEAH, TRIBES OF LEAH. Leah was the oldest daughter of **Laban** and the first wife of **Jacob**. She is also the eponymous ancestor of a tribal group among the Israelite **tribes**. The group comprises the tribes of **Reuben**, **Simeon**, **Levi**, **Judah**, **Issachar**, and **Zebulon** (Gen 29:31-30:24). The group contrasts the **Rachel** group of **Joseph** (or **Ephraim** and **Manasseh**) and the tributary tribes of **Dan**, **Naphtali**, **Gad**, and **Asher**. Previous scholarship used this partition of the Israelite tribes into two family groups to construct a prehistory according to which the Leah tribes constituted a separate and older tribal group that settled in **Palestine** before the Rachel group. Such speculation has mainly been given up by modern scholarship.

LEBANON. The name of the mountaineous territory north of **Palestine** and the homeland of the **Phoenicians**. Lebanon was never an independent political unity in ancient times, but it was famous because of its mountains, and the cedar trees growing on the slopes of the mountains, a renowned source of wood for building products in the ancient Near East. From Lebanon **Solomon** imported cedar timber for the construction of his palace in **Jerusalem**, and Phoenician craftsmen to work the wood. One of the buildings in the palace complex was named "the House of Forest of Lebanon" (1 Kgs 7:2).

LEVI, LEVITES. A son of **Jacob** and **Leah** and the eponymous ancestor of the **tribe** of Levi. Although **Genesis** portrays Levi as an active person, who together with his brother **Simeon** killed the inhabitants of **Shechem** (Gen 34), his descendants are best known as forming a tribe of **priests**, the **Levites**, who because of their loyalty to **Moses'** cause—Moses himself was from the Tribe of Levi— were chosen among the Israelite tribes to be their priests. Accordingly, this tribe had no territory of its own, although a number of cities were set aside as **Levitical cities** (Num 35:1-8; see also Josh 21). Old Testament scholarship has cast doubts on the existence of a secular tribe of Levi and often considers the stories about the secular Levites to be the outcome of a literary reflection that placed the original Levites in ancient **Israel** within the tribal system of Israel (*see* **Twelve tribe system**).

The history of the Levites within ancient **Israel** is illustrated in an unsatisfying way by the Old Testament. They may have represented the priesthood at local shrines and temples but according to 2 Kings, these shrines were closed down by King **Josiah**, and the Levites moved to the royal **temple at Jerusalem**, where they were allowed to serve in less important functions (2 Kgs 23:8-9). How far this information reflects pre-exilic conditions in Jerusalem is unknown, as archaeological evidence indicates that **Josiah's reform** did not bring an end to local worship. It is possible that the decline of the Levites has to do with the growing power of the **Aaronite** and especially the **Zadokite** priesthoods.

LEVITICAL CITIES. As a **tribe** of **priests**, the Levites were not allowed a territory of their own. However, a series of **cities** within the Israelite tribal territory was reserved for the use of the Levites, including **Hebron**, **Libnah**, and **Beth-Shemesh** in **Judah**, and **Gibeon**, **Geba**, and **Anatot** in **Benjamin**, and **Shechem** and **Gezer** in **Ephraim**. The list of Levitical cities is very comprehensive and includes many of the most important cities of ancient **Israel** (Josh 21).

LEVITICUS, BOOK. The third Book of **Moses**. Leviticus consists mainly of religious law and law collections. As such it has little bearing on the history of ancient **Israel**. However, many of the laws reflect customs and habits. Leviticus thereby contributes to the understanding of Israelite society in ancient times. Generally, scholars consider Leviticus to be a late composition belonging to the priestly stratum of the Pentateuch dating from the post-exilic period, although some scholars have recently proposed a date already before the destruction of **Jerusalem** and its **temple** in 587 B.C.E.

LIBNAH. A city in the Judean **Shephelah**, conquered by **Joshua** (Josh 10:29-30). It was made part of the tribal territory of **Judah** (Josh 15:42), and included among the **Levitical cities** (Josh 21:13). It revolted against **Jehoram** of Judah (2 Kgs 8:22), and served as base for **Sennacherib** during his campaign against **Hezekiah** of Judah in 701 B.C.E. (2 Kgs 19:8). It is identified with either Tell es-Safi close to Beth-Shemesh or Tell Bornat c. 10 kilometers east of the modern city of Kirjath-Gat.

LINEAGE. In anthropological literature, the lineage is a major kinship organization in traditional societies, placed below the level of the **tribe** but over the **family**. Anthropologists often see the lineage as the most important political organization in acephalous tribal societies, that is, tribes without a centralized authority like a chief. The lineage can be subdivided into so-called "minimal lineages," and a number of lineages can constitute a maximal lineage counting as much as several thousand people. The members of a lineage reckon their descent from a common ancestor and they should at least in theory know exactly the genealogy that constitutes them as members of their lineage. In scholarly literature about ancient Israel, the lineage is often confused with the **clan**, partly because the borderline between a clan and a lineage has never been made clear by anthropologists. In Hebrew, the level of the lineage is most likely defined as the *mishpaha*.

LOT. The nephew of **Abraham** and the son of **Haran** who joined his father on his journey to **Canaan**. When they separated, Lot moved to **Sodom** but was spared the fate of the Sodomites by the angels of the Lord. Later, Lot became the original ancestor of the **Ammonites** and **Moabites**.

LUZ. According to the story about **Jacob's** dream, Luz was the ancient name of **Bethel** (Gen 28:19). The name of Luz is not attested outside of the Old Testament.

- M -

MAACAH (PERSON). The name of several persons—men as well as women—in the Old Testament. Among the best known are Maacah, the **Geshurite** wife of **David** and the mother of **Absalom**, Absalom's daughter Maacah, the wife of **Rehoboam** and the mother of King **Abijah**, and Maacah, the wife of Abijah and the mother of **Asa**.

MAACAH (PLACE). *See* ARAM-MAACAH.

MACHIR. The son of **Manasseh** (Gen 50:23) and the eponymous ancestor of a tribal segment among the Israelite **tribes**. Machir is considered a segment of the tribe of Manasseh. However, in the Song of **Deborah**, Machir appears as an independent tribe from the central highland of **Palestine**. According to other traditions Machir's home was in **Transjordan**.

MAHANAIM. A city in Transjordan where **Jacob** met the angel of God (Gen 32:2-3—ET 32:1-2). Here he divided his family into two sections before his meeting with **Esau** (Gen 32:8-11—ET 32:7-10). Both stories function as popular explanations of the name of Mahanaim being interpreted as "two camps." **Ishboshet** was elected king at Mahanaim (2 Sam 2:8-9), and **David** retreated to Mahanaim when he was forced out of **Jerusalem** by **Absalom**. Here he established his temporary base (2 Sam 17:24-18:5). In the time of King **Solomon**, Mahanaim was the center of one of his provinces (1 Kgs 4:14). Mahanaim is usually identified with Telul ed Dhabab el-garbi on the Jabbok River. It has never been excavated.

MAKKEDAH. A **Canaanite** city conquered by **Joshua** (Josh 10:28). Later it became part of the tribal territory of **Judah** (Josh 15:41). Although the narrative in Josh 10 indicates a location in the **Shephelah** west of **Jerusalem**, its present location is unknown.

MAMRE. The place where **Abraham** lived and entertained God (Gen 18). It is also the name of one of Abraham's **Amorite** allies (Gen 14:13.24). It is normally identified with Ramat el-halil 4 kilometers north of **Hebron**.

MANASSEH (KING). King of **Judah** 697-642 B.C.E. In spite of his 55 years on the throne, Manasseh is considered the worst ever king of Judah and he is seen as the main reason for the impending destruction of **Jerusalem** and its **temple**, although, historically, Manasseh had nothing to do with these events (2 Kgs 21:1-18). The authors of the **Books of Chronicles** have problems understanding why Manasseh was allowed such a long reign—in their eyes a sign of the Lord's blessing. Accordingly they invented a totally unlikely story about an **Assyrian** attack on Judah that led to the **deportation** of Manasseh in chains to **Babylon**. From Babylon Manasseh returned a new and pious man and was allowed to stay on his throne (2 Chron 33:10-13). Assyrian documents from the time of **Esarhaddon** say that he was a loyal vassal of Assyria, and he was probably able to regain from the Assyrians the parts of **Hezekiah's** kingdom which they had removed from Judah in 701 B.C.E. *See also* SENNACHERIB'S SIEGE OF JERUSALEM.

MANASSEH (TRIBE). **Joseph's** first son with Asenat, the daughter of the **priest** of On (Gen 46:20), the brother of **Ephraim** and the eponymous ancestor of the **tribe** of Manasseh. He lost his father's blessing to his brother, something that has been understood as a reflection on the secondary position of the tribe of Manasseh in comparison to the tribe of **Ephraim**. On the other hand, all the capitals of the **Kingdom of Israel** were situated within Manassite territory: **Shechem, Tirzah,** and **Samaria.** Manasseh's tribal territory, between modern Nablus and the **Jezreel Valley,** was a fruitful area dominated by rolling hills and broad valleys. According to the Old Testament, Manasseh was divided into more segments, and half of the tribe was supposed to have lived in **Transjordan** under the name of **Machir.** This may be either a secondary historical development or just literary reflection as other sources indicate that Machir was an independent tribe.

MARESHA. A city in the Judean foothills normally located at Tell Sandahanna. Maresha was fortified by **Rehoboam** (2 Chron 11:8). **Chronicles** also refer to a battle at Maresha between Zera the Nubian and King **Asa** of **Judah** (2 Chron 14:8-9). It was partly excavated in 1900.

MAXIMALISM. A term used to refer to the representatives of a school of biblical historians interested in extracting as much historical information from the narratives of the Old Testament as possible. Representing mainstream scholarship at the beginning of the 21st century, they agree with the so-called **minimalists** on most when it comes to **Israel's** history before the introduction of the monarchy but take a firm stand when it comes to the historicity of **David** and **Solomon.** Generally, they date the major part of biblical historical literature as included in the **Pentateuch** and the **Deuteronomistic History** to the late pre-exilic period.

MEDIA. A **kingdom** on the Iranian plateau. Media appears in **Assyrian** records of the ninth century B.C.E. It was incorporated into the Assyrian Empire in the time of **Tiglath-pileser III,** but regained its independence c. 650 B.C.E. and became one of the architects of the downfall of Assyria. Its capital was Ekhbatana. About 550 B.C.E. it was incorporated into **Cyrus's** empire and became part of **Persia.** The Old Testament has difficulties distinguishing between the Medes and the Persians, and sometimes reckons a Persian king to be a Median. Thus **Darius** in the **Book of Daniel** is called a Mede, although he was a Persian king.

MEGIDDO. An important city at the western end of the **Valley of Jezreel**, in a strategic position where one of the most important ancient routes through **Palestine** crosses the **Carmel** range. The king of Megiddo was killed in a battle with **Joshua** (Josh 12:21) but, although it was located within the tribal territory of **Manasseh** (Josh 17:11), the Israelites did not conquer the city (Judg 1:27). The battle between **Sisera** and **Deborah** and **Barak** took place close to Megiddo (Judg 5:19). **Solomon** included the city in his provincial arrangements (1 Kgs 4:12) and fortified the city (1 Kgs 9:15). Belonging to its later history, **Ahaziah** died from his wounds at Megiddo, and **Josiah** was killed by **Pharaoh Necho** defending the pass through the Carmel at Megiddo (2 Kgs 23:29).

Megiddo is located on Tel Megiddo (previously Tell el Mutesellim) c. 45 kilometers southeast of modern Haifa. Settlement at Megiddo goes back to the Neolithic period. In the Chalcolithic period an unfortified settlement was established that developed into a heavily fortified city in the Early Bronze Age. After a period of decline, Megiddo achieved new importance in the Middle Bronze Age but was conquered in 1479 B.C.E. by Thutmose III, and remained in Egyptian possession for the duration of the Late Bronze Age. Also in the Iron Age, a city with massive **fortifications** existed at this place, a victim to the expedition of **Pharaoh Shishak**. In the time of the Neo-Assyrian (*see* **Assyria and Babylonia**) Empire, Megiddo was made the center of the Assyrian province of Magiddu. Megiddo was abandoned in the fourth century B.C.E. Megiddo has for a hundred years been excavated by three major archaeological expeditions, the last one still ongoing.

MEHOLA. The home town of **Saul**'s son-in-law and second husband of **Michal** (1 Sam 18:19). *See also* ABEL.

MELCHIZEDEK. When **Abraham** returned from his victory over the four great kings (Gen 14), he was met by Melchizedek, the king of Salem and the priest of the most high, and paid tribute to this king (Gen 14:18-20). The story is totally legendary but has been interpreted as a reference to a pre-Israelite **Jebussite Jerusalem**.

MENAHEM. King of **Israel** c. 744-736 B.C.E. Menahem resided at **Tirzah** but turned against **Shallum** in **Samaria** who only a month before had murdered his master, King **Zechariah,** the last king of the **House of Jehu.** In 738 B.C.E., as **Tiglath-pileser III** turned to the west, Menahem paid a heavy tribute to the king of **Assyria** (2 Kgs 15:13-22). The tribute is recorded both in the Old Testament and in Assyrian sources.

MEPHIBOSHET. 1. The invalid son of **Jonathan** who was spared by **David** (2 Sam 4:4; 9,1-8). Like the name of **Saul's** son **Ishboshet,** Mephiboshet is a pejorative for his real name, Meribbaal, substituting Baal (name of a god) with *boshet,* "evil." He was accused of having supported **Absalom** and lost half of his possessions (2 Sam 19:24-30).
2. A son of Saul and Rizpah who was on David's order executed at **Gibeon** (2 Sam 21:8).

MERAB. **Saul's** oldest daughter chosen to become the wife of **David.** Instead she was given in marriage to **Adriel** from **Mehola** (1 Sam 18:17-19) while David married **Michal,** her younger sister. Her children were executed by the **Gibeonites** on David's order (2 Sam 21:8-9).

MERENPTAH. Egyptian **Pharaoh** 1213-1203 B.C.E., the son of **Ramesses II,** whose victory stele from his fifth year includes the first known mention of **Israel** in any ancient Near Eastern **inscription.** *See also* ISRAEL STELE.

MERODAK-BALADAN. The Hebrew rendering of the **Akkadian** name Marduk-apal-iddina, the Babylonian adversary of several Assyrian (*see* **Assyria and Babylonia**) kings including **Sargon** and **Sennacherib.** The Old Testament refers to negotiations between **Hezekiah** of **Judah** and **Merodak-Baladan,** probably in connection with Hezekiah's rebellion against the Assyrians 705-701 B.C.E. (2 Kgs 20:12-19). He was finally driven out of **Babylon** by Sennacherib in 701 B.C.E.

MEROM, WATERS OF. The scene of the battle between a **Canaanite** coalition headed by King **Jabin** of **Hazor** and the Israelites under **Joshua** (Josh 11). It was located in Upper **Galilee** north or northwest of Lake Kinnereth and often identified with Meron, although other candidates have been proposed.

MESHA AND THE MESHA INSCRIPTION. King of **Moab** in the second half of the ninth century B.C.E. and the author of the Mesha inscription.

A. *Mesha in the Old Testament.* In contrast to Mesha's own version of his life, the Old Testament tells the story of a combined Israelite and Judean campaign in the days of **Jehoshaphat** of **Judah** and **Jehoram** of **Israel** against Mesha. The allied army succeeded in reaching Mesha's capital at Kir-Hareshet. Here Mesha sacrificed his son to his god, Kemosh, whereupon the Israelite-Judean army returned in dismay (2 Kgs 3).

B. *Mesha and the Mesha inscription.* The Mesha **inscription** is the most important royal inscription ever found in **Transjordan**. The stele carrying the inscription that was found in 1868 C.E. was composed by King Mesha of Moab honoring his god, Kemosh, because Kemosh no longer allowed the enemy to plague Moab. According to Mesha's inscription, the foe of Moab was King **Omri** of **Israel**, and his son, who is not mentioned by name. Mesha had liberated Moab from the yoke of the Israelites and vanquished its enemies. Israel was destroyed. The tribe of **Gad**, which since eternity had occupied Ataroth (see also Num 32:3.34), was seemingly exterminated by Mesha when he conquered the city and put a ban on its inhabitants. Other localities near **Dibon** and Ataroth were also conquered and turned into Moabite strongholds.

The historical importance of this inscription cannot be exaggerated, although it is not always easy to interpret the evidence. Thus the connection between the Mesha inscription and the story in 2 Kings 3 about King Jehoshaphat's and King Jehoram's campaign in Moab is not very clear. According to Mesha, the Israelites ruled Moab for 40 years, including Omri's reign and half the time of his son. However, according to 2 Kings 3, Mesha only rebelled after **Ahab**'s death. It is possible to solve the puzzle if the "40 years" are understood to be a round number (in the meaning of "many years") and the reference to the son of Omri as not involving mighty King Ahab. It seems likely that the title "son of Omri" became an honorary one for Omri's successors as long as the official dynastic name of Israel was "the **house of Omri.**" 2 Kings 3 may after all record the same events as Mesha in his inscription, although from an Israelite perspective. 2 Kings 3 and Mesha's inscription agree on one thing: that Israel did not conquer Moab in Jehoram's days.

The cultural information of the inscription is also important. The lord of history is Kemosh, the god of Moab—as Yahweh is the lord of history in the Old Testament. The note about the ban (in Hebrew and Moabite called *herem*) placed on the inhabitants of Ataroth can directly be likened to similar information in the Old Testament, for example, in the conquest narratives in the **Book of Joshua**. The Mesha inscription is currently part of the archaeological exhibition of the Louvre Museum in Paris.

MESOPOTAMIA. (Meaning "between the rivers"). *See* ASSYRIA AND BABYLONIA.

MICAH. From **Moreshet** in the Judean hill lands. His book belongs among the Minor Prophets of the Old Testament. He is supposed to have prophesied in the time of **Jotham, Ahaz,** and **Hezekiah** (Mic 1:1). His prophecies include severe criticism of social injustice. He is therefore considered an important firsthand witness to the social disorder of his time.

MICAIAH SON OF IMLAH. When the king of **Israel** asked his assembly of **prophets** for advice before going to war against **Aram,** he received the unanimous answer that he should go—not a single one of the 400 prophets assembled at the court opposed his plans. Therefore Micaiah was brought from the royal prison before the king and asked to give a true answer. Reluctantly Micaiah is forced to prophesy the truth to the king: if he goes to war, he will be killed and his army destroyed. Immediately, Micaiah was sent back to his cell (1 Kgs 22).

MICHAL. The youngest daughter of King **Saul** (1 Sam 14:49). She married **David** (1 Sam 18:17-21) and helped him to escape from Saul by cheating her father (1 Sam 19:1-17) but was given in marriage by her father to Paltiel from Gallim (1 Sam 25:44). During his negotiations with **Abner,** David demanded that Michal must be given back to him. As a consequence she was against her will handed over to David (2 Sam 3:12-16). When David brought the

Ark of the Covenant to **Jerusalem,** she ridiculed his behavior but was left barren as a punishment (2 Sam 6:20-23).

In the tradition about the execution of the seven sons of Saul (2 Sam 22), Michal is in the Hebrew Bible mentioned as the wife of **Adriel** from **Mehola,** whose five children the **Gibeonites** hang. Modern translations normally emend Michal to **Merab,** Saul's oldest daughter.

MICHMASH. An important place at a mountain pass c. 15 kilometers north of **Jerusalem.** Here **Saul's** son **Jonathan** surprised the **Philistines** and killed their outpost. Michmash can be identified with the Arab village of Mukilometersash that has preserved the name.

MIDIAN, MIDIANITES. According to the Old Testament, the Midianites were a camel-breeding nomadic people. Relations between the Midianites and **Israel** were in prehistoric times sometimes friendly, sometimes hostile. The eponymous ancestor of the Midianites is a son of Keturah (Gen 25:2). **Jacob's** beloved son **Joseph** was sold by his unfaithful brothers to Midianite merchants (Gen 37:28; they are in the same connection also called "Ishmaelites" [*see* **Ishmael**]). At a later date, during his escape from **Egypt,** Moses sought and found security in the home of the "priest of Midian" and here he married his daughter **Zipporah** (Exod 2:11-22). The relations between the Israelites and the Midianites turned to the worst at **Beth-Peor,** where the Israelites fornicated with Midianite women (Num 25). The final important story about the Midianites belongs to the **Period of the Judges,** when the judge **Gideon** had to fight against intruding Midianite camel nomads.

The information about Midian in the Old Testament is historically not very precise and also tendentious and may reflect memories of Midian long after the disappearance of the Midianites from history. The Midianites joined the coalition of Ishmaelite tribes that roamed the desert of **Syria** and northern Arabia. The historical Midian was partly a settled society including some important fortified **cities** located in the northwestern part of the Arabian Peninsula. Their society may have existed from the 13th century to the beginning of the first millennium B.C.E. Their language was an early variant of the later Arabic. Their civilization included a number of elements borrowed from neighboring cultures (Egyptian as well as Anatolian traits), certainly the result of their importance in international trade.

MIGRATION. *See* DESERT, MIGRATIONS IN THE DESERT.

MIGRATION MODEL. *See* SETTLEMENT OF ISRAEL.

MILLO. Or the House of Millo. A locality in **Jerusalem**. So far, several interpretations of Millo—probably meaning "the filling"—have been proposed but none universally accepted. Two locations of the Millo may be given preference: 1. Millo constituted the saddle on the ridge between the Temple Mount and the City of David located south of the temple complex, now filled up, or 2. Millo refers to the terrace system on the eastern slope of the City of David, occupied by several buildings located on an artificially constructed system of terraces.

MINIMALISM. A term used to refer to a recent trend among contemporary students of the history of ancient **Israel**. Skepticism constitutes the basic attitude of the so-called minimalists toward the historical reliability of the narratives of the Old Testament. The minimalists maintain that the books of the Old Testament include literature that is generally of a very late date, that is, the **Persian** period or later, and that they represent a view of **Israel's** past as seen through the eyes of Judaism that constructed its past without much regard for historical exactitude. The biblical narratives are fundamentally regarded as literature, not as historical reports. The main representatives of the circle of minimalists are Philip R. Davies, Niels Peter Lemche, and Thomas L. Thompson.

MIRIAM. The sister of **Moses** and **Aaron**, and named a **prophet**. During the migration (*see* **Desert, Migrations in the Desert**) of the Israelites in the desert, Miriam in alliance with **Aaron** opposed **Moses** at Hazeroth because of his marriage with an Ethiopian woman but received her deserved punishment for her offense from God (Num 12). She was buried in the desert of Sin (Num 20:1). The victory hymn in Exod 15:21 is attributed to Miriam by the Old Testament historiographers.

MIZPAH, MIZPEH. The name (meaning "watchtower") of several cities in ancient **Israel**. The most important was Mizpah of **Benjamin** (Josh 18:26). It is mentioned a number of times in narratives relating to the history of **Israel** before the introduction of the monarchy, sometimes as the place where the Israelite army assembled before a campaign. Thus, the army met at Mizpah during the war against Benjamin (Judges 19-21), and **Samuel** assembled his army here before moving against the **Philistines** (1 Sam 7). **Saul** was elected king at Mizpah (1 Sam 10:17-25). Mizpah was fortified by **Asa** (1 Kgs 15:22). After the fall of **Jerusalem** in 587 B.C.E., Mizpah became the center of the Babylonian (*see* **Assyria and Babylonia**) administration and the residence of **Gedaliah**. It is usually located at Tell en-Nasbeh, c. 12 kilometers north of Jerusalem. The place was excavated in the 1920s where a city dating back to the early Iron Age was discovered.

MOAB, MOABITES. The name of a state and its inhabitants located in **Transjordan**, to the east of the Dead Sea between the Zered River in the south and **Heshbon** in the north, altogether c. 2500 square kilometers. In the Old Testament, Moab sometimes acts as the enemy of the Israelites, sometimes as their friend. During their migrations (*see* **Desert, Migrations in the Desert**), the Israelites had to fight their way through Moabite territory (Num 22-24), but they also had intercourse with Moabite women (Num 25). The royal house of **Judah** was partly of Moabite origin as **David** was a descendant of the Moabite woman **Ruth**. When he fled from **Saul**, David brought his family to a safe harbor in Moab (1 Sam 22:3-5), but after having become king of **Israel**, he conquered Moab and killed a major part of its male population (2 Sam 8:2). Finally King **Jehoram** of Israel and King **Jehoahaz** of Judah led a campaign against King **Mesha** of Moab.

Moab may have been mentioned in ancient Near Eastern documents from the Middle Bronze Age. Egyptian sources of the Late Bronze Age refer to Moab. The Moabite state was established in the ninth century B.C.E., when Mesha liberated Moab from Israel. It was subdued by the **Assyrians** in 734-732 B.C.E. After that no records exist as to its further history.

MONARCHY, PERIOD OF. In the Old Testament, the period from the election of **Saul** as king of **Israel** to the destruction of **Jerusalem** and the fall of the **House of David**. In classical biblical scholarship the Period of the Monarchy covers a little more than 400 years, from c. 1000 to 587 B.C.E. The Monarchy can be subdivided into a prelude under Saul, who according to the Old Testament reigned for only two years, although this information has been doubted, as it appears in a seemingly broken context (1 Sam 13:1). The glorious period of the **United Monarchy** follows after Saul. Now all of Israel was for almost 80 years ruled by **David** and **Solomon**. In this period, Israel was not only united but also expanded beyond its traditional borders to include also the nations to the east of the **Jordan River**, and large parts of **Syria**. Some traditions even say that its northeastern border was on the banks of the **Euphrates**. This period lasted according to critical scholarship from c. 1000 to 932 B.C.E. The next phase opened with the dissolution of Solomon's kingdom into two Israelite states, the small **Kingdom of Judah** and the far bigger **Kingdom of Israel**. The empire was at the same time lost, as the **Ammonites, Moabites,** and **Edomites** regained their independence, and the **Aramaeans** of Syria threw away the yoke of the Israelite kings of Jerusalem.

The time of the two independent kingdoms was also a period of decline, although in the ninth century the Kingdom of Israel under the **House of Omri** regained some of the former greatness of the kingdom of David and Solomon. Internal strife between the two Israelite kingdoms only contributed to the decline. Most of the territories outside **Palestine** were lost to the Aramaeans, and the route to **Eloth** that had been the harbor from where Solomon had sent out his ships to foreign countries was blocked by the Edomites. The end came first to the Kingdom of Israel that succumbed to the power of **Assyria** in 722 B.C.E. after a large part of its population was **deported** to **Mesopotamia**. Later followed the destruction of the Kingdom of Judah that surrendered to the army of **Nebuchadnezzar** in 587 B.C.E. while at the same time Jerusalem was utterly destroyed, its king sent into captivity in Mesopotamia, and its population carried away into exile.

Although this has for long been the official version of the history of the Period of the Monarchy that can be found in most textbooks on the history of ancient Israel, historians have by now started a revision of the history of this period that has already changed it considerably. While it is acknowledged that nothing is known about the time of Saul, as no source from his time has survived except the Old Testament, it has at the same time become clear that the biblical image of the great Israelite state of the 10th century B.C.E. has little to do with political and economic circumstances in Palestine at that time. Thus, it is even being discussed whether a settlement existed at Jerusalem in the 10th century B.C.E. Instead of speaking of an Israelite empire, one should rather talk of the existence in central Palestine of an Israelite chiefdom, or principality of a limited geographical extent. The history of the two kingdoms of Israel and Judah is also being revised. While it seems likely that Israel under **Omri** and **Ahab** developed into a major player in southwestern Asia in the ninth century B.C.E., there are few traces of an organized state south of Omri's kingdom.

It seems now likely that a state in the proper sense of the word only arose in Judah in the late ninth or early eighth century B.C.E. This state, whose first economic if not political center was the city of **Lachish**, was soon crippled by **Sennacherib**, who attacked and destroyed most of the country except Jerusalem in 701 B.C.E. (*see* **Sennacherib's siege of Jerusalem**). In the following 70 years, Judah was a vassal of Assyria, although Jerusalem at the same time grew to new greatness both in size and in ideology for having survived Sennacherib's siege of the city. When Assyria withdrew from the Levant toward the end of the seventh century B.C.E., the **Egyptians** and after them the Babylonians took over. The king of Jerusalem may for a short time have mixed in international political affairs. But ultimately it spelled the end of the by now quasi-independent Kingdom of Judah. Instead of being impregnable to foreign attacks, Jerusalem was conquered twice by the Babylonians, in 597 and 587 B.C.E.

MORDECAI. The stepfather of **Esther**, who was instrumental in saving the **Jews** from the scheming of evil **Haman**.

MORESHET. The hometown of the **prophet Micah**, also called Moreshet-Gath, often identified as Tell ej-Judeideh c. 10 kilometers northeast of **Lachish**.

MORIAH. In the story in Genesis 22 about the sacrifice of **Isaac**, Moriah is the place of sacrifice, although Isaac was spared at the last moment. In 2 Chron 3:1, Moriah is identified with the **Temple Mount** in **Jerusalem**. The **Samaritan** tradition disagrees with this identification and claims that their holy mountain **Garizim** is the true place to look for Moriah.

MOSES. The central figure in the literature of the Old Testament from the **Book of Exodus** to **Deuteronomy**, and the hero of Israel's liberation from **Egypt**. According to the biblical narrative, Moses, who was of **Levite** parentage, was saved from the fate of the Israelite male children by being exposed in a basket on the Nile, where he was found by the **Pharaoh**'s daughter. Although brought up at the Pharaoh's court, Moses remained faithful to his people and was forced to flee for his life for having killed an Egyptian official. During his stay in the desert, he married a **Midianite** woman, **Zipporah**, the daughter of "the priest of Midian," and he was called by God in the burning bush to save his people **Israel** from the hands of the Egyptians (Exod 3). Assisted by his brother **Aaron**, Moses returned to Egypt and confronted the Pharaoh, demanding him to allow the Israelites to leave Egypt. When the Pharaoh refused, God struck Egypt with ten plagues. Then the Pharaoh thought it wise to let the Israelites go, although he soon regretted his leniency. When Pharaoh pursued the Israelites, the Israelites through Moses' intermediation walked through the **Sea of Reeds** and gained safety in the **Sinai** Peninsula while the Pharaoh perished in the waters of the sea (Exod 3-15).

At Sinai, Moses became the intermediary between the Lord and Israel, bringing the law of God to Israel while he at the same time supervised the establishment of the **covenant** between God and Israel (Exod 19-34). After he had finished his presentation of the law to Israel, for 40 years Moses led his people through the desert to the borders of **Canaan**, a country he himself was not allowed to enter. After a farewell speech that covers most of the Book of Deuteronomy, Moses climbed Mount **Nebo** to look over the future country of the Israelites. After that he died and was buried in a grave unknown to man (Num 10-Deut 34).

In the Old Testament, Moses appears in several capacities. First and foremost, he was the undisputed hero of early Israel, who on occasion led the Israelites in battle against the **Amorites** and Midianites. He is also described as a great leader of men who at times had to stand up to protest and revolt even from his own family (Num 12). He was also acting as a **prophet** and the spokesman of the Lord, and in this capacity he served as a mediator who turned God's anger away from his people. He was sometimes a magician who could strike water from a rock (Num 20:1-13), and he was a **priest**.

Aside from the five books of Moses, Moses only appears sporadically in the Old Testament. Hellenistic Jewish sources know of Moses as the real founder of the **temple in Jerusalem**, a tradition probably reflected in the note about his staff, Nehushtan, that was removed from the temple and destroyed in the days of King **Hezekiah** of **Judah** (2 Kings 18:4).

Although the tradition about Moses in the Old Testament is both complex and comprehensive, it is almost impossible to say anything about the historical Moses. Scholars have, on one hand, emphasized the importance of his unusual name—most likely a shortened form of an Egyptian name like Ramose (Ramessses), or Thutmose—while, on the other, they point to the information about the unknown grave of Moses in Moab (*see* **Moab, Moabites**). Too many miracles are included in his story, including the miraculous rescue from the waters of the Nile—a motif also found in other ancient sagas about heroes and founders of nations, as in **Mesopotamia** the legendary **Sargon**, the founder of the Empire of Akkad, and in Italy Romulus and Remus, the founders of Rome. Although it is impossible to say that he never lived, it is likewise impossible to present anything historically verifiable relevant to his life. Quasi-scholarly literature has sometimes ventured to establish connections between Moses and various characters of the Egyptian New Kingdom but, although people of Levantine origin sometimes obtained high positions in Egypt in the time of the Egyptian Empire in Asia, none of these identifications can be sustained by evidence.

– N –

NAAMAN. An **Aramaean** commander who as a leper consulted the **prophet Elisha** and was cured. Converted to the God of **Israel**, he brought back to Aram two mule loads of earth in order that he should also in the future be able to worship the Lord on Israelite soil (2 Kgs 5). The story about Naaman is part of the **Elijah** and Elisha cycle of prophetic narratives (1 Kgs 17-2 Kgs 9).

NABAL. (meaning "fool") A wealthy person from Maon in **Judah**, a place close to **Hebron**, rich in sheep and goats. When **David** demanded protection money from Nabal, he flatly refused the demand. However, when David pressed home his demand, **Abigail**, Nabal's wife, paid. When Nabal heard about the danger he had been saved from, he died from a stroke (2 Sam 25).

NABONIDUS. The last king of **Babylonia** (559-539 B.C.E.). Nabonidus, whose hometown was probably **Haran** in Upper **Mesopotamia**, usurped with the help of his son **Belshazzar** the throne of Babylonia and removed its ruling house. In opposition to the powerful priesthood of **Babylon**'s city god Marduk, Nabonidus favored the cult of the god Sin, the god of Haran, restoring sanctuaries in the Babylonian province including the ancient **Ur**. Not very much is known about his reign, except that he stayed away from Babylon for a period of eight years, living in the desert oasis of **Tema**. During his time in Tema, his son Belshazzar ruled in his place in Babylon. In 539 B.C.E., Nabonidus perished in connection with **Cyrus**'s conquest of Babylon, probably betrayed by the grandees of Babylon and the priesthood of Marduk. In tradition, he remained a controversial person, on the one hand praised for his piety, and on the other considered a religious fantast and fanatic. In the last capacity, Nabonidus appears in a late tradition such as "the prayer of Nabonidus" found among the Dead Sea Scrolls, and he is most likely also the source of inspiration for the description of **Nebuchadnezzar**'s madness in the **Book of Daniel** (Dan 4:25-34).

NABOTH. An Israelite nobleman from **Jezreel**, whose vineyard became the cause of his death, provoked by a fake process started by Queen **Jezebel** (1 Kgs 21). The treacherous execution of Naboth was seen as one of the main reasons for the fall of the **House of Omri.**

NADAB. 1. Oldest son of **Aaron**, who together with his brother Abihu, **Moses**, Aaron, and 70 Israelites nobles went up to see the Lord at **Sinai** (Exod 24:9). He was killed together with his brother because he had misbehaved in ritual matters (Lev 10:1-2). 2. King of **Israel** 911-910 B.C.E. He succeeded **Jeroboam**, the first king of the independent Israel, but soon after, while leading the Israelite army against the Philistine town of **Gibbethon**, was killed by **Baasha** who consequently exterminated the whole family of Jeroboam (1 Kgs 15:25-31), according to the Old Testament as a fulfillment of the curse put upon Jeroboam by the **prophet Ahijah** from **Shiloh** (1 Kgs 14:6-11; 15:29).

NAHASH. A king of **Ammon** whose war against **Jabesh** in **Gilead** provoked a reaction from **Saul**. Saul rescued the city and was chosen to be king of **Israel** (1 Sam 11). Nahash was later allied to **David** (2 Sam 10:1-2).

NAPHTALI. The second son of **Jacob** and Bilhah, and the eponymous ancestor of the **tribe** of Naphtali. In the **Blessing of Jacob**, Naphtali is said to be a "hind to let loose" (Gen 49:21), and in the **Blessing of Moses** he is described as one who is to conquer land (Deut 33:23). Naphtali's tribal area was fruitful and productive, the region close to Mount **Tabor** in eastern **Galilee**, bordering on the **Jordan River**. The account of the Israelite victory over the **Canaanites** in Judges 4-5 is the only tradition pertinent to the history of Naphtali before the introduction of the monarchy. Here Naphtali acted in alliance with **Zebulon**. In the **Period of the Monarchy**, Naphtali constituted one of **Solomon**'s provinces (1 Kgs 4:15). The tribal territory of Naphtali was lost to Israel after the **Assyrian** reorganization of its provinces in the west in 732 B.C.E.

NATHAN. A **prophet** at the court of **David**. It is said that Nathan was responsible for having stopped the king's plan for building a temple (2 Sam 7), but he also foresaw an eternal kingdom for David and his descendants. On the negative side, Nathan accused the king of having instigated the killing of **Uriah** after having made Uriah's wife **Bathsheba** pregnant (2 Sam 12). As David's sons fought for the throne, Nathan sided with the winning side and **Solomon** (1 Kgs 1). Although most if not all of the information about Nathan is legendary, his portrayal in the **Books of Samuel** is interesting as a testimony to the importance of the prophets as the spokespersons of Yahweh. The prophets are described as the king's superior advisor and indeed as a more important person than the king himself. It is in accordance with this view of the prophet's historical role that so much importance has been attached to the promise of Nathan to David in 2 Samuel 7 that his descendants will form an eternally ruling dynasty, if they keep the commandments of the Lord. It has often been assumed that the first part of this promise is old. It established the rights of the Davidic family to rule **Jerusalem** and **Judah**. It also appears in Ps 89:28-30 and 132:12. In Psalm 89, the possession of the throne is made dependent on the same conditions as in 2 Samuel 7. The promise of Nathan may therefore have been composed by the later deuteronomistic authors (*see also* **Deuteronomistic History**), who are supposed to have written 2 Samuel in order to show why the Davidic kingdom succumbed to foreign powers.

NATION, CONCEPT OF. The concept of the nation in antiquity was most clearly expressed by the Greek historiographer Herodotus (fifth century B.C.E.). His definition of the nation includes three criteria: a common blood, a common language, and a common culture or religion. The concept of nation in the Old Testament shares two of these criteria, the idea of a common blood and a common religion. It departs from the Greek definition by stressing the importance of a common land, the land of **Israel**, but disregards the demand for a common language, a sensible correction, as the Israelites spoke a dialect belonging to the **Amorite** language family shared with only a few local varieties by the **Phoenicians**, the **Moabites**, the **Ammonites**, and the **Edomites**. The modern concept of the nation and ethnicity departs considerably from the ancient ones, defining an ethnic group (nation) in a dynamic and changing way as a group of people who regard themselves as belonging to a certain group or nation, in contrast to other people who are not reckoned to be members of this group and do not regard themselves as members.

NEBO. A mountain east of the **Jordan River** opposite **Jericho.** Although **Moses** was expressly forbidden to enter **Canaan,** he was allowed to climb this mountain in order to have at least a view of the land of **Israel.** Here Moses died and was buried.

NEBUCHADNEZZAR, NEBUCHADREZZAR. The second king of the Neo-Babylonian Empire (605-562 B.C.E.). As crown prince he led the Babylonian army to victory against the Egyptians at **Charchemish** in 605 B.C.E. When his father died, he went home to **Babylon** and was crowned king. The next few years he spent in **Syria** forcing the major Syrian cities, including **Damascus,** to submit to Babylonian rule. A setback in 601 B.C.E., when he turned against **Egypt,** may have led to the revolt that ended in 597 B.C.E. with the first conquest of **Jerusalem** and the **deportation** of King **Jehoiachin** and a number of Judean citizens, including the future **prophet Ezekiel.** A new vassal king, **Zedekiah,** was installed on **Judah**'s throne, but when he revolted, Nebuchadnezzar finally made up with his Judean adversaries. He conquered Jerusalem in 587 B.C.E., had the royal family of Zedekiah executed at **Riblah,** and deported a large section of the Judean population. Little is known about the latter part of his reign except that for many years he laid siege to **Tyre** (585-573 B.C.E.), however without any success.

NEBUZARADAN. The Babylonian officer of **Nebuchadnezzar** who was entrusted with the destruction of **Jerusalem** and its **temple** in 587 B.C.E. (2 Kgs 25; see also Jer 39). Among his duties was to supervise the **deportation** of the leading Judeans to their death at **Riblah,** and of ordinary Judeans to their future home in **Mesopotamia.** He was instructed to save **Jeremiah** and send him to **Gedaliah** at **Mizpah** (Jer 40).

NECHO, NEKO. The Hebrew rendering of the Egyptian **Pharaoh** Nekau (c. 610-595 B.C.E.). He is mentioned in the Old Testament in connection with **Josiah**'s death at **Megiddo** in 609 B.C.E., when

Josiah unsuccessfully tried to block the pass at Megiddo in front of the advancing Egyptian army on its way toward **Charchemish**, where Necho's forces were routed by the **Babylonian** army (2 Kgs 23:29).

NEGEB. Or the Negeb of **Judah**, includes southern **Palestine**, and probably also parts of northern **Sinai**. The precise borders of this desertlike territory are difficult to establish, but the center of the biblical Negeb was the territory between **Beersheba** and **Arad**. Historically, the Negeb was settled in the Early Bronze Age, and after the general demographic breakdown at the end of this period, it was resettled in the Middle Bronze Age. However, the Late Bronze Age saw a Negeb largely stripped of towns and villages. In the early part of the Iron Age, some resettlement took place. The first millennium witnessed a resurrection of city culture with a major center established at Beersheba. At the end of the Iron Age, the Negeb seems to have been the center of conflict between the **Kingdom of Judah** and the **Edomites**, the Edomites successively reducing Judean presence in the Negeb. In the Old Testament, the Negeb was visited by the **patriarchs** who occasionally lived here. It was allotted to the tribe of **Simeon** as its territory (Josh 19:1-9), although when Judah swallowed up Simeon, it became Judah's territory, hence the name "the Negeb of Judah" (e.g., 2 Sam 24:7).

NEHEMIAH, THE BOOK OF NEHEMIAH. Nehemiah served at the **Persian** court at **Susa** as a high-ranking official. When he was informed about the conditions of the **Jews in Jerusalem**, living in a ruined city without walls and gates, he decided to travel there and obtained permission from **Artaxerxes**, the king of Persia. When he arrived in Jerusalem, secretly and in the middle of the night, he inspected the ruined walls. After having consulted the leading men of the city, the work could begin, although Nehemiah was constantly opposed by three important persons, **Sanballat the Horonite**, the **Tobiah the Ammonite**, and the **Arab Geshem**. In spite of their obstruction, Nehemiah managed to finish the rebuilding of Jerusalem's walls within the short span of 52 days. Nehemiah also had to attend to other problems, such as a **famine**, that threatened the survival of the population, and the problem of repopulating Jerusalem. The last problem was solved by moving people from neighboring communities to Jerusalem, while at the same time it became the residence of the leading families of the area. After twelve years Nehemiah could return in peace to his home in Persia, but had to go back to Jerusalem in order to finally settle old scores with the followers of Sanballat and Tobiah, now also including Nehemiah's former ally, the high priest **Eliashib**.

Historians generally accept the narrative of the Book of Nehemiah as a historical document including first-rate information about conditions in Judea in the fifth century B.C.E. As such, it narrates about a mission from Persia to Judea that took place around 450 B.C.E., in the time of Artaxerxes I. Nehemiah's book has, however, been compromised by the **Ezra** tradition that interrupts the flow of the narrative and has secondarily been inserted by redactors who considered Ezra a contemporary of Nehemiah, although it is generally accepted that Ezra only visited Jerusalem half a century after Nehemiah had ended his mission there.

NINEVEH. The capital of the Neo-Assyrian Empire (*see* **Assyria and Babylonia**) c. 700-612 B.C.E., located across the **Tigris River** from modern Mosul in northern Iraq. The city could trace its origins a long way back but achieved importance in the first millennium when **Sennacherib** chose it as his new residence. In those days, it was a huge city of not 120,000 inhabitants as claimed by the Book of **Jonah** (Jonah 4:11) but at least 300,000 inhabitants. In antiquity, the fall of Nineveh in 612 B.C.E. to a coalition of **Babylonian** and **Median** armies became proverbial.

NIPPUR. An ancient city of **Mesopotamia** some 150 kilometers south of Baghdad. **Tel-Abib**, the home of many deported people from **Jerusalem** and **Judah**, was located close to Nippur.

NOB. A city of **Benjamin** in the vicinity of **Jerusalem** and the home of a family of **priests** with roots going back to the sanctuary of **Shiloh**. When **David** fled from **Saul**, **Ahimelech**, the priest of Nob, supplied him with food and **Goliath**'s sword. As a consequence, Saul had the priesthood of Nob executed. Only **Abiatar** escaped (1 Sam 22). Its present location is unknown.

NOMADS. *See* ECONOMY.

NORTHERN KINGDOM. In scholarly literature one of the terms used to refer to the **Kingdom of Israel.**

NUBIA. *See* CUSH.

NUMBERS, BOOK. The fourth **Book of Moses.** Its name derives from the censuses that open the book. The first section (Num 1-10) includes the final part of the **Sinai** legislation, but in Numbers 10, the story about the desert migrations (*see* **Desert, Migrations in the Desert**) starts again. This time the narrative takes the Israelites from Mount Sinai where they stopped in the **Book of Exodus** 19 through the desert to the borders of **Canaan.** Thus Numbers 36— the final chapter of the **Pentateuch**—leaves the Israelites standing on the eastern bank of the **Jordan River,** ready to enter the Promised Land. The original plan was that the Israelites should move on from Sinai to southern **Palestine,** but after having heard the reports of Moses' spies (Num 13-14), they lost faith and were condemned to continue their travels in the wilderness for another 40 years. During their migration east of Palestine, they encountered numerous foreign peoples and nations, including the **Edomites,** the **Moabites,** and the **Amorites.** They either fought against these foes or circumvented them.

- O -

OFFICERS OF DAVID AND SOLOMON. The Old Testament includes four lists of the officers of **David** and **Solomon** (2 Sam 8:16-18; 20:23-26; 1 Kgs 4:1-6, and 1 Chron 18:14-17). David's officers were limited in number, consisting of a chief of the army, a secretary of state, two **priests,** a scribe, and the chief of the guard. Later the supervisor of public works and one more priest were added to the list. David's system of **administration** is sometimes believed to have been organized according to an Egyptian model, although the rather primitive organization speaks against this theory. Solomon added to the list by introducing a second scribe, a few more priests, a number of provincial governors, and their chief. Whether historical or not, the lists reflect a very limited royal administrative center. All the officers belonged to the inner circle of the king. Although it was enlarged at a later date, it never grew into a comprehensive body of officers of many ranks. Evidently, in the pre-Hellenistic period, there was no need for extensive bureaucratic systems. Only when the Hellenistic cities developed intro metropolises, did the society become so complicated that it had to be supported by an extensive organization of public servants.

OG. The giant king of **Bashan** in the days of **Moses** who was defeated and killed when he opposed the Israelite migration through his kingdom (Num 21:33-35). He belonged among the **Rephaim,** one of **Canaan's** pre-Israelite nations.

OMRI. King of **Israel** c. 886-875 B.C.E. Omri, whose name seems to be a mixture of Arabic and Hebrew elements (probably meaning "The life Yahweh has given"), was acting general, probably a mercenary of **Arab** origin, of the Israelite forces besieging the **Philistine city** of **Gibbethon,** when his master **Elah** was murdered by **Zimri,** the head of the guard. The army did not accept Zimri's coup and elected Omri to be its new king. Omri turned on Zimri at **Tirzah,** and put an end to his reign that had lasted for only seven days. The Old Testament has little to say about Omri, and most of the information is negative (1 Kgs 16:15-28). Apart from the story of his ascension, the Old Testament includes notes about the civil war between Omri and **Tibni** and about his construction of a new capital at **Samaria.** This meager information cannot conceal that he was one of the great figures in the history of the **Kingdom of Israel** who secured his kingdom by diplomacy and by war. Thus his son, **Ahab,** married a Tyrian princess, **Jezebel,** and he severely hampered the aspirations of the **Moabites** in **Transjordan.** When he died, he left Israel as one of the major powers of **Syria** and **Palestine,** ready to take upon itself the obligation of putting a (temporary) end to **Assyrian** imperial aspirations.

Assyrian **inscriptions** constitute an indirect testimony of Omri's importance. For more than a hundred years, the Assyrians regularly called the **Northern Kingdom** "the **House of Omri.**" Also, a king not belonging to his dynasty was called "son of Omri." Thus **Jehu,** who physically exterminated the dynasty of Omri, was to the Assyrians a "son of Omri."

OMRI, HOUSE OF. The royal house of the **Kingdom of Israel** that ruled the country between 886 and 842 B.C.E. The dynasty was probably of **Arab** origin (*see* **Omri**). The following kings belonged to this dynasty: Omri, **Ahab, Ahaziah,** and **Jehoram.** It was a prosperous period in Israel's history and a time when Israel became one of the major powers of the southeastern part of western Asia that entertained excellent diplomatic relations with its neighbors in **Syria** and **Phoenicia.** Its importance is reflected by the fact that the dynastic name of the Kingdom of Israel, "The House of Omri," remained in use until the eve of the fall of **Samaria** in 722 B.C.E.

OPHEL. (Meaning "hill"), the name of the ancient part of **Jerusalem** located south of the Temple Mount (*see* **Temple, Temple of Jerusalem**) and north of the city of **David.** In contemporary usage, Ophel is often used about the spur that leads from the Temple mount down to the pool of **Siloam.**

OPHIR. The goal of **Solomon's** overseas trade enterprises by ships departing from **Ezion-geber.** Its precise location is still the subject of debate, although a place along the Arabian coast—perhaps in modern Yemen—is generally preferred.

OREB AND ZEEB. Two **Midianite** princes who were caught and executed by **Gideon** (Judg 7:25) on the Rock of Oreb and the winepress of Zeeb, evidently a note based on etiological tales (*see* **etiological narrative**).

OTHNIEL. The first **judge** of **Israel** who liberated Israel from **Cushan-rishataim,** the king of **Aram-Naharaim** (Judg 3:7-11). Othniel is called the brother of Kenaz and **Caleb's** nephew who conquered **Debir** and won the daughter of Caleb as his wife (Josh 15:15-19). Othniel as well as Caleb and Kenaz are probably names of **tribes** or segments of tribes that became part of the tribe of **Judah.** The note about Othniel may be nothing more than an exemplary story introducing the **Period of the Judges.** It has hardly any historical background.

- P -

PADDAN-ARAM. The name of the **Haran** region, the home of **Abraham's Mesopotamian** relatives. It is generally assumed to be a variant of the name of **Aram-Naharaim.**

PALACE. In ancient **Palestine** and **Syria,** the palace was the center of the state. The king resided in the palace but it also housed the **administration** and directed the **economy.** At least in the Late Bronze Age it also included industrial factories like shops for the production of fine pottery and other crafts. Thus scholars speak—relating to the Late Bronze Age—of a palace economy where the king functioned more like the manager of a business enterprise than as a king in the modern sense of the word. The description of **Solomon's** palace complex in Jerusalem shows that this function of the palace also survived into the Iron Age.

PALESTINE. The ancient Greek, Roman, and Christian name of the country otherwise known in the Old Testament as, respectively, **Canaan,** the Promised Land, and the Land of **Israel.** The name of Palestine has been known at least since **Assyrian** documents as a reference probably to the coastal plain inhabited by the **Philistines** who gave their name to the country. In the days of the Greek historiographer Herodotus (5th century B.C.E.), Palestine could be used as the name of the territory between **Syria** and **Egypt,** meaning most likely all of Palestine. The Romans inherited the name from the **Greeks** and used it, although they knew of other terms including Judea for the political organizations that existed in Palestine. In Christian usage the name was common until the establishment of the modern state of Israel in 1948. Thus the British mandate that ruled the territory between the two world wars was called Palestine.

Although of limited size (c. 28,000 square kilometers), Palestine includes a variety of regions and great ecological contrasts. It also includes the lowest places on the inhabited earth, where, at the southern end of the Dead Sea, it goes down to almost 400 meters below sea level. Moving from north to south, Palestine borders in the north on **Lebanon.** This part of the country is mainly a mountain area, sometimes called Upper **Galilee,** but the mountains are intersected by fertile valleys that open up in the east to the Huleh Valley north of Lake Kinnereth, in the south to the **Jezreel** Valley, and in the west to the Esdraelon Plain, or the Plain of **Acco**. When moving from west to east through the central part of the country, the western part is taken up by the coastal plain, or the Plain of Sharon, the homeland of the Philistines. Before moving into the central mountains of Palestine, the traveler has to pass the **Shephelah**, a low ridge separating the coast from the mountains. The central mountains allow a relatively easy passage, only in one place rising to more than 1,000 meters. East of the watershed follows an abrupt descent into the Jordan Valley, a rift valley, running along its course below sea level.

The climate is subtropical with very hot summers, and fairly cold winters, at least in the mountains. A normal year will produce enough rainwater for extensive agriculture. Drought has, however, always been a problem, and on the average two or three years within a decade the country would suffer from lack of rain and **famine**. An estimate of the size of the early Palestinian population employing traditional agricultural techniques would be between 500,000 and 750,000 persons.

PALMS, CITY OF. Occasionally used as another name for **Jericho** (Deut 34:3).

PARAN, DESERT OF. The desert territory in the northern part of the **Sinai** Peninsula. Paran was the base of the Israelites when **Moses** sent out spies to explore the country (Num 12-13). When he fled from **Saul, David** also spent some time in Paran (1 Sam 25:1).

PATRIACHS, PERIOD OF THE PATRIARCHS. The Old Testament considers the patriarchs to be the early ancestors of ancient **Israel**. While living in **Mesopotamia, Abraham**, the first patriarch, was chosen by God to be the father of a great nation. Abraham moved to **Canaan**, the Promised Land, but his son **Isaac**, Israel's second patriarch, renewed relations with the family in Mesopotamia through his marriage. Isaac fathered **Jacob**, whose sons became the apical ancestors of Israel's twelve **tribes**. Jacob's second name was Israel, a name given to him personally by God (Gen 32:28). Jacob left Canaan with his family and moved to **Egypt**

where he died, but he was buried in the cave of his ancestors at **Hebron**—an indication that Canaan remained the Promised Land to Jacob's descendants, the future Israelites (Gen 59:13).

The Period of the Patriarchs has always kindled the imagination of readers of the Old Testament, and until a generation ago it was almost universally taken to constitute a historical part of Israel's past, considered as such also by most biblical scholars. Although scholars accepted that a large share of the patriarchal stories (roughly Gen 12-50) had to be relegated to myth and legend, they were of the opinion that a historical core was still present and reflected the ancient history of the people of Israel. As knowledge about the ancient Near East grew, this position became more difficult to maintain. First of all, it became harder to find a period where the patriarchs would fit in. Proposals ran from the Early Bronze Age to the Late Bronze Age. Secondly, obvious anachronisms such as the patriarchs' use of the domesticated camel—a development in animal husbandry that belonged to the Early Iron Age, that is, the end of the second millennium B.C.E.—became more and more obtrusive. The fairytale-like content of the patriarchal narratives also became bothersome. Such legendary stories have the patriarchs negotiating with the **Pharaoh** almost as if they were equals, something far from the realities of the Egyptian court in the third and second millennia B.C.E. Accordingly, modern scholarship—aside from its most conservative elements—has given up the idea of considering the time of the patriarchs to be a historical period. Instead it considers the patriarchal narratives to be stories about the past and the early heroes of the Israelite society not very different from similar stories among other nations. In this way, the Period of the Patriarchs is a pious construction by later historiographers who used the patriarchs to create ethnical coherence among their contemporaries.

PATRONAGE SOCIETY. A sociopolitical system that distinguishes theoretically between two kinds of people, the patrons and their clients. While it was the official political system of the Roman republic, and has been considered a specialized Roman way of organizing their society, the patronage system has roots that reach far back in history and is still very much in evidence in the Mediterranean world. The system seems to thrive in societies without an organized bureaucracy and a centralized state organization and provides a security system that establishes ties between the rich and the poor and thus juridical security also for poor people who in states without a proper police force to protect its citizens are left without protection if not allied to a patron of importance. The traditional Near Eastern society has often been understood as based on the existence of **tribes**, but it may be that the patronage system has been much more important in the daily life of people, including traditional Israelite society. The importance of the system, which is not very much in evidence in the literature of the Old Testament, may be reflected by the **covenant** at **Sinai** that probably copies ancient Near Eastern treaties between vassal kings and their overlords, the great kings (*see* **kingdom**). According to the biblical covenant, God acts as the patron and protector of **Israel**, while Israel is commanded to remain faithful to the Lord or it will be punished.

PEKAH. The son of Remaliah and king of **Israel** c. 734-731 B.C.E. (the text about the reign of 20 years of Pekah in 2 Kings 15:27 has been corrupted). Pekah changed the policies of the Kingdom of Israel in a fundamental way when he reversed his alliances and united with the **Aramaeans** of **Damascus** against **Assyria**. His choice of new allies could not have been worse. Assyria was in his time ruled by **Tiglath-pileser III**—probably the ablest king of the Assyrian Empire. Tiglath-pileser dealt with the rebellion in the west in his usual effective way, conducting a campaign to Syria and **Palestine** that in 732 B.C.E. led to the practical dissolution of the **Kingdom of Israel**. Most of the territory of Israel was put under the direct control of Assyrian governors. Pekah was killed in his palace as the result of a rebellion among his retainers and replaced by his son, who was, according to Tiglath-pileser's **inscriptions**, placed on the throne of **Samaria** as a vassal of the king of Assyria (cf. 2 Kings 15:29-31). According to the Old Testament, Pekah and his allies tried to press **Judah** to join the anti-Assyrian coalition—without any success: **Ahaziah** of Judah called for Assyrian help against his northern neighbor. Although Tiglath-pileser in his **annals** says nothing about this invitation, it cannot be excluded that he saw it as an opportunity to settle affairs in the southern Levant.

PEKAIAH. King of **Israel** c. 735-734 B.C.E. (2 Kings 15:23-26). Pekaiah was the son of King **Menahem** of Israel and may have continued his father's pro-**Assyrian** policies that, among other things, involved a heavy tribute paid by Menahem to **Tiglath-pileser III** of **Assyria**. A rebellion in his palace was his undoing. He was replaced by his retainer, **Pekah**, who soon changed his sound foreign policy and brought havoc on his own country.

PELETHITES. See CHERETHITES AND PELETHITES.

PENTATEUCH. In scholarly literature the usual way to refer to the first part of the Old Testament, the five **Books of Moses**, respectively the Books of **Genesis, Exodus, Leviticus, Numbers,** and **Deuteronomy**. In the Hebrew Bible it is also called "the Law" (the *Torah*). The Pentateuch covers the early history of humankind, tells the story of the election of **Israel's** patriarchs, **Abraham, Isaac,** and **Jacob,** and how Israel first migrated to **Egypt,** and thereafter escaped from the oppression of the **Pharaoh**. It includes the **covenant** and legislation at **Sinai**, and the migrations in the desert (*see* **Desert, Migrations in the Desert**). The narrative stops at the moment when the Israelites prepared to cross the **Jordan River** to enter their Promised Land.

The Pentateuch is a composite piece of literature made up of several different strands of tradition. In order to disentangle the composition history of the Pentateuch, scholars during the 19th and 20th centuries proposed that basically four sources are present in this work. In the original formulation of the theory, the oldest layer or source was named the "Yahwist" (based on its use of the name of God), the second source was called the "Elohist" (after Hebrew *elohim,* "God"), and the third source was attributed to a priestly writer. These three sources were found all over the first four Book of Moses, representing independent versions of Israel's early history, mixed together by a redactor into one coherent work. The fourth was considered to be **deuteronomistic,** and responsible for the fifth Book of Moses, the Deuteronomy. The Yahwist was considered the oldest source, originating perhaps in the 10th century B.C.E.; the Elohist was reckoned to be somewhat later, belonging to the ninth or eighth century B.C.E. The priestly writing was considered Jewish, and part of the literary and mental history of early

Judaism, while the deuteronomistic strand belonged to the sixth century at the earliest.

Modern scholarship has revised this theory of the literary history of the Pentateuch considerably. The scholarly view of the character of the individual sources and their relationship to each other has changed fundamentally, and the dating of the individual sources been lowered. Thus scholars have recently proposed dates for the Yahwist in the sixth, fifth, or even fourth or third centuries B.C.E. They also now see the Elohist source to be close to the Yahwist in outlook and general attitude to Israel's history, and accordingly contemporary with the Yahwist. A trend especially popular among Israeli scholars moves in the opposite direction and proposes to see the priestly writing as pre-exilic, that is, from the seventh century B.C.E.

PENUEL. A place east of the **Jordan River,** on the banks of the **Jabbok** River where **Jacob** wrestled with God (Gen 32:24-32). The **judge Gideon** destroyed the city and killed its inhabitants because they refused to assist him when he fought against the **Midianites** (Judg 8:8-9.17). Jeroboam fortified the city (1 Kings 12:25). Penuel is normally identified with Tell edh-Dhabah esh-Sherqiyeh but has never been excavated.

PEOPLE. *See also* NATION.

PERIZZITES. One of **Canaan's** pre-Israelite nations (Gen 15:20). Nothing particular is known about the Perizzites.

PERSIA, PERSIAN EMPIRE. An enormous empire that between c. 540 and 330 B.C.E. ruled the ancient Near East from the western part of India to **Egypt** and Libya. The creator of this empire was **Cyrus** II (559-530 B.C.E.), the founder of the **Achaemenid** dynasty that ruled the Persian Empire to its very end. From his base in Fars in modern Iran, Cyrus broke up the empire of the Medes (*see* **Media**), and went on to conquer **Babylon** and win control over the Neo-Babylonian Empire (539 B.C.E.). He also succeeded in reducing Asia Minor, including the Greek cities along its western coast, to submission to Persian rule, thereby establishing the conditions for the future clash with the **Greeks.** Cyrus died during a campaign against Bachtria, modern Afghanistan, but his successors managed to enlarge his empire by also including Egypt and pushing the borders of the empire across the Indus River into India itself. Only in 490 B.C.E. at Marathon, and again at Salamis and Plataia (480-479 B.C.E.), was the Persian expansion stopped when Persia's navies and armies were crushed by the coalition of Greek states under the leadership of Athens and Sparta.

The Persian Empire was for its time well organized with highly elaborate monarchical centers at **Susa**, and Persepolis in southern Persia. The king was the "king of kings." He was the supreme commander of all Persian armed forces and the undisputable master of his state. Economically, he relied on taxes imposed on imperial provinces, although local rule was exerted by *satraps*, provincial governors who as time went by became more and more independent of their imperial master. In this way, the satrapial provinces were highly autonomous but checked by an elaborate system of imperial spies (the "eyes and ears of the king") that was in evidence all over the empire. These satrapies, as they were named, were subdivided into minor provinces. Thus **Palestine** was until the arrival of **Nehemiah** governed by a Persian governor residing at **Samaria**, who was responsible to the satrap of the province of *Eber-Nahri* ("Beyond-the-River"), the Middle Eastern territories to the west of the **Euphrates**.

The Persian rule was considered, according to the standards of that time, lenient in allowing local customs and ethnicities to continue—a situation reflected by the Old Testament tradition about the Persians. Thus Cyrus allowed the **Jews** to return to **Jerusalem** in order to reestablish their society that had been crushed by the Babylonians. In spite of this, the history of Persia was not one of peace. Several rebellions endangered Persian rule, not least in Egypt, and the aftermath of the wars against the Greeks led to a partial restoration of Greek rule over western Asia Minor. Xenophon's famous *Anabasis*, the story of 5,000 Greek mercenaries who were employed by a Persian officer against his royal master, signals the inherent weakness of the Persian Empire: although ending up trapped in central **Mesopotamia**—almost at the heartland of the Persian Empire—the Greeks succeeded in fighting their way right through Asia Minor to the Black Sea where they were picked up by ships and returned home. When Alexander the Great attacked Persia, the Persian Empire crumbled within a couple of years, and was succeeded by a series of Macedonian kingdoms.

PHARAOH. The title of the king of **Egypt** in the Old Testament. Meaning in Egyptian "the Great House," its attestation begins in the third millennium B.C.E. denoting the palace in Memphis. Later, in the first millennium it became a title of the Egyptian king. The usage in the Old Testament reflects the final stage in its development.

PHILISTINES. The people of the coastal plain that gave the name to **Palestine**, that is, the "country of the Philistines." They originated among the so-called **"Sea Peoples,"** members of a migration of probably Aegean origin that at the end of the Late Bronze Age hit the Near East partly by sea, partly overland. In Egyptian sources, where they are called *prst* (ancient Egyptian did not have a special sign for *–l–* but rendered an *–l–* with a *–r–*), they turn up in the **inscriptions** of Ramesses III (c. 1187-1156 B.C.E.). In his inscriptions Ramesses III boasts of having destroyed the invading Sea Peoples, including the Philistines. It is generally assumed that Ramesses III, after having defeated the Philistines, granted them a new home in southern Palestine, then still part of the Egyptian Empire. Here they organized in a number of small states, in the Old Testament described as the five cities of the Philistines: **Gaza, Ashkelon, Ashdod, Ekron,** and **Gath,** but also including a series of settlements at least as far north as Tell Qasile, now within the city boundaries of modern Tel Aviv. The Philistines were never subdued by the Israelite kingdoms but remained independent until the **Assyrian** conquest toward the end of the eighth century B.C.E. The Assyrians called them *Palashtu,* a name that was taken over by the Greeks, and after them the Romans, and extended to include further parts of the country.

In the Old Testament, the Philistines turned up in the **Period of the Judges** as the enemies of **Israel.** The **Samson** narrative centers on the state of war between the Philistines and the Israelite tribe of **Dan.** Although the Philistines caught Samson, he was able to crush his opponents gathered at Gaza. Later, the monarchy was introduced to counter the threat from the Philistines, whom **Saul** initially fought successfully. Saul lost his life in combat against the

Philistines in the battle at **Gilboa,** but his successor **David,** who at a certain time had found asylum among the Philistines at Gath, settled affairs with the Philistines without ever conquering their land. The later history of the Hebrew kingdoms mentions a number of incidents between Israel and the Philistines, but the Philistines never again threatened the domination of the Israelites over the central mountain massif of Palestine.

PHOENICIA, PHOENICIANS. The Greek name of the Levantine coast of the Mediterranean and its inhabitants. The Greek name, meaning "purple" or "crimson," may refer to the manufacturing of purple colors in Phoenicia. Phoenicia embraced the coastal regions between, roughly, **Ugarit** in the north and **Acco** in the south. The Phoenicians are widely referred to in Egyptian, Mesopotamian, and Greek sources and also appear frequently on the pages of the Old Testament. **Inscriptions** from the Phoenician homeland are, however, few and far between.

As the name of the region and its inhabitants is attributed to them by foreigners, the ethnicity of the Phoenicians is uncertain, and it is most unlikely that they ever understood themselves to constitute a nation. Thus the Phoenicians never created a major state but their political society was organized as a series of **city**-states. Some of them obtained regional importance but none of them was able to extend its rule over all of Phoenicia.

The problem with the proper ethnic terminology sometimes induces scholars to let the history of the Phoenicians begin after 1200 B.C.E., after the breakdown of the political and economic system of the Late Bronze Age. Although the direction of Phoenician history changed in the Iron Age, it did not start there but reaches back into the Early Bronze Age when at least one of the major Phoenician cities became an important trade partner for the Egyptian **Pharaohs,** providing them with especially precious timber for building projects. Little is known about the history of the Phoenicians in the Middle Bronze Age until, at the beginning of the Late Bronze Age, they became the subjects of **Egypt.** The political situation of Phoenicia is probably best illustrated by the **Amarna letters** from the 14th century B.C.E. that include several letters from Phoenician rulers, not least from **Tyre** and **Byblos.**

After the breakdown of the empires of the Late Bronze Age, and after the interruption of international trade mainly in the hands of first Minoan and later Mycenean tradesmen, the Phoenicians were to experience their finest hour when they began to spread their trade activities all over the Mediterranean, founding colonies in such far-off regions as Spain, Corsica, Sicily, and North Africa—the most famous being Carthago, founded by the Tyrians near the modern city of Tunis. Political developments made them subjects first to **Assyrian**, then Babylonian, and finally **Persian** rule, but their new masters never seriously interfered with their trade activities, vital also to the economic welfare of the empires. The Phoenicians acted as brokers and middlemen allowing goods to flow from the western Mediterranean via their excellent harbors into the Syrian and Mesopotamian hinterland. The hardest blow to Phoenician well-being was probably delivered by Alexander the Great when he conquered and destroyed Tyre in 332 B.C.E., a city formerly believed to be impossible to subdue.

The Old Testament includes several references to the Phoenicians, although according to the political importance of the city of Tyre in the first millennium, they are normally referred to as Tyrians. Thus, the Tyrian king **Hiram** assisted **Solomon** in constructing the royal **palace** and **temple** (1 Kgs 9:10-14), and the dynasty of **Omri** was bound to the royal house of Tyre in marriage, when **Ahab** married the notorious Tyrian princess **Jezebel**. The prophet Ezekiel includes a series of attacks on Tyre and its king and prophecies that in a fundamental way will conquer and destroy the city (Hez 25-28). But although Nebuchadnezzar laid siege to the city for 25 years, he never succeeded in reducing it to serfdom.

PITHOM. In the **Book of Exodus**, Pithom, meaning "the house of Atum," is one of the storage cities in Egypt built by the Israelites (Exod 1:11). Its exact location is disputed, most scholars preferring Tell esh-Maskhuta, but a minority Tell er-Rabatah in northeastern Egypt. Although Tell esh-Maskhuta has roots far back in Egyptian history, no city existed at this place in the Late Bronze Age, when the exodus is supposed to have taken place. The city was rebuilt as late as the seventh century B.C.E., making it likely that the note about the storage cities has its historical background in a much later period than the one envisaged by the biblical text itself.

POTIPHAR. Moses' first master in **Egypt**, and the captain of the "butchers," evidently the palace guard of the **Pharaoh**. The name is Egyptian and well attested in the first millennium B.C.E.

PRIESTS. The political power of priests within a polytheistic environment, that is, with temples and shrines belonging to a great diversity of deities, can hardly be exaggerated. On the other hand, although it is known that ancient **Israel** was not a monotheistic society—not even the Old Testament claims it to be—the Old Testament does not allow for much detail about the role played by priests in the policies of the day except that the leading priests at the royal shrines in **Jerusalem** (*see also* **Temple, Temple of Jerusalem**) and elsewhere could sometimes act as the advisors of the kings, as for example, **Abiatar** did to **David**. However, in the historical literature of the Old Testament, this role as an advisor is generally played by the **prophets**, otherwise known from the ancient Near East as a rather low-ranking part of the priesthood.

Priesthood in the Old Testament can be subdivided into a number of priestly lines. The Zadokite priesthood represented the priestly elite. They claimed to be the descendants of **Zadok** and had monopolized the office of the **high priest** at Jerusalem. Below them stood the **Levites**, who were also functioning as priests at shrines distributed all over the land of Israel. Their importance seemingly diminished as the cult of Yahweh became the only official one, and they were—at least in the account of **Josiah's reform**—removed from local sanctuaries and moved to Jerusalem, where they were reduced to less important functions. This narrative may reflect the rise of the Aaronite priesthood (*see also* **Aaron**) to prominence, although details from this history are unknown. Chronicles (*see* **Chronicles, Books of**) know of more priestly functions and groups but evidently their knowledge concerns post-exilic conditions and not pre-exilic ones.

PROPHETS. Prophets are known from all over the Near East in antiquity as belonging to the system of predictions very much favored by the people of that time. In spite of their reputation in the Old Testament, they were generally low status soothsayers, ranked behind professional groups such as astrologists and **priests** providing oracles based on special features of the sacrifice. They were, however, feared for being unpredictable. Thus, the reports from ancient Mari on the **Euphrates**, dating back to the 18th century B.C.E., provide excellent comparative material elucidating the functions of prophets who also interfered in matters of state. When a prophet arose—often without any forewarning—he was immediately arrested and put into custody until his prophecy was verified. In the Old Testament, evidence of the same official attitude toward prophets can be found in the story about **Micaiah**, the son of Imlah, held in prison in **Samaria** (1 Kgs 22). When the king's colloquium of prophets in unison recommended a campaign against **Aram**, Micaiah was brought from the prison to tell the king the truth. When he delivered a devastating forecast of defeat, he was immediately returned to prison. The persecution of prophets is also one of the basic themes of the **Elijah-Elisha** cycle of narratives (1 Kgs 17-2 Kgs 9) that also describes the political impact of prophets opposing the decisions of their royal masters. Several prophets of the Old Testament, from **Samuel** to **Jeremiah**, were politically active, and no king would be without his prophet or prophets who would guide him in all matters of importance. Thus, the prophet **Nathan** was a trusted member of **David's** court, and the person who interfered when David had **Uriah** killed in order to marry his widow (2 Sam 12). Another prophet, **Ahijah** from **Shiloh**, promised **Jeroboam** that he should inherit the greater part of **Solomon's** kingdom (1 Kgs 11).

The great prophets of the Old Testament, such as **Isaiah** and Jeremiah, were both active in policies and fearlessly opposed the foreign policies of their kings. Several scenes in the books carrying their names show how the prophets stood up in confrontation with the king and his officers, sometimes risking their lives. Another prophet, **Amos**, was banned from the **Kingdom of Israel** when he rose against the royal Israelite sanctuary at **Bethel**.

Women could also appear as prophets. Thus the **judge Deborah** is called a prophet, and in Jeremiah's days, a prophet called **Hulda** was active (2 Kgs 22:14-20), apparently formulating a message not very different from the one of Jeremiah.

PROVINCES IN ISRAEL. **Solomon** is said to have been the first king of **Israel** to introduce a provincial system in his kingdom (1 Kgs 4:7-19) (*see also* **Governors**). This system constituted an intentional departure from the old **tribal** system as the borders of the provinces did not coincide with the tribal territories. At a later date, the **Assyrians** in the time of **Tiglath-pileser III** created a rather different provincial system, when they reduced the territory of the **Kingdom of Israel** to **Samaria** and its surrounding countryside because of an Israelite rebellion against the Assyrians. Then the provinces like Makidu **(Megiddo)** and Galaza **(Gilead)** were led by Assyrians governors. The description of the tribal territories in the **Book of Joshua** (Josh 13-19) is sometimes taken to reflect a provincial organization set up by **Josiah.**

PUL. An alternative name of the **Assyrian** king **Tiglath-pileser III** (2 Kgs 15:19).

- Q -

QARQAR. The place of a battle between the **Assyrian** army of Shalmaneser III (858-823) and a coalition of states from **Syria** and **Palestine.** Qarqar has not yet been identified with certainty but was located in the Orontes Valley in Syria. The importance of this battle is not limited to its outcome—the coalition managed temporarily to stop the **Assyrian** advance to the west—but the date of the battle has been linked to a solar eclipse that happened that year. This coincidence has made the battle a sort of pivotal point in the establishment of ancient Near Eastern **chronology** of the early first millennium B.C.E.

- R -

RABBA AMMON. The capital of the **Amonites**, and identical with modern Amman, the capital of the Kingdom of Jordan. According to the Old Testament, **David** conquered Rabba, but in the ninth century the Ammonites were again in possession of the city. So far no archaeological excavations have been conducted that may inform about the age of the city, although there are indications that no city was founded in this place before the Iron Age.

RAB-SARIS. An **Assyrian** officer who participates in **Rab-shakeh's** mission to **Jerusalem** (2 Kgs 18:17). The name is a title meaning probably "the chief eunuch," or perhaps more likely "the chief of the head," in other words, the chief of the king's bodyguard.

RAB-SHAKEH. An **Assyrian** officer in the service of **Sennacherib**. He was sent together with **Tartan** and **Rab-saris** by Sennacherib from **Lachish** against **Jerusalem** with an army to force **Hezekiah** to surrender. Standing in front of the walls of Jerusalem, he delivered a famous intimidating speech to the people of Jerusalem comparing the God of little Jerusalem to the mighty gods of **Hamath** and Arpad who yielded to Assyrian power. His mission was unsuccessful and he returned to the Assyrian camp that had moved to **Libnah** (2 Kgs 18:17-37; 19:8). Rab-shakeh's name—as is the case of the names of two officers who joined him on his mission—is not a personal name but the Hebrew form of an Assyrian title meaning either "chief butler" or "chief officer."

RACHEL, TRIBES OF RACHEL. Rachel was the favorite wife of **Jacob**, and the daughter of **Laban**. She was the mother of **Joseph** and **Benjamin**. She died and was buried near **Bethlehem** (Gen 35:16-20). Thus she is the ancestor of the two Israelite tribes of Joseph (and through him of **Ephraim** and **Manasseh**) sometimes reckoned by scholarship to constitute a separate Israelite tribal group that arrived in **Canaan** after the **Leah** tribal group had already settled.

RAHAB. A **Canaanite** prostitute living in **Jericho**. When **Joshua** sent his spies to Jericho they found shelter in Rahab's house (Josh 2). As a reward, Rahab and her family were spared when the Israelites conquered Jericho and killed its inhabitants (Josh 6).

RAMAH. ("Height"). The name of several localities in ancient Israel. The most important is Ramah, the hometown of the **prophet Samuel**. It is normally identified with er-Ram c. 6 kilometers north of **Jerusalem**.

RAMESES. City and region in **Egypt** where **Jacob** and his family settled (Gen 47:11). The city of Rameses, in Egyptian Piramese, has been identified as Khatana-Qantir in the northeastern part of the delta of the Nile, founded by **Ramesses II** (1279-1212 B.C.E.), and turned into the northern residence of the **Pharaohs** of the 19th and 20th dynasties. According to the **Book of Exodus**, the Israelites were employed as builders of this city (Exod 1:11).

RAMESSES II. Egyptian **Pharaoh** (1279-1213 B.C.E.) of the New Kingdom. Although never mentioned in the Old Testament, many scholars think he was the Pharaoh at the time of the **Exodus** of the Israelites. The note about the Israelites building the city of **Rameses** before the Exodus (Exod 1:11) provides the main reason for this identification. Historically, Ramesses II was without doubt the mightiest ruler of the late Egyptian Empire, and the person who checked the **Hittite** advance into **Syria**, but historically he has no relation to any exodus of the Israelites having the Pharaoh drowning with his army in the waters of the **Sea of Reeds** (Exod 14).

RAMOTH-GILEAD. A city in **Transjordan** in the territory of the tribe of **Gad** (Josh 20:8). It was the center of one of **Solomon**'s administrative districts (1 Kgs 4:13). At Ramoth the king of **Israel** died in battle with the **Aramaeans** after having been warned by **Micaiah**, the son of Imlah (1 Kgs 22). Also at Ramoth **Jehoram** of Israel received the wound that made him an easy victim of **Jehu**'s putsch (2 Kgs 8:28-29; 9:15), and at Ramoth Jehu was anointed king of Israel by a **prophet** sent out by **Elisha** (2 Kgs 9:1-13). Its present location may be at Tell Ramith c. 8 kilometers south of Ramtha on the modern Jordanian-Syrian border.

REBECCA. The wife of the **patriarch Isaac** and the sister of **Laban**. When **Abraham** sent his servant to his **Mesopotamian** relatives, Rebecca received him amicably at the city's well. After negotiating the marriage with her family, the servant brought her back to Abraham and Isaac (Gen 24). Rebecca became the mother of **Jacob** and **Esau**, and the protector of Jacob after he had deceived Esau and managed to persuade Isaac to send Jacob to Laban (Gen 27).

RECHAB, RECHABITES. An ascetic movement that derived their ancestry from **Jonadab**, the son of Rechab, a staunch supporter of **Jehu**'s putsch (2 Kgs 10:15-17). The Book of **Jeremiah** presents an impression of their anti-urban way of life (Jer 35). They scorned wine and declined to live in houses, thus displaying an ideal of a nomadic life that sometimes surfaces in the Old Testament, for example, in the Book of **Hoshea**.

RED SEA/REED SEA. The Red Sea divides Africa from the Arabian Peninsula. It is the traditional English translation—following the ancient Greek translation of the Old Testament—of the Hebrew phrase *Jam Suph*, indicating the point where the waters divided in front of **Moses** and the Israelites fleeing from **Egypt** (Exod 14). *Jam Suph*, however, does not mean the Red Sea, but the Reed Sea, which has led scholars to look elsewhere for the point of the Israelite crossing of the Sea. Here the Bitter Lake, now part of the Suez Canal complex, has been the object of special interest. *See also* SEA OF REEDS.

REHOBOAM. The third king of **Judah**, the son and successor of **Solomon** (932-916 B.C.E.). When Solomon died, Rehoboam received an empire in the stage of dissolution. The Israelite kingdom had already lost several provinces in **Transjordan** and **Syria**, and discontent was brewing among the northern **tribes** of **Israel**. Rehoboam traveled to **Shechem** in order to meet the representatives of the tribes, and when he answered their plea for more freedom with harsh threats, the northern tribes revolted and elected **Jeroboam** to be their king (1 Kgs 11). Rehoboam was left with **Judah** and a part of **Benjamin**. A few years later Rehoboam lost the temple (*see* **Temple, Temple of Jerusalem**) treasure to marauding **Pharaoh Shishak** (1 Kgs 14:25-26). No other information has survived from Rehoboam's time except that he fortified a number of cities in Judah including **Bethlehem, Lachish**, and **Hebron** (2 Chron 11:6-11).

RELIGION AND THE POLITICAL ROLE OF RELIGION. In a society like ancient Israel, it was difficult to distinguish between the religious and secular sphere. The state had a religious legitimacy, the king being the elected, not by his people but by the gods. Thus **Saul** was anointed king by the **prophet Samuel**, and when Saul was rejected by the same Samuel, he anointed **David** to be the next king according to the instructions of God. All kings of the Old

Testament received an evaluation of their reign that primarily concerned their behavior vis-à-vis the God of **Israel**. Being kings by the grace of God, the kings in ancient Israel were also in a position to profit from the religious foundation of their kingdom. Thus the **temple of Jerusalem** was located within the **palace** compound and functioned also as a royal chapel where the king played a major religious role. In this way religion was a major factor in the political life. **Priests** and prophets were important persons, sometimes cooperating with the kings, at other times directly confronting their kings and challenging their way of handling policies.

Although the Old Testament presents a picture of an Israelite society with only one god, Yahweh, as its legitimate divine master, it is an established fact that the religious reality of ancient Israel was of a different nature. The names of several gods of ancient Palestine appear in **inscriptions**, many as part of names carried also by people living within the territories of the Israelite state. Recently found inscriptions have also made it likely that Yahweh was not a single god, having a goddess, Asherah, at his side. Ancient Israel was definitely a polytheistic society, and only later tradition saw it as a society that originally only worshipped one god, but as time went by also turned to other gods forsaking its oath to Yahweh, the God of Israel.

REPHAITES. One of **Canaan**'s pre-Israelite nations (Gen 15:20). The references in the Old Testament to the Rephaites can be divided into two sections, the first reckoning them to be the giants of ancient times, the second the spirits of the dead. The second usage is confirmed also by texts from **Ugarit**, referring to the Rephaites as the deceased spirits of ancient kings, and **Phoenician inscriptions**. This information is not contradictory. The Rephaites are the spirits of the heroes of the past, and these heroes were giants in Israelite tradition as well as in traditions from other parts of the world. There is no reason to look for a historical people of the name of Rephaites.

REUBEN. The oldest son of **Jacob** and **Leah**, and the eponymous ancestor of the tribe of Reuben, who according to the **Blessing of Jacob** lost his position because he went to his father's bed (Gen 49:4). In the story of **Joseph**, Reuben, like his brother, **Judah**, tried to save the life of **Joseph** (Gen 37). The note in the Blessing of Jacob and the parallel note in the **Blessing of Moses** (Deut 33:6) indicate that in historical times this tribe was in an inferior position, having lost its territory in **Transjordan** to the tribe of **Gad**.

REUEL. One of the names of **Moses'** father-in-law (*see* **Jethro**).

REVOLUTION MODEL. *See* SETTLEMENT OF ISRAEL.

REZIN. The last king of independent **Damascus** and the ally of King **Pekah** of **Israel**. Not much is known about his reign, except that c. 735 B.C.E. he initiated a rebellion against **Tiglath-pileser III** of **Assyria** that also included Israel, **Tyre**, and the **Philistines**. When the coalition turned to **Judah** and invited King **Ahaz** to join it, Ahaz refused and called in Tiglath-pileser to help him against his neighbors—thereby providing the Assyrians with a direct opportunity to settle matters in the west. According to the Old Testament, Damascus was sacked and Rezin killed (2 Kgs 16:9).

REZON. The son of Eliadad, an **Aramaean** from Zobah, who according to the Old Testament fled from his master, King **Hadadezer** of **Aram-Zobah**. Rezon became the chief of a gang of bandits who sometime during the reign of **Solomon** entered **Damascus** and ruled "all of **Syria**" (1 Kgs 11:23-25). Rezon has left no inscriptions and no source tells about his importance for the history of Damascus.

RIBLAH. A city of **Syria** "in the land of **Hamath**" (2 Kgs 25:20-21) on the Orontes River that rose to importance in the seventh century. **Nebuchadnezzar** resided at Riblah when first the royal family of **Judah** and second the important captives from **Jerusalem** were brought in front of him. Here he executed the sons of **Zedekiah** and blinded Zedekiah. Later he also executed a number of leading Judeans at Riblah (2 Kgs 25).

ROADS. The history of **Israel** and **Palestine** is dominated by the fact that Palestine was a crossroad of major routes of trade leading from **Egypt** to **Mesopotamia**. The strategic importance of the country is reflected by the many armies that crossed its borders and the many battles that were fought on its soil. Of course, the international trade brought some benefits to the country. However, because it was never possible to establish a political unit including all of Palestine that might have controlled the trade routes through the country, the effects of the trade were sometimes more negative than positive, the traders bringing with them the armies of their employers. The most important route—the so-called "Via Maris"—started in Egypt at the fortress of Sile and continued along the Palestinian coast to the **Carmel** range. Here some narrow and dangerous passes allowed for passage. At **Megiddo** the road split into two routes, one leading across the **Jezreel Valley** and eastward to **Beth-Shan** and **Transjordan**, the other bypassing **Tabor** and **Hazor** in Upper **Galilee** and leading onward to **Damascus**. A second road connected the central mountains running from **Beersheba** via **Hebron, Jerusalem, Shechem,** and **Samaria** to the Jezreel Valley in the north. The east-west route over the central hill land was less important, starting in the **Jordan** Valley and continuing north of Jerusalem down to the coastal plain via **Gibeon** and **Beth-Horon**.

ROYAL STAMPS. *See* SEALS AND STAMPS.

RUTH. A **Moabite** woman who became the great-grandmother of **David** (Ruth 4:21-22). The book that carries her name describes her as a woman who, although a foreigner, remained faithful to her deceased husband. Applying a stratagem of her own, she forced the wealthy Boaz to marry her. The story is highly literary and most likely without historical value, but it presents a heroic figure of a foreign woman who by transgressing the normal rules of womanhood saved **Israel**.

- S -

SALEM. When **Abraham** returned from his victory over the great kings, he was met by **Melchizedek**, the king of Salem and the **priest** of the most high (Gen 14:18-20). This Salem is in the Old Testament identified with **Jerusalem** (Ps 76:2 [Hebrew 76:3]). It has been proposed to look for Salem elsewhere, for example, in the environs of **Shechem**, but this is a most unlikely proposal as no place has turned up in this area likely to represent a **city** with a famous temple.

SAMARIA. The capital of the **Kingdom of Israel**, also the name of this kingdom, located at the village of Sebastiye c. 80 kilometers north of **Jerusalem**. It was founded by **Omri**, who bought the place from Shemer (1 Kgs 16:24) and moved his capital from **Tirzah** to this place. It remained the capital of Israel until 722 B.C.E., when it was conquered and destroyed by the **Assyrians** and its inhabitants **deported** to **Mesopotamia** (2 Kgs 17:5-6). **Sargon** rebuilt the **city** and made it a provincial center. It continued in this capacity for the next centuries into the **Persian** period, when **Sanballat**, the governor of Samaria, opposed **Nehemiah**'s plans for reconstructing Jerusalem. The city was excavated before World War I, and again between 1931 and 1935. The remains of a royal city were found that extended down to the Hellenistic-Roman period, when the city was renamed Sebaste (preserved in the present name of the Arab settlement) honoring the Emperor Augustus. Recent reinterpretations of the archaeological evidence have questioned the version of the city's origin in the Old Testament, as traces of occupation predating Omri have surfaced at Samaria.

SAMARIA OSTRACA. A collection of inscribed ostraca found near the **palace** at **Samaria**, dating from the first half of the eighth century B.C.E. The texts are generally very short. They mention a number of people and places close to Samaria. They obviously functioned as an accounting system recording deliveries of wine and oil to the royal palace. They provide exceptional insight into the organization of the palace economy in the time of the House of **Jehu**.

SAMARITANS. According to the Old Testament, the inhabitants of the territory of the former **Kingdom of Israel** constituted a population of mixed origins. The center of the later Samaritans, who were named after **Samaria,** the capital of the Kingdom Israel, was at the old Israelite city of **Shechem**, but they represented the descendants of a mixed population of foreign origin that was deported to the territory of Samaria by the **Assyrians**, who had removed the original

Israelite population to faraway countries. Thus, the Samaritans were not considered Israelites and their claims of belonging to **Judaism** were rejected by the official tradition. Although little is known about the early history of the Samaritans—in modern times a small sect of some hundred people—this "authorized" version of their history may be in for a revision.

While **Jerusalem** and **Judah** were utterly destroyed in 587 B.C.E. by the Babylonians, the territory of Samaria was left almost untouched by the events of the early sixth century B.C.E. This means that the tradition originating in this part of the country that had once been the center of the Kingdom of Israel was left undisturbed by external events. It is therefore possible that many records about ancient Israel in the Old Testament were transmitted within a Samaritan environment but at a later date usurped by the tradition of Jerusalem. In Jewish tradition, the Samaritans broke with Jerusalem and claimed—of course illegitimately—that the true abode of God should not be sought in Jerusalem but at **Garizim**, close to Shechem. It has now been proposed to revise this version of the break between Judaism and the Samaritans as it seems more likely that they were forcefully removed from the center of Judaism, while at the same time their tradition was usurped and manipulated by early Judaism.

SAMSON. (Meaning "little sun"). A hero of the **tribe** of **Dan**, who was a **judge** in **Israel** and fought against the **Philistines** to the moment when he died. He is the "superman" of the Old Testament, and his exploits surpassed normal human possibilities. Yet, his downfall was a woman, **Delilah**, who enticed him to disclose the secrets of his superhuman strength to the Philistines who captured and blinded him. His end was spectacular, when he brought down the temple of Dagon at **Gaza** and crushed thousands of Philistines under its ruins. The Samson narratives from one end to the other are legends of the heroic kind also told by other nations. The closest parallels to the narrative about Samson are the **Mesopotamian** story of Gilgamesh and the Greek tradition about Heracles, also the victims of treacherous women.

SAMUEL. The son of Elkanah and Hannah, and a **prophet** and **judge** in **Israel**. Samuel, whose story is told in 1 **Book of Samuel**, was as a boy handed over to the temple of **Shiloh** by his parents and grew up in the family of **Eli the priest**. He is a transitory figure linking the **Period of the Judges** to the following era of the **Hebrew kingdom**. Against his will, Samuel was obliged by God to anoint **Saul** to be king of **Israel,** but he broke with the king who had transgressed a prohibition formulated by Samuel not to touch the war booty from Saul's campaign against the **Amalekites** (1 Sam 15). Instead of Saul, **David** was anointed king by Samuel. As of this point, Samuel vanished from history. He died while Saul was still acting as king (1 Sam 25), but was awakened from the death by Saul on the eve of the battle at **Gilboa** where Saul was to lose his life (1 Sam 28).

SAMUEL, BOOKS OF. The two Books of Samuel cover the history of ancient **Israel** from the time of **Eli the judge** to the closing part of **David's** reign. They can be divided roughly into three sections. The first describes the life and career of the **prophet Samuel** until he anoints David to be king over Israel (1 Sam 16), the second part includes the story of David's ascension to the throne of Israel (1 Sam 17-2 Sam 7), and the third and final part covers the later and tragic history of the fight for the succession after David (*see* **Succession History**). This third part also includes the two first chapters of the 1 Book of Kings (2 Sam 8-20; 1 Kgs 1-2). King **Saul** is the central figure of the 1 Samuel. His story begins in 1 Sam 9 and ends in 1 Sam 31, but it has been broken up and integrated into the stories about Samuel and young David. Formerly it was a widespread opinion among scholars that most of the narratives about Saul and David included important historical source material for the study of Israelite history toward the end of its **tribal** history and in the early days of the monarchy. Although scholars have not totally given up the possibility of historical recollections, historical analyses of the Samuel, Saul, and David traditions have given way to literate analyses that emphasize the fairytale-like character of the story of David's ascension to the throne, and the novelistic character of the story of his family tragedy.

SANBALLAT THE HORONITE. A governor of **Samaria** in Persian service, and the opponent of **Nehemiah's** plans for rebuilding **Jerusalem** (Neh 2:10.19). His name is Babylonian ("Sin gives life"), but his daughter was married into the family of the **high priest** in Jerusalem (Neh 13:28) and he may have been of Jewish orientation, probably from **Beth-Horon**. He joined the party of **Tobiah the Ammonite**, and accused Nehemiah of high treason (see also Neh 6:5-7). Sanballat is known from the **Elephantine papyri from Egypt**. These and other documents show that he was succeeded in office by his son and grandson, and that his family may have been in office until Alexander's conquest (331 B.C.E.).

SARAH. The wife of **Abraham**, and his half sister. Sarah, whose name was originally Sarai, had married Abraham before he left his family in order to travel to **Canaan**. She is described as a very beautiful woman, a fact that endangered Abraham's survival when he left Canaan for **Egypt**. Sarah was brought to the **Pharaoh**'s harem and only the intervention of the Lord saved her from being absorbed among the wives of the Pharaoh (Gen 12). She was barren but was promised a son by God personally (Gen 18). Within the promised time, she gave birth to her son **Isaac**. She was buried in the cave Abraham bought from **Ephron** the **Hittite** at **Hebron** (Gen 23).

SARGON. Name of two Mesopotamian kings. The name—in Akkadian Sharrukin—means "the legitimate king."
1. King of **Akkad** who between 2335 and 2279 founded a **Mesopotamian** empire. To posterity, Sargon was the ideal king endowed with legendary if not mythological heroic abilities. Nothing was known about his parentage, but in later times a story was told that shows a remarkable similarity to the one about the birth of **Moses** in the **Book of Exodus**. In later tradition, Sargon was reckoned the archetypical beneficent king while his nephew—the equally capable Naram-Sin—became the symbol of the tragic, if not evil king who transgressed the limits between man and God.
2. King of **Assyria** (721-705 B.C.E.). Sargon is sometimes considered the conqueror of **Samaria** (722 B.C.E.). The chronology speaks against bestowing him with this honor that rightfully belongs to his predecessor, **Shalmanesar V**. As the consequence of a successful putsch against his predecessor, he usurped the throne of Assyria. He used his time well. He consolidated and enlarged the power of Assyria on all fronts. His campaign to Cyprus was fa-

mous. From here he received tribute. He entertained relations with the Phrygian King Mita—the Midas of Greek literature. In **Syria** and **Palestine** he generally continued the policies of his predecessors, changing the independent or quasi-independent states into Assyrian provinces. He was the mastermind behind great **deportations** that involved large parts of the Syrian and Palestinian population: in 721 B.C.E. from Samaria, and ten years later from the territory of the **Philistines**. Here he had to quell a series of rebellions between 713 and 711 B.C.E. centering on the Philistine city of **Ashdod**. Sargon built a new capital, Dursharrukin (Khorsabad), which was given up in the days of his son when the capital moved to **Nineveh**.

SAUL. The son of Kish and **Israel's** first king. Three traditions tell about his enthronement. He was anointed by the **prophet Samuel** (1 Sam 9-10:16), the lot fell on him when the Israelites demanded a king (1 Sam 10:17-27), and he was chosen by his army after the rescue of **Jabesh** in **Gilead** (1 Sam 11). Saul became king in order to fight the **Philistines**. At first he successfully campaigned against the Philistines (1 Sam 13-14), but he soon broke with Samuel (1 Sam 15) who anointed **David** as the new king of Israel (1 Sam 16). David was employed by Saul as a singer, but after having defeated **Goliath** he became the king's esquire, and later son-in-law. The latter part of Saul's reign resulted in disaster. The break with David was final, and the war against the Philistines ended tragically at **Gilboa** where Saul and his sons lost their lives (1 Sam 31).

SEA OF REEDS. The traditional place of the **Exodus**. Its exact location is disputed as some biblical references point to a location on the Gulf of Aqaba, while other information speaks in favor of a more western location such as the Bitter Lake east of the delta of the Nile, or the bay of Suez. The Greek translation renders the Sea of Reeds as the **Red Sea**.

SEA PEOPLES. At the end of the Late Bronze Age (c. 1200 B.C.E.), the ancient Near East experienced an invasion of raiders, for a large part of Aegean origin, who with their ships struck the Levantine coast at several points, leaving destruction and chaos behind them. When the Sea Peoples finally approached **Egypt**, they were crushed in a sea battle by Ramesses III (c. 1187-1156 B.C.E.), who has on his monuments in both text and pictures commemorated his victory. The **Philistines** belonged to the Sea Peoples.

SEALS AND STAMPS. In the ancient Near East handwritten signatures on documents were unknown. Instead of handwritten personal documentation, people employed seals stamped into documents of clay written in cuneiform writing, or pressed into pieces of clay attached to documents of other forms, that is, papyri. Hundreds of such seals and stamps have turned up in excavations in **Palestine**, sometimes including an amazing amount of information about religion as well as history. Seals may be private or relating to public servants, even on the highest level. Thus, one of the most famous specimens from Palestine belongs to "Shema, the servant of Jeroboam," found at **Megiddo** (but now lost), probably a high-ranking official of **Jeroboam I** or **Jeroboam II**. A hoard of seal impressions was found in Jerusalem including names of officials from the last part of the independent Judean state: among others, seals belonging to **Hezekiah** the king of **Judah**, to Jerahmeel, the son of the king, and to **Baruch**, identified as the scribe of **Jeremiah**.

A special group of stamps from the eighth century B.C.E. reads "belonging to the king." These stamps were impressed into jars probably containing products from royal estates in Judah. These stamps may in the following century have been replaced by another official category of "rosette seals," probably following an **Assyrian** pattern. Seal impressions from the **Persian** period include the name of the Persian province of *Jehud*, that is, Judah.

SEIR, THE MOUNTAINS OF SEIR. Seir, meaning "hairy," appears in the Old Testament as another name for **Edom**, or a part of Edom (Gen 36:6-8.9).

SENNACHERIB. The son of **Sargon**, king of **Assyria** (704-681 B.C.E.), famous especially because of his siege of **Jerusalem** in 701 B.C.E. (*see* **Sennacherib's siege of Jerusalem**). On his ascension to the throne Sennecherib was forced to confront a widespread rebellion. Its center was Babylonia and its leader **Merodak-Baladan**. **Judah**'s rebellion against the Assyrians may be part of this anti-Assyrian revolt. Sennacherib put an end to the revolt when he totally destroyed **Babylon**, the center of world civilization—an act which shocked his contemporaries. In compensation for the loss of the great metropolis of Babylon, Sennacherib enlarged and adorned the city of **Nineveh** and turned it into the new capital of the Assyrian Empire. According to the Old Testament, Sennacherib was murdered by Adrammelek and Sareser—Assyrian documents indicate that they were Sennacherib's sons. The reason for the murder is not known, except that **Esarhaddon**, Sennacherib's favored son, was his appointed successor. For posterity, Sennacherib was the archetypical Assyrian king embodying arrogance and cruelty.

SENNACHERIB'S SIEGE OF JERUSALEM. In 701 B.C.E., **Sennacherib** reacted to the rebellion in **Palestine** instigated by **Hezekiah**. Two versions of the campaign survive: the one in the Old Testament, and Sennacherib's own report written the year after his return. They are basically in agreement, although different as far as detail goes. Sennacherib marched down the coast of **Palestine** removing and installing local kings at his pleasure. When he reached **Ashkelon**, he turned against an Egyptian army led by **Tirharka** and vanquished it at Eltekeh on the coastal plain. The next stage of his campaign was to bottle up Hezekiah "like a bird in its cage" in **Jerusalem**, while he subdued the other cities of Hezekiah's kingdom, including mighty **Lachish**, a feat depicted on the walls of his royal palace (the reliefs are now in the British Museum in London). In order to escape his fate, Hezekiah paid a heavy tribute, which included his daughters, to Sennacherib who pulled his forces back without destroying Jerusalem. In the account of the Old Testament, the tribute was not quite so heavy—the daughters of Hezekiah are excluded from the list (2 Kgs 16:13-16). The Old Testament adds the tale of the miraculous escape for Jerusalem, when the angel of God during the night killed 185,000 **Assyrian** soldiers resting in their camp (2 Kgs 19:35). The salvation of Jerusalem from destruction became a major theme in the Old Testament, and may have caused the disaster that destroyed the city a little more than a century later, making its population overconfident in the ability of the city to defend itself.

SEPTUAGINT. The Greek translation of the Old Testament traditionally dated to the beginning of the third century B.C.E. Although largely a translation of the **Hebrew** Bible, it differs considerably not only in its choice of books included in the Septuagint, but also at times in the version of a Hebrew biblical book used as the basis of the translation. Prior to the discovery of the Dead Sea manuscripts, the Septuagint represented the oldest surviving version of the Old Testament, its oldest manuscripts predating the manuscripts of the Hebrew Bible by several centuries.

SEREIAH. The name of several important officers in the **Kingdom of Judah.** Among the more important are 1. Seraiah the **high priest** in the **temple of Jerusalem** when **Nebuchadnezzar** conquered the city, and 2. An officer in the service of King **Zedekiah,** who is ordered by the king to read aloud **Jeremiah**'s prophecy against **Babylon** (Jer 51:59).

SETTLEMENT OF ISRAEL. The story of **Israel**'s settlement in **Canaan** is told by the **Book of Joshua.** After having occupied the territories east of the **Jordan River,** where two-and-a-half **tribes, Reuben, Gad,** and half of **Manasseh,** also sometimes called **Machir,** were to have their future homeland, the Israelite tribes crossed the Jordan River and began conquering Israel's new land. First the Canaanite cities of **Jericho** and **Ai** fell victim to the Israelite forces, then the inhabitants of **Gibeon** lured the Israelites into a treaty that in practice reduced the Gibeonites to servants of the Israelites. After having subdued these three Canaanite cities, the Israelites continued to conquer the southern part of the country. At first Joshua crushed a Canaanite coalition under the command of the five kings of **Jerusalem, Hebron, Jarmuth, Lachish,** and **Eglon;** then he proceeded to conquer **Makkedah, Libnah, Lachish, Gezer, Eglon, Hebron,** and **Debir.** After having subdued the south, Joshua turned against the north and a Canaanite coalition headed by **Jabin,** the king of **Hazor.** This coalition was also beaten by the Israelites and Hazor was conquered and destroyed. After having completed the conquest that did not include the **Philistine** territory in southwestern **Palestine** and the **Phoenicians** in the north, Joshua distributed the conquered territory among the nine-and-a-half Israelite tribes.

The **Book of Judges** includes a different version of Israel's conquest, attributing it to individual Israelite tribes but also stressing the Canaanite enclaves that were not conquered by the Israelites, notably Jerusalem (Judg 1).

In recent generations, scholars have been increasingly reluctant to accept the picture of Israel's settlement in Canaan provided by the Old Testament as historically reliable. Thus, it has sometimes been stressed that the corrections to the Book of Joshua in the opening chapter of the Book of Judges delivers a much more likely situation report after the conquest. The conquest itself has generally been placed at the end of the 13th century B.C.E. In scholarly literature it is possible to distinguish between four hypotheses about the settlement: the conquest model, the migration model, the revolution model, and the evolution model.

The conquest model, according to which Israel simply conquered Canaan from the Canaanites, mainly as described in the Book of Joshua but often accepting the modifications to the conquest presented in Judges 1. Nowadays, few apart from the most conservative, or evangelical scholars subscribe to this hypothesis. It is beset with too many problems to be true. Basically, the stories of the conquests of Jericho, Ai, and the reduction of Gibeon cannot be correct from a historian's point of view. Archaeology has brought about a fundamental revision of the information in the Book of Joshua: Jericho was destroyed c. 1550 B.C.E., probably in the wake of Egyptian campaigning in Canaan after the expulsion of the **Hyksos** from **Egypt**, that is, several centuries before the traditional date of Joshua. Furthermore, at the end of the 13th century B.C.E., the city of Ai had been in ruins for a thousand years, and, finally, the city of Gibeon was not founded before the 12th century B.C.E. The cultural continuity that existed in Palestine between the Late Bronze Age civilization and the Early Iron Age civilization also argues against a fundamental change in the demography of the country. Finally, the Book of Joshua—but also Judges 1—completely disregard the presence of the Egyptians in Canaan that was at the end of the 13th century B.C.E. still a part of Egypt's possessions in western Asia. Recent attempts to date the conquest to an earlier period than that usually accepted only lead to even bigger problems having to reconcile the biblical narrative with archaeological and textual evidence. The presence of the **Amarna letters** especially provides an excellent overview of Palestinian civilization and political organization in the century before the time of the Israelites, and they show not the slightest evidence of an Israelite presence in Canaan in the fourth century B.C.E. Although defended by important scholars of the 20th century, the theory of the Israelite military conquest of Canaan has generally been given up and substituted with other theories.

The migration model, fundamentally associated with the German scholar Albrecht Alt, denies that a sweeping Israelite conquest of Canaan ever took place. The Israelite settlement in Canaan was the result of the annual migration pattern of nomads living to the south and east of Palestine. Thus there was not a military campaign that put Canaan into the hands of the Israelites but a prolonged sociological process that lasted at least for a generation. During the first phase of Israelite presence in Canaan, the Israelites were a minority living at the fringe of Canaanite society. Only after some time did they grow in number and were able to subdue the Canaanites, a process that ended with David's conquest of Jerusalem. Although the model is historically and sociologically better founded than the conquest model, it fails to explain the peculiarity of the Israelite tradition, especially its religion. Thus many scholars have seen a core tradition about **Moses** and the **Exodus** from Egypt, allowing for a few Israelites under the guidance of Moses to have brought the tradition of Yahweh to Canaan. They therefore leave room for a third explanation, the revolution model.

The revolution model was originally formulated by the American scholar George E. Mendenhall. Because archaeology has made it clear that there was no cultural break that indicated that a new Israelite population had arrived in Canaan and certainly no destruction of the sites mentioned by the Book of Joshua and connected to the Israelite conquest there, it is necessary to reconsider the conquest model and the Mosaic tradition. Instead of conquest or migration, basically a foreign affair that left a new people in possession of Palestine, the Israelite conquest of Palestine began as a revolution, probably inspired by Moses and his followers carrying the tradition of Yahweh and the liberation of the oppressed to Canaan. The bulk of the Israelite population was Canaanite peasants who revolted against the oppression from their Canaanite overlords and set up an egalitarian Yahwistic society.

The evolution model, finally, rejects the revolution model as an expression of modern romantic thinking. Otherwise it keeps the main ingredients of the revolution hypothesis, including the idea that the Israelites originated in Palestine. It operates with a cultural continuum between the Palestinian population of the Late Bronze Age and of the Early Iron Age but generally sees Yahwism as a religious and ideological element that only developed in the course of Israelite history. Nowadays, most scholars have given up the revolution model and the present debate is between the migration and the evolution models.

SHALLUM. King of **Israel** for one month (752 B.C.E.) who murdered his predecessor **Zechariah** but was himself killed by **Menahem** (2 Kgs 15:10-15). The name of Shallum is also used as an alternative name of King Jehoahaz of **Judah** (*see* **Jehoahaz 2**).

SHALMANESAR V. King of **Assyria** 726-722 B.C.E. and the conqueror of **Samaria** in 722 B.C.E., when **Hoshea** the king of Samaria withheld his tribute and negotiated with the **Egyptians**. Hoshea was arrested, and his capital destroyed (2 Kgs 17:1-41).

SHAMGAR. A **judge** who killed 600 **Philistines** with an ox-goad (Judg 3:31). It has been conjected that he was a **Horite**, since his name is not a Semitic one. He is also mentioned in the Song of **Deborah** more as a highwayman than a judge (5:6).

SHAPHAN. A secretary of the state of **Judah** who was instrumental in connection with **Josiah's reform**, and brought the newly discovered law book from the **temple** to the king (2 Kgs 22). He may be the same as the Shaphan who acted as one of **Jeremiah**'s protectors (Jer 26:24), and whose grandson was **Gedaliah**.

SHEBA (PERSON). A **Benjaminite** who headed a revolt against **David** (2 Sam 20). Sheba's war cry, "We have no share in David / no lot in the son of Jesse. / Every man to his tent, O Israel," was the same as used against **Rehoboam** (1 Sam 20:1; see also 1 Kgs 12:16), an indication of a similar discontent among the tribes of **Israel** against David as those that led to the dissolution of his kingdom. The revolt met with little success. Sheba was defeated by

Joab and pursued to the very north of the country, to **Abel-Beth-Maacah**. Here he was killed by the inhabitants of the city.

SHEBA, QUEEN OF. An Arabian queen who visited **Solomon** in **Jerusalem** (1 Kgs 10). Her kingdom is usually located in the southwestern part of the Arabian Peninsula where in the ninth century a center of trade arose specializing in aromatics, especially incense. Although the story of the Queen of Sheba is highly legendary, it is a testimony of the importance of Sheba in the first millennium B.C.E. for the international trade between India and the ancient Near East.

SHECHEM (CITY). One of the most important cities of the Old Testament. Located at Tell Balata just to the east of modern Nablus, the Hellenistic Roman continuation of the ancient city. **Abraham** built an altar at Shechem (Gen 12:6-7). **Jacob's** sons **Simeon** and **Levi** killed its male population in revenge for their sister **Dinah's** dishonor (Gen 34). After the conquest, **Joshua** summoned the leaders of **Israel** to Shechem for his farewell speech (Josh 24). **Gideon's** son **Abimelech** destroyed Shechem (Judg 9), and the kingdom of **Solomon** was divided in two after negotiations between the northern tribes and Solomon's successor **Rehoboam** failed (1 Kgs 12). In the **Persian** and Hellenistic-Roman periods, Shechem became the home of the **Samaritans**.

Shechem was extensively excavated in a series of campaigns before World War I, during the British mandate, and again in the 1960s. The remains of a large, strongly fortified **city** were unearthed that go back to the Chalcolithic period. It was not settled in the Early Bronze Age, but in the Middle Bronze Age a major city was built here, mentioned in the Egyptian **Execration Texts**. It was destroyed c. 1500 B.C.E. but soon after rebuilt. It played an important role in the Amarna period (*see* **Amarna and the Amarna letters**) in the second half of the fourth century B.C.E. when its ruler, Labayu, gained notoriety among his colleagues—several Amarna letters including some of Labayu himself mention Shechem. It was destroyed again toward the end of the 12th century B.C.E. and only began to recover in the 10th century B.C.E., only to be destroyed yet another time by the **Assyrians** when they overran the **Kingdom** of **Israel**. Thereafter it gradually lost its importance until forsaken in the Persian period (fifth century B.C.E.).

SHECHEM (PERSON). The son of **Hamor** and the molester of **Jacob**'s daughter **Dinah**. His father negotiated a marriage between Shechem and Dinah but was killed together with the male population of his city by Dinah's brothers **Simeon** and **Levi** who would not accept a peaceful solution to the dishonoring of their sister (Gen 34).

SHEPHELAH. Although the Spephelah is mentioned at least 20 times in the Hebrew text of the Old Testament, it is translated in English in a number of different ways, for example, as the "vale" (1 Kgs 10:27 [KJV]), or as "the hills" (e.g., Josh 10:40). It is a characteristic feature of the geography of **Palestine**, a low ridge running from north to south along the coastal plain and separating the plain from the central mountains of Palestine. It was the home of a great many **cities**, including perhaps the most important, **Lachish**. From a military point of view, the Shephelah did not represent any obstacle to an invading army, but from an economic point of view, its many fertile valleys provided some of the best living conditions of ancient Palestine.

SHESHBAZZAR. The first **Persian** governor of **Judah** who according to the Old Testament started the rebuilding of the **temple** in **Jerusalem**. After 20 years little had happened (Ezra 5:14-16). No other evidence about Sheshbazzar has survived apart from the title "prince of Judah" (Ezra 1:8), a title that has led to many speculations about the identity of this person.

SHILOH. An important city in the traditions of the Old Testament located in the mountains of **Ephraim** between **Jerusalem** and Nablus (**Shechem**) some 20 kilometers north of Jerusalem. The name has been preserved by the local Arab name of the ruined city, Tell Seilun.

When the conquest of **Canaan** was completed, **Joshua** distributed the land of Canaan between **Israel**'s twelve **tribes** at Shiloh (Josh 18). He summoned the representatives of the tribes to Shiloh and delivered his farewell speech here (Josh 22-23). In the **Period** of the Judges, when the tribe of Benjamin was almost annihilated, its young men were allowed to carry away unmarried women who participated in the dance at Shiloh (Judg 21). The prophet Samuel grew up in the temple of Yahweh at Shiloh (1 Sam 1-3). In this temple the Ark of the Covenant had its home, but it was lost in the battle at Ebenezer, where the Philistines conquered it and killed the sons of Eli, the priest of Shiloh (1 Sam 4). Little is known about the fate of Shiloh after the introduction of the monarchy. The prophet Ahijah, who announced to Jeroboam the division of the kingdom of Solomon, had his home at Shiloh (1 Kgs 11:26-40). Finally, the prophet Jeremiah referred to the example of the temple of Shiloh in a prophecy concerning the ultimate fate of Solomon's temple (Jer 7:1-15).

Shiloh was excavated in the 1920s, again in 1963, and finally in the 1980s. It was founded during the Middle Bronze Age but deserted during the Late Bronze Age. In the Early Iron Age (12-11th centuries B.C.E.) Shiloh was temporarily rebuilt but destroyed shortly thereafter. No city worth mentioning could be found on this spot during the Period of the Monarchy (*see* **Monarchy, Period of**).

SHIMEI. The son of Gera, from the tribe of Benjamin and of the family of Saul. When David fled from Absalom and approached Shimei's hometown, Shimei went out to curse David as the murderer of the house of Saul (2 Sam 16:5-8). Among his advice to Solomon on his deathbed, David encouraged his son to execute Shimei, advice which Solomon followed at the first possible opportunity (1 Kgs 2:8-9.36-46).

SHINAR. A name for Mesopotamia, especially Babylonia, used occasionally in the Old Testament. The Old Testament Shinar may reflect an Assyrian term for Sumer.

SHISHAK. The biblical adaption of Egyptian Sheshonq, a Pharaoh who ruled Egypt c. 945-924 B.C.E. Shishak was the founder of the 22nd—Libyan—dynasty. He tried to restore Egyptian power and glory in western Asia and claimed to have led a campaign to Palestine. In his inscription commemorating this campaign in Palestine, he boasts of having destroyed and conquered at least 150 Palestinian cities. He does not mention **Jerusalem** or other places in **Judah**, something that contradicts the claim of the Old Testament that he plundered the **temple** of **Solomon** (1 Kgs 14:25-26). Although the historiographers of the Old Testament know about Shishak's campaign in King **Rehoboam**'s fifth year, they evidently did not dispose of any details relating to the campaign.

SHITTIM, alternatively **ABEL-SHITTIM.** The final station during the **migration** of the Israelites from **Egypt** to **Canaan**, located on the eastern bank of the **Jordan River.** Here, **Joshua** prepared for the campaign in Canaan (Num 33:49; Josh 2:1). Its present location is disputed.

SHUNEM. A **city** in the territory of **Issachar** (Josh 19:18), normally identified with modern Sulam on the southern slope of the Hill of Moreh where remains stretching from the Middle Bronze Age to Arab times have been found. Shunem is included in an **Egyptian** list of conquered **Palestinian** cities from the time of Thutmose III (15th century B.C.E.) to **Shishak** (10th century). According to an **Amarna letter**, Labayu of **Shechem** plundered Shunem. In the Old Testament, **Abishag**, the girl who was picked to revitalize ailing King **David**, came from Shunem (1 Kgs 1:3), and in Shunem the **prophet Elisha** brought the dead son of the widow back to life (2 Kgs 4:8-27).

SIDDIM, VALLEY OF. The place where the four great kings led by **Chedorlaomer** fought against the kings of **Sodom, Gomorrah,** Admah, Zeboiim, and Bela (Gen 14:10-11), by the author of Genesis 14 considered to be the Dead Sea.

SIDON. An important city of **Phoenicia** halfway between Beirut and **Tyre,** modern Saida. Sidon is known from ancient sources dating from the Late Bronze Age, although it is likely that it was already an important harbor and city before that time. At the beginning of the Iron Age, Sidon was undoubtedly the center of Phoenicia, and its name was also in later documents used about all of Phoenicia, although it had lost it political independence first to the Tyrians, and then successively to the **Assyrians,** the **Babylonians,** the **Persians,** and the Macedonians. In the Old Testament, Sidon is reckoned as part of the tribal territory of **Asher**, although it was never an Israelite city (Josh 13:6; 19:28; Judg 1:31).

SIHON. The **Amorite** king of **Transjordan** who opposed **Moses** and the Israelites when they asked for permission to cross through his country to **Canaan**. As a consequence, the Israelites fought against Sihon, conquering all of his cities including **Heshbon**, his capital (Num 21:21-31). His kingdom is believed to have embraced the territory between **Jabbok** in the north and **Moab** in the south. The account in the Old Testament of this war is highly legendary. Heshbon was not inhabited in the Late Bronze Age, and the Amorites hardly constituted a historical nation when these events are believed to have happened.

SILOAM, POOL OF. Ancient **Jerusalem**, located on the southeastern hill of modern Jerusalem, was devoid of springs except for the **Gihon** Spring at the bottom of the Kedron Valley. In case of siege, the procurement of water was mandatory to the survival of the city, and traditionally, the inhabitants of Jerusalem had gained access to Gihon through an elaborate system of tunnels that led down to the spring. In King **Hezekiah's** days, a tunnel was constructed that led the water from the spring to a pool built at the southern end of the city (2 Kgs 20:20). This pool was to become the most important factor in the water supply of Jerusalem for centuries to come. In commemoration of the construction of the tunnel, an **inscription** was placed where the workers carving out the tunnel met under the massif that supported the city of Jerusalem. *See also* SILOAM INSCRIPTION.

SILOAM INSCRIPTION. An **inscription** found in the subterranean water canal that leads water from the Spring of **Gihon** on **Jerusalem's** eastern side to the **Pool of Siloam** at the south end of the **Ophel** spur. The inscription commemorates the moment when two working teams met underground and opened the passage through the tunnel. It is widely accepted that the inscription relates to the note in 2 Kings that **Hezekiah** constructed the water canal, probably in expectation of the coming **Assyrian** attack on his kingdom in 701 B.C.E. (2 Kgs 20:20). A recent attempt to date the inscription to the Hasmonean period has been rejected by the majority of scholars. The inscription is today on display in the Archaeological Museum in Istanbul.

SIMEON. Jacob's second son with **Leah** and the eponymous ancestor of the **tribe** of **Simeon.** The **Blessing of Jacob** condemns Simeon for being a man of violence whose descendants shall be dispersed among the tribes of **Israel** (Gen 49:5-7). This remark obviously points to Simeon's behavior in the story of the rape of **Dinah,** when he together with his brother **Levi** killed the male population of **Shechem** (Gen 34). It also reflects the situation of the tribe of Simeon. The territory of this tribe was in the northern part of the **Negeb** desert (Josh 19:1-9), a territory otherwise attributed to **Judah** (Josh 15). It is likely that Simeon at an early date lost its independence to the tribe or tribal coalition called Judah. It is placed at the beginning of the tribal lists in Genesis together with **Reuben** and Levi, probably because these three tribes shared a similar fate: they did not survive as independent tribes into the historical period of ancient Israel.

SIN, WILDERNESS OF. A desert in the northwestern part of the **Sinai** Peninsula transversed by the Israelites after the **Exodus** (Exod 16:1). Its exact boundaries are not known.

SINAI. In ancient times, a desert and a mountain on the peninsula, now carrying the name of Sinai. The exact location of the mountain is disputed, but Christian tradition has since the fourth century C.E. identified it with the 2,285-meter-high *Djebel Musa* (Arabic "the mountain of Moses") in central southern Sinai. The Israelites moved through this area after having escaped from **Egypt,** and here they received the law and the **covenant** from God (Exod 19-34). Other biblical traditions combine the origin of **Israel**'s faith with Sinai.

In ancient times, the Sinai formed a natural border separating Egypt from western Asia. It was a place of copper mining, and **inscriptions** dating from c. 1500 B.C.E. have been found here at *Serabit el Khadem* using the so-called "Proto-Sinaitic" alphabet, possibly a forerunner of the West-Semitic alphabets, including **Phoenician** and Hebrew.

SISERA. The main opponent of **Deborah** and **Barak** in Judges 4-5. According to Judges 4, Sisera is the general of **Jabin**, the **Canaanite** king of **Hazor**; in Judges 5, Sisera is simply the leader of the coalition of Canaanite princes. The two accounts agree on the vital facts that Sisera lost the battle and had to flee for his life but was murdered sleeping in the **Kenite** woman **Jael**'s tent. The tradition of Judges 4 may have been mixed with the account of **Joshua**'s battle with Jabin of Hazor (Josh 11). Sisera's home **Haroshet-hagoim** ("Harosheth of the gentiles"), has not been located.

SO. An **Egyptian** king whose support King **Hoshea** of **Israel** asked for without success (2 Kgs 17:4). The identity of this king is disputed. The most likely proposal is to see So not as a personal name but as the name of the political center of the 24th dynasty; in Egyptian Sau (Greek Sais).

SODOM. A legendary city in the **Jordan** Valley, destroyed by God because of its wickedness (Gen 19). In spite of the combined efforts of many researchers, Sodom has never been found and there is little chance of finding any Sodom; it is not a real city but the proverbial wicked city of ancient tales and the narrative about the destruction of Sodom is literature, not history.

SOLOMON. The second son of **David** and **Bathsheba**, King of Israel c.960-932 B.C.E. Solomon, supported by the **prophet Nathan**, the commander of the guard **Benaiah**, and his mother, became king of Israel after a tense competition with his older brother **Adonijah**, whose followers were the old trusted officers of David, **Abiatar** and **Joab** (1 Kgs 1-2). The account in the Old Testament of his reign is fairly comprehensive (1 Kgs 3-11). His building projects in **Jerusalem**, including the **palace** complex and the **temple**, get the lion's share of the Solomon narrative (1 Kgs 5-8). He called upon the support of **Hiram**, the king of **Tyre**, requesting building materials and artisans. He also needed the help of Hiram for his overseas trade projects out of **Ezion-geber**, but had to pay a heavy price for Hiram's assistance, handing over several villages in northwestern **Galilee** to Tyre.

Solomon is described as a great king receiving guests as important as the **queen of Sheba** (1 Kgs 10). He married a daughter of **Pharaoh** and received **Gezer** as a dowry. He also fortified a number of important cities of his kingdom, including Gezer, **Hazor**, and **Megiddo**. He is described as a wise and just king listening to the complaints of his subjects. At the same time, dark clouds were rising on the horizon as sections of his empire started to break away, such as **Damascus** and **Edom**. Among his adversaries, the **Ephraimite** nobleman **Jeroboam** fled for safety to Egypt. Egypt evidently played a double game supporting Solomon, on one hand, and people in opposition to his reign, on the other, apart from Jeroboam also **Hadad**, the future king of Edom. Solomon died peacefully and was buried in Jerusalem.

Historians have recently questioned the image of Solomon's time created by the historiographers of the Old Testament. Jerusalem was hardly a glorious imperial capital in the 10th century B.C.E. Archaeologists formerly believed to have discovered his **fortifications** at Gezer, Hazor, and Megiddo but these remains are now generally dated to the time of **Omri** and **Ahab**. The queen of Sheba came from a kingdom that probably did not exist in the 10th century. In short, although Solomon may have been an important figure in the development of the history of Jerusalem and **Judah**, the biblical historiographers created an image of Solomon's greatness that is probably more legendary than historical.

SOLOMON'S CHRONICLE. The Old Testament **Books of Kings** include several references to the **Chronicles of the Kings of Israel** and the **Chronicles of the Kings of Judah**. There are also occasionally references to other works of that genre. Among these one finds Solomon's Chronicles (1 Kgs 11:41).

SOUTHERN KINGDOM. In scholarly literature one of the terms used about the **Kingdom of Judah**.

STAMPS. *See* SEALS AND STAMPS.

SUCCESSION HISTORY. The story of the strife within **David's** family for the succession to the throne, spanning 2 Samuel 8 (eventually 2 Sam 7) to 1 Kings 2. It opens with the affair between

David and **Bathsheba** and adds the tragedies of **Amnon** and **Tamar**, and of **Absalom**, and ends with the debacle following **Solomon**'s ascension to the throne that led to the execution not only of a number of David's followers, but also of **Adonijah**, another son of David. The Succession History has sometimes been taken to be an eyewitness account going back to the 10th century B.C.E. In modern scholarship it is generally considered a sophisticated literary composition of a much later date.

SUCCOTH. 1. A **city** in northeastern **Egypt** and the first station of the Israelites during the **Exodus** (Exod 12:37), sometimes identified with present-day Tell el-Maskhuta c. 16 kilometers west of modern Ismailia. 2. A city at the **Jabbok** just east of the **Jordan River**, said to be founded by **Jacob** (Gen 33:17). It was part of **Gad**'s tribal territory (Josh 13:27). It is mentioned in the **Gideon** story as a place punished by Gideon (Judg 8:5-17). It is normally located at Tell Deir 'Alla.

SUSA. The capital of **Elam**, located in the northwestern part of Iran. It was sacked by **Ashurbanipal**, but rebuilt and transformed into the capital of **Persia**. The narrative about **Esther**, who as the queen of Persia saves the **Jews**, is located at Susa.

SYRIA. Since the Greek translations of the Old Testament in antiquity the common translation of the Hebrew term **Aram**. Although in evidence as early as in Herodotus's History, the term has no equivalent in the ancient Near East. In the Greek tradition, it can be used for the territory between **Egypt** and the **Euphrates** River, roughly including the modern states of Israel, Lebanon, and Syria. The origin of the term is uncertain but some scholars see it as a late Greek variant for **Assyria**.

Syria's history goes back to the dawn of history although little is known about the details before the second half of the third millennium B.C.E. **Mesopotamian** rulers occasionally boast of campaigns to Syria, but the earliest historically solid corpus of information about Syria turned up as late as the 1970s during excavations at **Ebla** c. 45 kilometers south of Aleppo. It may be that the characteristics of Syrian history were already in evidence as early as the days of Ebla, including the existence of two major centers competing for power over Syria. In the second millennium the two great powers of Syria were Aleppo, in the north, and Qatna, in the south. During the second part of the second millennium, however, foreign powers took over the control of Syria, at first the **Egyptians**, and then the **Hittites**. After the breakdown of imperial control, Syria regained its political independence, and two new Syrian states appeared competing for control: in the north **Charchemish**, and in the south **Damascus**. This independence was short-lived as Syria in the eighth century B.C.E. succumbed to attacks from **Assyria**, followed by **Babylonia**, and again from **Persia**. After Alexander's conquest, Syria became part of the Seleucid Empire, and when this was destroyed by the Romans, the Roman Empire.

SYRO-EPHRAIMITE WAR. The current name of the war between the **Kingdom of Israel** and **Tiglath-pileser III** between 734 and 732 B.C.E. During this war, **Damascus** and Israel united against the **Assyrians**. They appealed to **Ahaz** of **Judah** for his support, but he refused and called in the Assyrians to help him against his northern neighbor. The war ended in 732 B.C.E. with the destruction of Damascus and the establishment of a series of Assyrian provinces in northern **Palestine** and **Transjordan**.

- T -

TAANACH. A city located at Tel Taanech c. 8 kilometers southeast of **Megiddo**. The city was conquered by **Joshua** (Josh 12:21) although another source says that the Israelites were not able to conquer the city (Judg 1:27). According to the **Song of Deborah**, Taanach was close to the scene of the battle between **Barak** and **Sisera** (Judg 5:19). The city was the possession of **Manasseh**, although it was located within the tribal territory of **Issachar** and **Asher** (Josh 17:11). In **Solomon**'s time it became part of his fifth district (1 Kgs 4:12). Taanach was excavated at the beginning of the 20th century, and again in the 1960s and 1980s. It was founded in the Early Bronze Age, which represented the heyday of the settlement. It was partially rebuilt during the Middle Bronze Age, and appears in Thutmose III's war report from the battle of **Megiddo**

(15th century). One **Amarna Letter** comes from Taanach, although several other cuneiform texts have been found here relevant to the history of the city. The Iron Age city was destroyed by **Shishak** and included in his list of conquered cities.

TABAL. (Meaning "no good," a pejorative rendering of the proper name Tabel, "God is good"). He appears in connection with the **Syro-Ephraimite War** as the father of an otherwise unknown contender for the throne of **Judah** supported by **Israel** and **Damascus** (Isa 7:6).

TABEL. A **Persian** official residing at **Samaria** who in the time of **Artaxerxes II** opposed the rebuilding of **Jerusalem** (Ezra 4:7).

TABOR. A mountain in the eastern part of the **Jezreel Valley** c. 600 meters high, on the border between the **tribes of Naphtali, Zebulon,** and **Issachar,** and the rallying point of the Israelite forces before the battle against **Sisera** (Judg 4). It may have served as a local shrine for the tribes of northern Israel.

TADMOR. The pre-Hellenistic name of the great oasis of Palmyra in the Syrian desert. The name of Tadmor also occurs in **Assyrian inscriptions** of the eighth century B.C.E.

TAHPANHES. An Egyptian city in the eastern part of the delta of the Nile, located at present Tell Defunna (recalling its Greek name of Daphne). After the murder of **Gedaliah,** a group of Judeans looked for a safe place in Tahpanhes (Jer 43:7), and also **Jeremiah** joined the refugees, although very much against his own will (Jer 43:8; 46:14). Excavations have unearthed an elaborate **fortress** from the time of Psamtik I (664-610 B.c.E.).

TAMAR. (Meaning "palm tree"). The name of four women in the Old Testament. The more important are 1. Tamar, the daughter-in-law of **Jacob's** son **Judah** (Gen 38). When her husband died without an heir, Tamar seduced her father-in-law, who had denied her offspring with a second son of his. She became pregnant by Judah and was the mother of the twins Pharez and Zerah. The genealogy of the family of **David** reckons Pharez as an ancestor of the royal house of **Judah**. 2. The daughter of David who was raped by her half brother **Amnon**. Another brother, **Absalom**, killed Amnon in revenge for the wrong done to his sister (2 Sam 13).

TARSHISH. One of the sons of **Javan** (Gen 10:4). Because Javan represents the **Greeks**, the location of Tarshish has been sought in the Mediterranean where several candidates ranging from the eastern Mediterranean to Spain, including Carthage, have been proposed. Ships heading for Tarshish were also running out of **Eziongeber**. Therefore a Tarshish-ship may mean a ship able to travel on the open sea.

TARTAN. An **Assyrian** officer who joined **Rab-shakeh** on his mission to **Jerusalem** (2 Kgs 18:17). The name is a title meaning perhaps "commander in chief" of the Assyrian army.

TECHOA. A small town of **Judah** on the fringe of the Desert of Judah, and the home of the **prophet Amos**. It is located at Khirbet Tekua a few kilometers southeast of **Bethlehem**.

TEL-ABIB. Place of settlement of exiled Judeans. The **prophet Ezekiel** belonged to this group (Ezek 3:15). It was located on the bank of the canal of Chebar, Akkadian Kabaru, running through the ancient city of Nippur in central **Mesopotamia**. Mesopotamian documents from the fifth century testify to the presence of people carrying West-Semitic names living in this region.

TEMA. The son of **Ishmael** (Gen 25:15), and an oasis and city in northern **Arabia**. It was an important center of trade and caravaneering. For a period of ten years, it was also the residence of King **Nabonidus** of Babylonia (*see* **Assyria and Babylonia**).

TEMAN. The name of a region, probably the northern part of **Edom** (see also Amos 1:12). In other references Teman is synonymous with Edom. The name means "south."

TEMPLE, TEMPLE OF JERUSALEM. In ancient societies, temples functioned as the center of **religion**. However, they were much more than that. Often they had—because there was no division between the sacral and secular world—decisive political as well as economic importance. The Old Testament is well aware of this significance of the temple. Thus, before the monarchy, the army of Israel assembled at temples, for example, at **Mizpah** or **Bethel** (Judg 20:1.18). King **David's** first act as king of **Jerusalem** was to bring back the old religious shrine, the **Ark of the Covenant**, to his newly acquired capital and install it in the sanctuary which he put up there at **Arauna's threshing ground** (2 Sam 6). He did not manage to erect a proper temple—that was a task left to his son **Solomon**, who according to the biblical tradition built an elaborate temple located next to his royal **palace**. Following this pattern of emphasizing the importance of temple construction, Jeroboam established as one of his first deeds as king over Israel royal sanctuaries at Bethel and **Dan**, officially to prevent his subjects from going to Jerusalem to worship the Lord and thus turn away from his rule (1 Kgs 12). When **Josiah**, the king of **Judah**, regained control over parts of the territory belonging to the former **Kingdom of Israel**, he demolished the temple at Bethel, and in this way showed that the country had a new master and a new center of its religion (2 Kgs 23:15-18).

A by-product of this political interest in the temple was the repeated concern of kings for rebuilding and repairing the temple. In the **Deuteronomistic History**, a king of Judah is measured according to his benevolent acts in favor of the temple. Thus, among the kings praised by the deuteronomistic (*see* **Deuteronomism**) composer of the **Books of Kings**, David ordered the temple built, and Solomon carried out his order. **Asa** cared for the temple and reformed its cult (1 Kgs 15:9-15), **Joash** repaired the temple, **Hezekiah** reformed the cult (2 Kgs 18:4-5)—according to **Chronicles** he also celebrated Passover in the temple (2 Chron 31)—and Josiah both repaired the temple and reformed its cult (2 Kgs 22-23).

The economic importance of the temple is evident. Thus the kings of Judah repeatedly had to strip the temple of its treasures to pay off foreign invaders, for example, when **Pharaoh Shishak** attacked Jerusalem after Solomon's death (1 Kgs 14:25-26) and again when **Hazael** prepared for an attack on Jerusalem (2 Kgs 12:18-19) while **Jehoash** of Israel, after having defeated **Amaziah** of Judah at **Beth-Shemesh**, moved on to Jerusalem and looted the temple treasuries (2 Kgs 14:8-14). In 587 B.C.E., **Nebuchadnezzar** went even further by not only plundering the temple of Jerusalem, but also burning it down to the ground—he had already plundered it ten years before when for the first time he conquered Jerusalem (2 Kgs 24:13). After the **Babylonian Exile**, in a society without a king, the temple of Jerusalem gained even more importance and the **high priest** became one of the most, if not the most, influential person of the country. Some scholars have described the post-exilic society as a "temple burger society," or a "theocracy," where the high priest of Yahweh at Jerusalem was the real master of Judea.

THEBEZ. The city where **Abimelech** met his death at the hand of a woman (Judg 9:50). It is identified with modern Tubas c. 20 kilometers northeast of **Shechem**.

TIBNI. The son of Ginath who was chosen king by half of **Israel** in opposition to **Omri**. Tibni lost and was killed (1 Kgs 17:21-22). It has sometimes been conjectured that Tibni represented old Israelite families who opposed Omri's rule, Omri being a soldier of foreign (probably **Arab**) origins.

TIDAL. The king of Goyim, one of the four great kings who were defeated by **Abraham** in the Valley of **Siddim** (Gen 14). Often identified with the **Hittite** royal name of Tudhaliya.

TIGLATH-PILESER III. King of **Assyria** 744-727 B.C.E. and the real creator of the Neo-Assyrian Empire, who changed the direction of Assyrian expansionist policies from occasional campaigns into a calculated campaign of conquest and reorganization of foreign countries, including the establishment of Assyrian provinces and large-scale **deportations**. He began to put pressure on **Syria** and **Palestine** after having subdued Urartu (Ararat) in Asia Minor in 743 B.C.E. Already in 738 B.C.E. he received tribute from **Menahem** of Israel. Between 734 and 733 B.C.E. he was confronted by a coalition of Syrian and Palestinian powers including **Damascus** and **Israel**. After an abortive attempt in 733 B.C.E. he conquered Damascus in 732 B.C.E., and forcibly reduced the Kingdom of Israel into a city-state of **Samaria** (*see* **Syro-Ephraimite War**). He ended his career by settling issues in Babylonia, which was ruled by an Assyrian vice king.

TIGRIS. One of the two great rivers that runs through **Mesopotamia** (*see also* **Euphrates**). It runs to the east of the Euphrates, from southeastern Turkey to the Persian Gulf. Although in many respects a more imposing and dangerous river than the Euphrates, the Tigris in the mind of the people of **Syria** never obtained the position as the great border to the east that was hold by the Euphrates. Along its upper course, the great cities of **Assyria** were located, including Ashur and **Nineveh.** Tigris is included among the four rivers of the world that take their offspring in Paradise (Gen 2:10-14).

TIMNA'. Often associated in popular literature with King **Solomon's** mines, although nothing indicates that any king of **Israel** was active mining at Timna' in the 10th century, the date usually associated with **David** and Solomon. Timna' is located c. 30 kilometers north of modern Elath on the Gulf of Aqaba. The Timna' area provides plenty of opportunities for copper mining, and such activity is in evidence from the Chalcolithic period to the Roman period, although a gap is conspicuous in the Late Bronze and Early Iron Age.

TIMNATH-SERAH (VARIANT: TIMNATH-HERES). A place in **Ephraim** where **Joshua** was buried (Josh 24:30; Judg 2:9). It has been proposed that Timnath-Serah is located at Khirbet Tibnah c. 24 kilometers southwest of **Shechem.**

TIRHARKAH (TAHARQA). The fourth **Pharaoh** of the Nubian 25th dynasty, king of **Egypt** 690-664 B.C.E. According to 2 Kings, Tirharkah, the king of **Cush** (that is, Nubia), involved Egypt in the events of the year 701 B.C.E., when **Sennacherib** led his victorious army to the gates of **Jerusalem** (2 Kgs 19:9). Sennacherib mentions the episode in his **annals** and recounts how his army destroyed the Egyptian force at the battle of Eltekeh in **Palestine.** Since Tirharkah only assumed kingship more than a decade after the battle of Eltekeh, it has been assumed that the Old Testament historiographer made a mistake. Otherwise, Tirharkah may have acted as the general of his predecessor Shebitqo. At the end of his reign, Tirharqa was forced out of Egypt by **Assyrian** armies.

TIRZAH. A city of **Manasseh,** and the third capital of **Jeroboam I** (1 Kgs 12:25). It was the capital of the **Kingdom of Israel** until the time of **Omri**, who moved the capital to **Samaria**. Tirzah is located at Tell el-Far'ah some 12 kilometers northeast of Nablus. It was excavated in the 1950s and traces of settlements were unearthed reaching back into the Chalcolitic period. In the Early Bronze Age a fortified **city** existed here. It was rebuilt in the Middle Bronze Age but was destroyed in the 16th century B.C.E. and not rebuilt as a city before the Iron Age. The city may have experienced a setback after it lost its status as capital, although the evidence is inconclusive. It was destroyed by the **Assyrians** in 722 B.C.E. and never rebuilt.

TOBIAH THE AMMONITE (*see* **Ammon, Ammonites**). Together with **Sanballat the Horonite**, and **Geshem** the Arab, a fierce opponent of **Nehemiah's** restoration projects in **Jerusalem**. From the **Book of Nehemiah** it becomes clear how Tobiah, although a foreigner, through family connections had created a network that included large sections of the leading Judeans. The family of the Tobiads of the third century B.C.E. that resided in **Transjordan** may be the descendants of this Tobiah.

TOLA. A **judge** in **Israel** who was in office for 23 years. His tribal affiliation was **Issachar** (Judg 10:1-2). He belongs to the list of five judges (Judg 10:1-5; 12:8-15) who together judged Israel for 70 years but left no records about their exploits.

TRANSJORDAN. In scholarly literature dealing with the history of ancient **Israel**, Transjordan is a convenient term used about the territories east of the **Jordan River**. In this way it coincides with the territory of the modern Kingdom of Jordan, but it was never an independent political unity in ancient times.

TRIBAL LEAGUE. The Old Testament describes **Israel** before the introduction of the Hebrew monarchy as organized in a system of twelve **tribes** (*see* **Twelve tribe system**). Based on this information, biblical scholars proposed the idea of a sacral Israelite tribal league organized along the lines of the Greek **Amphictyony**, a religious as well as political defensive alliance that should protect the Israelite tribes against their enemies in the early days of Israelite presence in **Canaan**. Although the theory of the Israelite tribal league found almost universal acceptance when it was proposed, later historical studies have led to its total dismissal in modern biblical scholarship.

TRIBAL WARS. In the **Period of the Judges,** war among the Israelite **tribes** was not unheard of. Thus **Jephthah** from **Gilead** led the people of Gilead against the **Ephraimites** (Judg 12:1-6). The misbehavior of the inhabitants of **Gibeah** led to a war between **Benjamin** and the other Israelite tribes (Judg 19-21). During this war the tribe of Benjamin was almost wiped out. The narratives in the Old Testament about tribal wars are strongly colored by the ideology of the **twelve tribe system** of Israel.

TRIBE, TRIBAL SOCIETY. Tribe is a sociological term that is often used to characterize the organization of traditional people living in societies without a strong centralized government. Tribe is a most elusive term that covers a plethora of variations of social organization, including so-called "acephalous" societies, that is, societies without official leaders sometimes connected with an egalitarian ideology ("we are all brothers and the sons of one and the same father") as well as organizations ruled by chieftains and hierarchically structured. The Old Testament presents early Israel as organized in twelve tribes: **Reuben, Simeon, Gad, Ephraim, Manasseh** (variation: **Joseph** substitutes Ephraim and Manasseh), **Benjamin, Judah, Issachar, Zebulon, Dan, Asher,** and **Naphtali,** although the Old Testament knows of many more tribal names, like **Machir** and **Caleb.** The individual organization of each of these tribes is unknown.

TWELVE TRIBE SYSTEM. The Old Testament distributes the Israelites among twelve tribes, the descendants of **Jacob's** twelve sons. Basically the system appears in two different shapes. The first system includes the tribes of **Reuben, Simeon, Levi, Judah, Zebulon, Issachar, Dan, Gad, Asher, Naphtali, Joseph,** and **Benjamin** (e.g., in Gen 49). In the second system Levi, the tribe of **priests,** has been substituted by **Ephraim** and **Manasseh.** Although some scholars have speculated about the historical changes that may have brought about the change of system, it is more likely that the difference is mainly a literary one, centering on the narrative in the

Book of Exodus about the **Levites** being installed as priests in **Israel** and making them different from the other tribes of Israel (Exod 32:29). The **Blessing of Jacob** (Gen 49) and the **Blessing of Moses** (Deut 33) include sayings about the individual tribes that have been taken as very old characterizations of the twelve tribes of Israel. However, the Song of **Deborah** leaves the impression that the twelve tribe system is schematic and of limited historical value, as the Israelite tribes included more tribes than the official twelve.

TYRE. An important **Phoenician city.** Originally an island, it changed into a peninsula when Alexander the Great built a dam from the coast that reached Tyre. Tyre has a history that reaches back into the Early Bronze Age. In the Middle Bronze Age it was a city of importance mentioned in the Egyptian **Execration Texts.** It was still an important city during the Late Bronze Age but rose to prominence among the Phoenician cities in the beginning of the first millennium B.C.E., when it subdued **Sidon** to the north. Beginning in the 10th century B.C.E., Tyre became the mother city of an extended network of Phoenician colonies all over the Mediterranean, including as its most important colony Carthage, in modern Tunisia. In the Old Testament, Tyre was the ally of **Solomon** but also a competitor for the control of the coastal region north of the **Carmel** ridge. The relations between Tyre and **Israel** were strengthened in the time of the dynasty of **Omri** when **Jezebel**, the daughter of the Tyrian king **Ethbaal** or Ittobaal, married **Ahab** of Israel. In later biblical traditions Tyre became the epitome of arrogance and its fall was predicted although not accomplished before the days of Alexander the Great.

- U -

UGARIT. Although never mentioned in the Old Testament, Ugarit has become one of the most important places in the ancient Near East for the understanding of ancient **Israel**, its society, and culture since the discovery of extensive written sources at Ugarit after 1929 when modern excavations began on Tell Ras Shamra, a few kilometers from modern Latakiye in **Syria.** Historically speaking, in the Late Bronze Age Ugarit was a flourishing Syrian seaport that was destroyed together with many other sites at the beginning of the 12th century B.C.E., perhaps in connection with the arrival of the **Sea Peoples**. The extensive archives from Ugarit are written in a peculiar cuneiform alphabet very different from Akkadian cuneiform but related to later **Phoenician** script. Apart from ample evidence about administration, economy, and foreign relations, they include the only epic texts that have so far survived from ancient Syria and **Palestine**. These texts have been of the outmost importance for more than 70 years for the study of ancient Israelite religion.

UNITED MONARCHY. In scholarly literature often used as the name of the kingdom of **David** and **Solomon** (*see* also **Empire of David and Solomon**).

UR OF THE CHALDAEANS. A city in lower **Mesopotamia**, identical with modern Tell Muqqajjar. Its history of settlement goes back to the fifth millennium B.C.E., although its period of greatness belonged to the late fourth millennium and most of the third millennium B.C.E. Although it lost its political importance in the second millennium and never regained it, Ur was considered a classical center of Mesopotamian culture, and a natural place to look for the original home of the Old Testament family of **patriarchs** (Gen 11:28.31). The addition of "**Chaldaea**" in the Old Testament to the name of Ur reflects its political situation after its territory became part of Chaldaea, no earlier than 1000-900 B.C.E.

URIAH. A **Hittite**. One of **David's heroes** (2 Sam 23:39) and the husband of **Bathsheba**, who denied that he was part of David's scheming when the king had made Bathsheba pregnant. As a consequence, David ordered **Joab** to make sure that Uriah was killed on the battlefield. Joab complied with his master's wish and placed Uriah in an exposed position where he was killed (2 Sam 11).

UZZIAH. King of **Judah** (769-741 B.C.E.) who reinforced **Eloth**, after his father **Amaziah** had conquered it from **Edom** (2 Kgs 14:21). In his later years he contracted leprosy and his son **Jotham** ruled in his name (2 Kgs 15:1-7). The **Books of Chronicles** add considerably to the Uzziah tradition by having him also defeating **Philistine** cities, and **Arab** tribes of the desert, and making **Moab** and **Ammon** tributaries of the **Kingdom of Judah.**

- W -

WARFARE. In the Old Testament war was considered inseparable from human life. Wars were always considered holy in one way or another. Whenever **Israel** fought a righteous battle, it was not Israel which fought but the God of Israel. The victory hymn of **Deborah** (*see* **Deborah, Song of**) provides a fine example of this ideology. Also the story in 1 Samuel (*see* **Samuel, Books of**) about the **Ark of the Covenant** that was carried into battle against the **Philistines** relates to this idea of the holy war. On the reverse side, when a battle was lost, it was never the God of Israel who lost it. On such occasions Israel and its kings had transgressed the will of the Lord and were accordingly punished by defeat. Wars were cruel, including mass executions of prisoners and the total extermination of the enemy, men, women, and children. The Hebrew technical term was *herem,* the ban of God imposed on the enemy, spelling disaster for Israel's vanquished foes. Thus, when **Joshua** conquered **Jericho** and **Ai,** he placed a ban on these sites. No one escaped their fate, except in Jericho's case: the prostitute **Rahab** who had assisted Joshua's spies (Joshua 2; 6).

Rather little is known about the development of warfare in ancient Israel. In Late Bronze Age western Asia, including **Palestine,** war was the business of professional, mostly relatively small armies. The main body of the army consisted of infantry, assisted by a corps of chariots. Only the great powers of that time, such as **Egypt** or the **Hittite** Empire, disposed over larger and more specialized military organizations, including light as well as heavy infantry, and an extensive amount of chariots driven by a very specialized elite corps of charioteers. In the Early Iron Age, a rabble of loosely organized tribesmen took over from the professionals, without any indication of specialization into different types of weaponry.

During the time of the **Hebrew kingdom**, the specialized organization reappeared as seen, for example, in the description of **Solomon**'s military system (1 Kgs 9:15-23). However, the real change in warfare came with the arrival of the heavy armored **Assyrian** armies in the Levant in the ninth-eighth centuries. The Assyrians managed to create the most specialized military body the ancient Near East had ever seen, including light and heavy infantry, specialist corps of archers, stone slingers, horsemen, and charioteers. The Assyrians were also innovative when it came to the construction of siege machinery, although they never achieved the professionalism in the procurement of such items as the later Hellenistic and Roman armies. Thus, **Nebuchadnezzar**, the king of **Babylon**, laid siege to **Tyre** for 25 years without any success at all. New developments only occurred in the fifth century when **Persian** local rulers began to employ **Greek** hoplites as mercenaries making use of their superior training and morale. The difference between the by now traditional Near Eastern military organization and the Greco-Roman military was exhibited when Alexander the Great crushed the Persian Empire within a couple of years and after that when Rome repeated his success, this time defeating the kingdoms established by Alexander's generals.

The Old Testament says close to nothing about warfare at sea. The kingdoms of Israel and **Judah** did not possess a navy. When the imperial powers of Assyria or Persia planned campaigns at sea, they turned to the **Phoenicians** for help.

WATER SYSTEMS. *See* FORTIFICATIONS.

- X -

XERXES I. King of **Persia** 486-465 B.C.E. In Greek tradition Xerxes was the tragic hero who sent his army and navy to destruction during the Persian Wars (480-479 B.C.E.). He is also the tragic hero of Aeschylus's tragedy *Persai*. The Old Testament renders Xerxes' name as **Ahasuerus**. In the **Book of Daniel**, without any historical justification, he is reckoned the father of **Darius** I (Dan 9:1). He is the Persian king of the Book of **Esther**. A second Xerxes was killed a few months after having ascended to the throne (423 B.C.E.), but he is not mentioned by the Old Testament.

- Z -

ZADOK. The son of **Ahitub** and the father of **Ahimaaz** and one of **David's** leading **priests**. He remained loyal to David during **Absalom's** rebellion but sided with **Solomon** against **Adonijah**. When his colleague and competitor **Abiatar** was banished to **Anatot**, Zadok inherited his office and position. Zadok served as the apical ancestor of the line of the **high priests** of Jerusalem. In post-exilic times his descendants, the Zadokite priestly family, became by far the most powerful clerical group at the **temple of Jerusalem**. It is sometimes suggested that Zadok was in reality related to the pre-Israelite royal house of **Jerusalem**. His name appears as part of the names of **Canaanite** kings related to Jerusalem or **Salem**, such as **Melchizedek** (Gen 14:18) and **Adoni-zedek** (Josh 10:1). By sparing an offspring of the former royal house, David was able to maintain good relations between his own Israelites and the **Jebusites**, the former inhabitants of Jerusalem, or so it is assumed.

ZEBAH AND ZALMUNNA. Two kings of the **Midianites**. When he defeated the Midianites, **Gideon** captured the two Midianite princes and had them executed because they had killed his brothers at **Tabor** (Judg 8).

ZEBUL. (Meaning "prince"). A champion of **Abimelech** living in **Shechem**. When **Gaal** raised the population of Shechem against Abimelech, Zebul reported the rebellion to Abimelech who returned to Shechem and put an end to it (Judg 9).

ZEBULON. A son of **Jacob** and **Leah**, and the eponymous ancestor of the **tribe** of Zebulon. The Old Testament mostly has positive things to say about Zebulon, although it has little in the way of solid information to present. The tribe of Zebulon is said to live close to **Sidon** in **Phoenicia**. Its territory was in southwestern **Galilee**. The Zebulonites were active defending their territory against the **Canaanites** (Judg 4-5) and the **Midianites** (Judg 6). The territory was lost to **Assyria** after 732 B.C.E.

ZECHARIAH. (Meaning "Yahweh remembers"). King of **Israel** c. 753-752 B.C.E. Although the son of **Jeroboam II**, and ruling in a seemingly prosperous time for the kingdom of Israel in the mid eighth century B.C.E., Zechariah was murdered by **Shallum** after a reign of only six months (2 Kgs 15:8-12).

ZECHARIAH, PROPHET. According to the witness of the prophetic book carrying the **prophet's** name, Zechariah functioned as a prophet in the years following the **Babylonian exile**. Some of his prophecies relate to the activity of **Zerubbabel** and the **high priest Joshua** and the rebuilding of the **temple of Jerusalem**.

ZEDEKIAH. (Meaning "Yahweh is righteous"). King of **Judah** (597-587 B.C.E.), son of **Josiah**. He succeeded his nephew King **Jehoiachin** in 597 B.C.E. when **Nebuchadnezzar** removed the royal family of Judah and sent it into exile in **Babylon**. As his personal choice, Nebuchadnezzar chose Zedekiah to be the successor to the throne of Judah and changed his name from Mattaniah to Zedekiah (2 Kgs 24:17). Probably inspired by the visit of **Pharaoh** Apries (Wahibre) to **Palestine** in 589 B.C.E., Zedekiah revolted against his Babylonian master. Nebuchadnezzar reacted immediately. Shortly thereafter his army laid siege to **Jerusalem**, and after 18 months, the city fell. Zedekiah was caught and brought to **Riblah** and his children executed. Blinded, Zedekiah was carried away to Babylon. Nothing more is known about his fate.

ZERUBBABEL. A Babylonian Jew who returned to **Jerusalem** in 538 B.C.E. after the exile (Ezra 2:2). Here he functioned as **Persian** governor and was active in the rebuilding of the **temple of Jerusalem**. The name means "the seed of Babylon," but he was of royal Judean descent, the son of Shealtiel, who was son of **Jehoiachim**, king of **Judah**, who was carried into exile in 597 B.C.E. He is sometimes without proper evidence identified with **Sheshbazzar** (cf. Ezra 1:8) who carried the same title as Zerubbabel. The biblical sources have nothing to say about Zerubbabel's fate after c. 520 B.C.E., a fact that has led scholars to propose all sorts of mishaps,

for example, that he was arrested and executed by his Persian overlords.

ZERUIAH'S SONS. Three mighty warriors of the family of **David**,
namely **Joab**, **Abishai**, and **Asahel**. Their mother was Zeruiah, the
sister of David (1 Chron 2:16).

ZIBA. A servant of **Saul**, entrusted by **David** with the administration
of **Mephiboshet's** property. By betraying Mephibosphet, Ziba acquired his possessions but had to give half of them back, when Mephiboshet defended himself in front of the king (2 Sam 9; 16:1-4;
19:24-30).

ZIGGURAT. *See* BABEL, TOWER.

ZIGLAG. A city of the **Negeb** in the tribal territory of **Judah** (Josh
15:31). Ziglag was the home base of **David** when he was in **Philistine** service. It was his personal fief granted him by **Achish**, the
king of **Gath**. As such it remained in the possession of the king of
Judah after David's time (1 Sam 27:6). Its present location has not
been firmly established. Most scholars prefer Tell esh-Shari'a between **Beersheba** and **Gaza**, where excavations made between
1972 and 1982 discovered a city with remains going back to the
Chalcolithic period, but also with ample remains from the Bronze
and Iron Age.

ZIMRI. Zimri, a commander in the army of **Baasha**, who slew **Elah**,
his master, exterminated the house of Baasha, and made himself
king of **Israel** (886 B.C.E.). After a reign of only seven days, Zimri
committed suicide when **Omri** laid siege to the **city** of **Tirzah**.

ZION. Another name for **Jerusalem** or a district of the **city**, probably
originally a **fortress** within the city. Today, the name is linked with
the southwestern hill of Jerusalem, including the traditional place
of **David's** grave.

ZIPH. A city in the territory of **Judah**, located at Tell Zif c. 8 kilometers southeast of **Hebron**. It served as a refuge for **David** fleeing

from **Saul**, but David was betrayed by the citizens of Ziph (1 Sam 23:14-24; 26:1). It was fortified by **Rehoboam** (2 Chron 11:8).

ZIPPORAH. Moses' **Midianite** wife, the daughter of **Jethro (Reuel)**, the priest of **Midian**, who saved her husband in the enigmatic text about the blood-bridegroom (Exod 4:24-26).

ZOBAH. *See* ARAM-ZOBAH.

Bibliography

Contents

Introduction

It is characteristic of the study of ancient Israel that much of the discussion takes place in connection with commentaries on the biblical books of the Old Testament. A list of relevant commentaries for all thirty-four volumes of the Old Testament would create a lack of balance of this bibliography and only partly be relevant to the lexicon presented here. Information about the biblical books and sources can be found in the general studies listed below. Otherwise, the bibliography puts special weight on monographs, including a number of seminal articles in scholarly journals listed here. As a general rule, the selection of books and articles is arbitrary and to a certain degree reflecting the position of the author of this dictionary, but I have tried to present a mixture of mainstream literature, conservative contributions, and contributions from the so-called school of minimalism at the forefront of the present discussion among biblical scholars.

Dictionaries

Freedman, David N., ed. *The Anchor Bible Dictionary*, 1-6. New York: Doubleday, 1992.
Görg, Manfred, and Bernhard Lang, eds. *Neues Bibel-Lexikon*, I-III. Zürich: Benziger, 1991-2001.

Journals

Biblica, Rome: Pontifical Biblical Institute.
Biblical Archaeologist (now continued as Near Eastern Archaeology).
Biblical Archaeologist Review. Washington, D.C.: The Biblical Archaeology Society.
Bulletin of the American Schools of Oriental Research. Winona Lake, Ind.: Eisenbrauns.
Hadashot Arkheologiyot: Excavations and Surveys in Israel. Jerusalem: Israel Exploration Society.

Israel Exploration Journal. Jerusalem: Israel Exploration Society.

Journal for the Study of the Old Testament. Sheffield: Sheffield Academic Press.

Journal of Biblical Literature. Atlanta: Society of Biblical Literature.

Journal of Near Eastern Studies. Chicago: University of Chicago Press.

Levant. London: Council for British Research in the Levant.

Near Eastern Archaeology. Boston: The American Schools of Oriental Research.

Palestine Exploration Quarterly. London: The Palestine Exploration Fund.

Revue Biblique. Paris: J. Gabalda.

Scandinavian Journal of the Old Testament. Oslo: Taylor & Francis.

Tel Aviv. Tel Aviv: University of Tel Aviv: Sonia and Marco Nadler Institute of Archaeology.

Vetus Testamentum. Leiden: E. J. Brill.

Zeitschrift des Deutschen Palästina-Vereins. Wiesbaden: Otto Harrassowitz.

Zeitschrift für die alttestamentliche Wissenschaft. Berlin: Walter de Gruyter.

General Studies

Baker, David W., and Bill T. Arnold. *The Face of Old Testament Studies: A Survey of Contemporary Approaches.* Grand Rapids, Mich.: Baker Books, 1999.

Clements, R. E., ed. *The World of Ancient Israel: Sociological, Anthropological and Political Perspectives.* Cambridge: Cambridge University Press, 1989.

Kee, Howard C., John Rogerson, Eric M. Meyers, and Anthony J. Saldarini, eds. *The Cambridge Companion to the Bible.* Cambridge: Cambridge University Press, 1997.

Rogerson, John, and Philip Davies. *The Old Testament World.* Cambridge: Cambridge University Press, 1989.

Sources

Collections of Sources

Davies, G. I. *Ancient Hebrew Inscriptions: Corpus and Concordance*. Cambridge: Cambridge University Press, 1991.

Donner, Herbert, and Walter Röllig. *Kanaanäische und aramäische Inschriften. Mit einem Beitrag von O. Rössler*. I-III. Wiesbaden: Otto Harrassowitz, 1962-1964.

Gibson, John C. L. *Textbook of Syrian Semitic Inscriptions*, I-III. Oxford: Clarendon Press, 1971-1982.

Gogel, Sandra Landis. *A Grammar of Epigraphic Hebrew*. SBL Resources for Biblical Study, 23. Atlanta: Scholars Press, 1998.

Hallo, William W., and K. Lawson Younger, eds. *The Context of Scripture*, I-III. Leiden: E. J. Brill, 1997-2002.

Kaiser, Otto, ed. *Texte aus dem Umwelt des Alten Testaments*, I-III & Ergänzungsband. Gütersloh: Gütersloher Verlagshaus, 1981-2001.

Lemaire, André. *Inscriptions hébraïques*, I. *Les ostraca*. Littérature anciennes du Proche-Orient, 9. Paris: Éditions du Cerf, 1977.

Parker, Simon B., ed. *Society of Biblical Literature Writings from the Ancient World*:
1: Wente, Edward. *Letters from Ancient Egypt*. Atlanta: Scholars Press, 1990.
2: Hoffner, Harry A. *Hittite Myths*. Atlanta: Scholars Press, 1990.
3: Michalowski, Piotr. *Letters from Early Mesopotamia*. Atlanta: Scholars Press, 1993.
6: Roth, Martha T. *Law Collections from Mesopotamia and Asia Minor*. 2nd ed. Atlanta: Scholars Press, 1997.
7: Beckman, Gary. *Hittite Diplomatic Texts*. 2nd ed. Atlanta: Scholars Press, 1999.
9: Parker, Simon B. *Ugaritic Narrative Poetry*. Atlanta: Scholars Press, 1997.

Pritchard, James B. *Ancient Near Eastern Texts Relating to the Old Testament*. 3rd ed. With a Supplement. Princeton, N.J.: Princeton, University Press, 1969.

Renz, Johannes. *Handbuch der Althebräischen Epigraphik*, I, II/1, III. Darmstadt: Wissenschaftliche Buchgesellschaft, 1995.

Josephus

The Jewish Antiquities, I-XX, in 10 volumes, translated by H. St. J. Thackeray, Ralph Marcus, Allen Wikgren, and L. H. Feldman. The Loeb Classical Library. Cambridge, Mass.: Harvard University Press; London: Heineman, 1930-1965.

Amarna Letters

Knudtzon, J. A. *Die El-Amarna Tafeln mit Einleitung und Erläuterungen herausgegeben. Anmerkungen und Register bearbeitet von Otto Weber und Erich Ebeling.* Vorderasiatische Bibliothek. Neudruck der Ausgabe 1915. Aalen: Otto Zeller Verlagsbuchhandlung, 1964.

Liverani, Mario. *Le lettere di el-Amarna.* Testi del Vicino oriente antico, 3:1-2. Brescia, 1998.

Moran, William L. *The Amarna Letters.* Baltimore: Johns Hopkins University Press, 1992.

———. *Amarna Studies. Collected Writings.* Edited by John Huehnergaard and Shlomo Izre'el. Harvard Semitic Museum Publications, 54. Winona Lake, Ind.: Eisenbrauns, 2003.

Rainey, Anson F. *El Amarna Tablets 359-379. Supplement to J. A. Knudtzon, Die El-Amarna Tafeln.* Alter Orient Und Altes Testament, 8. Kevalaer and Neukirchen-Vluyn: Verlag Butzon & Bercker and Neukirchener Verlag des Erziehungsvereins, 1970.

Merenptah Inscription

Ahlström, Gösta W., and Diana Edelman. "Merneptah's Israel." *Journal of Near Eastern Studies* 44 (1985): 59-61.

Engel, Hartmut. "Die Siegesstele des Mernephtah." *Biblica* 60 (1979): 373-399.

Fecht, G. "Die Israelstele: Gestalt und Aussage." In Manfred Görg, ed. *Fontes atque pontes: Eine Festgabe für Hellmut Brunner.* Wiesbaden: Otto Harrassowitz, 1983:106-38.

Hjelm, Ingrid, and Thomas L. Thompson. "The Victory Song of Merneptah, Israel and the People of Palestine." *Journal for the Study of the Old Testament* 27 (2002): 3-18.

Hornung, Erik. "Die Israelstele des Mernephtah." In Manfred Görg, ed. *Fontes atque pontes: Eine Festgabe für Hellmut Brunner.* Wiesbaden: Otto Harrassowitz, 1983: 224-33.

Singer, Itamar. "Merneptah's Campaign to Canaan and the Egyptian Occupation of the Southern Coastal Plain in the Ramesside Period." *Bulletin of the American Schools of Oriental Research* 269 (1988): 1-10.

Spiegelberg, W. "Der Siegeshymnus des merneptah auf der Flinders Petrie-Stele." *Zeitschrift für ägyptische Sprache und Altertumskunde* 34 (1896): 1-25.

Stager, Lawrence E. "Merneptah, Israel and Sea Peoples: New Light on an Old Relief." *Eretz-Israel* 18 (1985): 59-64.

Mesha Inscription

Dearman, J. Andrew. *Studies in the Mesha Inscription and Moab.* Atlanta: Scholars Press, 1989.

Na'aman, Nadab. "King Mesha and the Foundation of the Moabite Monarchy." *Israel Exploration Journal* 47 (1997): 83-92.

Smelik, K. A. "King Mesha's Inscription: Between History and Fiction." In *Converting the Past: Studies in Ancient Israelite and Moabite Historiography.* Oudtestamentische Studien, 28. Leiden: E. J. Brill, 1992: 59-92.

Thompson, Thomas L. "A Testimony of the Good King: Reading the Mesha Stele." In L. L. Grabbe, ed. *European Seminar in Historical Method*, 5. Sheffield: Sheffield Academic Press (forthcoming).

Dan Inscription

Athas, George. *The Tell Dan Inscription: A Reappraisal and a New Interpretation.* Journal for the Study of the Old Testament Supplement Series, 360/Copenhagen International Seminar, 12. Sheffield: Sheffield Academic Press, 2003.

Becking, Bob, "Did Jehu Write the Tel Dan Inscription?" *Scandinavian Journal of the Old Testament* 13 (1999): 187-201.

Biran, Avraham, and Joseph Naveh. "An Aramaic Stele Fragment from Tel Dan." *Israel Exploration Journal* 43 (1993): 81-98.

———. "The Tel Dan Inscription: A New Fragment." *Israel Exploration Journal* 45 (1995): 1-18.

Cryer, Frederick H. "On the Recently-Discovered 'House of David' Inscription." *Scandinavian Journal of the Old Testament* 8 (1994): 3-19.

——. "King Hadad." *Scandinavian Journal of the Old Testament* 9 (1995): 223-35.

Garbini, Giovanni. "L'iscrizione aramaica di Tel Dan." *Atti della Accademia Nazionale dei Lincei.* Anno CCCXCI (1994): 461-71.

Gmirkin, Russell. "Tool Slippage and the Tel Dan Inscription." *Scandinavian Journal of the Old Testament* 16 (2002): 293-308.

Lemaire, André. "The Tel Dan Stela as a Piece of Royal Historiography." *Journal for the Study of the Old Testament* 81 (1998): 3-14.

Lemche, Niels Peter. "Bemerkungen über einen Paradigmenwechsel aus Anlass einer neuentdeckten Inschrift." In Manfred Weippert and Stefan Timm, eds. *Meilenstein. Festgabe für Herbert Donner.* Ägypten und Altes Testament, 30. Wiesbaden: Otto Harrassowitz, 1995: 99-108.

——. "'House of David': The Tel Dan Inscriptions." In Philip R. Davies and Thomas L. Thompson, eds. *Jerusalem in History.* Sheffield: Continuum, 2003 (forthcoming).

Lemche, Niels Peter, and Thomas L. Thompson. "Did Biran Kill David? The Bible in the Light of Archaeology." *Journal for the Study of the Old Testament* 64 (1994): 3-22.

Wesselius, Jan-Wim. "The First Royal Inscription from Ancient Israel: The Tel Dan Inscription Reconsidered." *Scandinavian Journal of the Old Testament* 13 (1999): 163-86.

Samaria Ostraca

Noth, Martin. "Das Krongut der israelitischen Könige und seine Verwaltung." *Zeitschrift des Deutschen Palästina-Vereins* 50 (1927): 211-44 (reprinted in Martin Noth, *Aufsätze zur biblischen Landes- und Altertumskunde. Herausgegeben von Hans Walter Wolff,* I-II. Neukirchen: Neukirchener Verlag, 1971: 159-82).

Rainey, Anson F. "The Samaria Ostraca in the Light of Fresh Evidence." *Palestine Exploration Quarterly* 99 (1967): 32-41.

Reisner, George Andrew, Clarence Fisher, and David Gordon Lyon. *Harvard Excavations at Samaria,* 1-2. Cambridge, Mass.: Harvard University Press, 1924.

Shea, William H. "The Date and Significance of the Samaria Ostraca." *Israel Exploration Journal* 27 (1977): 16-27.

Arad Ostraca

Aharoni, Yohanan. *Arad Inscriptions.* Ed. Anson F. Rainey. Jerusalem: Israel Exploration Society, 1981.

Pardee, Dennis. "Letters from Tel Arad." *Ugarit-Forschungen* 10 (1978): 289-336.

Siloam Inscription

Hendel, Ronald. "The Date of the Siloam Inscription: A Rejoinder to Rogerson and Davies." *Biblical Archaeologist* 59 (1996): 233-37.

Rogerson, John, and Philip R. Davies. "Was the Siloam Tunnel Built by Hezekiah?" *Biblical Archaeologist* 59 (1996): 138-49.

Sasson, V. "The Siloam Tunnel Inscription." *Palestine Exploration Quarterly* 114 (1982): 111-17.

Lachish Letters

Cross, Frank Moore. "A Literate Soldier: Lachish Letter III." In Ann Kort and Scott Morschauser, eds. *Biblical and Related Studies Presented to Samuel Iwry.* Winona Lake, Ind.: Eisenbrauns, 1985: 41-47.

Torczyner, Harry. *Lachish I: The Lachish Letters.* London: Oxford University Press, 1938.

Vaux, Roland de. "Les ostraca de lachish." *Revue Biblique* 48 (1939): 181-206.

Babylonian Chronicle

Wiseman, Dennis J. *Chronicles of Chaldean Kings (626-556 B.C.) in the British Museum.* London: Trustees of the British Museum, 1956.

Elephantine Papyri

Porten, B. *Archives from Elephantine.* Berkeley: University of California Press, 1968.

Seals and Stamps

Avigad, Nahman, and Benjamin Sass. *Corpus of West Semitic Stamp Seals.* Jerusalem: Israel Academy of Sciences and Humanities, Israel Exploration Society, and Institute of Archaeology, Hebrew University, 1997.

History in Israel and the Ancient Near East

Barr, James. *History and Ideology in the Old Testament: Biblical Studies at the End of a Millennium.* Oxford: Oxford University Press, 2000.

Boshoff, Willem, Eben Scheffler, and Izak Spangenberg. *Ancient Israelite Literature in Context.* Pretoria: Protea Book House, 2000.

Dentan, R. C., ed. *The Idea of History in the Ancient Near East.* New Haven, Conn.: Yale University Press, 1955 (reprint Winona Lake, Ind.: Eisenbrauns 1983).

Kuhrt, Amélie. "Israelite and Near Eastern Historiography." In A. Lemaire and M. Sæbø, eds. *Congress Volume Oslo 1998.* Supplements to Vetus Testamentum, 80. Leiden: E. J. Brill, 2000: 257-79.

Lemche, Niels Peter. *Die Vorgeschichte Israels. Von den Anfängen bis zum Ausgang des 13. Jahrhunderts v. Chr.* Biblische Enzyklopädie, 1. Stuttgart: W. Kohlhammer, 1996 (*Prelude to Israel's Past: Background and Beginnings of Israelite History and Identity.* Peabody, Mass.: Hendrickson Publishers, 1998).

Liverani, Mario. "Memorandum on the Approach to Historiographic Texts." *Orientalia n.s.* 42 (1973): 178-94.

Long, V. Philip, David W. Baker, and Gordon J. Wenham, eds. *Windows into Old Testament History: Evidence, Argument, and the Crisis of "Biblical Israel."* Grand Rapids, Mich.: William B. Eerdmans, 2002.

Thompson, Thomas L. *The Early History of the Israelite People. From the Written and Archaeological Sources.* Studies in the History of the Ancient Near East IV. Leiden: E. J. Brill, 1992.

———. *The Bible in History. How Writers Create a Past.* London: Jonathan Cape, 1999 (N. American edition: *The Mythic Past: Bibli-*

cal Archaeology and the Myth of Israel. New York: Basic Books, 1999).

Van Seters, John. *In Search of History. Historiography in the Ancient World and the Origins of Biblical History.* New Haven, Conn.: Yale University Press, 1983 (reprint Winona Lake, Ind.: Eisenbrauns, 1997).

———. *Prologue to History: The Yahwist as Historian in Genesis.* Louisville, Ky.: Westminster/John Knox Press, 1992.

———. *The Life of Moses: The Yahwist as Historian in Exodus-Numbers.* Kampen: Kok Pharos, 1994.

Younger, K. Lawson. *Ancient Conquest Accounts: A Study in Ancient Near Eastern and Biblical History Writing.* Journal for the Study of the Old Testament Supplement Series, 98. Sheffield: Sheffield Academic Press, 1990.

History of the Ancient Near East

Bierbrier, Morris L. *Historical Dictionary of Ancient Egypt.* Historical Dictionaries of Ancient Civilizations and Historical Eras, No. 1. Lanham, Md.: Scarecrow, 1999.

Boardman, John, I. E. S. Edwards, H. G. L. Hammond, and E. Sollberger. *The Cambridge Ancient History.* III, 1-2. 2nd edition. Cambridge: Cambridge University Press, 1982.

Boardman, John, H. G. L. Hammond, D. M. Lewis, and M. Ostwald. *The Cambridge Ancient History.* IV. 2nd edition. Cambridge: Cambridge University Press, 1988.

Briant, Pierre. *Histoire de l'empire Perse de Cyrus à Alexandre.* Paris: Fayard, 1996 (*From Cyrus to Alexander: A History of the Persian Empire.* Winona Lake, Ind.: Eisenbrauns, 2002).

Cassin, Elena, Jean Bottéro, and Jean Vercoutter, eds. *Die altorientalischen Reiche 1: Vom Paläolithicum bis zur Mitte des 2. Jahrtausends.* Fischer Weltgeschichte 2. Frankfurt a.M.: Fischer Bücherei, 1965.

———. *Die altorientalischen Reiche 2: Das Ende des 2. Jahrtausends.* Fischer Weltgeschichte 3: Frankfurt a.M.: Fischer Bücherei, 1966.

———. *Die altorientalischen Reiche 3. Die erste Hälfte des 1. Jahrtausends.* Fischer Weltgeschichte 4. Frankfurt a.M.: Fischer Bücherei, 1967.

Edwards, I. E. S., C. J. Gadd, and N. G. L. Hammond, eds. *The Cambridge Ancient History*. I, i-ii and II, i-ii. 3rd ed. Cambridge: Cambridge University Press, 1970-1975.

Grimal, Nicolas. *A History of Ancient Egypt*. Oxford: Blackwell, 1992.

Klengel, Horst, ed. *Kulturgeschichte des alten Vorderasien*. Berlin: Akademie-Verlag, 1989.

Kuhrt, Amélie: *The Ancient Near East c. 3000-330 BC*, I-II. London: Routledge, 1995.

Leick, Gwendolyn. *Historical Dictionary of Mesopotamia*. Historical Dictionaries of Ancient Civilizations and Historical Eras, 9. Lanham, Md.: Scarecrow, 2003.

Liverani, Mario. "The Collapse of the Near Eastern Regional System at the End of the Bronze Age. The Case of Syria." In W. Rowlands, M. T. Larsen and K. Kristiansen, eds. *Centre and Periphery in the Ancient World*. Cambridge: Cambridge University Press, 1987: 66-73.

———. *Antico Oriente. Storia, Societa, economia*. Rome: Editio Laterza, 1988.

Sasson, Jack M., ed. *Civilizations of the Ancient Near East* I-IV. New York: Simon & Schuster/Macmillan, 1995.

Snell, Daniel C. *Life in the Ancient Near East 3100-332 B.C.E* New Haven, Conn.: Yale University Press, 1997.

Trigger, Bruce G. *Ancient Egypt: A Social History*. Cambridge: Cambridge University Press, 1983.

Hyksos

Beckerath, Jürgen von. *Untersuchungen zur politischen Geschichte der Zweiten Zwischenzeit in Ägypten*. Ägyptologische Forschungen Glückstadt: J. J. Augustin, 1964.

Bietak, Manfred. *Avaris the Capital of the Hyksos: Recent Excavations at Tell el-Daba*. London: British Museum Press, 1996.

Van Seters, John. *The Hyksos: A New Investigation*. New Haven, Conn.: Yale University Press, 1991.

Habiru-Hebrew

Bottéro, Jean. *Le problème des Habiru à la 4e rencontre assyriologique internationale.* Paris: Imprimerie nationale, 1954.

Greenberg, Moshe. *The Hab/piru.* New Haven, Conn.: American Oriental Society, 1955.

Lemche, Niels Peter. "'Hebrew' as a National Name for Israel." *Studia Theologica* 33 (1979): 1-23.

Loretz, Oswald. *Habiru-Hebräer: Eine sozio-linguistische Studie über die Herkunft des Gentiliziums 'ibrî vom Appellativum* habiru. Beiheft zur Zeitschrift für die alttestamentlischen Wissenschaft, 160. Berlin: Walter de Gruyter, 1984.

Na'aman, Nadav. "Hapiru and Hebrews: The Transfer of a Social Term to the Literary Sphere." *Journal of Near Eastern Studies* 45 (1986): 271-88.

The Philistines and the Sea People

Bunimowitz, Shlomo. "Problems in the 'Ethnic' Identification of the Philistine Material Culture." *Tel Aviv* 17 (1990): 210-22.

Dothan, Trude. *The Philistines and Their Material Culture.* New Haven, Conn.: Yale University Press, 1982.

Dothan, Trude, and Moshe Dothan. *People of the* Sea. New York: Macmillan, 1992.

Margalith, Othniel. *The Sea Peoples in the Bible.* Wiesbaden: Otto Harrassowitz, 1994.

Noort, Ed. *Die Seevölker in Palästina.* Kampen: Kok Pharos, 1994.

Sandars, N. K. *The Sea Peoples: Warriors of the Ancient Mediterranean 1250-1150 BC.* London: Thames and Hudson, 1978.

Singer, Itamar. "Egyptians, Canaanites, and Philistines in the Period of the Emergence of Israel." In Israel Finkelstein, and Nadav Na'aman eds. *From Nomadism to Monarchy. Archaeological and Historical Aspects of Early Israel.* Yad Izhak Ben-Zvi. Jerusalem: Israel Exploration Society, 1994: 282-338.

Palestine before Israel

Gerstenblith, P. *The Levant at the Beginning of the Middle Bronze Age.* American Schools of Oriental Research Dissertation Series, 5. Winona Lake, Ind.: Eisenbrauns, 1983.

Kempinski, Aharon. *Megiddo: A City-State and Royal Centre in North Israel.* Munich: C. H. Beck, 1989.

Lemche, Niels Peter. *The Canaanites and Their Land: The Tradition of the Canaanites.* Journal for the Study of the Old Testament, Supplement Series, 110. 2nd ed. Sheffield: Sheffield Academic Press, 1999.

Marfoe, Leon. "The Integrative Transformation: Patterns of Socio-Political Organization in Southern Syria." *Bulletin of the American Schools of Oriental Research* 234 (1979): 1-42.

Israel, Palestine, and the Ancient Near East

Bartlett, John R. *Edom and the Edomites.* Journal for the Study of the Old Testament, Supplement Series, 77. Sheffield: JSOT Press, 1989.

Bienkowski, P., ed. *Early Edom and Moab. The Beginning of the Iron Age in Southern Jordan.* Sheffield Archaeological Monographs, 7. Sheffield: J. R. Collis, 1992.

Coogan, Michael D., ed. *The Oxford History of the Biblical World.* Oxford: Oxford University Press, 1998.

Dion, Paul.-E. *Les Araméens à l'age du fér: histoire politique et structure sociales.* Études Bibliques, nouvelle série, 34. Paris: J. Gabalda, 1997.

Edelman, Diana Vikander, ed. *You Shall Not Abhor an Edomite for He is Your Brother: Edom and Seir in History and Tradition.* Archaeology and Biblical Studies, 3. Atlanta: Scholars Press, 1995.

Ephal, Israel. *The Ancient Arabs: Nomads on the Borders of the Fertile Crescent 9th-5th Centuries B.C.* Jerusalem: Magnes Press, 1982.

Görg, Manfred. *Die Beziehungen zwischen Israel dem alten Israel und Ägypten. Von den Anfängen bis zum Exil.* Erträge der Forschung, 290. Darmstadt: Wissenschaftliche Buchgesellschaft, 1997.

Harden, Donald. *The Phoenicians.* Harmondsworth, Middlesex: Penguin Books, 1971.

Heinz, Marlies. *Altsyrien und Libanon. Geschichte, Wirtschaft und Kultur vom Neolithikum bis Nebukadnezar.* Darmstadt: Wissenschaftliche Buchgesellschaft, 2002.

Helck, Wolfgang. *Die Beziehungen Ägyptens zu Vorderasien im 3. und 2. Jahrtausend v.chr.* Ägyptologische Abhandlungen, 5. Wiesbaden: Otto Harrassowitz, 1962 (2nd ed., 1971).

Heltzer, Michael. *The Rural Community in Ancient Ugarit.* Wiesbaden: Dr. Ludwig Reichert Verlag, 1976.

Hoerth, Alfred J., Gerald L. Mattingly, and Edwin M. Yamauchi. *Peoples of the Old Testament World.* Cambridge: Lutterworth Press and Baker Books, 1996.

Hübner, Ulrich. *Die Ammoniter. Untersuchungen zur Geschichte, Kultur und Religion eines transjordanischen Volkes im 1. Jahrhundert v.chr.* Abhandlungen des Deutschen Palästina-Vereins, 16. Wiesbaden: Otto Harrassowitz, 1993.

Kitchen, Kenneth A. *The Third Intermediary Period in Egypt (1100-650 B.C.).* Revised edition. Warminster: Aris & Phillips, 1995.

Klengel, Horst. *Syria: 3000-300 BC. A Handbook of Political History.* Berlin: Akademie Verlag, 1992.

Knauf, Ernst Axel. *Ismael: Untersuchungen zur Geschichte Palästinas und Nordarabiens im 1. Jahrtausend v. Chr.* 2., erweiterte Auflage. Abhandlungen des Deutschen Palästina-Vereins. Wiesbaden: Otto Harrassowitz, 1989.

———. *Midian. Untersuchungen zur Geschichte Palästinas und Nordarabiens am Ende des 2. Jahrtausends v. Chr.* Abhandlungen des Deutschen Palästina-Vereins. Wiesbaden: Otto Harrassowitz, 1988.

Malamat, Abraham. *Mari and the Bible.* Studies in the History and Culture of the Ancient Near East, 12. Leiden: E. J. Brill, 1998.

Moscati, Sabatino, ed. *The Phoenicians.* New York: Rizzoli, 2000.

Pitard, Wayne T. *Ancient Damascus.* Winona Lake, Ind.: Eisenbrauns, 1987.

Redford, Donald B. *Egypt and Canaan in the New Kingdom.* Beer-Sheva IV. Beer-Sheba: Ben-Gurion University of the Negev Press, 1990.

———. *Egypt, Canaan and Israel in Ancient Times.* Princeton, N.J.: Princeton University Press, 1992.

Sawyer, John F. A., and David J. A. Clines, eds. *Midian, Moab and Edom: The History and Archaeology of Late Bronze and Iron Age*

Jordan and North-West Arabia. Journal for the Study of the Old Testament, Supplement Series, 23. Sheffield: JSOT Press, 1983.

Schipper, Bernd Ulrich. *Israel und Ägypten in der Königszeit: Die kulturellen Kontakte von Salomo bis zum Fall Jerusalems.* Orbis Biblicus et Orientalis, 170. Freiburg Schweiz: Universitätsverlag; Göttingen, Vandenhoeck & Ruprecht, 1999.

Simons, J. *Handbook for the Study of Egyptian Topographical Lists Relating to Western Asia.* Leiden: E. J. Brill, 1937.

Timm, Stefan. *Moab zwischen den Mächten: Studien zu historischen Denkmälern und Texten.* Ägypten und Altes Testament, 17. Wiesbaden: Otto Harrassowitz, 1989.

Wiseman, Dennis J., ed. *Peoples of Old Testament Times.* Oxford: Oxford University Press, 1973.

Worschech, Udo. *Die Beziehungen Moabs zu Israel und Ägypten in der Eisenzeit: Siedlungsarchäologische u. siedlungshistorische Untersuchungen im Kernland Moabs (Ard el-Kerak).* Ägypten und Altes Testament, 18. Wiesbaden: Otto Harrassowitz, 1990.

Archaeology of Israel

Encyclopedias

Meyers, Erik M., ed. *The Oxford Encyclopedia of Archaeology in the Near East.* Oxford: Oxford University Press, 1997.

Negev, Avraham, and Shimon Gibson. *Archaeological Encyclopedia of the Holy Land.* Revised edition. New York: Continuum, 2001.

Stern, Ephraim, ed. *The New Encyclopedia of Archaeological Excavations in the Holy Land.* Jerusalem: Israel Exploration Society, 1993.

Studies

Ben-Tor, Amon, ed. *The Archaeology of Ancient Israel.* New Haven, Conn.: Yale University Press, 1992.

Dever, William G. *Recent Archaeological Discoveries and Biblical Research.* Seattle: University of Washington Press, 1990.

———. *What Did the Biblical Writers Know and When Did They Know It: What Archaeology Can Tell Us about the Reality of Ancient Israel.* Grand Rapids, Mich.: William B. Eerdmans, 2001.

Finkelstein, Israel. *The Archaeology of the Israelite Settlement.* Jerusalem: Israel Exploration Society, 1988.

———. *Living on the Fringe: The Archaeology and History of the Negev, Sinai and Neighbouring Regions in the Bronze and Iron Ages.* Monographs in Mediterranean Archaeology, 6. Sheffield: Sheffield Academic Press, 1995.

Finkelstein, Israel, and Zvi Lederman, eds. *Highlands of Many Cultures: The Southern Samaria Survey: The Sites,* I-II. Tel Aviv: Sonia and Marco Nadler Institute of Archaeology, 1997.

Finkelstein, Israel, and Neil Asher Silberman. *The Bible Unearthed: Archaeology's New Vision of Ancient Israel and the Origin of Its Sacred Texts.* New York: The Free Press, 2001.

Fritz, Volkmar. *An Introduction to Biblical Archaeology.* Journal for the Study of the Old Testament, Supplement Series, 172. Sheffield: JSOT Press, 1994.

Jamieson-Drake, David W. *Scribes and Schools in Monarchic Israel: A Socio-Archeological Approach.* Journal for the Study of the Old Testament. Supplement Series, 109, The Social World of Biblical Antiquity Series, 9. Sheffield: Almond Press, 1991.

Kenyon, Kathleen M. *Archaeology in the Holy Land.* 4th ed. London: Ernest Benn, 1979.

Levy, Thomas E., ed. *The Archaeology of the Society in the Holy Land.* London: Leicester University Press, 1995.

Mazar, Amihai. *Archaeology of the Land of the Bible 10,000-586 B.C.E.* The Anchor Bible Reference Library. New York: Doubleday, 1990.

Pritchard, James B. *Gibeon, Where the Sun Stood Still: The Discovery of a Biblical City.* Princeton, N.J.: Princeton University Press, 1962.

Silberman, Neil Asher. *Digging for God and Country: Exploration in the Holy Land 1799-1917.* New York: Doubleday, 1982.

Silberman, Neil Asher, and David Small. *The Archaeology of Israel: Constructing the Past, Interpreting the Present.* Journal for the Study of the Old Testament, Supplement Series, 237. Sheffield: Sheffield Academic Press, 1997.

Skjeggestad, Marit. *Facts in the Ground? Biblical History in Archaeological Interpretation of the Iron Age in Palestine.* Oslo: Oslo University, 2001.

Stern, Ephraim. *Archaeology of the Land of the Bible. II: The Assyrian, Babylonian, and Persian Periods 732-332 BCE.* New York: Doubleday, 2001.

Tappy, Ron E. *The Archaeology of Israelite Samaria, I: Early Iron Age Through the Ninth Century B.C.E.* Atlanta: Scholars Press, 1992.

Weippert, Helga. *Palästina in vorhellenistischer Zeit. Mit einem Beitrag von Leo Mildenberg. Handbuch der Archäologie Vorderasien II:* I. Munich: C. H. Beck'sche Verlagsbuchhandlung, 1988.

History of Israel

History Writing in Ancient Israel

Amit, Yairah. *History and Ideology: An Introduction to Historiography in the Hebrew Bible.* The Biblical Seminar, 60. Sheffield: Sheffield Academic Press, 1999.

Brettler, Marc Zvi. *The Creation of History in Ancient Israel.* London: Routledge, 1995.

Edelman, Diana Vikander, ed. *The Fabric of History: Text, Artifact and Israel's Past.* Journal for the Study of the Old Testament, Supplement Series, 127. Sheffield: JSOT Press, 1991.

Grabbe, Lester L. *Did Moses Speak Attic? Jewish Historiography and Scripture in the Hellenistic Period.* Journal for the Study of the Old Testament, Supplement Series, 317. European Seminar in Historical Methodology, 3. Sheffield: Sheffield Academic Press, 1997.

Halpern, Baruch. *The First Historians, The Hebrew Bible and History.* San Francisco: Harper & Row, 1988.

Lemaire, André. *Les écoles et la formation de la Bible dans l'ancien Israël.* Orbis Biblicus et orientalis, 39. Fribourg Suisse: Éditions universitaires, and Göttingen: Vandenhoeck and Ruprecht, 1981.

Long, V. Philip, ed. *Israel's Past in Present Research. Essays on Ancient Historiography.* Sources for Biblical and Theological Study, 7. Winona Lake, Indi.: Eisenbrauns, 1999.

Malamat, Abraham. "Die Frühgeschichte Israels: Eine methodologische Studie." *Theologische Zeitschrift* 39 (1983): 1-16.

Nielsen, Flemming A. J. *The Tragedy in History: Herodotus and the Deuteronomistic History.* Journal for the Study of the Old Testament,

Supplement Series, 251, Copenhagen International Seminar, 4. Sheffield: Sheffield Academic Press, 1997.

Rad, Gerhard von. "Der Anfang der Geschichtsschreibung im alten Israel." *Archiv für Kulturgeschichte* 32 (1944): 1-42 ("The Beginning of Historical Writing in Ancient Israel." In Gerhard von Rad. *The Problem of the Hexateuch and Other Essays*. New York: McGraw-Hill, 1966: 205-21).

Smith, Morton. *Palestinian Parties and Politics That Shaped the Old Testament*. New York: Columbia University Press, 1971 (reprint London: SCM Press, 1987).

Wellhausen, Julius. *Prolegomena to the History of Ancient Israel, with an Introduction by W. Robertson Smith and a Preface by Douglas A. Knight*. Atlanta: Scholars Press, 1994.

Wesselius, Jan-Win. *The Origin of the History of Israel: Herodotus' Histories as Blueprint for the First Book of the Bible*. Journal for the Study of the Old Testament, Supplement Series, 345. Sheffield: Sheffield Academic Press, 2002.

General Works and Collections

Ahlstöm, Gösta W. *Who Were the Israelites?* Winona Lake, Ind.: Eisenbrauns, 1986.

———. *The History of Ancient Palestine from the Palaeolithic Period to Alexander's Conquest. With a Contribution by Gary. O. Rollefson.* Ed. Diana Edelman. *Journal for the Study of the Old Testament*, Supplement Series, 146. Sheffield: Sheffield Academic Press, 1993.

Albertz, Rainer. *A History of Israelite Religion in the Old Testament Period*, I-II. London: SCM Press, 1994.

Albright, William F. *From the Stone Age to Christianity: Monotheism and the Historical Process*, 2nd ed. Garden City, N.Y.: Doubleday, 1957.

———. *The Biblical Period from Abraham to Ezra*. New York: Harper & Row, 1963.

Alt, Albrecht. *Kleine Schriften zur Geschichte* Israels, I-III. Munich: C. H. Beck'sche Verlagsbuchhandlung, 1953-1959.

———. *Essays on Old Testament History and Religion*. Trans. R. A. Wilson. The Biblical Seminar. Sheffield: JSOT Press, 1989.

Anderson, Bernhard W. *The Living World of the Old Testament*. 4th ed. Harlow: Longman, 1988.

Bordreuil, Pierre, and Françoise Briquel-Chatonnet. *Le temps de la Bible*. Paris: Gallimard, 2000.

Bright, John. *A History of Israel*. The Old Testament Library. London: SCM Press, 1960 (4th ed., Louisville, Ky.: Westminster-John Knox Press, 2000).

Davies, Philip R. *In Search of "Ancient" Israel*. Journal for the Study of the Old Testament, Supplement Series, 148. Sheffield: Sheffield Academic Press, 1992.

Donner, Herbert. *Geschichte des Volkes Israel und seiner Nachbarn in Grundzügen*, I-II. Göttingen: Vandenhoeck & Ruprecht, 1984-1986.

Garbini, Giovanni. *History and Ideology in Ancient Israel*. London: SCM Press, 1988.

Grabbe, Lester L., ed. *Can a "History of Israel" Be Written?* Journal for the Study of the Old Testament, Supplement Series, 245. European Seminar in Historical Methodology, 1. Sheffield: Sheffield Academic Press, 1997.

Gunneweh, Antonius H. J. *Geschichte Israels bis Bar Kochba*. Stuttgart: W. Kohlhammer, 1972.

Hayes, John H., and J. Maxwell Miller, eds. *Israelite and Judaean History*. Old Testament Library. London: SCM Press, 1977.

Herrmann, Siegfried. *A History of Israel in Old Testament Times*. 2nd ed. Philadelphia: Fortress Press, 1981.

Knauf, Ernst Axel. *Die Umwelt des Alten Testaments*. Neue Stuttgarter Kommentar, Altes Testament, 29. Stuttgart: Verlag Katholisches Bibelwerk, 1994.

Knauf, Ernst Axel, and Andre de Pury. *Geschichte Israel*. Stuttgart: Kohlhammer, 2003.

Knoll, K. L. *Canaan and Israel in Antiquity: An Introduction*. The Biblical Seminar, 83. Sheffield: Sheffield Academic Press, 2001.

Isserlin, B. S. J. *The Israelites*. Minneapolis: Fortress Press, 2001.

Lemche, Niels Peter. *Ancient Israel: A New History of Israelite Society*. The Biblical Seminar. Sheffield: JSOT Press, 1988.

———. *The Israelites in History and Tradition*. Library of Ancient Israel. London: SPCK, and Louisville, Ky: John Knox Press, 1998.

Miller, J. Maxwell, and John H. Hayes. *A History of Ancient Israel and Judah*. Philadelphia: Westminster Press, 1986.

Noth, Martin. *The History of Israel*. 2nd ed. London: Black, 1959.

———. *Aufsätze zur biblischen Landes- und Altertumskunde.* Herausgegeben von Hans Walter Wolff, I–II. Neukirchen: Neukirchener Verlag, 1971.

Shanks, Hershel, ed. *Ancient Israel: A Short History from Abraham to the Roman Destruction of the Temple.* Washington, D.C.: Biblical Archaeological Society, and Englewood Cliffs, N.J.: Prentice Hall, 1988.

Soggin, J. Alberto. *An Introduction to the History of Israel and Judah.* 3rd ed. London: SCM Press, 1999.

Vaux, Roland de. *Histoire ancienne d'Israël, I: Des origines à l'installation en Canaan.* Paris: Librairie Lecoffre, J. Gabalda et Cie, Éditeurs, 1971.

———. *Histoire ancienne d'Israël, II: La période des juges.* Paris: Librairie Lecoffre, J. Gabalda et Cie, Éditeurs, 1973.

———. *The Early History of Israel to the Period of the Judges.* London: Datton, Longman & Todd, 1978.

Whitelam, Keith W. *The Invention of Ancient Israel: The Silencing of Palestinian History.* London: Routledge, 1996.

Chronology

Andersen, Knud Tage. "Noch einmal: Die Chronologie von Israel und Juda." *Scandinavian Journal of the Old Testament* 3/1 (1989): 1–45.

Bickerman, Ed. J. *Chronology on the Ancient World.* Rev. ed. London: Thames and Hudson, 1980.

Cryer, Frederick H. "To the One of Fictive Music: OT Chronology and History." *Scandinavian Journal of the Old Testament* 1/2 (1987): 1–27.

Hayes, John H., and Paul K. Hooker. *A New Chronology for the Kings of Israel and Judah and Its Implications for Biblical History and Literature.* Atlanta: John Knox Press, 1988.

Thiele, Edwin R. *The Mysterious Numbers of the Hebrew Kings.* New Rev. ed.. Grand Rapids, Mich.: Kregel, 1994.

Geography and Historical Geography

Aharoni, Yohanan. *The Land of the Bible. A Historical Geography.* Translated from the Hebrew by A. F. Rainey. London: Burns & Oates, 1968.

Aharoni, Yohanan, Michael Avi-Yonah, Anson F. Rainey, and Ze'ev Safrai. *The Carta Bible Atlas*. 4th ed. Jerusalem: Carta, and Winona Lake, Ind.: Eisenbrauns, 2003.

Avi-Yonah, Michael. *The Holy Land from the Persian to the Arab Conquest (536 B.C. to A.D. 640)*. Grand Rapids, Mich.: Baker Book House, 1966.

Bahat, Dan, with Chaim T. Rubinstein. *The Illustrated Atlas of Jerusalem*. New York: Simon & Schuster, 1990.

Baly, Dennis. *The Geography of the Bible: A Study in Historical Geography*. London: Lutterworth Press, 1964.

Dorsey, David A. *The Roads and Highways of Ancient Israel*. Baltimore: Johns Hopkins University Press, 1991.

Frank, H. T. and J. Monson eds. *Student Map Manual. Historical Geography of the Bible Lands*. Jerusalem: Pictorial Archive (Near Eastern History), 1983 (1979).

Galil, Gershon, and Moshe Weinfeld, eds. *Studies in Historical Geography and Biblical Historiography Presented to Zechariah Kallai*. Supplements to Vetus Testamentum, 81. Leiden: E. J. Brill, 2000.

Höhne, Ernst. *Palästina. Historisch-Archäologische Karte. Zwei vierzehnfarbige Blätter 1:300000. Mit Einführung und Register*. Göttingen: Vandenhoeck & Ruprecht, 1981.

Kallai, Zechariah. *Historical Geography of the Bible: The Tribal Territories of Israel*. Jerusalem: The Magnes Press, and Leiden: E. J. Brill, 1986.

Karmon, Yehuda. *Israel. Eine geographische Landeskunde*. Wissenschaftliche Länderkunden 22. Darmstadt: Wissenschaftliche Buchgesellschaft, 1983.

Keel, Othmar, and Max Küchler. *Orte und Landschaften der Bibel. Ein Handbuch und Studien-reiseführer zum Heiligen Land, II: Der Süden*. Zürich: Benziger, and Göttingen: Vandenhoeck & Ruprecht, 1982.

Keel, Othmar, Max Küchler, and Christoph Uehlinger. *Orte und Landschaften der Bibel. Ein Handbuch und Studien-reiseführer zum Heiligen Land, I: Geographisch-geschichtliche Landeskunde*. Zürich: Benziger, and Göttingen: Vandenhoeck & Ruprecht, 1984.

May, Herbert G. *Oxford Bible Atlas*. 3rd edition. London: Oxford University Press, 1985.

Mittmann, Siegfried, and Götz Schmitt, eds. *Tübinger Bibelatlas*. Stuttgart: Deutsche Bibelgesellschaft, 2001.

Na'aman, Nadav. *Borders and Districts in Biblical Historiography. Seven Studies in Biblical Geographical Lists*. Jerusalem Biblical Studies, 4. Jerusalem: Simor Ltd., 1986.

Pritchard, James B. *Herders grosser Bibel Atlas*. Freiburg: Herder, 1996.

Strange, John. *Stuttgarter Bibelatlas: Historische Karten der biblischen Welt*. Stuttgart: Deutsche Bibelgesellschaft, 1998.

Sociology—Society

Borowski, Oded. *Agriculture in Iron Age Israel*. Winona Lake, Ind.: Eisenbrauns, 1987.

Brett, M. G., ed. *Ethnicity and the Bible*. Biblical Interpretation, 19. Leiden: E. J. Brill, 1996.

Briant, Pierre. *Etat et pasteurs au Moyen-Orient ancient*. Cambridge: Cambridge University Press, and Paris: Editions de la Maison des sciences de l'homme, 1982.

Carter, Charles E., and Carol L. Meyers, eds. *Community, Identity, and Ideology: Social Science Approaches to the Hebrew Bible*. Sources for Biblical and Theological Study, 6. Winona Lake, Ind.: Eisenbrauns, 1996.

Fritz, Volkmar. *Die Stadt im alten Israel*. Munich: Verlag C. H. Beck, 1990.

Gottwald, Norman K. *The Hebrew Bible in Its Social World and in Ours*. The Society of Biblical Literature, Semeian Studies. Atlanta: Scholars Press, 1993.

———. *The Politics of Ancient Israel*. Library of Ancient Israel. Louisville, Ky: Westminster/John Knox Press, 2001.

Heltzer, Michael. *The Suteans. With a Contribution by Shoshane Arbeli*. Naples: Istituto Universitario Orientale, 1981.

Hopkins, David C. *The Highlands of Canaan. Agricultural Life in the Early Iron Age*. The Social World of Biblical Antiquity Series, 3. Sheffield: Almond Press, 1985.

King, Philip J., and Lawrence E. Stager: *Life in Biblical Israel. Library of Ancient Israel*. Louisville, Ky: Westminster/John Knox Press, 2001.

McNutt, Paula. *The Forging of Israel. Iron Technology, Symbolism, and Tradition in Ancient Society.* The Social World of Biblical Antiquity Series, 8, Journal for the Study of the Old Testament Supplement Series, 108. Sheffield: Almond Press, 1990.

———. *Reconstructing the Society of Ancient Israel.* Library of Ancient Israel. Louisville, Ky.: Westminster/John Knox Press, 1999.

Noth, Martin. *Die Welt des Alten Testaments.* 4. Auflage. Berlin: Alfred Töpelmann, 1962.

Pedersen, Johannes. *Israel. Its Life and Culture* I-II. Oxford: Oxford University Press, 1926-1947.

Reviv, Hanoch. *The Elders in Ancient Israel: A Study of a Biblical Institution.* Jerusalem: Magnes Press, 1989.

Rogerson, John W. *Anthropology and the Old Testament.* Oxford: Basil Blackwell, 1978.

Sneed, Mark R., ed. *Concepts of Class in Ancient Israel.* South Florida Studies in the History of Judaism, 201. Atlanta: Scholars Press, 1999.

Sparks, Kenton L. *Ethnicity and Identity in Ancient Israel: Prolegomena to the Study of Ethnic Sentiments and Their Expression in the Hebrew Bible.* Winona Lake, Ind.: Eisenbrauns, 1998.

Staubli, Thomas. *Das Image der Nomaden im Alten Israel und in der Ikonographie seiner sesshaften Nachbarn.* Orbis Biblicus et Orientalis, 107. Freiburg Schweiz: Universitätsverlag, and Göttingen: Vandenhoeck and Ruprecht, 1991.

Institutions

Blenkinsopp, Joseph. *Sage, Priest, Prophet: Religious and Intellectual Leasership in Ancient Israel.* Library of Ancient Israel. Louisville, Ky: Westminster/John Knox Press, 1995.

Buccellati, Giovanni. *Cities and Nations of Ancient Syria: An Essay on Political Institutions with Special Reference to the Israelite Kingdoms.* Studi Semitici, 26. Rome: Istituto di Studi del Vicino Oriente, 1967.

Nissinen, Martti, ed. *Prophecy in Its Ancient Near Eastern Context: Mesopotamian, Biblical, and Arabian Perspectives.* Society of Biblical Literature, Symposium Series, 13. Atlanta: Society of Biblical Literature, 2000.

Vaux, Roland de. *Les Institutions de l'Ancien Testament. I. Le nomadisme et ses survivances. Institutions familiales. Institutions civiles.* 2e edition revue. Paris: Les éditions du Cerf, 1961.

———. *Les Institutions de l'Ancien Testament. II. Institution militaires-Institutions religieuses.* Paris: Les éditions du Cerf, 1960. (*Ancient Israel.* London: Darton, Longman & Todd, 1962).

The Minimalist—Maximalist Controversy

Davies, Philip R. "Method and Madness: Some Suggestions on Doing History with the Bible." *Journal of Biblical Literature* 114 (1995): 699-705.

Grabbe, Lester L. "Writing Israel's History at the End of the Twentieth Century." In A. Lemaire and M. Sæbø, eds. *Congress Volume Oslo 1998.* Supplements to Vetus Testamentum, 80. Leiden: E. J. Brill, 2000: 203-18.

Halpern, Baruch. "Erasing History: The Minimalist Assault on Ancient Israel." In V. Philip Long, ed. *Israel's Past in Present Research. Essays on Ancient Historiography.* Sources for Biblical and Theological Study, 7. Winona Lake, Ind.: Eisenbrauns, 1999: 415-26.

Lemche, Niels Peter. "Is it Still Possible to Write a History of Ancient Israel." *Scandinavian Journal of the Old Testament* 8 (1994): 163-88. Reprinted in V. Philip Long, ed. *Israel's Past in Present Research. Essays on Ancient Historiography.* Sources for Biblical and Theological Study, 7. Winona Lake, Ind.: Eisenbrauns, 1999: 391-414.

———. "Ideology and the History of Ancient Israel." *Scandinavian Journal of the Old Testament* 14 (2000): 165-94.

Pasto, James. "When the End Is the Beginning? Or When the Biblical Past Is the Political Present: Some Thoughts on Ancient Israel, 'Post-Exilic Judaism,' and the Politics of Biblical Scholarship." *Scandinavian Journal of the Old Testament* 12 (1998): 157-202.

Provan, Ian W. "Ideologies, Literary and Critical Reflections on Recent Writing on the History of Israel." *Journal of Biblical Literature* 114 (1995): 585-606.

———. "In the Stable with the Dwarves: Testimony, Interpretation, Faith and the History of Israel." In A. Lemaire and M. Sæbø, eds. *Congress Volume Oslo 1998.* Supplements to Vetus Testamentum, 80. Leiden: E. J. Brill, 2000: 281-319.

Thompson, Thomas L. "A Neo-Albrightean School in History and Biblical Scholarship." *Journal of Biblical Literature* 114 (1995): 683-98.

Patriarchs

Albright, William F. "Abraham the Hebrew: A New Archaeological Interpretation." *Bulletin of the American Schools of Oriental Research* 163 (1961): 36-54.
Dever, William G. and W. Malcolm Clark. "The Patriarchal Traditions." In John H. Hayes and J. Maxwell Miller, eds. *Israelite and Judaean History*. Old Testament Library. London: SCM Press, 1977: 70-148.
Redford, Donald B. *A Study of the Biblical Joseph Story*. Supplements to Vetus Testamentum, 20. Leiden: E. J. Brill, 1970.
Thompson, Thomas L. *The Historicity of the Patriarchal Narratives: The Quest for the Historical Abraham*. Beiheft zur Zeitschrift fur die alttestamentliche Wissenschaft 133. Berlin: Walter de Gruyter, 1974 (repr. Harrisburg, Penn.: Trinity Press International, 2002).
Thompson, Thomas L. and Dorothy Irvin. "The Joseph and Moses Narratives." In John H. Hayes and J. Maxwell Miller, eds. *Israelite and Judaean History*. Old Testament Library. London: SCM Press, 1977: 149-212.
Van Seters, John. *Abraham in History and Tradition*. New Haven, Conn.: Yale University Press, 1975.
Vaux, Roland de. "The Hebrew Patriarchs and History." In V. Philip Long, ed. *Israel's Past in Present Research. Essays on Ancient Historiography*. Sources for Biblical and Theological Study, 7. Winona Lake, Ind.: Eisenbrauns, 1999: 470-79.

Exodus, Settlement of the Israelite Tribes, Period of the Judges

Ahituv, Shmuel, and Eliezer D. Oren. *The Origin of Early Israel— Current Debate: Biblical, Historical and Archaeological Perspectives*. Beer-Sheva, 12. Beer-Sheva: Ben-Gurion University of the Negev Press, 1998.
Albright, William F. "Archaeology and the Hebrew Conquest of Palestine." *Bulletin of the American Schools of Oriental Research* 58 (1935): 1-18.

———. "The Israelite Conquest in the Light of Archaeology." *Bulletin of the American Schools of Oriental Research* 74 (1939): 11-22.

Alt, Albrecht. "Die Landnahme der israeliten in Palästina." *Kleine Schriften zur Geschichte Israels*, I. Munich: C. H. Beck'sche Verlagsbuchhandlung, 1953: 89-125 ("The Settlements of the Israelites in Palestine." In Albrecht Alt. *Essays on Old Testament History and Religion*. The Biblical Seminar. Sheffield: JSOT Press, 1989: 177-221).

———. "Erwägungen über die Landnahme der Israeliten in Palästina." *Kleine Schriften zur Geschichte Israels*, I. Munich: C. H. Beck'sche Verlagsbuchhandlung, 1953: 126-75.

Coats, George W. *Moses: Heroic Man, Man of God*. Journal for the Study of the Old Testament, Supplement Series, 57. Sheffield: Sheffield Academic Press, 1988.

Coote, Robert B., and Keith W. Whitelam: *The Emergence of Early Israel in Historical Perspective*. The Social World of Biblical Antiquity Series, 5. Sheffield: Almond Press, 1987.

Finkelstein, Israel, and Nadav Na'aman, eds. *From Nomadism to Monarchy. Archaeological and Historical Aspects of Early Israel*. Yad Izhak Ben-Zvi. Jerusalem: Israel Exploration Society, 1994.

Freedman, David Noel, and David Frank Graf, eds. *Palestine in Transition: The Emergence of Ancient Israel*. The Social World of Biblical Antiquity Series, 1. Sheffield: Published in Association with the American Schools of Oriental Research by Almond Press, 1983.

Frerichs, Ernest S., and Leonard H. Lesko, eds. *Exodus: The Egyptian Evidence*. Winona Lake, Ind.: Eisenbrauns, 1997.

Fritz, Volkmar. *Die Entstehung Israels im 12. und 11. Jahrhundert v. Chr*. Biblische Enzyklopädie, 2. Stuttgart: W. Kohlhammer, 1996.

Gal, Zvi. *Lower Galilee during the Iron Age*. American Schools of Oriental Research Dissertation Series, 8. Winona Lake, Ind.: Eisenbrauns, 1992.

Geus, C. H. J. de. *The Tribes of Israel. An Investigation into Some of the Presuppositions of Martin Noth's Amphictyonic Hypothesis*. Studia Semitica Neerlandica, 18. Amsterdam: van Gorcum, 1976.

Givéon, Raphael. *Les Bédouins Shoshou des document égyptiens*. Documenta et monumenta Orientis Antiquii, 18. Leiden: E. J. Brill, 1971.

Gottwald, Norman K. *The Tribes of Yahweh. A Sociology of the Religion of Liberated Israel 1250-1050 B.C.* Maryknoll, N.Y.: Orbis Books, 1979.

Halpern, Baruch. *The Emergence of Israel in Canaan.* Society of Biblical Literature Monograph Series, 29. Chico, Calif.: Scholars Press, 1983.

Jericke, Detlef. *Die Landnahme im Negev: Protoisraelitischen Gruppen im Süden Palästinas. Eine archäologische und exegetische Studie.* Abhandlungen des Deutschen Palästina-Vereins. Wiesbaden: Otto Harrassowitz, 1997.

Herrmann, Siegfried. *Israels Aufenhalt in Ägypten.* Stuttgart: Verlag Katholisches Bibelwerk, 1970.

Kaufmann, Yehezkel. *The Biblical Account of the Conquest of Palestine.* Jerusalem: Magnes Press, 1953.

Lemche, Niels Peter. "Israel in the Period of the Judges—The Tribal League in Recent Discussion." *Studia Theologica* 38 (1984): 1-28.

———. *Early Israel: Anthropological and Historical Studies on the Israelite Society before the Monarchy.* Supplements to Vetus Testamentum, 37. Leiden: E. J. Brill, 1985.

———. "Early Israel Revisited." *Currents in Research: Biblical Studies* 4 (1996): 9-34.

Mayes, A. D. H. *Israel in the Period of the Judges.* London: SCM Press, 1974.

Mendenhall, George E. "The Hebrew Conquest of Palestine." *Biblical Archaeologist* 25 (1962): 66-87.

———. *The Tenth Generation. The Origin of the Biblical Tradition.* Baltimore: Johns Hopkins University Press, 1973.

Meyers, Carol. "Early Israel and the Rise of the Israelite Monarchy." In James G. Perdue, ed. *The Blackwell Companion to the Hebrew Bible.* Cambridge: Blackwell, 2001: 61-86.

Mittmann, Siegfried. *Beiträge zur Siedlungs- und Territorialgeschichte des nördlichen Ostjordanlandes.* Abhandlungen des Deutschen Palästina-Vereins, 2. Wiesbaden: Otto Harrassowitz, 1970.

Niemann, Hermann Michael. *Die Daniten. Studien zur Geschichte eines altisraelitischen Stammes.* Forschungen zur Religion und Literatur des Alten und Neuen Testaments, 135. Göttingen: Vandenhoeck & Ruprecht, 1985.

Noth, Martin. *Das System der Zwölf Stämme Israels.* Beiträge zur Wissenschaft vom Alten und Neuen Testament, 4:1. Stuttgart: W. Kohlhammer, 1930 (reprint, Darmstadt: Wissenschaftliche Buchgesellschaft, 1966).

Schmidt, Werner H. *Exodus, Sinai und Mose. Erwägungen zu Ex1-19 und 24.* Erträge der Forschung, 191. Darmstadt: Wissenschaftliche Buchgesellschaft, 1990.

Schunck, Klaus-Dietrich. *Benjamin. Untersuchungen zur Entstehung und Geschichte eines israelitischen Stammes.* Beiheft zur Zeitschrift für die alttestamentliche Wissenschaft, 86. Berlin: Alfred Töpelmann, 1963.

Shanks, Hershell, ed. *The Rise of Ancient Israel.* Washington, D.C.: Biblical Archaeology Society, 1992.

Shilo, Yigael. "The Four-Room House: Its Situation and Function in the Israelite City." *Israel Exploration Journal* 20 (1970): 180-90.

————. "The Casemate Wall, the Four Room House, and Early Planning in the Israelite City." *Bulletin of the American Schools of Oriental Research* 268 (1987): 3-16.

Stager, Lawrence E. "The Archaeology of the Family in Ancient Israel." *Bulletin of the American Schools of Oriental Research* 260 (1985): 1-35.

Weinfeld, Moshe. "The Period of Conquest and of Judges as seen by Earlier and Later Sources." *Vetus Testamentum* 17 (1967): 93-113.

Weippert, Manfred. *Die Landnahme der israelitischen Stämme in der neueren wissenschaftlichen Diskussion. Ein kritischer Bericht.* Forschungen zur Religion und Literatur des Alten und Neuen Testaments, 92. Göttingen: Vandenhoeck & Ruprecht, 1967 (*The Settlement of the Israelite Tribes in Palestine: A Critical Survey of Recent Scholarly Debate.* Studies in Biblical Theology Second Series, 21. London: SCM Press, 1971).

Yadin, Yigael. *Hazor. The Head of All Those Kingdoms with a Chapter on Israelite Megiddo.* The Schweich Lectures of the British Academy, 1970. London: Published for the British Academy by Oxford University Press, 1972.

Zobel, Hans-Jürgen. *Stammespruch und Geschichte.* Beiheft zur Zeitschrift für die alttestamentliche Wissenschaft, 95. Berlin: Alfred Töpelmann, 1965.

United Monarchy

Alt, Albrecht. "Die Staatenbildung der Israeliten in Palästina." In *Kleine Schriften zur Geschichte Israels*, II. Munich: C. H. Beck'sche Verlagsbuchhandlung, 1953: 1-65 ("The Formation of the Israelite State in Palestine." In Albrecht Alt. *Essays on Old Testament History and Religion*. The Biblical Seminar. Sheffield: JSOT Press, 1989: 171-237.

Ash, Paul S. *David, Solomon and Egypt: A Reassessment*. Journal for the Study of the Old Testament, Supplement Series, 297. Sheffield: Sheffield Academic Press, 1999.

Crüsemann, Frank. *Der Widerstand gegen das Königtum. Die anti-königlichen Texte des Alten Testamentes und der Kampf um den frühen israelitischen Staat.* Wissenschaftliche Monographien zum Alten und Neuen Testament, 49. Neukirchen-Vluyn: Neukirchener Verlag des Erziehungsvereins, 1978.

Dietrich, Walter. *Die frühe Königszeit in Israel. 10. Jahrhundert v. Chr.* Biblische Enzyklopädie, 3. Stuttgart: W. Kohlhammer, 1997.

———. *Von David zu den Deuteronomisten: Studien zu den Geschichtsüberlieferungen des Alten Testaments.* Beiträge zur Wissenschaft vom Alten und Neuen Testament, 156. Stuttgart: W. Kohlhammer, 2002.

Edelman, Diana Vikander. *King Saul in the Historiography of Judah.* Journal for the Study of the Old Testament, Supplement Series, 121. Sheffield: Sheffield Academic Press, 1991.

Finkelstein, Israel. "The Emergence of the Monarchy in Israel: The Environmental and Socio-economic Aspects." *Journal for the Study of the Old Testament* 44 (1989): 43-74.

———. "The Archaeology of the United Monarchy: An Alternative View." *Levant* 28 (1996): 177-87.

———. "State Formation in Israel and Judah: A Contrast in Context, A Contrast in Trajectory." *Near Eastern Archaeology* 62 (1999): 35-52.

Frick, F. S. *The Formation of the State in Ancient Israel. A Survey of Models and Theories.* The Social World of Biblical Antiquity Series, 4. Sheffield: Almond, 1985.

Friis, Heike. *Die Bedingungen für die Errichtung des Davidischen Reichs in Israel und seiner Umwelt.* Dielheimer Blätter zum Alten Testament und seiner Rezeption in der Alten Kirche Beiheft, 6. Heidelberg: Dielheimer Blätter, 1986.

Fritz, Volkmar, and Philip R. Davies, eds. *The Origins of the Israelite States*. Journal for the Study of the Old Testament, Supplement Series, 228. Sheffield: Sheffield Academic Press, 1996.

Halpern, Baruch. "The Uneasy Compromise: Israel between League and Monarchy." In Patrick D. Miller, Paul D. Hanson, and S. Dean McBride, eds. *Ancient Israelite Religion: Essays in Honor of Frank Moore Cross*. Philadelphia: Fortress Press, 1987: 59-96.

———. *David's Secret Demons: Messiah, Murderer, Traitor, King*. Grand Rapids, Mich.: William B. Eerdmans, 2001.

Handy, Lowell K., ed. *The Age of Solomon. Scholarship at the Turn of the Millennium*. Studies in the History and Culture of the Ancient Near East, XI. Leiden: E. J. Brill, 1997.

Knoppers, Gary N. *Two Nations under God: The Deuteronomistic History of Solomon and the Dual Monarchy*, 1: *The Reign of Solomon and the Rise of Jeroboam*. Harvard Semitic Monographs, 42. Atlanta: Scholars Press, 1993.

Levin, Christoph. *Der Sturz der Königin Atalja: Ein Kapitel zur Geschichte Judas im 9. Jahrhundert v. Chr.* Stuttgarter Bibelstudien, 105. Stuttgart: Verlag Katholisches Bibelwerk, 1982.

Long, V. P. *The Reign and Rejection of King Saul. A Case for Literary and Theological Coherence*. Society of Biblical Literature, Dissertation Series, 118. Atlanta: Scholars Press, 1989.

Mazar, Amihai. "Iron Age Chronology: A Reply to Israel Finkelstein." *Levant* 29 (1997): 157-67.

Na'aman, Nadab. "In Search of Reality behind the Accounts of David's Wars with Israel's Neighbours." *Israel Exploration Journal* 52 (2002): 200-24.

Neu, Rainer. *Von der Anarchie zum Staat Entwicklungsgeschichte Israels vom Nomadentum zur Monarchie im Spiegel der Ethnosoziologie*. Neukirchen: Neukirchener Verlag, 1992.

Nicholson, Sarah. *Three Faces of Saul: An Intertextual Approach to Biblical Tragedy*. Journal for the Study of the Old Testament, Supplement Series, 339. Sheffield: Sheffield Academic Press, 2002.

Niemann, Hermann Michael. *Herrschaft, Königtum und Staat: Skizzen zur soziokulturellen Entwicklung im monarchischen Israel*. Forschungen zum Alten Testament, 6. Tübingen: J. C. B. Mohr (Paul Siebeck), 1993.

Rost, Leonhard. *Die Überlieferung von der Thronfolge Davids*. Beiträge zur Wissenschaft des Alten und Neuen Testaments, III, 6. Stuttgart: W. Kohlhammer, 1926 (*The Succession to the Throne of David*. Sheffield: Almond Press, 1982).

Soggin, J. Alberto. "The Davidic—Solomonic Kingdom." In John H. Hayes, and J. Maxwell Miller, eds. *Israelite and Judaean History*. Old Testament Library. London: SCM Press, 1977: 332-80.

Wightman, G. J. "The Myth of Solomon." *Bulletin of the American Schools of Oriental Research* 277/278 (1990): 5-22.

The Hebrew Kingdoms

Ahlström, Gösta W. *Royal Administration and National Religion in Ancient Palestine*. Leiden: E. J. Brill, 1982.

Alt, Albrecht. "Das Königtum in den Reichen Israel und Juda." In *Kleine Schriften zur Geschichte Israels*, II. Munich: C. H. Beck'sche Verlagsbuchhandlung, 1953: 116-34 ("The Monarchy in Israel and Juda." In Albrecht Alt, *Essays on Old Testament History and Religion*. The Biblical Seminar. Sheffield: JSOT Press, 1989: 239-59.

Avishur, Y., and M. Heltzer. *Studies on the Royal Administration in Ancient Israel in the Light of Epigraphic Sources*. Tel Aviv: Archaeological Center Publications, 2000.

Becking, Bob. *The Fall of Samaria: An Historical and Archaeological Study*. Studies in the History of the Ancient Near East, 2. Leiden: E. J. Brill, 1992.

Broshi, Magen, and Israel Finkelstein. "The Population of Palestine in Iron Age II." *Bulletin of the American Schools of Oriental Research* 287 (1992): 47-60.

Conçalves, Francolino J. *L'expédition de Sennacherib en Palestine dans la littérature hébraïque ancienne*. Études Bibliques N.S. 7. Paris: Librairie Lecoffre, J. Gabalda et Cie éditeurs, 1986.

Donner, Herbert. *Israel unter den Völkern: Die Stellung der klassischen Propheten des 8. Jahrhunderts v. Chr. zur Aussenpolitik der Könige von Israel und Juda*. Supplements to Vetus Testamentum, 11. Leiden: E. J. Brill, 1964.

Evans, C. D. "Judah's Foreign Policy from Hezekiah to Josiah." In C. D. Evans, W. W. Hallo, and J. B. White, eds. *Scripture in Context: Essays on the Comparative Method*. Pittsburgh: Pickwick Press, 1980.

Hoppe, Leslie J. "The History of Israel in the Monarchic Period." In James G. Perdue, ed. *The Blackwell Companion to the Hebrew Bible.* Cambridge: Basil Blackwell, 2001: 87-101.

Lang, Bernhard. "The Social Organization of Peasant Poverty in Biblical Israel." *Journal for the Study of the Old Testament* 24 (1982): 47-63.

Lemche, Niels Peter. "Kings and Clients: On Loyalty between the Ruler and the Ruled in Ancient 'Israel'." *Semeia* 66 (1995): 119-32.

Lowery, R. H. *The Reforming Kings: Cult and Society in First Temple Judah.* Journal for the Study of the Old Testament, Supplement Series, 120. Sheffield: Sheffield Academic Press, 1991.

McKenzie, Stephen L. *The Trouble with Kings: The Composition of the Book of Kings in the Deuteronomistic History.* Supplements to Vetus Testamentum, 42: Leiden: E. J. Brill, 1991.

Mettinger, Tryggve N. D. *Solomonic State Officials. A Study of the Civil Government Officials of the Israelite Monarchy.* Coniectanea Biblica Old Testament Series, 5. Lund: CWK Gleerup, 1971.

Na'aman, Nadab. "Hezekiah's Fortified Cities and the *LMLK* Stamps." *Bulletin of the American Schools of Oriental Research* 261 (1986): 5-21.

———. "The Kingdom of Judah under Josiah." *Tel Aviv* 18 (1991): 3-71.

———. "Population Changes in Palestine following Assyrian Deportations." *Tel Aviv* 20 (1993): 104-24.

———. "Hezekiah and the Kings of Assyria." *Tel Aviv* 21 (1994): 235-254.

———. "The Deuteronomist and Voluntary Servitude to Foreign Powers." *Journal for the Study of the Old Testament* 65 (1995): 37-53.

Oded, Bustaney. *Mass Deportation and Deportees in the Neo-Assyrian Empire.* Wiesbaden: Ludwig Reichert, 1979.

———. "The Settlement of the Israelite and Judean Exiles in Mesopotamia in the 8th-6th Centuries BCE." In Gershon Galil, and Moshe Weinfeld, eds. *Studies in Historical Geography and Biblical Historiography Presented to Zechariah Kallai.* Supplements to Vetus testamentum, 81. Leiden: E. J. Brill, 2000: 91-103.

Olivier, Hannes. "In Search of a Capital for the Northern Kingdom." *Journal of Northwest Semitic Languages* 11 (1983): 117-32.

Reinhold, G. G. G. *Die Beziehung Altisraels zu den aramäischen Staaten in der israelitisch-judäischen Königszeit.* Europäische Hochschulschriften, XXIII: 368. Frankfurt a.M.: Peter Lang, 1989.

Schoors, Antoon. *Die Königsreiche Israel und Juda im 8. und 7. Jahrhundert v. Chr.* Biblische Enzyklopädie, 5. Stuttgart: W. Kohlhammer, 1998.

Schulte, H. "The End of the Omride Dynasty: Social-Ethical Observations on the Subject of Power and Violence." In Douglas A. Knight, ed. *Ethics and Politics in the Hebrew Bible.* Atlanta: Scholars Press, 1994: 133-48.

Spieckermann, Hermann. *Juda unter Assur in der Sargonidenzeit.* Forschungen zur Religion und Literatur des Alten und Neuen Testaments, 129. Göttingen: Vandenhoeck & Ruprecht, 1982.

Sweeney, Marvin A. *King Josiah of Judah: The Lost Messiah of Israel.* Oxford: Oxford University Press, 2001.

Timm, Stefan. *Die Dynastie Omri. Quellen und Untersuchungen zur Geschichte Israels im 9. Jahrhundert vor Christus.* Forschungen zur Religion und Literatur des Alten und Neuen Testaments, 124. Göttingen: Vandenhoeck & Ruprecht, 1982.

Ussishkin, David. *The Conquest of Lachish by Sennacherib.* Tel Aviv: Tel Aviv University, Institute of Archaeology, 1982.

Vogt, E. *Der Aufstand Hiskias und die Belagerung Jerusalems 701 v. Chr.* Analecta Biblica, 106. Rome: Pontificium Institutum Biblicum, 1986.

Welten, Peter. *Die Königs-Stempel: Ein Beitrag zur militärpolitik Judas unter Hiskia und Josia.* Abhandlungen des Deutschen Palästina-Vereins. Wiesbaden: Otto Harrassowitz, 1969.

———. *Geschichte und Geschichtsdarstellung in den Chronikbüchern.* Wissenschaftliche Monographien zum Alten und Neuen Testament, 42. Neukirchen: Neukirchener Verlag, 1972.

Younger, K. Lawson. "The Deportation of the Israelites." *Journal of Biblical Literature* 117 (1998): 201-27.

Exile

Ackroyd, Peter. *Exile and Restoration: A Study of Hebrew Thought of the Sixth Century BC.* London: SCM Press, 1968.

———. *Israel unter Babylon and Persia.* Oxford: Oxford University Press, 1970.

Albertz, Rainer. *Die Exilszeit. 6. Jahrhundert v. Chr.* Biblische Enzy-klopädie, 7. Stuttgart: W. Kohlhammer, 2001.

Barstad, Hans M. *The Myth of the Empty Land. A Study in the History and Archaeology of Judah during the "Exilic" Period.* Symbolae osloenses, 28. Oslo: Scandinavian University Press, 1996.

Carroll, Robert P. "Exile, Restoration, and Colony: Judah in the Per-sian Period. In James G. Perdue, ed. *The Blackwell Companion to the Hebrew Bible.* Cambridge: Basil Blackwell, 2001: 102-16.

Grabbe, Lester L. *Leading Captivity Captive: "The Exile" as History and Ideology.* European Seminar in Historical Methodology, 2. Shef-field: Sheffield Academic Press, 1998.

Janssen, E. *Juda in der Exilszeit: Ein Beitrag zur Frage der Entste-hung des Judentums.* Forschungen zur religion und Literatur des Al-ten und Neuen Testaments, 69. Göttingen: Vandenhoeck & Ruprecht, 1956.

Lipschits, Oded. *The Fall and Rise of Jerusalem.* (forthcoming)

Lipschits, Oded, and Joseph Blenkinsopp, eds. *Judah and the Judaeans in the Neo-Babylonian Period.* Winona Lake, Ind.: Eisen-brauns, 2003.

Oded, Bustaney. "Observations on the Israelite/Judaean Exiles in Mesopotamia during the Eighth-Sixth Centuries BCE." In K. van Lerberghe and Anton Schoors, eds. *Immigration and Emigration within the Ancient Near East. Studies E. Lipinski.* Leuven: Peeters, 1995: 205-12.

Zadok, Ran. *The Jews in Babylonia during the Chaldean and Achae-minidian Periods according to the Babylonian Sources.* Haifa: Uni-versity of Haifa, 1979.

Restoration, Persian Period

Bedford, Peter Ross. *Temple Restauration in Early Achaemenid Judah.* Supplements to the Journal of Judaism, 65. Leiden: E. J. Brill, 2001.

Berquist, J. L. *Judaism in Persia's Shadow. A Social and Historical Approach.* Minneapolis: Fortress Press, 1995.

Briant, Pierre. "Histoire impériale et historire régionale: à propos de l'histoire de Juda dans l'empire achéménide." In A. Lemaire and M. Sæbø, eds. *Congress Volume Oslo 1998.* Supplements to Vetus Tes-tamentum, 80. Leiden: E. J. Brill, 2000: 235-45.

Carter, C. *The Emergence of Yehud in the Persian Period: A Social and Demographical Study.* Journal for the Study of the Old Testament. Supplementary Studies, 294. Sheffield: Sheffield Academic Press, 1999.

Davies, Philip R., ed. *Second Temple Studies. 1: Persian Period.* Journal for the Study of the Old Testament, Supplement Series, 117. Sheffield: Sheffield Academic Press, 1991.

Eskenazi, Tamara C., and Kent H. Richards. *Second Temple Studies. 2: Temple and Community in the Persian Period.* Journal for the Study of the Old Testament, Supplement Series, 175. Sheffield: Sheffield Academic Press, 1994.

Galling, Kurt. *Studien zur Geschichte Israels im persischen Zeitalter.* Tübingen: J. C. B. Mohr (Paul Siebeck), 1964.

Grabbe, Lester L. *Judaism from Cyrus to Hadrian,* I-II. Minneapolis: Fortress Press, 1992.

Hoglund, K. *Achaemenid Imperial Administration in Syria-Palestine and the Missions of Ezra and Nehemia.* Atlanta: Scholars Press, 1992.

Kuhrt, Amélie. "The Cyrus Cylinder and Achaemenid Imperial Policy." *Journal for the Study of the Old Testament* 25 (1983): 83-97.

Meyers, Eric M. "The Persian Period and the Judean Restoration: From Zerubbabel to Nehemiah." In Patrick D. Miller, Paul D. Hanson, and S. Dean McBride, eds. *Ancient Israelite Religion: Essays in Honor of Frank Moore Cross.* Philadelphia: Fortress Press, 1987: 509-22.

Pastor, Jack. *Land and Economy in Ancient Palestine.* London: Routledge, 1997.

Smith, D. L., and Norman K. Gottwald. *The Religion of the Landless. The Social Context of the Babylonian Exile.* Houston: HarperCollins, 1989.

Stern, Ephraim. *Material Culture of the Land of the Bible in the Persian Period 538-332 B.C.* Jerusalem: David Brown Books, 1982.

Weinberg, Joel. *The Citizen-Temple Community.* Journal for the Study of the Old Testament, Supplement Series, 151. Sheffield: Sheffield Academic Press, 1992.

Willi, Thomas. *Juda—Jehud—Israel: Studien zum Selbstverständnis des Judentums in persischer Zeit.* Forschungen zum Alten Testament, 12. Tübingen: J. C. B. Mohr (Paul Siebeck), 1995.

Williamson, Hugh. "Judah and the Jews." In M. Brosius and A. Kuhrt, eds. *Studies in Persian History: Esssays in Memory of David M. Lewis.* Leiden: E. J. Brill, 1998: 145-63.

About the Author

Niels Peter Lemche (Dr.theol., University of Copenhagen) is professor of theology at the University of Copenhagen. He studied theology and oriental languages at the University of Copenhagen and went on to teach as an assistant professor at the University of Aarhus. He finished his doctoral thesis on early Israel in 1984 and moved back to Copenhagen as a professor of theology in 1987. He has also taught at the Universities of Hamburg and Stellenbosch. His research revolves around historical and socioanthropological subjects, and he has published several monographs and more than a hundred articles dealing with ancient Israel and the ancient Near East. Dr. Lemche has received many grants and was head of the Copenhagen Dead Sea Scrolls Initiative between 1996 and 1999. At present he is director of the Ph.D. program of the School in Religious Studies at the University of Copenhagen.